Children and War

Past and Present

Edited by Helga Embacher, Grazia Prontera, Albert Lichtblau,
Johannes-Dieter Steinert, Wolfgang Aschauer, Darek Galasinski,
and John Buckley

 Helion & Company Ltd

Helion & Company Limited
26 Willow Road
Solihull
West Midlands
B91 1UE
England
Tel. 0121 705 3393
Fax 0121 711 4075
Email: info@helion.co.uk
Website: www.helion.co.uk
Twitter: @helionbooks
Visit our blog http://blog.helion.co.uk/

Published by Helion & Company 2013. Reprinted in paperback 2016

Designed and typeset by Farr out Publications, Wokingham, Berkshire
Cover designed by Paul Hewitt, Battlefield Design (www.battlefield-design.co.uk)
Printed by Lightning Source, Milton Keynes, Buckinghamshire

Text © individual contributors.
For © of images see credits within the book.

ISBN 978-1-911096-71-9

British Library Cataloguing-in-Publication Data.
A catalogue record for this book is available from the British Library.

Front cover: Painting of an eleven year old girl's representations of war experiences. Rear cover: 14-year old Józefa Glazowska, 'Children of War' Exhibition, 2001; Young Soldier of Warsaw, 'Children of War' Exhibition, 2001.

For details of other military history titles published by Helion & Company Limited contact the above address, or visit our website: http://www.helion.co.uk.

We always welcome receiving book proposals from prospective authors.

Contents

List of images

List of contributors

Affiliations (in 2010)

Marie Claire Lefort und Carl Bouchard
Marie-Claire Lefort, M.A. in history, Université de Montréal, Canada.
Carl Bouchard, Associate Professor of History, Université de Montréal,
Canada.

Nicholas Stargardt
Nicholas Stargardt, Professor of Modern European History, Magdalen
College, University of Oxford, UK.

Sara Valentina Di Palma
Sara Valentina Di Palma, Research Associate in Contemporary History,
University of Sienna, Italy.

Patricia Heberer Rice
Patricia Heberer Rice, Historian, Center for Advanced Holocaust Studies,
United States Holocaust Memorial Museum in Washington DC, USA.

Irina Rebrova
Irina Rebrova, Assistant Professor of History, Kuban State Technological
University, Russia.

Hanna Ulatowska
Hanna K. Ulatowska, Professor of Communication Disorders and
Neurolinguistics, University of Texas at Dallas, USA.

Matthias Franz
Matthias Franz, Professor of Psychosomatic Medicine, Heinrich-Heine-

University Düsseldorf, Germany.

Carolyn Kay
Carolyn Kay, Professor of History, Trent University, Ontario, Canada.

Yvonne Kozlovsky Golan
Yvonne Kozlovsky Golan, Head of the Graduate Programme for Culture and Film Studies, University of Haifa, Israel.

Jane Rice
Jane Rice, MA in Anthropology and Social Research, University of Aberdeen, MSc in Forced Migration, University of Oxford, UK.

Hideyuki Okano
Hideyuki Okano, PhD candidate, Graduate School of Human Sciences, University of Osaka, Japan.

Loukianos Hassiotis
Loukianos Hassiotis, Lecturer in Modern and Contemporary European History, Aristotle University of Thessaloniki, Greece.

Janusz Wrobel
Janusz Wróbel, Historian, Institute of National Remembrance, Poland.

Christina Ryan
Christine Ryan, Lecturer in Politics and Global Studies, University of Winchester, UK.

Laurene Graziani
Laurene Graziani, PhD candidate in International Public Law, Center of International and European Research and Studies (CERIC), University Paul Cézanne Aix-Marseille III, France.

Editors

Wolfgang Auschauer, Assistant Professor, Division of Sociology and Cultural Science, University of Salzburg, Austria.

John Buckley, Professor of Military History, University of Wolverhampton, UK.

Helga Embacher, Associate Professor of History, University of Salzburg, Austria.

Darek Galasinski, Professor of Discourse and Cultural Studies, University of Wolverhampton, UK.

Albert Lichtblau, Associate Professor of History, University of Salzburg, Austria.

Grazia Prontera, Assistant Professor, Division of Modern European History, University of Salzburg, Austria.

Johannes-Dieter Steinert, Professor of Modern European History and Migration Studies, University of Wolverhampton, UK.

Introduction

Helga Embacher and Johannes-Dieter Steinert

The amount of international research on "Children and War" carried out by academics, governmental and non-governmental organizations and other institutions has continually increased in recent years. At the same time there has been growing public interest in how children experience military conflicts and how their lives have been affected by war and its aftermath. In light of the many brutal post-colonialist civil wars or "new wars" especially in Africa and Asia, child soldiers have gained increased attention.[1] NGOs emphasize the multiple roles of children in contemporary wars and genocides. Lately, former child soldiers have also begun to speak out.[2] With the so-called war on terror in Afghanistan and Iraq, children have received attention as refugees and victims, often killed by landmines.[3] Many were shocked when fifteen-year-old Malala Yousafzai was shot by Taliban as punishment for her fight for girls' education in October 2012.[4] With the Second Intifada in Israel (that began in autumn 2000) and the wars in Gaza (2009 and 2012), images of Palestinian children killed during the riots and as the result of Israeli counter attacks as well as of Israeli children killed in Palestinian suicide attacks or running for shelter dominated news coverage worldwide. The ongoing debate in Europe about refugees—many of them children and young adults from Africa and Asia —has again brought the situation of children to the attention of a broad

---

1 For example, Alcinda Honwana, *Child Soldiers in Africa*, Philadelphia, 2006; Christin Voß, *Kindersoldat(inn)en. Ein Phänomen der Gegenwart und Zukunft?*, Mönchengladbach 2011; David M. Rosen, *Armies for the Young, Children Soldiers in War and Terrorism*, New Brunswick, New Jersey and London, 2005; Sabine von Schorlemer, *Kindersoldaten und bewaffneter Konflikt. Nukleus eines umfassenden Schutzregimes der Vereinten Nationen* (Dresdner Schriften zu Recht und Politik der Vereinten Nationen 9), Frankfurt am Main 2009.
2 e.g Ishmael Beah, *A Long Way Gone: Memoirs of a Boy Soldier*, Sarah Crichton Books 2007 (German translation: *Rückkehr ins Leben. Ich war Kindersoldat*, Frankfurt/New York 2007).
3 For example, on December 17, 2012, twelve girls were killed by landmines while collecting wood.
4 "Thousands call for Nobel peace prize for Malala Yousafzai. Politicians urged to back nomination of 15-year-old girl shot by Taliban while campaigning for girls' education in Pakistan", in: *The Guardian*, 9.11.2012.

audience.[5] This new sensitivity, however, masks the fact that children have always been part of wars as victims and survivors being instrumentalized by various stakeholders. Even if they did not take part in actions directly, they were deeply involved and confronted with long-term effects.

In addition to this attention focused on the fate of children in "new wars", the history of the Holocaust and World War II has also increasingly been written from the perspective of children, particularly over the last few decades. In the postwar period, Holocaust literature dealt primarily with adult survivors of concentration camps. Some of them were prominent writers and artists, and became creators of important testimonial works. Studies on the subject of Jewish exile also neglected children's narratives for many years. Since the 1980s and 1990s, the number of memoirs written by child survivors has steadily increased. This special focus on children has to be explained by the changing of the generational guard among the survivors. Those who speak out now and publish their memoirs experienced the Holocaust as children. This new focus on children is also reflected by memorials installed in recent years in Liverpool Station in London, at the Berlin Friedrichsstraße train station, in Rotterdam and at the Westbahnhof in Vienna to commemorate the *Kindertransport*. A similar generational change took place in the societies of the perpetrators: Germans and Austrians who experienced the war as children took over the role of war witnesses from the soldiers of the German *Wehrmacht*. Thus, the impact of World War II on children and on their lives afterwards is given special consideration. Moreover, intensified focus on children's experiences and their strategies for dealing with what they went through is evident in Eastern Europe as well.[6] In recent years studies about the difficult situation of children have been published and discussed at conferences.[7]

This collection of original essays contain a selection of papers given at the international multidisciplinary conference on 'Children and War: Past and Present', held at the University of Salzburg from 30 September to 2 October 2010, jointly organized by colleagues from the universities of Salzburg and Wolverhampton. The conference brought together around 150 young and established scholars, practitioners in the field and representatives of governmental and non-governmental organizations and institutions. Topics ranged from the experience of war, flight, displacement and resettlement,

5   For example, Dima Zito, *Zwischen Angst und Hoffnung. Kindersoldaten als Flüchtlinge in Deutschland*, Ibbenbühren 2009.
6   See, for example, Ignes Hopfer, Geraubte Identität, *Die gewaltsame „Eindeutschung" von polnischen Kindern in der NS-Zeit*, Wien 2010. In December 2012, the conference *War Children in the Post-war. A West-East perspective on child policies, child experiences and war childhood remembrance cultures in Europe since 1945* took place in Vienna.
7   See, for example, the conference *Besatzungskinder in Österreich und Deutschland* at the Diplomatische Akademie Wien, September 27, 2012.

relief and rehabilitation work, gender issues, persecution, trafficking, abuse and prostitution, trauma and amnesia, the trans-generational impact of persecution, individual and collective memory, educational issues, films and documentaries, artistic and literary approaches, to remembrance and memorials, and questions of theory and methodology.

For this book, we have selected fifteen (out of some 120) papers. They have been structured into three chapters: 1) Experiences of Children in War, 2) Representations of Children in War and 3) Children in War: An Institutional Perspective. Though the main focus is on World War II with respect to experiences of Jewish as well as non-Jewish children; research on children's experiences in World War I and in post-colonial and contemporary wars in Africa are presented as well. Scholars from different academic disciplines, practitioners in the field, and representatives of governmental and non-governmental institutions approached this sensitive subject from different angles and in various methodological ways. Thus, it again became clear that children's experiences are very different from those of grown-ups and that there is still a research desideratum.

Part One: Experiences of Children in War

The first section, Experiences of Children in War, shows how children expressed their experiences in letters, memoirs and diaries during and after World War I and World War II and how children remember the war. Most of the authors also deal with various long-term psychological effects of wars.

In the first chapter, *Marie Claire Lefort* und *Carl Bouch* analyze a corpus of more than two hundred letters sent by French children to Woodrow Wilson, who arrived on French soil in December 1918. They discuss how children represented French and American soldiers, how they depicted the enemies as a result of what they had learned about them during the war and also according to their personal encounters with the enemy. In their very emotional letters, the US president seemed omnipotent, generous, rich, unselfish and powerful. They also confessed to him their nightmares and suppressed emotions, such as the victory of the Germans.

Nicholas Stargardt shows that war was not only something that had happened to children. Using the example of children's games, he demonstrates that children simultaneously protected themselves from and adapted to a reality in which they recognized their enemies as the image of victorious strength and their parents as impotent failure. Children's games as well as their other precocious activities demonstrated that they were not just mute and traumatized witnesses of this war. They found new roles for themselves and adapted with a speed that shocked many adults.

Using documents and children's memoirs, *Sara Valentina Di Palma* reconstructs stages and various aspects of children's persecution in camps such as arrival, camp life, births and medical experiments, resistance, survival and memory. Thus, she demonstrates that life experiences by children, and especially their perception, are different from those of adults. Based on the postwar difficulties children were confronted with after their survival, the paper also explains why the majority of testimonies of child survivors have appeared only since the 1980s.

Patricia Heberer Rice provides a unique insight into the experiences and viewpoints of children in the Theresienstadt family camp and the Birkenau extermination camp. Using the unpublished diary of the Czech boy, Michael Kraus, written immediately after the war, she scrutinizes a special group of prisoners, the "Birkenau Boys", who survived the camp as "runners" (*Läufer*) assigned to convey communications and supplies among officials in the core of the extermination camp. The diary also demonstrates that liberation did not end the Holocaust odyssey of many Jewish children.

Based on a collaborative oral history research project, *Irina Rebrova* discusses the daily life experienced by children during World War II in Northern Caucasus. She analyzes the way her interview partners remember the structure and function of their families, interpersonal relationships and how they were integrated into the world of the adults. The author concludes with an important finding: that the patriarchal family model that was predominant during the whole Soviet period became stronger during wartime. What children feared most was the loss of their families.

Hanna Ulatowska's paper is based on interviews with two non-Jewish Polish children who survived Auschwitz. She analyzes how children construct their legacy through testimonies, publications and social activism in such organizations as the Association of Child Survivors of Concentration Camps in Warsaw, founded in 1989.

Based on two quantitative empirical studies conducted in Germany, *Matthias Franz* discusses the long-term impact of World War II-related fatherlessness on childhood. He demonstrates that depression, mistrust and social phobia, anxiety in particular, were significantly enhanced among the adult children of war. As he shows, World War II had an enormous biographical impact on a big segment of postwar German society.

Part Two: Representations of Children in War

The second section of the book analyzes how children are represented in different wars using the example of children's literature in World War I and the representation of child survivors in the postwar cinema. Based on post-colonial and contemporary wars in Africa, images of girl and boy soldiers created by the media, NGOs and governments as well as trends in how they are represented in contemporary research are analyzed.

Carolyn Kay's paper is based on books created during World War I to explain and justify the war to children. She shows how these publications glorified war heroes like General Paul von Hindenburg and depicted the Russians as bullies needing a good thrashing. Just as astonishing is the "breezy" manner in which they depict the war, showing it as a game in which the good must prevail and German soldiers are invincible.

Yvonne Kozlovsky Golan analyzes the representation of the lives of Jewish child survivors in international postwar cinema. She concludes that the representation of children in films reflects the way a nation views the Holocaust. Analyzing European films, she identifies a process of "Christianization" and "iconization" of Jewish children to make it easier for viewers to identify with them.

Jane Rice examines how female child soldiers were represented in the media, by NGOs and by governments during the Cold War and post-Cold War conflicts. Focusing on the war of independence in Mozambique in the 1960s, the recent civil war in Sierra Leone and the ongoing Colombian civil war, she shows that girls join armed groups for multiple and often complex and competing reasons.

Hideyuki Okano examines three images of boy soldiers that are popular among scholars and represent their specific ways of thinking. He warns of one-sided interpretations of soldiers such as passive "victims with no future" or as "rational men" being recruited through a patron-client relationship for economic reasons. To understand the complexity of this phenomenon, he suggests an interdisciplinary approach to understand what the other disciplines explore and how these understandings are related to scholars' own findings.

Part Three: Children in War: An Institutional Perspective

The last section of the book concentrates on various institutions such as welfare organizations and NGOs dealing with children in different wars. Important questions raised in the papers are how institutions not only supported but also instrumentalized children and—concerning contemporary conflicts—how the international community has to face the question of international justice and adapt to children's needs.

It begins with *Loukianos Hassiotis'* paper about child welfare in Spain and Greece during and after the civil wars. He shows that in both countries, the so-called children's issue became part of the political agenda of the conflicting camps. They soon realized that children should be "saved" both for humanitarian reasons and for the success of their own struggle. Thus, relief institutions not only supported children but also tried to create loyal citizens.

Janusz Wróbel followed the lives of Polish children who were deported with their parents from Poland to Siberia where they suffered hunger, disease and humiliation. From there they were evacuated to Iran in 1942. With the help of the Polish government, they were transferred to various other countries in the Middle East, to South Africa and to Mexico. Many of them lost their families and were unable to return to Poland after the war.

Based on field studies involving 33 non-governmental agency workers and civil society members in Southern Sudan conducted between 2007 and 2008, *Christine Ryan* examines their approaches to and interaction with child soldiers. She discusses the weakness of NGOs' approaches and brings out the dissimilarities in interpretations of the interests of child soldiers.

The main question *Laurene Graziani* addresses in her paper is how to make international justice a reality for children affected by armed conflicts. She gives an overview of the different mechanisms that were established in recent years to protest war-affected children and thus demonstrates the huge gap between theoretical concepts and real-world practice.

Many friends, colleagues and institutions have supported our work during the last years. Without their generosity and commitment the conference and this publication would not have been possible. We would like to thank our universities, the University of Salzburg and the University of Wolverhampton, the City of Salzburg and the Province of Salzburg. A special thanks to Astrid Rössler of the Green Party. For their practical help and support during the conference we thank Salzburg students Barbara Huber, Filip Fetko, Ute Palemetshofer, Stefan Pitzer, Lorence Salas Kastilio, Veronika Aschenbrenner, Magdalena Oberpeilsteiner, Sonja Unteregger, and Katharina Wimmer. Thanks are also due to Richard Hammond for assiduous and careful editing of the text. Last but not least, our warmest thanks to Nadine Ernsting for her untiring work and commitment.

Part One   **Experiences of Children in War**

1   War and Postwar in Kids' Words: Letters from French Children to Woodrow Wilson (1918-1919)

Carl Bouchard and Marie-Claire Lefort,
Université de Montréal (Canada)

The bells that rang on the morning of 11 November 1918 called an end to the fighting on the Western Front, but not the end of the conflict in many ways, nor the suffering and deprivation for much of the European population. Although sometimes not officially at peace, nations nevertheless slowly entered the transitional period from wartime to peacetime. While the pain of the losses and suffering perpetuated hatred towards the enemy, with whom belligerents now had to learn to live with once again, it also nourished an intense desire for peace, calm and a return to normality.

This research is based on the concept of *'sortie de guerre'*, a stimulating research theme that has recently emerged in French historiography. In the footsteps of John Horne's seminal work on cultural mobilisation,[1] re-mobilisation and de-mobilisation in war and postwar-time, Bruno Cabanes, Stéphane Audoin-Rouzeau, Guillaume Pickety and other researchers intend to look at how French and Europeans societies, in social and cultural terms, 'got out of the war'.[2] One way of doing so is to uncover the persistence of wartime discursive constructions in the months and years that followed the end of the war. Bruno Cabanes, for instance, looking at various European postwar episodes in the 20th century, argues that the *sortie de guerre* 'is fundamentally a violent period governed by representations of hatred forged during the war'.[3] According to Cabanes this internalized violence has been put aside by historiography, which traditionally emphasized the pacifist outburst

---

1   J. Horne, 'Démobilisations culturelles après la Grande Guerre', *14-18 Aujourd'hui, Today, Heute.*
2   B. Cabanes, G. Picketty, 'Sortir de la guerre: jalons pour une histoire en chantier', *Histoire@ Politique. Politique, culture, société*; S. Audoin-Rouzeau, C. Prochasson, *Sortir de la Grande Guerre: le monde et l'après-1918*; S. Claisse, T. Lemoine, *Comment (se) sortir de la grande guerre?: regards sur quelques pays "vainqueurs": la Belgique, la France et la Grande-Bretagne*; B. Cabanes, 'Sortir de la Première Guerre mondiale (1918-début des années 1920)', in B. Cabanes, É. Husson (eds), *Les sociétés en guerre 1911-1946.*
3   Cabane, Picketty, 'Sortir de la guerre', p. 2.

when looking at the interwar period. Our research builds on this argument by examining French children's feelings towards war and the upcoming peace in late 1918 and early 1919. For this purpose we collected 240 children's letters sent to the American President Woodrow Wilson in the weeks following the Armistice.

The symbolic impact of the American president's arrival on French soil in December 1918, prior to the opening of the Peace Conference, was tremendous.[4] As the first sitting American president to visit Europe, he was greeted by a jubilant crowd at every stop and more than a million people in Paris on 15 December 1918. Newspaper coverage was similarly phenomenal. One hundred and thirty-six communes dedicated a street or a public place to the President's name, the most famous being Avenue du Président Wilson, formerly Avenue Trocadéro, in Paris.[5] Wilson was a genuine icon at the end of the war and his popularity—at least on the first months following the Armistice—lay across a wide range of the political spectrum and not just on the left, as has often been said since Pierre Miquel published his work on French public opinion and the Versailles Treaty.[6] By joining the Entente in April 1917, Wilson's country directly contributed to victory over the Central Powers, and his Fourteen Points of January 1918 laid the groundwork for the upcoming peace. Wilson finally proposed to "reform" international relations and subject them to the judgment of global public opinion. In short, he carried much of the task of making the Great War 'the war to end all wars'. Rarely has a single individual borne such responsibility.

Even though thousands of men and women from all over Europe, Canada and the US wrote to President Wilson, the vast majority came from France. What moved such a great number of the French to write to a foreign head of state? Many explanations may be put forward, from the culturally strong letter-writing practice in France, to the physical proximity of Wilson who stayed in this country for close to six months from the end of 1918.[7] Even though, as Eren Manela has brilliantly showed, Wilson's popularity was a worldwide phenomenon,[8] the 'Wilsonmania' was more intense in France than anywhere else, perhaps because Wilson was seen as a new version of the mythical *providential man* that would come and save France again from

4   E. Fordham, 'From Whitman to Wilson: French Attitudes towards American Around the Time of the Great War', in L. Passerini (ed.), *Across the Atlantic: Cultural Exchanges Between Europe and the United States*.

5   J. Bouvier, *Les noms de rues disent la ville*, p. 149.

6   P. Miquel, *La paix de Versailles et l'opinion publique française*.

7   M. Hanna, 'A Republic of Letters: The Epistolary Tradition in France during World War I', *The American Historical Review*.

8   E. Manela, *The Wilsonian Moment. Self-Determination and the International Origins of Anticolonial Nationalism*.

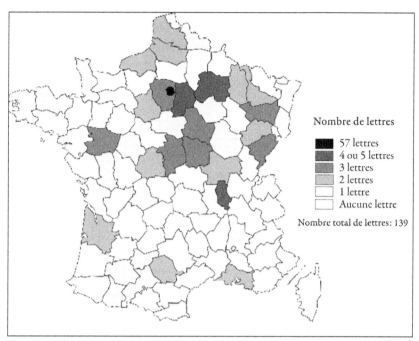

Fig. 1.1: Origin of the individual letters sent to Wilson.
(Library of Congress, Washington DC)

despair.[9] The novelty was that this providential man, for the first time, came not from France but from abroad. Indeed, in the wake of the war, there was in France the profound and often concealed belief that the country's future as a great power depended heavily upon the coming peace settlement in which Wilson was the key actor. But beyond those sociological and psychological explanations, the epistolary frenzy regarding Wilson was, more prosaically, a sign of sincere gratitude for the American participation in the war and the victory, a gratitude that the childrens' letters rightly reflect.

All the letters in this corpus were sent to Wilson from November 1918 to February 1919. We listed 141 individual letters.[10] The children's ages varied from 7 to 16 years old, the latter being considered at that time in France as the moment of transition from childhood to adulthood.[11] Six out of 10 children told Wilson his/her age, which gives us an average of 11 years old. As Figure

---

9   R. Girardet, *Mythes et mythologies politiques.*

10 71 from boys, 63 from girls and 7 letters written jointly by a boy and a girl, generally siblings.

11 M. Pignot, *Allons enfants de la patrie? Filles et garçons dans la Grande Guerre: expériences communes, construction du genre et invention des pères (France 1914-1920).*

1.1 shows, 40% of the individual letters come from the Seine department, i.e. Paris and the surrounding area. Overall a great majority of the letters come from the northern half of France, especially from the north-eastern war-occupied zones. Manon Pignot has shown through her examination of children's diaries during the war that the further the children were from the front, the less they seemed preoccupied by the war,[12] and our study tends to confirm this point of view.

The corpus is completed by 99 school letters. It is likely that the French Department of Education asked schools to send a standard letter of appreciation to the American President, as 80% of them are composed of the same sentences with very few variations:

To Mister Wilson, President of the United States of America. The children from [name of school] are pleased to send to Mister Wilson their most cordial, respectful and grateful salute. Long live President Wilson! Long live the United States!'[13] Each of these letters were carefully signed by all the class children and their teacher. Considering the low number of school letters received during the first two months, few schools seem to have answered what appeared to be a national class homework, which is surprising considering the high proportion of left-wing and radical teachers; usually seen as Wilson's most ardent supporters in France.[14]

Children used many strategies to get the President's interest and sympathy. We will see throughout this chapter that some rhetorical tropes are very common, like the humility with which they present themselves.[15] While this humbleness is a common and quite conventional tactic—largely used for instance in supplicant letters[16]—it is not the only one. One clever girl from Marseille, Andrée Fischer, chose to send her letter to Wilson's wife in the hope of getting his autograph, on the basis that the First Lady had more free time than her husband.[17] For their part, twelve children sent a letter in English, probably because this would give them a better chance of being read, but also as a sign of admiration and interest for American culture.[18] Simone Diénis, one of the few young girls who wrote in English, was pleased to say that on her twelfth birthday she bade welcome to the President and, significantly, concluded her letter by depicting herself as 'a little French girl who likes the Americans very

---

12 Pignot, *Allons enfants de la patrie?*, p. 214.
13 All quotations have been translated from French to English unless indicated.
14 M. Siegel, *The Moral Disarmament of France: Education, Pacifism, and Patriotism, 1914-1940*.
15 Like "I'm just a young boy"; "I'm a poor orphan", "My father has died in the trenches", etc.
16 S. Fitzpatrick, 'Supplicants and Citizens: Public Letter-Writing in Soviet Russia in the 1930s', *Slavic Review*.
17 Andrée Fischer to Edith Wilson, December 12, 1918. All the letters come from the *Papers of Woodrow Wilson* (series 5D and 5F) archived at the Library of Congress in Washington.
18 See an example, appendix #1.

much'.[19] Otherwise, most children wrote their letter in their mother tongue, without apparently asking themselves if Wilson or any one of its secretaries could read French. This was perfectly normal since only a fraction of the French population could actually read or write in English.

Individual letters focused, though not exclusively, on four major subjects. Letters were variously 1) Expressions of gratitude to Wilson for the US involvement in the war and the victory; 2) letters of welcome, like Diénis, to the American President to Paris; 3) requests for personal assistance or material aid, and; 4) finally, like that of Andrée Fischer, requests for an autograph or a signed photograph of the President that they could keep in their war-scrapbook. Of course, many letters dealt with a combination of these subjects. In all cases, whatever the letter's topic or length, children, as they shared their thoughts and hopes with the American President, all say something about the way they lived through the war, about what they retained of the war discourse and propaganda, and about how they viewed Wilson's role in this nebulous period between war and peace.

The following three sections will highlight important themes that children addressed in their letters to Wilson, first the soldiers' representation, then the representation of the German enemy and lastly the way children talked to Wilson about war and peace.

1. Soldiers' representation

'I'm the daughter of a brave man who fought to save Right, Justice and Liberty', wrote Marthe Dargent at the close end of 1918.[20] Like her, many children praise the soldiers and show admiration for what they have accomplished during the war.

As Mona Ozouf has argued, the French republican school system, established in the aftermath of the Franco-Prussian War of 1870-1871, was instrumental in forging the perception of the war and of French soldiers.[21] More recently, Stéphane Audoin-Rouzeau has shown in his book, *La guerre des enfants,* that education was part of a vast propaganda system aimed at culturally mobilizing the children for the war effort.[22] School offered an idealized vision of the conflict through various academic activities, the most obvious being dictations, lectures, and writing assignments. But the war also served, in France and in all belligerent countries, as a pedagogical tool in itself,

---

19 Simone Diénis to Wilson, 12 December 1919.
20 Marthe Dargent to Wilson, 29 December 1918.
21 M. Ozouf, *L'école de la France, Essais sur la Révolution, l'utopie et l'enseignement.*
22 S. Audoin-Rouzeau, *La guerre des enfants, 1914-1918: essai d'histoire culturelle.*

notably as a means of exploring geography, history or mathematics.[23] There was
no balanced information here : the French Poilus is systematically described
as a noble and courageous hero fighting for a just cause whereas the enemy is
either vile and cruel or clumsy and ridiculous. In all cases the French soldiers
win over their foes. Manon Pignot has argued that this kind of propaganda,
although largely infused in the child's world, was not equally internalized
by the children and, as the months and the years passed, enthusiasm faded.[24]
Our records nevertheless show that, as the war ended, children who wrote to
Wilson expressed sincere pride in their soldiers' achievements. Like the young
Marthe Dargent, who associates right, justice and liberty with the soldier's
figure, children convey many propaganda tropes learned in school.

There are, however, some differences between the representation of the
French and the American soldiers. Surprisingly, children express more
deference in their letters for the latter than for the former. The fact that they
wrote to the American President largely explains this discrepancy, but a
cultural bias seems also at play. Children, through the Republican system
of education, learned in History and Geography classes that the American
people was a young, prosperous and heroic nation, who fought for liberty and
the rule of law. The United States was seen as country of opportunity which,
as Jacques Portes has argued, epitomized modernity.[25] The French were also
quite impressed when the first 'Sammies' arrived in France, especially by the
American army's organizational capabilities and the quality of its equipment.[26]
French children thus recurrently described the American soldiers as 'healthy',[27]
'well equipped',[28] 'handsome',[29] and 'brave'.[30] Young Nicolas François was so
filled with admiration regarding the US troops that he even played down the
heroism of his own father: 'Even if my father, who was incorporated in your
First Army, received the cross and the stars, he's still nothing compared to
your good soldiers,' wrote François to Wilson. [31]

Children from the war-occupied zones of the northeastern France
insisted a great deal on the American role in their liberation. Their personal
experience plays of course a decisive part in their perception. Unlike other
children in France, they witnessed and directly suffered from the hardships

---

23 S. Cardinal, *Le discours de guerre tenu aux enfants montréalais au sujet de la Première Guerre mondiale entre 1914 et 1918.*
24 Pignot, *Allons enfants de la patrie?*, pp. 105-107.
25 J. Portes, *Une fascination réticente: les États-Unis dans l'opinion française.*
26 Y.-H. Nouailhat, *Les Américains à Nantes et Saint-Nazaire, 1917-1919*, pp. 191-93.
27 S. Mazerolle to Wilson, 14 December 1918.
28 Simone Gonnet to Wilson, 31 December 1918.
29 Germaine Ostenciaux to Wilson, 28 December 1918.
30 Denise Pichat to Wilson, 30 December 1918.
31 Nicolas François to Wilson, 20 December 1918.

of war, the destruction, the looting and the starvation.[32] Eighteen children explicitly mention to Wilson that they took refuge in other departments after the invasion of August 1914, which is undoubtedly a painful and traumatic experience for children who had to flee their house and hometown for an indefinite period of time. The armistice therefore came as an immense relief and the Americans were especially thanked for it. Hélène Jacques, a young refugee from the Meuse, wrote to Wilson: 'I always liked America very much and I like it more since its armies bravely defended my little village and my country.'[33] As for Simone Brun, she expressed her immense relief to Wilson: "You freed us from a long and terrible war. Without you, our benefactor, what would we be and what would have we become?"[34]

The soldiers' representation is sometimes defined by a direct encounter with the American troops. Many children built personal relationships with soldiers to a point that some even talked about them as 'friends'. They told Wilson about how their community generously offered hospitality to American troops arriving in their town or how their own family welcomed 'Sammies' at home. A child mentioned that the American soldiers were 'very nice and gentle and welcoming with children',[35] while a school letter declared that American soldiers 'pamper and spoil the children like big brothers towards their younger siblings'.[36] Numerous material aid requests sent to Wilson by poor children also reveal how wealthy and generous the Americans looked in the eyes of French.[37] The very young Paul Loubdé wrote in that sense to Wilson: 'I was told that you arrived in France along with a ship packed with toys, you'd be so kind to send me a train, soldiers and cavalry men, I'd be so happy and I'd love you very much, warm kisses.'[38] These testimonies all point to a discourse very much ingrained in France about the generosity and the material opulence of the United States. Not all the letters are as candid as Loubdé's but overall French children did have a very positive opinion of the Americans, because they helped France win the war but also at a more personal level, because of their positive attitude and behavior since arriving in France. We found only one exception, Maurice Leclerc, who complained to Wilson about an American soldier who stole his bike, but even then, the young boy is so grateful to the 'Sammies' that he only 'unwillingly hold[s] a grudge against the bicycle thief'.[39]

---

32 A. Becker, *Journaux de combattants et de civils de la France du Nord dans la Grande Guerre*.
33 Hélène Jacques to Wilson, 20 December 1918.
34 Simone Brun to Wilson, 3 January 1919.
35 Unknown to Wilson, 14 December 1918.
36 Pontenx-les-Gorges Public School to Wilson, 19 December 1918.
37 Nouailhat, *Les Américains à Nantes et Saint-Nazaire*, pp. 196-197.
38 Paul Loubdé to Wilson, 20 December 1918.
39 Maurice Leclerc to Wilson, 1st January 1919.

The seemingly close relationship thus built between the French and Americans through the hardship of war led some children to emphasize the long-lasting ties between both countries. Some historical symbols of friendship between the United States and France appear frequently in the letters, like drawings of the two countries' flags or reference to Lafayette and Rochambeau, two central French figures of the American Revolution.[40] A school letter thus reminded the President that 'In 1776 Rochambeau and Lafayette crossed the Atlantic to fight beside Washington. In 1917 the great Republic declared war on Germany to save the principles of Liberty, Justice, Law, Civilization and Humanity.'[41] As France helped the American colonies to free themselves from the British yoke, then the Americans naturally helped France win her liberty back from the German foe. The two sister republics already had a common history; they now had a common future.

Reference to French soldiers is of course recurrent in the letters. Children saw their fathers, their brothers, their uncles, their neighbors go to war; many didn't come back. Children put a stronger emphasis on the sacrifice and the heroism of the French soldiers than of the Americans. This is particularly the case in the orphans' letters who pay tribute to their lost fathers. Young Andrée Thelliez wrote: 'In spite of my grief, the idea that the death of my dear father contributed just a little to the liberation of our dear country is a kind of consolation.'[42] The burden of this sacrifice was heavy on the orphans' shoulders; they nevertheless adhered to the heroic value of death magnified by war propaganda. The idea that a soldier's sacrifice—not any soldier but a child's father—was justified for the sake of the country seems to have been internalized by children. It might have allowed them to support the grief of a relative loss.

Not all children stoically accepted the sacrifice of their beloved father. On Christmas Eve 1918 Raymond Cauet wrote these bitter and poignant words to Wilson: 'In this damned war the Boche barbarians killed my father [...] and all my family was imprisoned. I no longer have a godfather so I ask you Mister President if you would want to be mine.'[43] As for young Gilbert Gaillot, he depicted his misery to Wilson thus: 'My father is dead, he was murdered by the barbarians. We are totally ruined by the war and I am now an orphan.'[44] A father's death is already unbearable, but life becomes even worse when this loss throws the family into misery, as it often did at the time. The soldiers' sacrifice is therefore viewed in a quite different angle by these children whose material conditions dramatically deteriorate as a consequence

---

40 See appendix 2.
41 Leroux School to Wilson, 19 December 1918.
42 Andrée Thelliez to Wilson, 9 January 1919.
43 Raymond Cauet to Wilson, 24 December 1918.
44 Gilbert Gaillot to Wilson, 15 January 1919.

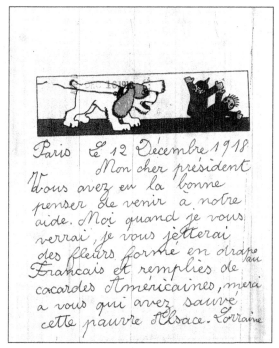

Fig. 1.2: Barking at the enemy. (Library of Congress, Washington DC)

of their father's death.

The two last citations highlight the personal distress of war orphans. Quite revealingly they also described the enemy as the *Boche* and as the 'barbarians'. Although almost every letter used such terms or similar, we can learn more about the children's personal experiences during the war in the ways they depicted the German foe to Wilson.

2. The enemy's representation

The enemy is depicted in the letters as the absolute opposite of an allied soldier: brutal, cruel and uncivilized. Derogatory terms like 'savage' and 'barbarians' are most common. Children also refer to the German's 'horrible *Kultur*'[45] or to the 'German servitude',[46] thus showing the penetration, even in the world of children, of the intense war propaganda against Germany originally intended for adults.

The letter reproduced in Figure 1.2 is therefore quite interesting. The very

---

45 Jean Domergue to Wilson, 20 December 1918.
46 Estela Perrin to Wilson, 24 December 1918.

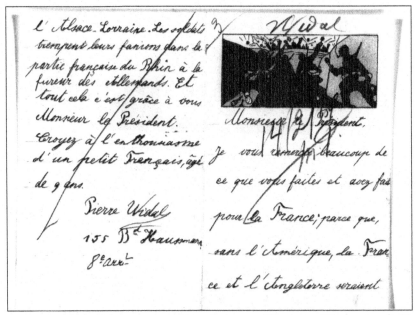

Fig. 1.3: Scene of violence and warfare. (Library of Congress, Washington DC)

young boy—considering the handwriting and the spelling mistakes—wrote his letter on stationary paper with a header representing a dog barking at terrified German toy soldiers. Although the scene looks at first benign and amusing, it does legitimise violence against the Germans as natural behavior, since the dog throws itself at the Germans—thus breaking his leash.

The second example reproduced in Figure 1.3 is even more impressive. Again, the stationary paper on which the child wrote his letter came with a header showing what is more often than not concealed to children, that is actual warfare. In this scene, four French *poilus* in their trenches are surprised by a German attack—the *poilu* on the right is still smoking his pipe—but they are able to drive back the enemy by throwing hand grenades at them. The four Germans are killed or severely wounded by the explosions.

These two examples are striking evidence of the penetration of a violent war discourse which seems to be both internalized and durable among the children whose letters we studied. Bruno Cabanes is definitely right about the persistence of verbal and graphic violence against the enemy in the weeks following the end of the conflict.[47]

Yet, this consensual and negative depiction of the enemy comes in a variety of forms. Refugees and orphans tended to accentuate their hatred of the

47 Cabanes, Picketty, 'Sortir de la guerre'.

foe, whereas the other children rather expressed their fear of the Germans. The children who suffered the most during the war put the entire fault on the Germans and are more vindictive against them. Writing on New Year's day, Marie-Thérèse Vasseur, who had to leave her home when the Germans arrived in her town, testified to Wilson:

> The *Boches* destroyed all of what my parents and grandparents owned. Those vile men did not even spare the children. I had a superb doll, a friend of my exile which I adored. They pushed the cruelty to the point of taking it from my arms in spite of my tears. They claimed that I could find another one in Paris.[48]

It was indeed a traumatizing experience for this eleven year-old girl who could not take this very comforting toy with her into her exile. Like in Vasseur's letter, reference to the enemy is often related to the destruction and looting. There is also a strong feeling of injustice among children who directly suffered pillaging. Some of the refugees learned at the very end of the war that their house had been destroyed; many were still in shock when they wrote to Wilson. Orphans expressed similar resentment towards the enemy, and sometimes called for vengeance and punishment: 'I am very happy', wrote Andrée Thelliez a month after her first letter [see above], 'that the instigators of this dreadful war that deprived us of our beloved father are now punished and that they will harshly expiate their fault for all the misfortune they have caused.'[49]

The children who did not personally suffer during the war showed less resentment. Their representation of the enemy mirrors war propaganda, which drew on the newly known atrocities and devastations committed in the liberated areas of France to depict Germans as dehumanized brutes.[50]

Most interestingly, depictions of the German enemy sometimes go along with the expression of a fear of France's defeat that children could not expose heretofore. The dreadful prospect of 'becoming German' is one of the letters' most fascinating themes. During the war, any thought related to the possible defeat of the French army was swiftly self-censored; the French could not express the slightest doubt about victory. Any private or public discourse vaguely related to defeat was perceived by the authorities as defeatism and, as it threatened the morale of the French population, could lead to criminal charges.[51] Now that the war was over, some did admit to the President their fear that France might have been defeated if it weren't for American military

---

48 Marie-Thérèse Vasseur to Wilson, 1st January 1919.
49 Andrée Thelliez to Wilson, 28 January 1919.
50 J. Horne, A. Kramer, *German Atrocities, 1914: A History of Denial*.
51 Series F⁷, 13371 at the Archives nationales de France contains many examples of French citizens who were tried and found guilty of defeatism.

intervention. Children were now free to expose the catastrophic scenarios they had imagined in case of defeat. 'Without your help', wrote 16-year old Germaine Ostenciaux, 'we would surely be German now, not of heart of course, but our land would be theirs.'[52] For his part, Pierre Widal was graphically precise when describing his fear of a German victory: 'Without America, France and England would have been defeated and the Germans would now be the masters of Paris. Everything would have been looted, the houses burned and the Parisians killed or tortured like the poor people in the North.'[53] Simone Gonnet summarizes in the same way: 'You prevented the spreading of devastation, cruelty and ruin on our beautiful France.'[54] These apocalyptical visions of a Germanized France are remarkable testimonies of the anxiety that affected the French population during the war. Children, who literally had nightmares about a German victory, had less trouble talking about it to Wilson, but it is likely that this unmentionable apprehension was shared by the adults as well.

The War and the Wilsonian peace

How did children talk about the war and about the peace to come? At the end of 1918, war was still prevailing over peace, as can be observed from the way children interpreted Wilson's role during and after the conflict.

Wilson was known for his work for peace; he embodied peace for millions of individuals. Yet, he is explicitly mentioned as a man of peace in only 19 children's letters whereas twice as many depicted him as a man of war. Although children praised the President as the man who ended the war, they never asked or talked to him about the ways he intended 'to end all wars': the self-determination of the peoples, the Fourteen Points and the League of Nations, all well-known themes of Wilsonianism, passed completely unnoticed by children, like if the political and ideological issues were of no interest to them. One might argue that this ignorance was the same for the bulk of the French population, for whom victory and peace were but the same word. Fernand Devot's words are typical of this sentiment: 'I am very happy that you gave us the victory and peace forever.'[55] In brief, victory over Germany *was* peace. When considering the way some children expressed to Wilson their terror of a Germanized France, it seems quite logical that getting the Germans out of the country was enough to call it peace.

Indeed, letters show that the children had a very down-to-earth vision of

---

52 Germaine Ostenciaux to Wilson, 28 December 1918.
53 Pierre Widal to Wilson, 14 February 1919.
54 Simone Gonnet to Wilson, 31 December 1918.
55 Fernand Devot to Wilson, 12 December 1918.

Fig. 1.4: André Taret's representation of peace. Note the spelling
of the President's name, "Vilson," which is an evidence of Wilson's
presence in the oral sphere—the letter "W" in French was traditionally
pronounced "V". (Library of Congress, Washington DC)

peace, which was by and large the return to normalcy and stability. 'Peace'
was therefore a sum of concrete things: the soldiers' demobilization, the
celebrations of victory, the return home for refugees, and the end of fear for
most of them. André Taret's drawing shown in Figure 1.4 illustrates this
feeling. Protected by peace and good fortune symbols, like the horseshoe and
the oak and olive tree branches, a quiet house and smooth water lay under
the flags of France and the United States which seem to protect them.[56]
Sending his new year's wishes to the President, André Taret's letter shows
how important the return to normalcy was for children. Peace for them was
called home.

In the corpus of letters, the conflict occupies more room than the coming
peace. Children still endured war conditions when they wrote to Wilson:
poverty, food deprivation and family separations plagued many. This reality
had an influence on their representation of the war, and only few depicted

56 André Taret to Wilson, letter not dated.

the war as a great patriotic enterprise. One of them is Nicolas François, who bombastically wrote: 'Thanks to you, our soldiers braved the hail of bullets, leaping on the battle ground proclaiming your name and your colors. That gave us Victory.'[57] More often, the war was seen like an intolerable burden, like in Andrée Thelliez's letter, whose father died at war: 'The horrible war that brought bloodshed to the nations has now ended.'[58] Children emphasized the suffering caused by the war and revealed their weariness, but they never questioned the principles promoted by France in the war. Thanks to the Americans, peace had arrived and Wilson is the new savior: 'Allow me, Mister President, to address to you the assurance of our admiration. You, our new redeemer, our savior who snatched ourselves from death by poverty, will never have enough people proclaiming your name,' emphatically wrote Georgette and Louise Racine.[59] Both sisters took refuge in Paris during the war without their family; they knew when writing to Wilson that they would find their mother again back home. For them, war meant the anguish of finding ways to survive. The legitimacy of France's war was never put into question: it was really the personal consequences of war, the deaths that it carried, its emotional and physical suffering, that were rejected by the children.

Conclusion

Children's letters to Wilson confirm Bruno Cabanes' argument about the persistence of discursive violence in the months following the end of the war. Children talked about the German enemy according to what they had learned about them during the war, but also according to their personal encounter with the enemy. They had internalized the war propaganda although this internalization was defined by their personal experience. Their cultural demobilization had not yet begun, especially in the case of orphans, who had first to deal with grief, and of refugees, whose return back home was only the first step towards a return to normalcy. We must keep in mind that the youngest of those who wrote to the American President had lived in war conditions up to half of their 'conscious' life. They would mentally relive and dream about their war experience for many years on.

Wilson's representation as a man of war clearly surpasses his representation as a man of peace. This is surprising considering that the latter view largely dominates in the adult world. Although very harsh regarding their enemy, adults combined their hatred with a sincere hope, with a kind of eschatological expectation that this horrible war would give way to real and lasting peace.

---

57 Nicolas François to Wilson, 20 December 1918.
58 Andrée Thelliez to Wilson, 28 January 1919.
59 Georgette et Louise Racine to Wilson, 20 December 1918.

Le 11 Décembre 1918.

ACK'D DEC 18 1918

My dear President,

I am very happy to tell you, that I am just 10 years old the day you arrive at Brest. The 13th Decembre is my anniversary and this year it is a double feast for me. I would like very much if you had sailed into St. Brieuc as our home is near the Port and I could have given you a bouquet of roses, and thanked you

Appendix 1
Fig. 1.5 and Fig. 1.6:
Child's letter written in English (except for the date). (Library of Congress, Washington DC)

for having finished the horrible war, where papa was Captain.
I have no luck at all as granny billeted many Americans, at her home, and I never went to see them.
I am the oldest of the family. I have a little brother, and two sisters. We all love you dearly and send you many kisses.
I hope you will enjoy your visit to France
Perhaps it will interest you to know that my uncle was bishop of Quebec.
I remain, Dear President, Yours affectionately
Alix de Pontbreand.

Appendix 2, Fig. 1.7: Symbols of Franco-American
friendship. (Library of Congress, Washington DC)

There is nothing equivalent in the children's letters, which never address the issue of peace other than a return to normalcy. Why, then, was Wilson so important to children if they did not talk to him about lasting peace?

For children, peace was a very concrete reality. The image of Wilson as a man of peace must give way in our minds to Wilson as benefactor, as savior, as a larger-than-life figure who could bring this tangible peace. He was the man who came to help France and gave victory to allied nations; therefore it was still he who, logically, would help the French population once the war was over. His image and his words were omnipresent in the media sphere. Children wrote to him because he seemed as omnipotent as the nation he represented: generous and rich, unselfish, powerful. They told him in simple words and in candid ways how they felt and how they made sense of the terrible experience they lived through. They also confessed to him concealed or suppressed emotions, such as their nightmare of a German victory. It is likely that hundreds of children also wrote to other important figures of the postwar period, especially French political men like President Poincaré or Premier Georges Clemenceau. We believe that it is unlikely though that they wrote to them in the same instinctive and emotional way as they did to Wilson, who represented the perfect man to listen to such confessions.

Bibliography

S. Audoin-Rouzeau, *La guerre des enfants, 1914-1918: essai d'histoire culturelle*, Paris, Armand-Colin, 1993.

S. Audoin-Rouzeau, C. Prochasson, *Sortir de la Grande Guerre: le monde et l'après-1918*, Paris, Tallandier, 2008.

A. Becker, *Journaux de combattants et de civils de la France du Nord dans la Grande Guerre*, Presses universitaires du Septentrion, 1998.

J. Bouvier, *Les noms de rues disent la ville*, Paris, Christine Bonneton, 2007.

B. Cabanes, 'Sortir de la Première Guerre mondiale (1918-début des années 1920)', in B. Cabanes, É. Husson (eds), *Les sociétés en guerre 1911-1946*. Paris, Armand Colin, 2003.

B. Cabanes, G. Picketty, 'Sortir de la guerre : jalons pour une histoire en chantier', *Histoire@Politique. Politique, culture, société*. Online. Available HTTP: http://histoire-politique.fr/index.php?numero=03&rub=dossier&item=22, (accessed 2007).

S. Cardinal, *Le discours de guerre tenu aux enfants montréalais au sujet de la Première Guerre mondiale entre 1914 et 1918*, M. A. Thesis (unpublished), Université de Montréal, 2009.

S. Claisse, T. Lemoine, *Comment (se) sortir de la grande guerre?: regards sur quelques pays "vainqueurs", la Belgique, la France et la Grande-Bretagne*, Paris, Harmattan, 2005.

S. Fitzpatrick, 'Supplicants and Citizens: Public Letter-Writing in Soviet Russia in the 1930s', *Slavic Review*, pp. 78-105, 1996, vol. 55.

E. Fordham, 'From Whitman to Wilson: French Attitudes towards American Around the Time of the Great War', in L. Passerini (ed.), *Across the Atlantic: Cultural Exchanges Between Europe and the United States*, Bruxelles, New York, P.I.E. P. Lang, 2000.

R. Girardat, *Mythes et mythologies politiques*, Paris, Éditions du Seuil, 1986.

M. Hanna, 'A Republic of Letters: The Epistolary Tradition in France during World War I', *The American Historical Review*, 1338-1361, 2003, vol. 108.

J. Horne, 'Démobilisations culturelles après la Grande Guerre', *14-18 Aujourd'hui, Today, Heute*, Clamecy, Noesis, 2002.

J. Horne, A. Kramer, *German Atrocities, 1914: A History of Denial*, New Haven, Yale University Press, 2001.

E. Manela, *The Wilsonian Moment. Self-Determination and the International Origins of Anticolonial Nationalism*, Oxford, Oxford University Press, 2007.

P. Miquel, *La paix de Versailles et l'opinion publique française*, Paris, Flammarion, 1972.

Y.-H. Nouailhat, *Les Américains à Nantes et Saint-Nazaire, 1917-1919*, Paris, Les Belles Lettres, 1972.

M. Ozouf, *L'école de la France, Essais sur la Révolution, l'utopie et l'enseignement*, Paris, Gallimard, 1963.

M. Pignot, *Allons enfants de la patrie? Filles et garçons dans la Grande Guerre: expériences communes, construction du genre et invention des pères (France 1914-1920).* Ph. D, EHESS, 2007.

J. Portes, *Une fascination réticente: les États-Unis dans l'opinion française*, Nancy, Presses universitaires de Nancy, 1990.

M. Siegel, *The Moral Disarmament of France: Education, Pacifism, and Patriotism, 1914-1940*, New York, Cambridge University Press, 2004.

2 Moments of Rupture: The Subjectivity of Children in the Second World War

Nicholas Stargardt

On Friday 26 November 1943, Marie Vassiltchikov[a] – or 'Missie', as she was universally known – walked through the foreign embassy quarter in Berlin, just to the south of the Tiergarten:

> We crossed over to Kurfürstenstrasse, where friends lived in almost every house; most of them had been hit too. The Oyarzabals' huge granite apartment building was a heap of stones. The corner of Nettelbeckstrasse (including our favourite little restaurant, the 'Taverna') had been literally pulverised, only small piles of rubble remaining. Wherever we looked, firemen and prisoners-of-war, most of them … Italians', were busy pumping air into the ruins, which meant that some people were still alive in the collapsed cellars.
>
> In front of another wrecked building a crowd was watching a young girl aged about sixteen. She was standing atop a pile of rubble, picking up bricks one by one, dusting them carefully and throwing them away again. Apparently her entire family was dead, buried underneath, and she had gone mad.[1]

In all wars, children are victims. The Second World War differed only in the unprecedented extent to which this was true. At least one million Jewish children perished in the 'final solution', and we still do not know how many of the 216,000 victims of medical killing were children. Children were shot by German soldiers and militia men in droves in occupied Poland and the Soviet Union. Starvation and disease killed the elderly and the very young throughout occupied Europe, but especially in the east. Children were incinerated with their mothers in the fire-storms of Hamburg, Dresden, Hildesheim, Darmstadt and a host of German cities, and were killed or froze to death in the mass flight of German civilians along the snow-bound roads from Silesia and East Prussia in 1945. Still greater numbers of children suffered in the war, losing their homes and belongings, their parents or

1 M. Vassiltchikov, *The Berlin Diaries, 1940-1945*, p. 118.

older siblings. Some were undoubtedly traumatised to the point where they were incapable of communicating with others, like the girl that 'Missie' Vassiltchikova saw dusting bricks above the place where her family lay buried, or the Polish girl who had to be taught to speak again after she was liberated from a concentration camp.[2]

For many others, trauma manifested itself later or less overwhelmingly, leaving them sufficiently unimpaired to study, enter professions, marry, raise children and love others. As many psycho-analysts and therapists have observed, it was often only decades later that they began the task of trying to express their buried memories, fears, and, in the case of the women survivors of the concentration camps whom Dinora Pines worked with, their suppressed rage. What interested me when I wrote about the war and the Holocaust in *Witnesses of War* was what we could learn about children's immediate experience at the time. But I think a project such as that only makes sense if we are also aware of the weight of our contemporary baggage, of cultural assumptions and the shapes that experiences have taken on in later memory. Nor, as you'll see, do I think we can ever completely escape into the historic past, unmediated by subsequent moments of recall, memory and cultural fashioning.[3]

I am very sceptical of a term which first entered mass circulation in the 1980s – 'collective trauma'. It promises to explain too much. It overwhelms its source material. With the best of empathetic intentions, our culture turns to notions like victimhood and social or collective trauma with an ease which creates enormous obstacles to understanding the past. Such terms are neither apolitical nor neutral. They give suffering a particular emotional colouring, highlighting innocence and recovery, what we might call the redemptive sides of pain, whilst casting destructive ones, such as hatred, rage and envy, into deep shadow. Recognition as a victim can also have a curiously disempowering effect, as historical subjects who were trying to make difficult calculations in terrible predicaments are turned into the passive objects of history.

National and personal redemption in the wake of defeat is not a new idea. In the 1920s, the political Right in Germany unanimously endorsed militant claims about the power of the 'blood sacrifice' made by those who had 'fallen' on the battle fields of the First World War, and the 1950s articulated a more pacifistic vision of national rebirth – in European countries on both sides of the Iron curtain – through economic and social reconstruction. In Germany, such ideas went out of fashion in the 1960s and then came under attack in the 1980s, as Germans increasingly came to see the Holocaust as the central event

2   K. Sosnowski, *The Tragedy of Children under Nazi Rule*, p. 167.
3   D. Pines, *A Woman's Unconscious Use of Her Body: A Psychoanalytical Perspective*; N. Stargardt, *Witnesses of War: Children's Lives under the Nazis*.

of the Second World War.

At just this time, 'collective trauma' entered mass circulation to give a sense of overall meaning to the stories of Holocaust survivors – and to underline society's duty to listen to them, to help them to 'break their silence'.[4] In the decades since then, 'collective trauma' has become the first term journalists reach for when they cover ethnic cleansing, wars and earthquakes, and it has also become the cultural gold standard of claims for recognition as victims. There is a limit to the number of occasions a whole society can stop and engage in rituals of commemoration and soul-searching.

In Norway, the collective term 'war children' has been used to refer rather specifically to the children born of German fathers and Norwegian mothers during and after the occupation: for them, as Kjersti Ericsson and Eva Simonsen showed, the 'trauma' that has to be overcome stems from postwar stigma and, in gaining a voice, they were also calling for social recognition and financial compensation. Fabrice Virgili has done similar work in France, and what these painful stories of individual discrimination by neighbours, the education and welfare system and even other relatives, shows, is that much of what constitutes 'trauma' has a postwar political and cultural history. It may have as much to do with societies that were not ready to listen, rather than with victims who were intrinsically unable to speak.[5]

In Germany, the subject of 'war children' has been amplified most loudly in the run-up to the commemorations of 8 May 1945 during the last few years. When Germans gathered to commemorate the 60th anniversary of the end of the Second World War in May 2005, the talk everywhere turned to the suffering of German civilians. In many respects, this is a present-centred pre-occupation, focusing on those aged 70 to 85 upwards, who report sleep deprivation, anxiety attacks, recurring nightmares and the resurgence of buried memories.[6] But classifying these individual stories as part of a general, 'collective trauma' endured by a whole generation of German children obviously also advances a claim to symbolic recognition. As an analytical term, 'collective trauma' tends to generate stronger moral responses than intellectual insight. It is not clear whether, or indeed why, all children should respond in the same ways: not all children emerged from the concentration camps or other sites of violence speechless. Nor, as it turns out on closer investigation,

4   T. Kushner, *The Holocaust and the Liberal Imagination: A Social and Cultural History*; P. Novick, *The Holocaust and Collective Memory: The American Experience*.
5   A. Warring, *Tyskerpiger: under besoettelse og retsopgør*; K. Ericsson, E. Simonsen (eds), *Children of World War II: The Hidden Enemy Legacy*; F. Virgili, *Nait ennemi: Les enfants de couples franco-allemands nés pendant la Seconde Guerre mondiale*.
6   H. Lorenz, *Kriegskinder: Das Schicksal einer Generation Kinder*; S. Bode, *Die vergessene Generation: Die Kriegskinder brechen ihr Schweigen*; H. Schulz, H. Radebold, J. Reulecke, *Söhne ohne Väter: Erfahrungen der Kriegsgeneration*.

did all children undergo the same 'collective' experiences in the first place.

In 1948, the directors of international children's villages gathered at Trogen in Switzerland to discuss their experience of working with war orphans. There was no consensus on what harm the children had suffered. Some considered that the violence they had witnessed was crucial, while others thought this had made little impression compared to their loss of family, concluding that their plight was similar to that of children who suffered such separations during peacetime. Some thought their memories needed to be repressed successfully for them to move on; others that they needed to express them through play therapy.[7] Over the next decade, Ernst Kris and Anna Freud, both editors of the new journal, *The Psychoanalytic Study of the Child*, pursued the subject further, Anna Freud's reflections were informed by what she had seen in the Hampstead war nurseries and from working with child survivors of the Theresienstadt camp. Returning to the familiar terrain of her long-running argument with Melanie Klein about the role of cognition and the oedipal conflict in developing a sense of self, she concluded that it was the loss of parental figures, rather than children's experience of violence which was central. This may seem a rather distant discussion now, but her work seems to have had a special reception in Germany, perhaps because her scattered essays on childhood and war were gathered together published as a single volume in German.[8] In any event, German analysts like Hartmut Radebold, who have pioneered the current discussion of 'war children', in fact lay great emphasis on the loss of fathers through the war. For him, absent fathers disproportionately affected the development of sons. There is of course a gender element to this, and the oral historian Dorothee Wierling has noted that protagonists of this self-styled 'war child generation' are predominantly men, who pursued successful careers in West Germany in the 1960s-90s.[9]

What interested me when I wrote about the war and the Holocaust from the point of view of children was to try to find ways back into the kinds of subjectivity they had developed at the time. There are major difficulties in recovering children's subjectivity, even of such a relatively recent past.

---

7   T. Brosse, *Homeless Children: Report of the Proceedings of the Conference of Directors of the Childrens Communities, Trogen, Switzerland*, p. 22, 27 and pp. 43-4.

8   See E. Kris, 'The Recovery of Childhood Memories in Psychoanalysis', *The Psychoanalytic Study of the Child*, pp. 54-88; A. Freud, 'An experiment in group upbringing', *The Writings of Anna Freud*, pp. 163-229; A. Freud, 'Child observation and prediction of development: A memorial lecture in honour of Ernst Kris', *The Writings of Anna Freud*, pp. 102-35; A. Freud and D. Burlingham, *Heimatlose Kinder*; John Bowlbys study of 200 British children under twelve, who had war-related problems, concluded that in one third of cases, evacuation rather than bombing was the cause: J. Bowlby, *Child Care and the Growth of Love*, p. 42.

9   H. Radebold, *Abwesende Väter und Kriegskindheit: Fortbestehende Folgen in Psychoanalysen*; also website for main publications: http://www.kriegskinder.de/trauma.php; D. Wierling, ,Kriegskinder: westdeutsch, bürgerlich, männlich?', in L. Seegers, J. Reulecke (eds), *Die 'Generation der Kriegskinder'. Historische Hintergründe und Deutungen*, pp. 141 – 155.

Surviving contemporary sources – such as children's letters, drawings, diaries, school work or adult observations, whether of children's games or of child psychiatric patients – are fragmentary and discontinuous. There is a danger that such complicated and fragile source material could be crushed to fit a simple, over-arching interpretation, and in the process, lose everything that was most striking and individual about it. Not surprisingly, I was very reluctant to use the term 'trauma' as an interpretative category, both because of the risks of this kind of 'force-fit' and because of its moral-political baggage. At the same time, I am very interested in a situation which is often to be found in cases of trauma, but is not exhausted by them: what I would call moments of emotional rupture.

In June 1943, fourteen-year-old Alfred Völkel wrote a short memoir of his childhood. He explained how he had grown up in foster care, at his grandmother's, and then from the age of ten – and the outbreak of the war – in a Bavarian children's home. He had finished school and hoped to become a clerk or a teacher, but had had to accept an apprenticeship to a book-binder instead, almost certainly a disappointment to his ambitions to join the white-collar lower middle class. Written on a single sheet of paper divided into two columns, Völkel's 'Lebenslauf' is one of those deceptively 'complete' documents, whose real significance – and incompleteness – only became apparent thanks to his subsequent testimony. He wrote it soon after being sent to the psychiatric asylum at Hadamar.[10]

The asylum, perched picturesquely on the hillside above the little town, overlooked the forgotten winding valley carved out by the river Lahn between Marburg and Frankfurt, an area of small tin mines, Catholic observance and rural poverty. In January 1941, it became one of the centres for the T-4 programme of killing psychiatric patients. By the time Alfred Völkel arrived at Hadamar, the T-4 personnel had been redeployed and the small gas chamber in the basement was not being used. Psychiatric patients were now being killed in ways which it was easier to disguise. Many adult patients were put on a diet of stinging nettle soup until they died of hunger-related disease. Killing children had been disguised from the start for fear of public outcry, with doctors and nursing staff using different cocktails of drugs: powdered luminal was mixed into the evening meals, children were injected with morphium-scopolamin, or given tablets of luminal and trional. With symptoms of acute pneumonia or bronchitis, death was often painful, dragged out over several days. Alfred Völkel was given the task of sorting the children's clothes in one of the attics. On his way there, he had to walk through the closed ward, where he heard the 'death rattles' of the twenty to thirty hungry and exhausted children as they battled for breath against the fluid flooding their lungs.

10 A. Völkel, 'Lebenslauf', 5031.

Völkel was not mentally disabled. He was, though he did not know it, half-Jewish, in Nazi-speak a 'first degree *Mischling*'. He had been sent to Hadamar alongside forty-one other half-Jewish children in a nationwide sweep of German children's homes. As the original group gradually dwindled to four boys and two girls, Alfred Völkel soon realised that each day that he was not called to the 'office' was 'a gift of life'.[11]

Thanks to the help of his immediate supervisor, Alfred managed to smuggle a letter to his uncle, Corporal Georg Völkel, who immediately wrote to the Director of the asylum. Using whatever leverage he had, he questioned whether Alfred was in fact a first or only a second degree *Mischling*, and pointed out that he, not the child's mother, had supported Alfred and was his legal guardian. Georg Völkel's commanding officer also wrote in support, vouchsafing him as 'a conscientious, dutiful and keen soldier'. But the *Oberleutnant* also confirmed that Völkel had mentioned disturbing rumours about the 'fate of asylum inmates', which were clearly causing him grave concern, and the officer suggested that the asylum should tighten its own security and prevent letters being smuggled out. In the end, it was the authority which had sent Alfred to Hadamar in the first place whose intervention proved decisive: the Nuremberg Youth Welfare department confirmed that they were indeed not his legal guardian, and so, although he had been in a Bavarian children's home, they had had no right to send him to Hadamar with the other *Mischling* children in state care. By the time this ruling arrived, four months had passed, and of the 42 children only Völkel and one other terrified boy were left.[12]

Alfred Völkel was able to go home – as we shall see, this was a recurring dream for children in war. There he rejoined the Hitler Youth, going on to

11 A. Völkel, 'Not just because I was a "bastard"', 5031.
12 Ibid.; Alfred Völkel survived because the Nuremberg Jugendamt declared that it did not have the right to decide his abode, because this still rested with his 'Aryan' mother, and so requested his return on 20 Sept. 1943; the same was true for one of the other children; the other three were siblings, whose uncle employed a lawyer to have them released, after he learned of the deaths of their three others siblings in Hadamar: Landeswohlfahrtsverband Hessen, B. Winter (eds), *"Verlegt nach Hadamar": Die Geschichte einer NS-"Euthanasie"-Anstalt*, p. 136; S. Scholz, R. Singer, 'Die Kinder in Hadamar', in: Roer and Henkel, *Psychiatrie im Faschismus*, pp. 229-35; on the whole development, see Sander, *Verwaltung des Krankenmordes*, pp. 542-4 and 654-68; individual files in LWV Hessen: K12/53, Horst S.; K12/252, Peter W.; K12/1013, Horst St.; K12/1023, Karlheinz Sch.; K12/1050, Willi St.; K12/1071, Edith Sp.; K12/1548, Elias R.; K12/1598, Emmi Sch.; K12/2166, Helmut W.; K12/2918, Ingeborg D.; K12/2957, Georg Br.; K12/3298, Egon H.; K12/3608, Wolfgang Fr.; K12/3615, Klaus Fr.; K12/3750, Leo C.; K 12/4769, Ruth B.; K12/5002, Manfred B.; K12/5017, Gerhard K.; K12/5021, Eleonore B.; K12/5028, Erika H.; K12/5030, Sigmund W.; K12/5031, Alfred Völkel; K12/5032, Günther P.; K12/5033, Günther H.; K12/5037, Amanda G.; K12/5038, Klara G.; K12/5039, Alfred G.; K12/5040, Edeltrud G.; K12/5046, Günther M.; K12/5047, Maria L.; K12/5054, Alfred R.; K12/5055, Hermann R.; K12/5056, Johann R.; K12/5057, Irma R.; K12/5058, Anna R.; K12/5059, Friedrich Z.; K12/5060, Jakob H.; K12/5061, Wolfgang H.; K12/5064 ,Manfred L.

serve in the German Army and be taken prisoner by the Allies. In 1996, fifty-three years after being sent there, he dared to visit Hadamar – still a functioning psychiatric asylum – again. Only after that did he contact the local archives and read a copy of his medical file. This was the first time that he realised that his father – a man he had never met – was Jewish and that this was the reason why he had been sent to Hadamar in the first place. If his Bavarian, Catholic maternal relatives had been careful to shield him from this knowledge and the social stigma it carried, it was his own mother's rejection he had always felt most keenly. As he wrote, he had been the 'bastard' child, 'scolded, punished, directed and shuttled from one orphanage to another'. He had seen almost nothing of her, even when he had lived in his grandmother's house. 'All I could see', Alfred wrote, 'was that my mother chose others over me – a stepfather and later two half siblings.' Alfred may have owed his life to the persistence of his mother's brother, but even a life-saving miracle could not undo the deep rejection he had experienced. For him, Nazi racism was etched into the most personal of all relationships, of mother and child. After the war, Alfred Völkel emigrated to the United States.

Völkel's case is significant in a number of ways, most obviously because he is one of a handful of children to be released from a killing centre like Hadamar; but it is also revealing for what it tells us about subjectivity. The complete document, the short contemporary autobiography, turns out to be a fragment, embedded in a process whose purpose was probably still obscured from Völkel at the point he wrote it. By contrast, his medical case file can explain the context and the process, retaining all the letters written by his uncle, his superior officer and the Nuremberg Youth Welfare Board. Yet even Völkel's later testimony almost certainly recaptures only sparse elements of how he experienced these events at the time. It is this broken mosaic, with its many lost and few retained fragments which accentuates a problem which itself is embedded in children's memories and ways of experiencing – namely a sense of the moments illuminating subjective experience being discrete; unintegrated into the kind of over-arching, connected narrative which adults can, and indeed often feel the need to, give. The fragmentary source and the isolated moment accentuate something which we are all probably already looking for when we study children and war; a sense of rupture.

Rupture is of course critical to memories of war and the Holocaust, and one of the things which is striking about it is the clarity and stability over a subsequent lifetime with which particular events are invested with this significance. One of the most revealing sets of sources are a collection of essays from the mid-1950s by West German teenagers who would have been aged four to seven when the events actually occurred. If their accounts are inevitably infused with later memory – one even wrote about what his mother told him later on – and bear the imprint of a broadly pacifist postwar outlook, they nonetheless evoke their younger selves at a point when they had still not yet left school or home to begin their adult lives. As a 16 year-old boy at the Burg Gymnasium in Essen wrote in February 1956,

> I was born just at the outbreak of war so that I cannot remember the first [war] years. But from my fifth year on, much is ineradicably etched in my memory. I sat through long nights of bombing in the cellar or bunker between shaking adults.[13]

Or as a boy at the working-class vocational school put it at the same time; 'Then it started in the bunker where people crouched in every corner and angle. With every bomb that fell the "Our Fathers" sounded louder'.[14] Having to endure months of twice or thrice nightly alarms under the entire flight path of the bomber fleets took its toll on sleep and nerves. These young children also had to learn fear from the adults around them, however much their mothers thought that they were protecting them by involving them in the purposeful routines of giving them small suitcases to pack and going to bed in their tracksuits so that they would be prepared for the alarms. These were lessons which had already been learned in Warsaw and London.

One Essen boy, born in 1940, traced his first memory back to the sound of the air-raid sirens as his parents roused him from his sleep. Another [15] older children recalled in early 1946 how during the raids on Berlin, they had quickly learned to listen for the different sounds, recognising the high explosive bombs from their 'Crash bang!!!' and the 'muffled crack' of the incendiaries, whose 'Clack, clack clack' reminded one child of 'when someone got a juicy slap.'[16]

In other respects, however, extreme experiences such as air raids seem to

---

13 Wilhelm Roessler-Archiv, Institut für Geschichte und Biographie der Fernuniversität Hagen: Burg-Gymnasium Essen (hereafter, RA), UII/516, anon., 16 yrs, 14 Feb. 1956, 1: 'Ich selbst war bei Ausbruch des Krieges gerade geboren, so daß ich mich an die ersten Jahre nicht erinnern kann. Vom fünften Lebensjahre an aber, steht mir vieles unerschütterlich ins Gedächtnis geschrieben. Lange Bombennächte hindurch saß ich zwischen zitternden Erwachsenen im Keller oder Bunker. Bei jedem Bombenabwurf oder Fliegerabsturz wankte der Boden.'
14 RA, Berufschule M2/6, 1, praying in bunker, 16 yrs, 21 Jan. 1956: 'Dann ging's ab in den Bunker wo die Menschen in allen Ecken und Winkeln hockten. Bei jeder Bombe die fiel ertönten die Vater Unser lauter.'
15 RA, Burg-Gymnasium Essen, UII/522, anon., b. 1940, 24.2.1956.
16 RA, Berufschule M2/6, 1, praying in bunker, 16 yrs, 21 Jan. 1956: 'Dann ging's ab in den Bunker wo die Menschen in allen Ecken und Winkeln hockten. Bei jeder Bombe die fiel ertönten die Vater Unser lauter.' Sounds in Prenzlauer Berg Museum des Kulturamtes Berlin and A. Gröschner (ed.), *Ich schlug meiner Mutter die Brennenden Funken ab: Berliner Schulaufsätze aus dem Jahr 1946*, p. 35: 'dumpfen Knall'; 'Klack, Klack, Klack'; Krach, bum!!!'; 'Hui! Wum!' Even in Berlin, where about a quarter of all German bunkers were built in the programme after the raids on Hamburg, there was capacity for only about 10% of city's population: O. Groehler, *Bombenkrieg gegen Deutschland*, pp. 238-54.

have widened the divide between younger and older children. Whilst younger ones played games, fell asleep and even waited for St Nikolaus in the air raid cellars, they also lacked a sense of what it all meant and why it was happening. By contrast, a fifteen year-old Berlin girl, Liselotte G, had increasing difficulties reconciling the events of the nights with her rather uneventful daily routine of a school-girl living in the quiet eastern suburbs of the capital. On 29 December 1943, she noted, 'It was another terrifying attack' and she had struggled to keep the composure she thought befitting for her ideal of 'the German woman', silently repeating to herself the prayer she had learned for her own confirmation nine months before.[17] By 3 January, she worried whether her religious faith would see her through and whether she could pass this test of 'self-sacrifice' which she felt was being demanded of her. Things were not helped by the fact that, instead of receiving positive confirmation of the retaliation Hitler had promised against England back in November, she instead had a long conversation with her defeatist Social Democratic father. He explained to her, in early January 1944, that Germany would be defeated and occupied by the Allies. Confused by the conflicting perspectives and moral demands, she insisted on seeing the patriotic as personal – asking herself if she was too weak to do what every German soldier at the front could do? 'No & I repeat no,' she declaimed silently to her diary. 'I can & will sacrifice myself.' And taking refuge in the Gothic mythology so beloved by Nazi propagandists:

> If victory is no longer to be had, then there is still honour', shouted Teja the Ostgoth, still fighting as he fell. Can one not shout to Germany's enemies: 'you can murder me, but you cannot kill me, for I am eternal![18]

Liselotte dramatised her need to understand war in adult moral and political terms – though one might note too the extent to which the Nazi regime was thrusting the adult world into a particularly teenage one, with its willingness for self-sacrifice and to make boundless commitments for a cause.

---

17 I. Hammer, S. zur Nieden (eds), *Sehr selten habe ich geweint: Briefe und Tagebücher aus dem Zweiten Weltkrieg von Menschen aus Berlin*, p. 288: Liselotte G., diary, 29 Dec. 1943:
'Mein schönstes Zier und Kleinod bist auf Erden du, Herr Jesu Christ, dich will ich lassen walten, u. alle Zeit in Lieb u. Leid in meinem Herzen halten.
Dein Lieb u. treu vor allem geht, kein Ding auf Erd so fest besteht, das muß ich frei bekennen, drum soll nicht Tod, nicht Angst, nicht Not von deiner Lieb mich trennen.
Dein Wort ist wahr u. trüget nicht u. hält gewiß, was es verspricht, im Tod u. auch im Leben.
Du bist nun mein u. ich bin dein, dir hab ich mich ergeben.'

18 Hammer, zur Nieden, *Sehr selten habe ich geweint*, pp. 289-290, 2 Jan. 1944: ' "Gilt es nicht mehr den Sieg, so gilt es doch die Ehre", rief Teja den untergehen noch kämpfenden Ostgoten zu. Kann man nicht doch den Feinden Deutschlands zurufen: Ihr könnt mich mörden, aber töten könnt ihr mich nicht, denn ich bin ewig!'

This was not, of course, a uniquely German experience, though in its mixture of Nazi, religious and even oppositional ideas, her variant on it clearly was. As the diaries and letters of teenage boys reveal too, this emphasis on cool composure under fire and patriotic self-sacrifice was sacralised by exchanging their Hitler Youth uniforms for those of anti-aircraft auxiliaries and later the *Volkssturm,* and remained potent parts of their sense of duty into the final weeks of the war.

Younger children, by contrast, marvelled at the bombing of their cities, thrilled by the vividness of the colours and wild beauty of the sights. One five-year-old girl, watching from her home outside Berlin as the planes flew in to bomb the city in 1943, remembered that 'the sight of the threatening and growling aeroplanes was such that I thought I was dreaming and in a magical world.'[19] Adults commented on this side of the air war more rarely: almost certainly, they were not immune to this aesthetic sense – soldiers, for example, wrote often about the beauty of burning and destruction. However, a sense of propriety held such responses in check when the victims were one's own neighbours, only for them to pop out in popular slang: the coloured, marker flares which slowly fell on their miniature parachutes were universally known as 'Christmas trees'.[20]

The bombing gave rise to new children's games. Collecting *Flak* splinters was particularly prized by boys, who traded them in their school yards just as their older brothers had once swapped cigarette cards. Some other games no longer made any sense at all: one six year-old girl found no fun anymore in one of her favourite games, jumping off the roof of the chicken hutch screaming 'Stucka!' as loudly as she could. She stopped playing the game after Essen was bombed in March 1943. The make-believe had all become too real.[21]

As they watched their houses burn and collapse in front of them, older children and adults had words for expressing their disbelief and their pain. They could find meaning in competing explanations – from 'Jewish retaliation' to a 'burden' sent by God to purify society from sin. Younger children did not have such meanings. Instead, it was the moment when their house was hit which was the meaning. Small children consoled themselves with the shoes, books and dolls which were rescued from the rubble, much as their mothers often counted the plates and glasses which had miraculously survived, as if

19 RA, Goetheschule Essen, OII, anon., b. 1938, 1: 'Durch das Auf- und Ableuchten der Positionslichter wurde der Anblick der drohenden und brummenden Flugzeuge so geschildert, daß ich dachte, ich träumte und wäre in einer Zauberwelt.'

20 A rare exception is Ursula von Kardorff, *Berliner Aufzeichnungen: Aus den Jahren 1942 bis 1945,* p. 159: 21 June 1944, on the swirling clouds of dust and flames after an air raid on Berlin as resembling 'das Fegefeuer auf mittelalterlichen Bildern' and 'Dabei war das Ganze zugleich von einer wilden Schönheit.'

21 *Flak* splinters in Harald H., MS, 1 (author's collection); 'Stuka' game in RA, UI/ no no., anon. 19 yrs., 16 Jan. 1956, pp. 2-3.

they stood for all that they had lost. But loss also divided small children from adults. What children did do was to construct their own chronologies of the war through key events; the moment when *their* war became real. When exactly their secure world collapsed became a defining moment, dividing the war from a previous 'golden age'. This remained remarkably constant against all subsequent reworkings of later experience.

For Jewish children in Germany, Austria and the Czech lands, that moment of chronological rupture came before the war, often with their emigration, especially if it involved family separations. For Poles, this often happened in 1939-40, with the mass shootings, deportations and – for Polish Jews – ghettoisation which followed the German invasion. For German children in the cities of the Rhineland and Ruhr, it came with the onset of heavy bombing in 1942 and 1943. For children in the eastern German provinces, that moment was usually the mass flights of 1945. For many other German and Austrian children growing up in the backwaters of the countryside, their intact and safe world did not end until occupation and the collapse of the Third Reich: for them, the events shaping their inner sense of time were more likely to be the capitulation of 8 May 1945 and the hunger years which followed than the Nazi period itself. There never was a homogeneous experience of this war. Any 'generational' experience always has to face the extreme inequalities of experience encapsulated in these three images of home or its loss:

Fritz Wandel and Karin Isolde Lehmann both lived in parts of Germany spared from Allied air raids, and where children's first and last experiences of the war often followed one another in rapid succession, leaving behind drastic inequalities of experience. The flight of Wandel's family from the Soviet Army, the movement of their 'trek' from right to left across the page following the east-west direction of maps, confronts the idyllic Lehmann home, protected until the very last, when French and German soldiers fought for control of their village in the Black Forest. For Zuzana Winterová, the loss of home is more complex, her ideal world – where children sit at the table, the mother cleans and father reads his paper in the armchair – is simultaneously preserved and, as she adds the banner of the newspaper, torn apart again. Instead of 'Tageszeitung', daily paper, she put 'Tagesbefehl', order of the day, a slip with which her evocation of the safe pre-Nazi world abruptly vanished and she found herself back in the Jewish transit camp and 'ghetto' of Theresienstadt.[22]

There is a different way of looking at moments of rupture. During and immediately after the War, adults across Europe were rattled and offended by the confidence and activity of children. From looking after younger siblings while their effectively single mothers went out to work, children took on ever greater responsibilities. They became beggars and smugglers to feed their

---

22 N. Stargardt, 'Children's Art of the Holocaust', *Past and Present*, pp. 192-235.

families. At some point – as their parents broke down in the starving Jewish ghettos, or as they fled before the Red Army in the snows of 1945, or while they hid in their cellars during bombing raids – many children shouldered premature responsibilities, often for the whole family.[23]

During wartime and post-war occupations, and in the Jewish ghettos, children had asserted themselves on the streets and market. They had had fewer norms to unlearn than adults and often more drive and energy to adapt. In these moments when the war became 'real', the integrity of their family worlds broke apart and children felt that they needed to patch them up again. But the same development also undermined their trust in the adult world and increased their sense of having to take responsibility for themselves. In 1945, the Polish State Institute of Mental Hygiene studied the war's moral and psychological harm through a large-scale questionnaire. Many children claimed to have learned the patriotic virtues from their parents, teachers and the Resistance. Yet just as many children admitted that they had learned to lie, steal and deceive, hate, treat authority with contempt, feel indifferent to all ideals, and even to have lost faith in the sanctity of human life. Set against the evidence of teenage drinking, sex, absenteeism from work, theft and black marketeering which welfare workers, juvenile courts and psychologists were reporting across the European continent, such surveys confirmed their belief that the war had destroyed children's innocence.[24] It had also taught these children how to survive. By 1946, German children were plying the black market too.[25] In this premature and 'wild' activity of children lay their capacity for treating the most extreme conditions as *normal*.

These specific moments shaped children's overall chronology of the war, establishing when the 'safe' or 'intact' world of childhood was destroyed. Critical to how this chronology ran was its *future* trajectory: if the family itself survived, as most German ones did, that became the central element of the tale; where the family itself was destroyed, as was often the case for the handful of Jewish children who survived the Holocaust, that shaped the tale.

There is one final way of exploring these moments of rupture, which is not

---

23 See Stargardt, *Witnesses of War*; on wartime Poland, see T. Szarota, *Warschau unter dem Hakenkreuz: Leben und Alltag im besetzten Warschau 1.10.1939 bis 31.7.1944*, pp. 101-130; G. S. Paulsson, *Secret City: The Hidden Jews of Warsaw, 1940-1945*, p. 26 and pp. 61-66.

24 Brosse, *War-handicapped Children*, pp. 19-20 and pp. 77-100; Sosnowski, *The Tragedy of Children under Nazi Rule*, pp. 165-71; H. Radomska-Strzemecka, 'Okupacja w oczach młodzieży', in J. Wnuk, H. Radomska-Strzemecka, *Dzieci polskie oskarżają (1939-1945)*, pp. 195-379.

25 D. Macardle, *Children of Europe: A Study of the Children of Liberated Countries: Their War-time Experiences, Their Reactions, and Their Needs, with a Note on Germany*, p. 287, citing *International Child Welfare Review*, 2, 1948, 3; C. Klessmann, *Die doppelte Staatsgründung: Deutsche Geschichte 1945-1955*, pp. 50-1; S. Meyer, E. Schulze, *Wie wir das alles geschafft haben: Alleinstehende Frauen berichten über ihr Leben nach 1945*, pp. 100-1: Mutti, kocht Mittag!; Stargardt, *Witnesses of War*, pp. 333-5; Meyer, Schulze, *Wie wir das alles geschafft haben*, pp. 103-8; A.L. Lloyd, „Germany's child smugglers", *Picture Post*, 4 Oct. 1947, cited in Macardle, *Children of Europe*, pp. 287-8.

dependent on future events and the survival of the children themselves. This is to consider how the war impacted on children's games. Whereas diaries and memories reveal moments of solitary introspection, play takes us back into the immediacy of children's group activities. With the rise of the black market came new games like 'coal thief and engine driver', which were played in Poland in 1940 and in Germany in 1946.[26] Children's games have a limited and historically repetitive repertoire, and for exactly this reason dramatic changes in the character and allocation of roles may be highly revealing. Throughout the second world war, children played war games. In Southern Westphalia in October 1939, Detlef was able to convey some of the excitement of his battles to his enlisted father, as the ten year-old described how his side had retaken their position under 'murderous fire'. His side had used sticks as hand grenades, but the enemy had thrown stones. Then Detlef had led the charge, his 'sabre' raised, putting the enemy temporarily to flight. As battle resumed, Detlef's side attacked once more and withstood a fierce counter-attack: 'None of us cried out and we won,' he wrote triumphantly to his father.[27]

There was nothing very new about this. Only the roles which the children competed for altered over time. Children in 1757 in Aachen or in Cologne in 1810 wanted to be the 'king' or the 'robber captain'. By the interwar period, German and Austrian children were playing *Räuber und Gendarmes*, cops and robbers.[28] Anything which is historically specific about children's games in central Europe during the second world war is only evident against the backdrop of these more general characteristics of children's playing.[29]

Defeat, occupation and imprisonment had an immediate impact upon children's games too. In Bromberg – or Bydgoszcz – four and six-year-olds soon began re-enacting the mass executions the Germans carried out on the town square in the first weeks of the occupation, acclaiming most those who cried, 'Poland has not yet perished!' In Warsaw, boys played at liberating prisoners,

---

26 M. Maschmann, *Account Rendered: A Dossier on my Former Self*, p. 121; Archiv der Akademie der Künste, Kempowski-Archiv, 4622, P. Laudan, 'Gefährdete Spiele', b 1935, 34: 'Kohlenklau und Lokomotivführer'.

27 H. Lange, B. Burkard (eds), *'Abends wenn wir essen fehlt uns immer einer': Kinder schreiben an die Väter 1939-1945*, p. 97-8: Detlef, 17 Oct. 1939: 'unter mörderisches Feuer' and 'ich mit vorgehaltenen Säbel stürmte vor' and 'Aber von uns heutle keiner, und wir siegten.'

28 Stargardt, 'Kinder zwischen Arbeit und Spiel', *Sozialwissenschaftliche Informationen*, pp. 123-130; E. Rosenhaft, *Beating the Fascists?*; H. Lessing, M. Liebel, *Wilde Cliquen*. The upper classes were the first to withdraw their children from such wild freedom of the streets at the turn of the eighteenth century, in a sense setting the precedence for the wholesale withdrawal of the middle classes from the streets into private recreational spaces in the last third of the nineteenth century: J. Schlumbohm, *Kinderstuben: Wie Kinder zu Bauern, Bürgern, Aristokraten wurden 1700-1850*, p. 222.

29 Archiv der Akademie der Künste, Kempowski-Archiv, 3024, Otto P., b. 1926, 'Himmel und Hölle: Eine Kreuzberger Kindheit', MS, pp. 59-60; J. David, *A Square of Sky: The Recollections of a Childhood*, pp. 111-14.

but they were also observed pretending to carry out Gestapo interrogations, slapping each others' faces in this 'wild' game. As reality invaded the make-believe, children were torn between models of heroic resistance and the allure of their conquerors.[30]

German children played at fighting the French, the English (never the British) and the Russians, but as in the older games of cops and robbers, the Germans always won. For the conquered, bringing the old games up to date often meant playing with real humiliations and immediate threats. In the Jewish ghetto in Vilna, children also began to play with a daily reality. There was only one main gate in and out of the ghetto, and each evening the Jewish police searched the Jewish workers as they returned from the workshops on the Lithuanian side of town for smuggled food, and although they risked being beaten for it, children often lingered near the gate in the hope of getting something. They also played at what they saw. As children enacted 'Going through the gate', Tzvia Kuretzka recalled:

> Two main characters were selected; Levas, the hated head of the Jewish gate guards, and Franz Murer, one of the most murderous Gestapo men. The rest of the children played the Jewish workers who tried to smuggle some food into the starving ghetto and the guards who attempted to find the contraband. While the Jewish gate guards search everyone 'Murer' comes, which propels the Jewish police to intensify its brutality and, at the same time, precipitates a tumult and panic among the 'workers.' They try desperately to toss away the small food packages, but 'Murer' finds some with the incriminating evidence and the 'workers' are put aside and later are whipped by the police.[31]

The two biggest boys got to play Franz Murer and Meir Levas, leaving it to the smaller ones to take the role of the adult Jewish workers, who, in reality, would often have included their own older brothers, sisters, aunts, uncles and parents. Like the adults they were playing, they were powerless to protect themselves from the blows rained upon them; in this case by the bigger, stronger children. As in the triumphant war games German children

---

30 For these games, see I. Flatsztejn-Gruda, *Byłam wtedy dzieckiem*, pp. 37-8; Polish Ministry of Information, *The German New Order in Poland*, p. 27; T. Szarota, *Warschau unter dem Hakenkreuz*, p. 100, citing Stanislaw Srokowski's diary for 20-21 June 1940: 'In einem Wohnblock in der Niemcewicz-Straße 9 in Warschau spielen die Kinder Gestapo. Ein wildes Spiel – und worin liegt es? Daß man sich gegenseitig ins Gesicht schlägt.'

31 Tzvia Kuretzka cited in: G. Eisen, *Children and Play in the Holocaust: Games among the Shadows*, p. 77. For the context of this game, see Y. Rudashevski, *The Diary of the Vilna Ghetto: June 1941-April 1943*, p. 113: 28 Dec. 1942; pp. 115-16: 1 Jan. 1943; see also p. 99: 26 Nov; pp. 126-27: 27 Jan. 1943, visits the ghetto furniture workshop and finds that the adult workers keep the children in line by threatening them with 'Dear Children, Murer will come and make a fuss.'; Y. Arad, *Ghetto in Flames: The Struggle and Destruction of the Jews in Vilna in the Holocaust*, pp. 304-5.

were playing at this time, power resided in the uniform. But the choice of role models was a stark one, as fear and detestation mingled with envy and longing. Where Detlef wanted to be just like his uncle and father in France, for these children being like their elders promised only fear and suffering.

For ten months from September 1943 till July 1944, several thousand Jews from the Theresienstadt ghetto were kept in a special section of Auschwitz-Birkenau known as the 'family camp'. This was just in case the SS were to open the camp to inspection by the International Red Cross. To the great envy of inmates in other sections of Birkenau, this so-called 'family camp' had special blocks for children, and the inmates were allowed to keep their hair and the clothes they had come in. The children played organised games and sang, even performing a full-length musical loosely based on Walt Disney's *Snow White*. One of the Czech kindergarten teachers in the family camp also noticed the games the younger children played when they thought no one was watching. They played 'Camp elder and Block elder', 'Roll call' and 'hats off'. They played the sick who were beaten for fainting during roll call, and they played the doctor who took their food away and refused to help them if they had nothing to give him in return.[32]

Games in concentration camps did not protect children from the reality around them by preserving an ideal world of make-believe. On the contrary, they reshaped their games to incorporate that reality. In doing so they drew the most extreme conclusion from the key lessons defeat and occupation taught all children. The first thing that defeated children witnessed was the sudden impotence of the adults they had grown up thinking were all-powerful. Power and success, the strivings of ambition and envy, were suddenly incorporated in their enemies. In some cases, children could imagine themselves as partisan fighters or members of one of the underground armies of the Resistance. But complete defeat and capitulation left few positive role models.

As the Third Reich crumbled in the rubble of Berlin during the last days of April and the first days of May 1945, German children began to express the dilemmas of their new predicament in their games. Before they had even emerged from their Berlin cellars, children started playing at being Russian soldiers. Waving make-believe pistols, they relieved each other of imaginary watches, crying, '*Uhri, uhri*' to mimic Red Army looters. As they assimilated the real and terrifying power of their enemies and masters into their games, these Berlin children were also enacting their own impotence and envy.[33]

Yet, the very fact of children's *play* leaves a degree of openness and ambiguity

---

32 . Otto Dov Kulka, evidence given on 30 July 1964 at the Auschwitz trial, and Hanna Hoffmann-Fischel report for Yad Vashem, both reprinted in I. Deutschkron (ed.), ... *Denn ihrer war die Hölle: Kinder in Gettos und Lagern*, p. 80 and p. 54; and Dokumentation des österreichischen Widerstandes, Vienna, 13243, Y. Bacon, interview with Ben-David Gershon, pp. 47–8.
33 Anneliese H.'s diary, 1 May 45, in E. Kuby, *The Russians and Berlin, 1945*, p. 226.

about the meaning of their games: what does it mean for children to consciously enact such scenarios? When, in May 1940, Emmanuel Ringelblum overheard an eight year-old Jewish boy in the Warsaw ghetto screaming, 'I want to steal, I want to rob, I want to eat, I want to be a German,' he was hearing the voice of pure desperation and rage.[34] But to *play* at robbing, stealing and being German was somehow different from this starving child's scream. Children knew it was a game, that one scenario that they could truly control, however powerless they might be in other respects. And then there were things they did not play at altogether – German children might enact Russian plunder, but not rape. Indeed, this pattern persisted later on: as German and Austrian children wrote about the end of the war over the next 50 years in school essays or unpublished memoirs, they might mention the ubiquity of rape but veered away from the subject again as soon as it touched on their own mothers.[35]

The 'family camp' in Birkenau was a rectangular barbed-wire enclosure situated within sight of three crematoria. Their chimneys belched out three and four metre high flames when in constant use. Whereas the adults attempted to ignore their proximity to the gas chambers, the children drew them directly into the fabric of their daily lives. The older ones played games with death, daring each other to run up to the electric fence and touch it with their finger tips, knowing the high voltage current was usually – but not always – switched off during the day time. One day one of their teachers came upon the younger children playing 'Gas chamber' outside their block. They had dug a hole and were throwing in one stone after the other. These were to be the people who were going into the crematorium and the children mimicked their cries. In one way, their game broke down here. Whereas in their normal games of 'Roll call', the little children may have had to submit to beatings for 'fainting', here no one jumped into the hole which was the gas chamber. They had to use stones instead.[36] Even the smaller children, who were routinely dragooned into playing roles where they were punished or beaten, could not be those people. We may surmise that to do so would, like playing at rape, have been too psychologically self-destructive. In any event,

---

34 J. Sloan (ed.), *Notes from the Warsaw Ghetto: The Journal of Emmanuel Ringelblum*, p. 39: 9 May 1940.

35 See Stargardt, *Witnesses of War*, pp. 321-3; A. Petö, 'Memory and the narrative of rape in Budapest and Vienna in 1945', in R. Bessel, D. Schumann (eds), *Life after Death: Approaches to a Cultural and Social History of Europe during the 1940s and 1950s*, pp. 133-4 and p. 138; I. Bandhauer Schöffmann, E. Hornung, 'Vom Dritten Reich zur Zweiten Republik', in D. F. Good, M. Grandner, M. J. Maynes (eds), *Frauen in Österreich: Beiträge zu ihrer Situation im 19. und 20. Jahrhundert*, pp. 232-3; also M. Baumgartner, 'Zwischen Mythos und Realität: Die Nachkriegsvergewaltigungen im sowjetisch-besetzten Mostviertel,' *Zeitschrift für Landeskunde von Niederösterreich*, p. 80.

36 Hoffmann-Fischel report for Yad Vashem, reprinted in Deutschkron, ... *Denn ihrer war die Hölle*, 54.

these unspoken limits to children's games suggest that, however much they may have envied their enemies, their primary drive was to adapt in order to survive.

The war was not just something that had happened to children. As they strove to survive in it and to parent their parents, it also tore apart their inner emotional world. Through their games, children simultaneously protected themselves from and adapted to a reality in which they recognized their enemies as the image of victorious strength and their parents as impotent failure. Children's games, as much as their other precocious activities, demonstrated that they were not just the mute and traumatised witnesses to this war. By its end, almost all European children had experienced military defeat and occupation. Once secure social structures became fluid, including that 'safe' realm of 'childhood' which so many pedagogues and social reformers had sought to create in the previous 120 years, in order to insulate children from violence. The level of violence and the policies of the German and Allied occupations could not have been more different, but everywhere adults and children alike became acquainted with hunger, cold and the powerlessness of adults. The 'time before' might seem like a lost 'golden age', but children found new roles for themselves and adapted with a speed and practicality which shocked many adults. In the process, they demonstrated just how profound were the social transformations wrought by Nazism and war: children found these things *normal*.

Bibliography

Y. Arad, *Ghetto in Flames: The Struggle and Destruction of the Jews in Vilna in the Holocaust*, Jerusalem, Yad Veshem Martyrs and Heroes Remembrance Authority, 1980.

I. Bandhauer Schöffmann, E. Hornung, 'Vom Dritten Reich zur Zweiten Republik', in D. F. Good, M. Grandner, M. J. Maynes (eds.), *Frauen in Österreich: Beiträge zu ihrer Situation im 19. und 20. Jahrhundert*, Vienna, Böhlau, 1994.

M. Baumgartner, 'Zwischen Mythos und Realität: Die Nachkriegsvergewaltigungen im sowjetisch-besetzten Mostviertel,' *Unsere Heimat/ Zeitschrift für Landeskunde von Niederösterreich*, 1993.

S. Bode, *Die vergessene Generation: Die Kriegskinder brechen ihr Schweigen*, Stuttgart, Klett-Cotta, 2004.

J. Bowlby, *Child Care and the Growth of Love*, Harmondsworth, Penguin, 1953.

T. Brosse, *Homeless Children: Report of the Proceedings of the Conference of Directors of the Childrens Communities, Trogen, Switzerland*, Paris, UNESCO, 1950.

T. Brosse, *War-handicapped Children*, Paris, UNESCO, 1950.

J. David, *A Square of Sky: Memoirs of a Wartime Childhood*, London, Eland, 1992.

I. Deutschkron (ed.), ... *Denn ihrer war die Hölle: Kinder in Gettos und Lagern*, Köln, Verlag für Wissenschaft und Politik, 1965.

G. Eisen, *Children and Play in the Holocaust: Games among the Shadows*, Amherst, University of Massachusetts Press, 1988.f

K. Ericsson, E. Simonsen (eds), *Children of World War II: The Hidden Enemy Legacy*, Oxford, Berg, 2005.

I. Flatsztejn-Gruda, *Byłam wtedy dzieckiem*, Lublin, Norbertinum, 2004.

A. Freud, 'An experiment in group upbringing', in A. Freud, *The Writings of Anna Freud* Volume 4, New York, International Universities Press, 1968.

A. Freud and D. Burlingham, *Heimatlose Kinder*, Frankfurt, Fischer, 1971.

A. Freud, 'Child observation and prediction of development: A memorial lecture in honour of Ernst Kris', in A. Freud, *The Writings of Anna Freud* Volume 5, New York, International Universities Press, 1974.

O. Groehler, *Bombenkrieg gegen Deutschland*, Berlin, Akademie-Verlag, 1990.

A. Gröschner (ed.), *Ich schlug meiner Mutter die Brennenden Funken ab: Berliner Schulaufsätze aus dem Jahr 1946*, Berlin, Kontext-Verlag, 1996.

I. Hammer, S. zur Nieden (eds.), *Sehr selten habe ich geweint: Briefe und Tagebücher aus dem Zweiten Weltkrieg von Menschen aus Berlin*, Zürich, Schweizer-Verlags-Haus, 1992.

U. von Kardorff, *Berliner Aufzeichnungen: Aus den Jahren 1942 bis 1945*, München, Biederstein, 1962.

C. Klessmann, *Die doppelte Staatsgründung: Deutsche Geschichte 1945-1955*, Bonn, Bonn : Bundeszentrale für Politische Bildung, 1982.

E. Kris, 'The Recovery of Childhood Memories in Psychoanalysis', in *The Psychoanalytic Study of the Child*, pp. 54-88, 1956, vol. 11.

E. Kuby, *The Russians and Berlin, 1945*, New York, Hill & Wang, 1968.

T. Kushner, *The Holocaust and the Liberal Imagination: A Social and Cultural History*, Oxford, Blackwell, 1994.

Landeswohlfahrtsverband Hessen, B. Winter (eds.), *"Verlegt nach Hadamar": Die Geschichte einer NS-"Euthanasie"-Anstalt*, Kassel ; Landeswohlfahrtsverband Hessen, 1991.

H. Lange, B. Burkard (eds.), *'Abends wenn wir essen fehlt uns immer einer': Kinder schreiben an die Väter 1939-1945*, Reinbek b. Hamburg, Rowohlt, 2000.

H. Lessing, M. Liebel, *Wilde Cliquen: Szenen einer anderen Arbeiterjugendbewegung*, Bensheim, Päd.extra Buchverlag, 1981.

H. Lorenz, *Kriegskinder: Das Schicksal einer Generation Kinder*, Berlin, List, 2005.

D. Macardle, *Children of Europe: A Study of the Children of Liberated Countries: Their War-time Experiences, Their Reactions, and Their Needs, with a Note on Germany*, London, Gollancz, 1951.

M. Maschmann, *Account Rendered: A Dossier on my Former Self*, London, Abelard-Schuman, 1965.

S. Meyer, E. Schulze, *Wie wir das alles geschafft haben: Alleinstehende Frauen berichten über ihr Leben nach 1945*, München, Beck, 1984.

P. Novick, *The Holocaust and Collective Memory: The American Experience*, London, Bloomsbury, 2000.

G. S. Paulsson, *Secret City: The Hidden Jews of Warsaw, 1940-1945*, New Haven, Yale University Press, 2002.

A. Petö, 'Memory and the narrative of rape in Budapest and Vienna in 1945', in R. Bessel, D. Schumann (eds.), *Life after Death: Approaches to a Cultural and Social History of Europe during the 1940s and 1950s*, London, German Historical Institute, 2003.

D. Pines, *A Woman's Unconscious Use of Her Body: A Psychoanalytical Perspective*, London, Virago Press, 1983.

Polish Ministry of Information, *The German New Order in Poland*, London, Hutchinson, 1941.

H. Radebold, *Abwesende Väter und Kriegskindheit: Fortbestehende Folgen in Psychoanalysen*, Göttingen, Vandenhoeck & Rupprecht, 2000.

H. Radomska-Strzemecka, 'Okupacja w oczach młodzieży', in J. Wnuk, H. Radomska-Strzemecka, *Dzieci polskie oskarżają (1939-1945)*, Warsaw, Pax, 1961.

E. Rosenhaft, *Beating the Fascists? The German Communists and political violence*, Cambridge, Cambridge University Press, 1983.

Y. Rudashevski, *The Diary of the Vilna Ghetto: June 1941-April 1943*, Tel-Aviv, Ghetto Fighters' House, 1973.

P. Sander, *Verwaltung des Krankenmordes*, Gießen, Psychosozial-Verlag, 2003.

J. Schlumbohm, *Kinderstuben: Wie Kinder zu Bauern, Bürgern, Aristokraten wurden 1700-1850*, München, Dt. Taschenbuch-Verlag, 1983.

S. Scholz, R. Singer, 'Die Kinder in Hadamar', in Roer and Henkel, *Psychiatrie im Faschismus*, Bonn, Psychiatrie-Verlag, 1986 (2nd ed., Frankfurt/Main, Mabuse-Verlag, 1996).

H. Schulz, H. Radebold, J. Reulecke, *Söhne ohne Väter: Erfahrungen der Kriegsgeneration*, Berlin, Links, 2004.

J. Sloan (ed.), *Notes from the Warsaw Ghetto: The Journal of Emmanuel Ringelblum*, New York, McGraw Hill, 1958.

K. Sosnowski, *The Tragedy of Children under Nazi Rule*, Poznán, Zachodnia Agencja Prasowa, 1962.

N. Stargardt, 'Children's Art of the Holocaust', *Past and Present*, pp.191-235, 1998.

N. Stargardt, *Witnesses of War: Children's Lives under the Nazis*. London, Cape, 2005.

T. Szarota, *Warschau unter dem Hakenkreuz: Leben und Alltag im besetzten Warschau 1.10.1939 bis 31.7.1944*, Paderborn, Ferdinand Schöningh Verlag, 1985.

M. Vassiltchikov, *The Berlin Diaries, 1940-1945*, New York, Vintage Books, 1985.

F. Virgili, *Naitre ennemi: Les enfants de couples franco-allemands nés pendant la Seconde Guerre mondiale*, Paris, Payot, 2009.

A. Warring, *Tyskerpiger: under besoettelse og retsopgør*, København : Gyldendal, 1994.

D. Wierling, ‚Kriegskinder: westdeutsch, bürgerlich, männlich?', in L. Seegers, J. Reulecke (eds.), *Die 'Generation der Kriegskinder'. Historische Hintergründe und Deutungen*, Gießen, Psychosozial-Verlag, 2009.

3   "We ate lace and swallowed earth". Children in Nazi camps

Sara Valentina Di Palma

Nazi camps: persecution policies towards children

Children were sent to all the three main types of concentration camps created by the Nazis: labour camps with their precarious and hard conditions and high mortality due to exhaustion, deprivation, and beatings; the two labour-and-extermination camps in Auschwitz-Birkenau and Majdanek, where the large numbers who did not pass the selection for work were killed; and the four extermination camps in Poland (Chełmno, Bełżec, Sobibór and Treblinka) where there was no work selection, only death by gas on arrival.[1]

Jewish children were sent primarily to extermination camps to be immediately killed, or to labour-and-extermination camps where, if they looked old and strong enough, they could pass selection and enter the camp. Sinti and Roma children and the youth of subjected populations arrived in labour-and-extermination camps and in labour camps. When racial persecution of the Sinti and Roma led to large-scale deportation, beginning in the spring of 1943, racial legislation was also applied to women at advanced stages of pregnancy, and to children and babies.[2]

There were several reasons behind the Nazi persecution of children. In the case of Jewish children, extermination derived from anti-Semitic ideology and was an integral part of the decision to kill a whole people; Sinti and Roma children's persecution initially combined racism and a fear of social deviance stemming from their nomadic life, to shift later on to the idea of their inferiority and their racial danger, as in the case of the Jews. This explains why the persecution of Sinti and Roma children first relied on compulsory sterilisation of youth to prevent new births, and later led to deportation and extermination.

---

1   R. Hilberg, *The Destruction of the European Jews*, vol. 2, chap. IX; W. SOFSKY, *The Order of Terror. The Concentration Camp*, pp. 28-43.
2   G. Lewy, *The Nazi Persecution of Gypsies*, pp. 218-221.

Finally, other children were murdered, together with adults, as part of Nazi racial policies towards the population of annexed and conquered countries, seen as *Untermenschen*, or "inferior people" to be deported (to clear the land for the *Volksdeutsche*, local inhabitants with proven Arian German blood) and whose work was to be exploited for the war effort to the point of exhaustion and death. This is what happened to children in war zones.[3]

Discrimination against the population of annexed and conquered countries in fact led to a stark drop in the birth rate and a sharp rise in mortality: the legal age for marriages was raised by law; abortions for Polish women were encouraged, even though it was otherwise forbidden by the Nazis; social welfare policies were not offered to illegitimate children, whose number increased due to the marriage restrictions; health care for pregnant women was reduced and Polish women's access to prenatal care precluded; infant diseases such as TB and rickets were not treated and rations for non-German children were reduced. The programming of mass deportation was begun in 1942 to some extent because even these measures came to be seen as inadequate.[4]

It has been estimated that almost 90 per cent of Jewish children who lived in Nazi Europe (about one and a half million) perished in the genocide.[5] It is more difficult to estimate the numbers of the other children murdered by the Nazis. Regarding the *Porrajmos* (a Romanès word meaning annihilation and devouring), the extermination of Sinti and Roma, numbers differ widely. The most common data refer to at least 200,000 victims[6]; it is impossible to know the exact number of persecuted and killed people because of the long historiographical silence and because of the simultaneous presence of various other forms of persecution, from mass executions to sterilization. There is also a lack of information about the number of European Sinti and Roma before the Nazi era and it is therefore difficult to extrapolate certain data.[7] Similar considerations affect children and teenagers from war zones, who were killed summarily above all by firing squads, and on which there are no specific studies.

It is likewise very difficult to establish the number and names of the

3   L.H. Nicholas, *Cruel World. The Chifdren of Europe in the Nazi Web*, p. 229.
4   Ibid, pp. 240-242.
5   D. Dwork, *Children with a Star. Jewish Youth in Nazi Europe*, pp. XI. On testimony, see C. Coquio, A. Kalisky (eds), *L'enfant et le génocide. Témoignages sur l'enfance pendant la Shoah*.
6   More careful estimates, even if partial, are in M. Zimmermann, 'La persecuzione nazista degli zingari', in M. Cattaruzza, M. Flores, S. Levis Sullam, E. Traverso (eds), *Storia della Shoah. La crisi dell'Europa, lo sterminio degli ebrei e la memoria del XX secolo*, pp. 763-785, here pp. 776-778.
7   After decades of indifference, for a long time the only historiographical study in the international context was D. Kenrick, G. Puxon, *The Destiny of Europe's Gypsies*. In the last twenty years, German historiography has started to update and rectify the data offered in Kenrick and Puxon: M. Zimmermann, *Rassenutopie und Genozid: Die nationalsozialistische ⊠Lösung der Zigeunerfrage⊠*. Regarding Anglo-Saxon historiography see Lewy, *The Nazi persecution*.

children deported to Nazi camps, as well as their fate. It is known for instance that there were several children in Majdanek, but babies up to three years old were registered on their mothers' cards.[8] In Auschwitz-Birkenau as well, reconstructing the data of about 1,300,000 deported people, it seems that some 234,000 among them were children (and among these 220,000 were Jews), but it is always difficult to be certain about either their names or their fates (gassing on arrival, entry into the camp or death), because children sent immediately to the gas chambers were not registered, and the ones who were registered are recorded in the file numerical series of the adults. Children were seldom recorded in a separate registry, but a reasonable estimate is that some 19,000 children and teenagers up to 18 years old died there. Compared to the approximately 400,000 persons who were registered in the camp, children selected to enter the camp amount to only five percent.[9]

In the extermination camps, built for the mass killing of European Jews, children had almost no chance of survival. Survivors amongst children are very rare, such as 15-year-old Stanislaw Szmajzner, who escaped during the revolt in Sobibór[10] or 13-year-old Simon Srebnik, left alive because the SS took a liking to his ability in running and singing. He was shot anyway, but somehow survived before Chełmno was abandoned.[11] In the labour-and-extermination camps of Auschwitz-Birkenau and Majdanek, the majority of Jewish children were killed on arrival. The camp was usually only a temporary situation, as Primo Levi writes in *The Truce*: "The children at Birkenau were like birds of passage: after a few days they were transferred to the Experiments Block, or directly to the gas chambers".[12]

Once at their destination, children belonging to all groups had almost no choices. Many mothers decided to go with their children to their deaths, while others may have saved themselves only at the terrible cost of having to abandon their children.[13] Where young children were officially forbidden, they were often secretly introduced, by drugging them with sleeping-pills, or by corrupting the guards, or with the help of prisoners belonging to the clandestine resistance networks.[14] The resistance in Auschwitz played a

8   B. Distel, 'Kinder und Jugendliche im nationalsozialistischen Verfolgungssystem', in E. Bamberger, A. Ehmann (eds), *Kinder und Jugendliche als Opfer des Holocaust, proceedings of the international conference held at the Haus der Wannseekonferenz, 12-14 December 1994*, pp. 53-63, here p. 61.
9   H. Kubica, 'Les enfants et les adolescents au KL Auschwitz', in F. Piper, T. Swiebocka (eds), *Auschwitz. Camp de concentration et d'extermination*, pp. 133-151, here pp. 133-136.
10   L. Beccaria Rolfi, B. Maida, *Il futuro spezzato. I nazisti contro i bambini*, p. 107.
11   C. Lanzmann, *Shoah. An Oral History of the Holocaust*, p. 15.
12   P. Levi, 'The Truce', in Idem., *If this is a Man – The Truce*, p. 199.
13   G. Melodia, 'Padri…madri…figli…', in G. Bellak, G. Melodia (eds), *Donne e bambini nei lager nazisti*, pp. 83-86.
14   See for instance Z. Zweig, *Il bambino di Buchenwald. Dal ghetto ai lager nel racconto di un padre*; Kubica, 'Les enfants et les adolescents', p. 150.

crucial role in saving Jewish children, in part by sending them to medical experiments in the hope that they might survive, in part by hiding them.[15]

Transport toward camps and arrival

The inhumane condition in camps was prefigured by the transports, already a first step in the selection and extermination of the weakest: the elderly and sick seldom survived after days without food and water, in the stink of faeces and dead bodies. If before the transport it was still possible to hope and believe in survival, any illusion died on the boxcars used for deportation, as Sultana remembers:

> The trip lasted forever, we all were standing or sitting but there was not room enough to lay down. There was a drum in a corner, which everybody used as a toilet; many died on the way, it was shocking, all the doors closed, nothing to eat nor to drink ... .[16]

When the transport took little time, the shock that faced children when they arrived was profoundly distressing, as the Sinti Otto Rosenberg remembers: "Then one morning, it could have been four or five in the morning, we were rousted out by SA and police".[17]

Between 1933 and 1938, Sinti and Roma children were in fact sent to several city camps, both to calm the local population's protests at the Sinti and Roma occupation of rural areas, and following the new Nazi programme of urban renewal. The camp where Otto was sent was created for the Olympic games in 1936, to present Berlin as a model city. This tightened policy of exclusion was also directed against other groups such as homosexuals – whose deportation had begun in 1934, but who were now interned in large numbers, mainly in Sachsenhausen and Buchenwald, just before the Olympics.[18] Even people living in private houses or on private land were deported, children such as Otto for example, to the camp of Marzahn. The place was terribly unhealthy, without fresh water or enough toilets, without power or heat;

---

15 Kubica , 'Les enfants et les adolescents', p. 150.
16 Testimony by Sultana Razon in S.V. Di Palma, *Bambini e adolescenti nella Shoah. Storia e memoria della persecuzione in Italia*, p. 241. Born in 1932 of Turkish Jewish parents, Sultana was interned at Ferramonti (Italy), confined at Taglio di Po, incarcerated at Rovigo, newly interned at Fossoli and from there deported to Bergen-Belsen, from whence she was taken to Turkey for an exchange for German prisoners a few days before liberation. She survived together with her family.
17 O. Rosenberg, *A Gypsy in Auschwitz*, p. 20. Otto was born in 1927 and survived Birkenau, Buchenwald and Bergen-Belsen, while his whole family was killed.
18 See the decree by H. Himmler for the Olympic games, in G. Grau (ed.), *Hidden Holocaust? Gay and Lesbian Persecution in Germany 1933-1945*, p. 59.

consequently several contagious diseases such as diphtheria, TB and scabies spread fast.[19]

"Life" in camp: hunger, work, games, violence

Liliana Segre remembers: "I suddenly learned the meaning of Camp. It meant death-cold-beatings-corporal punishment; it meant slavery; it meant humiliation-torture-experiments"[20]. Usually killed right after their arrival in labour-and-extermination camps, children might survive if they looked older or if they lied about their age to be included among the adults declared suitable for work.[21] Those who seemed too young and delicate were automatically selected for the gas chambers, while their relatives kept hoping that they were alive and had been sent to another destination.[22]

The youngest did not receive any special treatment, and to get their daily ration of food they had to wait in line with the other prisoners, trying not to be passed by those stronger and faster, thus finding themselves at the end of the queue when there was no food left. Worrying about *brot*, bread, and *dörrgemüse*, vegetable soup (just a liquid slop in which only the luckiest found some peels and small pieces of dry vegetables), occupied the whole day and was often present even in dreams. If in the first years prisoners could share one loaf of bread among four, by the spring of 1945 one single loaf had to suffice for 16 people. Soup rations as well were scarce and occasional, decided by the *Blockältester* according to his whim: sometimes a three litre pot had to feed five persons, sometimes even seven.[23] Ceija Stojka remembers her hunger in the final months in camp: "We ate lace and swallowed earth. If there is nothing you eat anything, even old clothes"[24]. Hunger could lead to death for imprudence, as happened when children were severely punished because they did not respect the rules, and queued for rations at two different

19 Lewy, *The Nazi persecution*, p. 22.
20 L. Segre, 'Un'infanzia perduta', in *Voci dalla Shoah testimonianze per non dimenticare*, pp. 49-63, here p. 57. The Italian Jewish girl Liliana, born in 1930 and deported to Auschwitz after being turned away from Switzerland, survived the Holocaust.
21 E. Wiesel, *Night*, pp. 28-29; E. Bruck, *Chi ti ama così*, pp. 25-26. Elie, born in 1928 in the village of Sighet, where Hungarian Jews lived in Romanian territory, was deported with his family to Auschwitz and to Buchenwald, where his father, the only relative who shared with him the suffering of the camp, did not live to liberation. The Jewish child Edith, born in 1932 in a Hungarian village near Ukraine and Slovakia, was deported in 1944, first to the Satoraljaujhely ghetto and then to Auschwitz, before being liberated at Bergen-Belsen.
22 H. Kugler Weiss, *Racconta! Fiume-Birkenau-Israele*, p. 52. Born in Fiume in 1928, the Jewish girl Hanna survived Auschwitz.
23 O. Lustig, *Dizionario del Lager*, pp. 36-37, 42-44.
24 C. Stojka, *Forse sogno di vivere. Una bambina rom a Bergen-Belsen*, p. 24. Ceija was born in 1933 in a Roma family living in Austria and survived Bergen-Belsen.

barracks.[25] The only extra food was often the crust on bottom of the cooking pots: children who helped and brought the pots back to the kitchen could scrape them.[26]

In most camps the bigger children were sent to work. Ida Marcheria remembers being sent to the *Kanada*, the warehouse for property confiscated at the prisoners' arrival; it was a place where it was possible to be warm and to find some necessities, but it was also full of risks:

> To be caught with a soap could entail a beating. But if an officer had seen a girl stealing a ring and found it hidden on her, he would have taken his gun and shot her point-blank without saying one single word. [27]

In some ways the most tragic aspect of the Nazi persecution against children is the resignation they developed for restrictions and suffering and their adaptation to the camp: 'in the few years that I had lived as a conscious person, my rights had been removed piece by piece, so that Auschwitz had a kind of logic to it', Ruth Klüger remembers.[28] The extreme experiences of the camp seemed so natural that many children assimilated them into their games, which emulated camp life: they would run among the dead bodies, or sing songs about humiliation, sacrifice and death; they played at digging graves or being the *Blockältester* or at the roll call or at being sick prisoners ill-treated by doctors, even at going into the gas chambers.[29] They sometimes played at eating, that is holding their spittle in their mouth for one minute and then swallowing it, pretending to have eaten and drunk.[30] Other games involved dares, showing bravery by making faces at the guards or by going to forbidden places like the mortuary.[31]

The adaptation to the absurd is shown by children's naturalness regarding death: they often had no memories of a life before the persecution and the

25 A. Novac, *The Beautiful Days of My Youth. My Six Months in Auschwitz and Plaszow*, pp. 131-132. Born in 1930, the Jewish girl Ana was deported to Auschwitz and from there to Płaszów, near Kraków, and again to Auschwitz until the first evacuations caused by the approaching Red Army. She was liberated and as an adult became a playwright.

26 J. Oberski, *Childhood*, p. 50. Born in Amsterdam in 1938, the Jewish child Jona was deported with his parents to Bergen-Belsen and he alone survived the Holocaust.

27 'Ida', in R. Olla, *Le non persone. Gli italiani nella Shoah*, pp. 7-34, here p. 19. See also her testimony in A. Pavia, A. Tiburzi, *Non perdonerò mai*, pp. 58-59. Ida Marcheria, born in 1929, being Jewish was deported to Auschwitz and survived, along with her younger sister Stella, who later committed suicide.

28 R. Klüger, *Still Alive: A Holocaust Girlhood Remembered*, p. 95. Ruth was born in Vienna in 1931 in a Jewish family. Deported with her mother to Terezín, Auschwitz and Christianstadt (satellite camp of Gross-Rosen), she survived the war and emigrated to the USA with her mother.

29 Distel, 'Kinder und Jugendliche', p. 65.

30 Marion Stokvis-Krieg in Dwork, *Children with a Star*, p. 142.

31 Oberski, *Childhood*, p. 74.

camp seemed normal to them. To this brutalisation, some prisoners reacted by trying to assure children minimal rights and a dignified existence: even if children were forbidden to study, courses were organised secretly where it was possible. This was the case for instance for Sultana Razon, a Jewish girl imprisoned in Bergen Belsen in an internal camp for foreign citizens belonging to neutral countries, since her family was from Turkey:

> We took French classes almost daily with a Greek polyglot, we used to write on any single piece of paper that we could find […] and we paid for these lessons, me and my sister paid three bowls of soup every week. [...] But this helped us a lot, because we had homework and things to do.[32]

The rule in camp was nevertheless the absence of any such rights and for children this meant that they could not study. Instead, children had a different practical schooling, the education of the camps. It consisted of learning as fast as possible how to live in that absurd world and then how to manage: to cover themselves in winter and to resist thirst in summer time; to work, but not so much as to weaken; to ration food and preserve it from thieves; to "organise": that is, obtain by barter or theft what was necessary to survive; and above all to find the moral strength to resist. It was a school of self-education, among which there were also sexually abused children, taken into camps and protected as lovers to satisfy the desires of the *Kapos*.[33]

Birth, experiments, death

If a woman could complete her pregnancy inside the camp, she would rarely see her child survive the camp itself, and babies often died right after their birth, sometimes with their mothers, both of them too weak to survive. The medical student Marie-José Chombart de Lauwe was chosen in 1944 to nurse the newborns in the *Kinderzimmer* in the women camp of Ravensbrück, where there were several children. There were not enough nappies, no baby bottles and above all no milk to keep the babies alive longer than three months. The death rate was very high and the few nurses in the nursery had to face helplessly the babies' death throes.[34] To spare their babies from being

---

32 Di Palma, *Bambini e adolescenti*, p. 243.
33 P. Caleffi, *Si fa presto a dire fame*, pp. 132-134; Levi, 'The Truce', pp. 200-202; D. P. Liggeri, 'I minorenni', in Bellak, Melodia (eds), *Donne e bambini*, p. 79. On this topic see B. Perz, 'Kinder und Jugendliche im Konzentrationslager Mauthausen und seinen Aussenlagern', in *Dachauer Hefte, Die Verfolgung von Kindern und Jugendlichen*, pp. 71-90, especially par. *Lagersexualität*, pp. 85-88; Kubica, 'Les enfants et les adolescents', p. 149.
34 M-J. Chombart de Lauwe, 'Condizione delle donne incinte e dei neonati nei campi di concentramento nazisti femminili', in L. Monaco (ed.), *La deportazione femminile nei lager nazisti*, Proceedings of the international conference, Turin, October 20-21 1994, pp. 75-87. On

used for cruel medical experiments, many new mothers decided to kill them by themselves or with the help of some charitable deported doctor, as in the case of doctor Maca Steinberg. She helped the young Jewish mother Ruth Elias to kill her daughter by supplying her with a morphine injection; the baby had been destined by SS doctor Josef Mengele for a slow and horrible death through starvation, to discover how long a baby could live without milk.[35]

In Auschwitz-Birkenau, from the establishment of the women's camp at the end of March 1942, the extermination of all pregnant women and babies usually took the form of drowning. Later on, abortions were practised without any concern for the month of pregnancy. Only in the so-called *Zigeunerlager* was it possible for Sinti and Roma women to give birth, and on March 11, 1943 the first baby girl was born there[36]. Babies usually died right after being born because of the impossibility of breastfeeding them and the lack of healthy conditions, as remembered by the garrison physician's clerk, Hermann Langbein.[37] Later on, only non-Jewish women in the women's camp in Birkenau were allowed to give birth, and on September 18, 1944 the first newborn girl, daughter of a woman from Cracow, was registered in the camp's registry.[38]

From August 1944, to keep pregnant women from hiding their pregnancy at the selection, women were told that all pregnant women would receive milk daily, but women who came forward were instead killed. After October 1944, Jewish children were not killed immediately after being born; even so a newborn Jewish girl had already been registered on February 21, 1944.[39] The principal concern was to tattoo the babies with a number immediately, so that when they died the number was correct on the camp's registry. Since their arms were too small, they were tattooed on their thigh.

Children in camps were often kept alive to be used in medical experiments, which involved brutal cruelties.[40] Among the worst event was the transport from Auschwitz to Neuengamme of twenty children for medical research on TB in January 1945. Seriously sick, the children were killed in April.

Sinti and Roma girls became the specific object of racial policies from

children in Ravensbrück see also B. Pawelke, 'Als Häftling geboren Kinder in Ravensbrück', in Bamberger, Ehmann (eds), *Kinder und Jugendliche*, pp. 93-106.

35 R. Elias, *Triumph of Hope. From Theresienstadt and Auschwitz to Israel*, pp. 149-152. On pregnant women in camps see G. Tedeschi, 'Caratteri specifici della deportazione femminile', in Monaco (ed.), *La deportazione femminile*, pp. 28-30.

36 Her name is Anna Malik. See D. Czech, *Kalendarium. Gli avvenimenti del campo di concentramento di Auschwitz-Birkenau 1939-1945*, p. 330.

37 H. Langbein, *People in Auschwitz*, pp. 236-237.

38 Czech, *Kalendarium*, p. 466.

39 Czech, *Kalendarium*, p. 552.

40 G. Schwarberg, *Der SS – Arzt und die Kinder vom Bullenhuser Damm*; Idem., *Meine zwanzig Kinder*; M.P. Bernicchia, *I 20 bambini di Bullenhuser Damm*.

1937 onwards. Psychiatrist Robert Ritter, who, beginning in 1926, lead the *Rassenhygienische und bevölkerunsgbiologische Forschungsstelle* (Institute for Race Hygiene and Population Biology) inside the Public Health Office of the Reich in Berlin, recommended the sterilisation of the whole Roma and Sinti population, starting at the age of twelve. Ritter then used genealogical mapping to program their subsequent extermination. He pushed for a mass killing of the whole population, but Himmler later decided to save the so-called "pure" Sinti and Roma whose Aryan origin was certified.[41] Sinti and Roma girls in camps were sterilised when they reached ten years old, first using X-rays, then with less expensive methods such as cervical injections. The Nazis believed in fact that Roma and Sinti children were sexually dissolute and had premature sexual relations or got involved in prostitution: sterilisation was therefore considered the "proper" prevention.[42]

Twins who arrived in Auschwitz-Birkenau were specifically chosen by Mengele for his medical experiments on Aryan race fertility. For this purpose, twins were photographed, measured, used for blood transfusions from one twin to the other and for other brutalities.[43] Children were the objects of other medical experiments on dwarfism and on various diseases before being killed by chloroform injections in their heart; afterwards, their organs were subjected to necropsy.

The two family camps in Birkenau

Children who lived inside the two family camps, one for Sinti and Roma and the other for Jews evacuated from Theresienstadt (Terezín), had a different life from others of the same age. Camp BIIb for persons coming from the ghetto-gathering and transit camp in Terezín (through which more than 15,000 children under 15 passed, with an average of 3,000 children at once, and from which at least 9,000 were sent to extermination camps)[44] was opened in September 1943 for men, women and children, who lived together but slept in different barracks. In spite of its difficulties, for a certain time smaller children in this camp were gathered in a day nursery where they received better food – heartier soup, beetroot jam, margarine and even butter – and could play.

The presence of a day nursery itself, called *Kindergarten*, was something

41 K. Reemtsma, *Sinti und Roma: Geschichte, Kultur und Gegenwart*, p. 103; Lewy, *The Nazi persecution*, pp. 135-140.
42 Zimmermann, 'La persecuzione', pp. 768-769; R. Gilsenbach, *Oh Django, sing deine Zorn!* Sinti und Roma unter den Deutschen, pp. 82-84.
43 Lustig, *Dizionario del Lager*, pp. 225-229.
44 R.M. Wlaschek, 'Kinder im Konzentrationslager Theresienstadt', in H. Weissová, *Zeichne, was Du siehst. Zeichnungen eines Kindes aus Theresienstadt/ Terezín*, pp. 145-149, here p. 146.

unique, together with the school for bigger children. Here children learned songs and poems, could play and follow some basic educational programmes.[45] The gym teacher Fredy Hirsch once obtained a barracks to be used as a school where children were obliged to learn German, but he let children learn drawing and build toys. Hirsch even managed to organise a performance of Snow White, where the young actors were applauded by the SS[46]! In March 1944 the family camp suffered a first liquidation, to be closed forever on July 11, 1944, with the killing of the last 4,000 prisoners.[47] Though children in the camp for families from Terezín lived better, even exceptionally compared to other children in camps, they ended in the same way, in the gas chambers.

One of the most dreadful camps in Birkenau was camp BIIe, called *Zigeunerlager*. It hosted Sinti and Roma prisoners from all over Europe. Among more than 200,000 Sinti and Roma victims of the Nazi persecution, around 23,000 passed through this camp, and more than 19,000 perished here between the end of February 1943 and the liquidation of the camp the night of August 2, 1944. That night, about 1,400 persons were deported to other camps, while the last 4,000 Sinti and Roma prisoners who did not pass the selection were sent to the gas chambers.[48]

In the *Zigeunerlager* prisoners lived in unusual conditions: they were not subjected to the initial selection and they lived together with their families, without taking part in the life of the camp, which consisted of morning roll call and exhausting work. They lived forgotten, without enough food and at the mercy of diseases that caused a mortality rate higher than in the other internal camps of Birkenau, as for instance during the typhus epidemic in May 1943. Children in particular contracted several diseases, including noma, a gangrenous stomatitis widespread among the youngest, caused by malnutrition and leading to a very high mortality. The garrison physician's clerk, Hermann Langbein, remembers seeing abandoned babies whose mothers were in their death throes, and mountains made of babies' and children's corpses:

> Six babies are lying on a pallet of straw; they can't be more than a few days old. What a sight! Scrawny limbs and bloated bellies. On the bunk beds next to them lie the mothers – emaciated and with burning eyes. One of them softly

45 Kubica, 'Les enfants et les adolescents', p. 138.
46 T. Todorov, *Facing the Extreme. Moral Life in the Concentration Camps*, pp. 209-210. On the family camp for Jews from Terezín in Birkenau see M. Kárny, M. Kárná, 'Kinder in Theresienstadt', in *Dachauer Hefte*, 1993, vol. 9, "Die Verfolgung von Kindern", pp. 14-31, here pp. 27-31; Beccaria Rolfi, Maida, *Il futuro spezzato*, p. 81; Distel, 'Kinder und Jugendliche im nationalsozialistischen Verfolgungssystem', p. 64.
47 Czech, *Kalendarium*, p. 634.
48 Ibid, pp. 647-649.

sings to herself. She is best off, she has lost her mind.[49]

Children were the first ones to die from typhus, dysentery and other diseases, and also from experiments carried out especially on twins. In Barracks 29 and 31, SS doctor Josef Mengele organised a day nursery and a day-care for children under six, where they could play and get high quality food such as milk and butter, before being used in medical experiments. When the camp was liquidated there were still seven pairs of twins alive from the over 60 who passed through Mengele's laboratory.[50] Of over 300 children born in the *Zigeunerlager*, none survived.

Moral resistance and alienation

Children in the camps were forced to mature rapidly, as in the case of those who entered the camp with a parent and saw their position reversed, being obliged to take care of the adult who was weaker and more apathetic[51]. The help given by children to their parents was not always just a burden: it may also have been accompanied by a feeling of guilt for not having been capable enough to protect the adult – for instance, nine-year-old Rysio refused food because he saw his father dying after the liberation of Buchenwald.[52] Faced with the need to survive, children could not think of anything else or react emotionally to what happened to them. "We did not even have our own thoughts", Ida Marcheria states[53], while Tatiana Bucci felt nothing at her mother's disappearance, even though she believed that her mother was dead.[54]

Generally speaking, very young children, who were not old enough to understand what was happening, faced life in camps with an alienated and detached behaviour, as if reality reached them filtered out and deadened. "I remember having neither cried nor laughed in Auschwitz", Tatiana says.[55] Nothing is left then but trying to survive: protect feet and legs, to 'organise' what is fundamental for life in the camps, to know how to save food by rationing it, to respect the rules as much as possible. Liliana Segre remembers

---

49 Langbein, *People in Auschwitz*, p. 237.

50 Ibid, p. 339.

51 T. Birger, *A Daughter's Gift of Love: A Holocaust Memoir*; the diary by Werner Galnik, in L. Holliday (ed.), *Children in the Holocaust and World War II: Their Secret Diaries*, pp. 55-65, here pp. 62-63. Trudi, a Jewish girl, was deported with her mother from the Kaunas ghetto to the Stutthof camp; both were liberated. Also a Jewish boy, Werner (born in 1933) survived the war together with his brother.

52 R. Minc, *L'inferno degli innocenti. I ragazzi ebrei nella bufera nazista*, pp. 36-37.

53 'Ida', in Olla, *Le non persone*, p. 17.

54 T. Marrone, *Meglio non sapere*, p. 46. The two Jewish little sisters Tatiana and Andra Bucci are the youngest Italians who survived Birkenau, born two years apart, Liliana, called Tatiana, in 1937 and Alessandra, called Andra, in 1939, and erroneously taken for twins in the camp.

55 Marrone, *Meglio*.

having reacted to the horror and the risk of brutalisation with a different defensive attitude: not refusing to think, but concentrating on nice thoughts and creating her own imaginary world, far from violence: "Running on a lawn, swimming in the Ligurian sea, picking flowers, seeing beautiful things in the sky. And I could be in another place"[56]. Ruth Klüger instead recited poems night and day, as if in their pattern more than in their poetical content lay the secret of some mental order which could oppose the chaos of the physical world.[57]

Memory during the persecution, memory of "survival", coming back from camps

Testimony by children is necessarily different from testimony by adults: very young people have different sensitivity and maturity, and their understanding of what they live is thus affected by the perspective of childhood. To understand what the Holocaust of children meant, it is therefore necessary to try to see events through children's eyes. As the Jewish writer Aharon Appelfeld underlines, children's memory is "not chronological, but abundant and mutable"[58], it changes with the passing of time and it often has a close and difficult relationship with the imagination. It is therefore arduous and perhaps even unfair to reconstruct childhood's experiences in the Holocaust on the basis of memory only, while it may be more useful to proceed by evocations and sensations: as Ruth Klüger reaffirms 'we do not think in a linear way'[59].

The groups of survivors who eventually fought to be recognized as victims of Nazi persecution were above all formed by former political prisoners and Jews. In both cases, the consciousness of a collective identity was strengthened thanks to an internal cohesion, to historiographical research and to the trials of former perpetrators. Memory of the *Porrajmos*, on the other hand, was long denied, both because Sinti and Roma were for a long time not recognized as a group persecuted for racial reasons, and because the Sinti and Roma culture itself is predominantly oral and therefore more fragmentary and more difficult to transpose. In addition, historiographical interest in this topic is relatively recent, and it is therefore difficult to find documents and even more so, testimonies. For all these reasons, the greatest number of testimonies found are those of Jewish children.[60]

56 E. Zuccalà, *Sopravvissuta ad Auschwitz. Liliana Segre fra le ultime testimoni della Shoah*, p. 46.
57 Klüger, *Still Alive*, p. 110.
58 A. Appelfeld, *The Story of a Life: A Memoir*, p. 86. Born in 1932 in Bucovina (today between Rumania and Ukraine), Aharon survived the ghetto, camp and living in hiding with hostile Ukrainian farmers, then alone in the woods; in the end he joined the Red Army.
59 R. Klüger interviewed by S.V. Di Palma, Wien, 13 September 2000.
60 There are some exceptions such as Stojka, *Forse sogno di vivere*.

Testimonies coeval to the Holocaust are few because, in addition to the psychological difficulty of dwelling on one's own suffering, life conditions were also very precarious. This makes the works done by Jewish children in Terezín (66 poems and about 4,000 drawings) particularly interesting.[61] The poems, written by older and more mature children, are characterized by a remarkable descriptive skill. Both drawings and poems mirror life in camps, or in contrast, depict dreams of a past life or of a desired future, both of them too distant. Among the most striking examples are the poems *Terezín* (1944), signed with the name Mif and whose author is unknown; *Terezín* (1943), signed with the name Teddy; *A sunny evening* (1944, anonymous); the drawing by Pavel Sonnenschein of the entrance to the fortress at Terezín; the drawing by Vladimir Flusser of sick people and death; the watercolour by Doris Weiserová of a warmly coloured butterfly; and the intimate winter landscape by Julie Ogulárová.[62]

A fundamental document is the collection of drawings by Helga Weissová-Hošková of life in Terezín from her entrance in the ghetto, depicted in minute, almost photographic, detail, as well as some drawings from the years 1945-46 of her experience in Birkenau and of the evacuation death march from Birkenau towards more western camps[63]. Helga supplied her drawings with captions and explanations which complete her writings from the same period.[64]

Children writing in the period right before or during the persecution in fact left diaries and letters as well. Their works are very different according to the age of their authors, content, experiences and context. The differences do not seem to be due to the children's origins. For all of them, writing represented a resistance – writing was forbidden, or very dangerous, and nevertheless leaving a testimony meant describing cruelties suffered and condemning the perpetrators. Writing could be also a diversion, a relief valve from the oppressive reality, an escapism or a kind of therapy. In a few cases, writing could save a child: thanks to her literary talent, Janina Hesheles was helped by some fellow prisoners in the Janowska camp to escape.[65]

One remarkable case is that of Ana Novac, a Jewish girl who collected the

---

61 M. De Micheli (ed.), *I bambini di Terezín. Poesie e disegni dal lager 1942-1944*; *Terezín, disegni e poesie dei bambini del campo di sterminio* (catalogue from the exhibition *Disegni e poesie dei bambini del campo di sterminio di Terezín*, promoted by Associazione Versiliese Italia-Cecoslovacchia, Regione Toscana, Amministrazione Provinciale di Pisa).

62 Poems are in De Micheli (ed.), *I bambini di Terezín*, respectively pp. 25, 19, 46; drawings are in *Terezín, disegni e poesie* quot, respectively pp. 25, 35, 17, 19.

63 H. Weissová, *Zeichne, was Du siehst. Zeichnungen eines Kindes aus Theresienstadt/ Terezín*. Helga (born in 1929) was deported, after Terezín, to other camps, but she lived to see the end of the war and was one of the few children to survive Terezín.

64 Part of her diary is in Holliday (ed.), *Children in the Holocaust*, pp. 73-78.

65 Holliday (ed.), *Children in the Holocaust*, pp. 67-72. Janina Hesheles, a Jewish Pole from Lviv born in 1931, began keeping a diary at ten years old, when her city was occupied. In hiding from 1943, she was able to survive.

pages of her diary, written in captivity, which she deciphered years later and only in part. Writing can be a filter through which to view and understand the terrible life in camp, so much so that, when Ana reread her pages years later and decided to transcribe and publish them, she affirmed: "All I knew about the camp was that I had been there [...] and that I made notes there"[66]. Another important diary was left by Petr Ginz, who died in Birkenau after being deported from Terezín, where he made several drawings and articles for the underground journal written by the children, *Vedem.*[67]

There are even fewer children who in the postwar chaos found the time, calm, force and motivation to write. Asked to forget, to re-enter a normality which often seemed not only impossible but even completely overturned, child survivors hid their torment.[68] After all, the end of the persecution was itself sudden and very different from what had been expected. The majority of the camp population was frequently evacuated and sent on death marches to more western camps, resulting in a very high mortality due to privation, fatigue and extermination.[69] In the camps, the liberators found people too weak and too tired who could neither feel anything nor respond to the idea of being still alive. In the eyes of the prisoners the liberation became an estranging fact, something not completely real.[70] Even when children were able to rejoice at the liberation, as 11-year-old Ceija remembers "very soon we had worries. Who survived? Who is still alive?"[71].

Children did not belong to the postwar world, and they did not recognize the surrounding environment: "return to Vienna was terribly sad. Everything was like before. In Auschwitz I had even thought that Auschwitz was everything, that there was nothing else left"[72]. Many hoped for a better society, but were often immediately disappointed, as in the case of Jordanit Ascoli:

> A girl said to me: "You cannot play with us because you are Jew". [ ] Her mother called her and spoke to her in a low voice. The child came back and said to me: "No, my mother told me that *now* you can play with us *even* if you are Jew"[73].

66 Novac, *The Beautiful Days*, p. 10.
67 C. Pressburger (ed.), *The Diary of Petr Ginz*. A Jewish boy, Petr was born in Prague in 1928 and died at sixteen at Birkenau after having passed through Terezín.
68 There are few exceptions such as the diary by Werner Galnik, in Holliday (ed.), *Children in the Holocaust* quot, pp. 55-65, already published in "Jewish Life" in April 1947.
69 Bruck, *Chi ti ama così*, p. 40.
70 Novac, *The Beautiful Days*, pp. 296-297.
71 Stojka, *Forse sogno di vivere*, pp. 49-50.
72 Ibid, p. 67.
73 Di Palma, *Bambini e adolescenti*, p. 222. Born in 1939, the Jewish child Jordanit fled to Switzerland in Sept. 1943 with her parents and two elder brothers.

Paul Aron Sandfort remembers when he and his mother went back to Denmark, where they found their house occupied by people who denied having stolen their property.[74] Edith Bruck as well, when she returned with her sister to the Hungarian village where they lived before being deported, was attacked with the name of "stinking Jews" by the family who was looking after their property.[75] Psychological assistance for survivors was unusual (as Trudi Birger says, "We were alone. There were no social workers or psychologists"[76]), and people who managed to find their relatives again did do not know how to communicate with them – "I was cumbersome, from the beginning" Liliana Segre remembers.[77] For many the camp would always be an open wound, as Ida Marcheria asserts: "anything happens, and you go back there"[78].

The situation of Sinti and Roma children was made worse by the peculiar weakness of their community after the war and by the destruction not only of lives but also of traditions and community links. Furthermore, old discriminatory measures against nomadic life became effective again in the aftermath, or were informally enforced by the police even in the absence of official laws, while the requests for restitution were largely denied or postponed[79], and all the old prejudices against Sinti and Roma people started up again[80]. These postwar difficulties explain in good measure why the majority of testimonies (those of Jewish children) have appeared only recently, since the 80s and 90s, when there has been less reticence. Many people decided to testify because of several factors: the increase in racism, the generation gap with a young public whose eventual disbelief would be less painful than the incredulity of those who lived during the extermination, the validation of one's own memories. The comparison that others have made with more recent events also defined as genocide has also been a factor, insomuch as many survivors decided to talk about their experiences during the Balkan wars in the 90s[81].

74 'Paul', in R. Olla, *Ancora ciliegie zio SS*, pp. 159-206, here p. 203. Paul Aron Sandfort, born Paul Rabinowitsch in Hamburg in 1930, survived Terezín and became a musician and poet. Decades after the end of the war he took the second name Aron, in memory of his father from whom he was separated at three years old, first by the divorce of his parents and then by the Holocaust.

75 Bruck, *Chi ti ama così*, p. 60.

76 Birger, *A Daughter's Gift of Love*, p. 170.

77 D. Padoan, *Come una rana d'inverno. Conversazioni con tre donne sopravvissute ad Auschwitz*, pp. 9-62, here p. 40.

78 'Ida', in Olla, *Le non persone*, p. 30.

79 Lewy, *The Nazi persecution*, pp. 202-204.

80 Stojka, *Forse sogno di vivere*, pp. 70-71.

81 G. Salmoni, *Una storia nella Storia. Ricordi e riflessioni di un testimone da Fossoli a Buchenwald*, p. 101. Gilberto Salmoni, an Italian Jew born in 1928, was captured with his family just before they reached safety in Switzerland; deported to Buchenwald with his brother, he survived the camp, while his parents and sister were sent to Birkenau and immediately assassinated in the gas chambers.

Bibliography

A. Appelfeld, *The Story of a Life: A Memoir*, New York, Schocken, 2004.

L. Beccaria Rolfi, B. Maida, *Il futuro spezzato. I nazisti contro i bambini*, Firenze, Giuntina, 1997.

M.P. Bernicchia, *I 20 bambini di Bullenhuser Damm*, Milano, Proedi Editore, 2004.

T. Birger, *A Daughter's Gift of Love: A Holocaust Memoir*, Philadelphia, Jewish Pubn Society, 1992.

E. Bruck, *Chi ti ama così*, Venezia, Marsilio, 1994 (English translation *Who Loves You Like This*, Philadelphia, Paul Dry Books, 2000).

P. Caleffi, *Si fa presto a dire fame*, Milano-Roma, Ed. Avanti!, 1961, pp. 132-134.

M-J.Chombart de Lauwe, 'Condizione delle donne incinte e dei neonati nei campi di concentramento nazisti femminili', in L. Monaco (ed.), *La deportazione femminile nei lager nazisti, proceedings of the international conference, Turin, October 20-21 1994*, Milano, Franco Angeli, 1995, pp. 75-87.

B. Coquio, A. Kalisky (eds), *L'enfant et le génocide. Témoignages sur l'enfance pendant la Shoah*, Paris, Robert Laffont, 2007.

D. Czech, *Kalendarium. Gli avvenimenti del campo di concentramento di Auschwitz-Birkenau 1939-1945*, Milano, Mimesis Edizioni, 2006.

M. De Micheli (ed.), *I bambini di Terezín. Poesie e disegni dal lager 1942-1944*, Milano, Feltrinelli, 1979.

S.V. Di Palma, *Bambini e adolescenti nella Shoah. Storia e memoria della persecuzione in Italia*, Milano, Unicopli, 2004.

B. Distel, 'Kinder und Jugendliche im nationalsozialistischen Verfolgungssystem', in E. Bamberger, A. Ehmann (eds), *Kinder und Jugendliche als Opfer des Holocaust, proceedings of the international conference held at the Haus der Wannseekonferenz, 12-14 December 1994*, Heidelberg, Dokumentationszentrum Deutscher Sinti und Roma in Zusammenarbeit mit der Gedenkstätte Haus der Wannseekonferenz, 1997, pp. 53-63.

D. Dwork, *Children with a Star. Jewish Youth in Nazi Europe*, New Heaven and London, Yale University Press, 1991.

R. Elias, *Triumph of Hope. From Theresienstadt and Auschwitz to Israel*, New York, John Wiley and Sons Inc., 1998.

R. Gilsenbach, *Oh Django, sing deine Zorn! Sinti und Roma unter den Deutschen*, Berlin, BasisDruck, 1993.

G. Grau (ed.), *Hidden Holocaust? Gay and Lesbian Persecution in Germany 1933-1945*, London, Cassell, 1995.

R. Hilberg, *The Destruction of the European Jews*, vol. 2, New Haven, Yale University Press, 2003.

L. Holliday (ed.), *Children in the Holocaust and World War II: Their Secret Diaries*, New York, Pocket Books, 1995.

'Ida', in R. OLLA, *Le non persone. Gli italiani nella Shoah*, Roma, Rai Eri, 1999, pp. 7-34.

M. Kárny, M. Kárná, 'Kinder in Theresienstadt', in *Dachauer Hefte*, 1993, vol. 9, 'Die Verfolgung von Kindern und Jugendlichen', pp. 14-31.

D. Kenrick, G. Puxon, *The Destiny of Europe's Gypsies*, New York, Basic Books, 1972.

L. Klüger, *Still Alive: A Holocaust Girlhood Remembered*, New York, The Feminist Press at the City University of New York, 2001.

H. Kubica, 'Les enfants et les adolescents au KL Auschwitz', in F. Piper, T. Swiebocka (eds), *Auschwitz. Camp de concentration et d'extermination*, Editions Le Musée d'Etat d'Auschwitz-Birkenau à Oswiecim, 1994.

H. Kugler Weiss, *Racconta! Fiume-Birkenau-Israele*, Firenze, Giuntina, 2006.

H. Langbein, *People in Auschwitz*, Chapel Hill and London, The University of North Carolina Press, 2004.

C. Lanzmann, *Shoah. An Oral History of the Holocaust*, New York, Pantheon Books, 1987.

P. Levi, 'The Truce', in Idem., *If this is a Man – The Truce*, London, Abacus, 2004.

G. Lewy, *The Nazi Persecution of Gypsies*, New York, Oxford University Press, 2000.

P. Liggeri, 'I minorenni', in G. Bellak, G. Melodia (eds), *Donne e bambini nei lager nazisti*, Milano, ANED, 1960, p. 79.

O. Lustig (1996), *Dizionario del Lager*, Firenze: La Nuova Italia Editrice. Online. Available in English http://isurvived.org/Lustig_Oliver-Dictionary.html (Access date).

T. Marrone, *Meglio non sapere*, Milano, Editori Laterza, 2003.

G. Melodia, 'Padri...madri...figli...', in G. Bellak, G. Melodia (eds), *Donne e bambini nei lager nazisti*, Milano, ANED, 1960, pp. 83-86.

R. Minc, *L'inferno degli innocenti. I ragazzi ebrei nella bufera nazista*, Milano, Massimo, 1969.

L.H. Nicholas, L.H., *Cruel World. The Children of Europe in the Nazi Web*, New York, Vintage Books, 2005.

A. Novac, *The Beautiful Days of My Youth. My Six Months in Auschwitz and Plaszow*, New York, Henry Holt & Company, 1997.

J. Oberski, *Childhood*, New York, Doubleday Books, 1983.

D. Padoan, *Come una rana d'inverno. Conversazioni con tre donne sopravvissute ad Auschwitz*, Milano, Bompiani, 2004.

'Paul', in R. OLLA, *Ancora ciliegie zio SS*, Roma, Rai Eri, 2001, pp. 159-206.

Pavia, A. Tiburzi, *Non perdonerò mai*, Portogruaro, Nuovadimensione, 2006.

B. Pawelke, 'Als Häftling geboren Kinder in Ravensbrück', in E. Bamberger,

A. Ehmann (eds), *Kinder und Jugendliche als Opfer des Holocaust, proceedings of the international conference held at the Haus der Wannseekonferenz, 12-14 December 1994*, Heidelberg, Dokumentationszentrum Deutscher Sinti und Roma in Zusammenarbeit mit der Gedenkstätte Haus der Wannseekonferenz, 1997, pp. 93-106. Essay published also in *Dachauer Hefte*, 1993, *Die Verfolgung von Kinder*, vol. 9, pp. 91-101.

B. Perz, 'Kinder und Jugendliche im Konzentrationslager Mauthausen und seinen Aussenlagern', in *Dachauer Hefte*, 1993, vol. 9, 'Die Verfolgung von Kindern und Jugendlichen', pp. 71-90.

C. Pressburger (ed.), *The Diary of Petr Ginz*, Boston, Atlantic Monthly Press, 2004.

K. Reemtsma, *Sinti und Roma: Geschichte, Kultur und Gegenwart*, München, Beck, 1996.

O. Rosenberg, *A Gypsy in Auschwitz*, London, London House, 1999.

G. Salmoni, *Una storia nella Storia. Ricordi e riflessioni di un testimone da Fossoli a Buchenwald*, Torino, Ega Editore, 2005.

G. Schwarberg, *Der SS – Arzt und die Kinder vom Bullenhuser Damm*, Göttingen, Steidl Verlag, 1988.

Idem., *Meine zwanzig Kinder*, Göttingen, Steidl Verlag, 1996.

L. Segre, *Un'infanzia perduta*, in *Voci dalla Shoah testimonianze per non dimenticare*, Firenze, La Nuova Italia Editrice, 1996, pp. 49-63.

W. Sofsky, *The Order of Terror. The Concentration Camp*, Princeton, Princeton University Press, 1997.

C. Stojka, *Forse sogno di vivere. Una bambina rom a Bergen-Belsen*, Firenze, Giuntina, 2007.

G. Tedeschi, 'Caratteri specifici della deportazione femminile', in L. Monaco (ed.), *La deportazione femminile nei lager nazisti*, Proceedings of the international conference, Turin, October 20-21 1994, Milano, Franco Angeli, 1995, pp. 28-30.

Terezín, disegni e poesie dei bambini del campo di sterminio (catalogue from the exhibition *Disegni e poesie dei bambini del campo di sterminio di Terezín*, promoted by Associazione Versiliese Italia-Cecoslovacchia, Regione Toscana, Amministrazione Provinciale di Pisa), Firenze, Grafiche Il Fiorino, s. d..

T. Todorov, *Facing the Extreme. Moral Life in the Concentration Camps*, New York, Holt Paperbacks, 1997.

H. Weissová, *Zeichne, was Du siehst. Zeichnungen eines Kindes aus Theresienstadt/Terezín*, Göttingen, Wallstein Verlag, 1998.

E. Wiesel, *Night*, New York, Bantam Books, 1982.

R.M. Wlaschek, 'Kinder im Konzentrationslager Theresienstadt', in H. Weissová, *Zeichne, was Du siehst. Zeichnungen eines Kindes aus Theresienstadt/Terezín*, Göttingen, Wallstein Verlag, 1998, pp. 145-149.

M. Zimmermann, *Rassenutopie und Genozid: Die nationalsozialistische 'Lösung der Zigeunerfrage'*, Hamburg, Christians, 1996.

Idem., 'La persecuzione nazista degli zingari', in M. Cattaruzza, M. Flores, S. Levis Sullam, E. Traverso (eds), *Storia della Shoah. La crisi dell'Europa, lo sterminio degli ebrei e la memoria del XX secolo*, vol. I, *La crisi dell'Europa e lo sterminio degli ebrei*, Torino, Utet, 2005, pp. 763-785.

E. Zuccalà, *Sopravvissuta ad Auschwitz. Liliana Segre fra le ultime testimoni della Shoah*, Milano, Paoline Editoriale Libri, 2005.

Z. Zweig, *Il bambino di Buchenwald. Dal ghetto ai lager nel racconto di un padre*, Bolsena, Massari Editore, 1998.

4   Running in Auschwitz: The Holocaust 'Diary' of Michael Kraus

Patricia Heberer Rice

Beginning in the autumn months of 1943, prisoners resident in Birkenau, the camp which housed the Auschwitz complex's killing center, were privy to a strange and puzzling sight. Those venturing near that area of the camp designated B II b could see young children—hundreds of them—playing, performing calisthenics, and engaging in study in the company of their teachers and caretakers. With the exception of those youngsters—many of them twins—whom camp physician Dr. Josef Mengele had selected for medical experimentation and housed in Block 10, there had been, practically speaking, no resident Jewish children in Birkenau.[1] The vast majority of young people arriving at Auschwitz perished immediately in the gas chambers. To Auschwitz prisoners, the image was jarring: unshorn and relatively well-fed youngsters gamboling about their blocks in civilian clothes. Where had these children come from and what were they doing in Birkenau?

The children in question belonged to a unique group of prisoners from the Terezin ghetto, who for nearly a year formed the 'Theresienstadt family camp.'[2] In September 1943, five thousand Czech Jews, among them over one thousand youngsters and adolescents, arrived at Auschwitz from Theresienstadt (Terezin).[3] Spared the customary 'selection', they were brought directly to a special part of the Birkenau quarantine area close to the main entrance gate. Placed within a separate barracks network, designated B II b, these Jews were processed as special prisoners; beside each of their names in the prisoner record stood the singular notation, 'SB6'.[4] Although they received tattooed prisoner numbers on their arms, their hair was not shorn, and they

---

1   N. Keren, 'The Family Camp', in Y. Gutman, M. Berenbaum (eds), *Anatomy of the Auschwitz Death Camp*, p. 431.
2   For a discussion of the 'Theresienstadt family camp', see Keren, 'The Family Camp'; N. Stargardt, *Witnesses of War: Children's Lives under the Nazis*, pp. 197-225.
3   H. Kubica, 'Children', in Y. Gutman, M. Berenbaum (eds), *Anatomy of the Auschwitz Death Camp*, p. 415.
4   Keren, 'The Family Camp', pp. 428-29.

were allowed to retain their civilian clothing. Men and women were housed in separate blocks, but prisoners could move freely within the small camp, and children could remain with their parents.[5] These Jews were not assigned to labor brigades and were allowed, even encouraged, to write letters as well as to receive correspondence and parcels from outside Auschwitz.

At the time no one understood the purpose of the 'family camp', or why its inhabitants received such preferential treatment. When a further group of five thousand Jews from Theresienstadt arrived at Birkenau in December 1943 and were added to their ranks, residents of the little camp could only infer from their privileged existence that their fate would be essentially different than that of other prisoners in the complex. However, on the night of March 7, 1944, exactly six months after the arrival of the first transport of Jews from Theresienstadt to the family camp, all surviving members from the initial September transport were assembled and taken to the gas chamber without the benefit of a 'selection'. Thereafter, the significance of the annotation 'SB6' in the Terezin Jews' prisoner records became clear: the code signified "*Sonderbehandlung*" ['special treatment'],[6] in this case gassing, within six months' time. Indeed all prisoners from the September transport were gassed precisely six months after their arrival at Birkenau. From this sequence of events, surviving prisoners from the December transport could surmise that six months after their arrival, they too would share the fate of their fellow family camp members.

What could explain the curious delay between arrival and gassing of these deportees from Theresienstadt, and why were those ultimately doomed to perish in the Crematorium kept under such privileged circumstances? Most historians believe that the answer to this question lies in the correspondence between Nazi authorities and officials of the International Committee of the Red Cross (ICRC). Succumbing to pressure following the deportation of Danish Jews to Theresienstadt, German administrators had arranged to allow representatives of the ICRC to inspect the Theresienstadt ghetto on June 23, 1944. Originally Nazi officials had planned to include a Red Cross visit to Auschwitz-Birkenau to the Committee's itinerary in order to deflect allegations that camps like Auschwitz represented industrialized killing centers which were claiming the lives of thousands of Jews and other persecutees. German authorities calculated that just as Theresienstadt became a sanitized 'model ghetto' for ICRC visitors, the Theresienstadt family camp 'would give the lie' to 'rumors' of the mass murder of European Jewry. International Red Cross members, however, were satisfied from their highly choreographed visit to

---

5   In late spring 1944, shortly before the liquidation of the family camp, a separate block was designated for children, so that they no longer slept in their parents' barracks.

6   A Nazi euphemism for execution or killing.

Theresienstadt that Jews transferred there remained in the ghetto and were relatively well cared for.[7] Correspondence from 'family camp' members in Birkenau to relatives and friends in Theresienstadt, relating their satisfactory conditions at the camp, furnished further evidence to neutral officials that the systematic murder of Jews in Auschwitz was 'unfounded speculation'. After ten months, the 'family camp' in Birkenau had served its purpose. In early July 1944, survivors of the camp's December 1943 transports, including hundreds of children, were put to a 'selection'. The majority of these prisoners were gassed, while the camp itself was liquidated.

One child who survived the destruction of the Theresienstadt family camp was Michal (today Michael) Kraus. In contrast to the hundreds of thousands of children who lived and died anonymously in the course of the Holocaust, we know a good deal about the young Kraus, because of the remarkable testament which the teenager created in the immediate postwar period. As a child, young Michal had shown promise as a writer and illustrator. He had kept a diary during the first years of his family's persecution in the former Czechoslovakia, but at Auschwitz his journal had been taken away and destroyed.[8] The youngster vowed that should he survive, he would reconstruct on paper 'the memories of those horrible times'.[9] Returning orphaned to Czechoslovakia in the summer of 1945, the teenager immediately began to record his Holocaust experiences in a three-volume chronicle, completed in 1947. Kraus's 'diary', which he dedicated to his slain parents, provides unique insight into the experiences and viewpoints of children during the Holocaust. Punctuated by remarkable illustrations, the journal is an extraordinary story of survival in the charnel world of the extermination camp.

Thirteen-year-old Michal Kraus arrived at Auschwitz with his parents from Theresienstadt in December 1943. An only child, the youngster had been raised in the Bohemian town of Nachod, where his father, Karl Kraus, was a physician. In December 1942, the Krauses, like many Czech Jews, were deported to Theresienstadt. Here Michal was separated from his parents and housed in a boy's home in the so-called Hannover Barracks.[10] In January 1943, the family narrowly missed deportation to Auschwitz, a fortunate escape, for only ten of the five thousand individuals who left with this transport survived the war. Precisely one year after their arrival at Theresienstadt, it was the Krauses' turn; in December 1943, they arrived with a transport of five thousand Jews from Terezin in Birkenau and were quickly absorbed within

7 J.-C. Favez, *The Red Cross and the Holocaust*.
8 A. Zapruder, *Salvaged Pages: Young Writers' Diaries of the Holocaust*, p. 445.
9 United States Holocaust Memorial Museum Archive, Acc. 2006.51 (Michael Kraus Collection), Diary of Michael (Michal) Kraus, 1945-1947, p. 5.
10 Ibid, p. 15.

Fig. 4.1: Michael Kraus's postwar drawing of Auschwitz's Crematorium I.
(United States Holocaust Memorial Museum, gift of Michael Kraus)

the 'Theresienstadt family camp'.[11]

For six months the Krauses lived there in relative safety. As a young boy, Michal was allowed to spend his time in the camp's *Kinderblock* [children's block], a haven in the very heart of the killing center. The *Kinderblock* was the brain child of Fredy Hirsch, who had served as deputy director for youth services in the Theresienstadt ghetto. Deported to Auschwitz with the September 1943 transport, he quickly gained the confidence of Nazi authorities. Hirsch used his status with camp officials to improve the lot of children assigned to the family camp. He acquired permission to construct a separate children's block (Block 31) where youngsters might receive educational instruction, engage in structured play, and obtain more appropriate and nutritious meals. The *Kinderblock* was the 'one oasis in our camp', recalled Hanna Hoffmann, a young and idealistic Czech-Jewish instructor in the children's block.[12] Youngsters under fourteen years old spent most of their waking hours in this area. Here they took their meals and washed themselves

11 Diary of Michael (Michal) Kraus, p. 32.
12 Hanna Hoffmann-Fischel, quoted in I. Deutschkron, *Denn ihrer war die Hölle: Kinder in Gettos und Lagern*, pp. 49-52.

daily, even in the coldest weather. Prisoners in the family camp were not exempt from the monotonous roll calls conducted twice daily in Auschwitz, but Hirsch arranged for his young charges to report to *Appell* [roll call] inside their block, a relative luxury, especially in inclement weather. There were calisthenics before instruction began, and children were also allowed time for games, sport and recreation. Youngsters spent the evening hours with their parents, and slept in the barracks of their father or mother, depending on their gender.[13] The hunger and deprivation which prevailed in the family camp prepared special challenges for the young teachers who sought to provide basic educational instruction to their pupils. Yet, as instructor Avi Fischer later recounted, when the children came together to play or sing in the afternoon, 'the barracks became a safe ship sailing through the vast spaces...' even in the midst of Birkenau.[14]

But this world into which children like Michal Kraus might escape, at least temporarily, from the horrors of the concentration camp, was not made to last. It had been six months since the December transport had brought the Krauses and five thousand other Terezin Jews to Auschwitz; the timeframe which Nazi officials allotted for each transport group to survive in the Theresienstadt family camp. In June 1944, Kraus's mother, Lotte, was transferred to Stutthof concentration camp near Danzig (Gdansk). In early July, camp officials moved to eliminate the family camp and subjected its residents to the 'selection' process. Most of the children, as 'useless eaters', went directly to the gas chamber.[15] Yet in the midst of the liquidation, a curious thing occurred. For reasons that are still unclear to us today, Birkenau camp physician Josef Mengele chose from among the family camp eighty-nine young boys, aged fourteen to sixteen, and decided to spare them. These 'Birkenau Boys', as they came to be known, were removed to the men's camp [*Männerlager*] and initially settled in the punishment block there.[16] From this vantage point the young Kraus could observe the gassing and incineration of friends and loved ones in the family camp, including his father, who was murdered on 11 July. Kraus wrote of that night in his memoir/diary:

> On 11 July, I did not sleep. The night was bright, the sky red. Of that—I cannot talk about it. On 11 July, they killed my father. I balled my fists, I cried, and I promised to avenge him. Many of us lost their loved ones that day.[...]
>
> The sky was burning! Yes, it really was! At night the windows of the block were completely red. All the crematoria worked in full swing. The gas chambers

---

13 Keren, 'The Family Camp', pp. 431-33.
14 Avi Fischer, quoted in Keren, 'The Family Camp', p. 435.
15 Ibid, p. 440.
16 See P. Heberer, *Children during the Holocaust*, p.165.

Fig. 4.2: Young Kraus's vision of the smoking crematorium
at Auschwitz's killing center, Birkenau. (United States
Holocaust Memorial Museum, gift of Michael Kraus)

continuously choked their victims. It was a slaughterhouse such as the world
had never seen. Tens of thousands went daily to the gas. They hounded them
out of the cattle cars directly to their deaths. And sometimes directly into the
flames. And that was what we were supposed to see in the camp![17]

Michal eventually lodged in the so-called *Unterkunft-Verwaltung;* the
housing administration. He and many of the 'Birkenau boys' were now
deployed as runners [*Läufer*], errand boys assigned to convey communications
and supplies among officials in the core of the extermination camp. Life for
young people in such settings was fraught with danger, particularly if those
youngsters, like Kraus, were separated from their parents. Young prisoners
suffered the same deprivation, overcrowding, and unsanitary conditions as
adult detainees did. Children more often lacked access to resources, such as
food and contraband material for barter, than did their grown-up counterparts,
and were more vulnerable to duplicity and abuse both from their guards and
from their fellow prisoners. In many camps, such as Auschwitz, children
under the age of fourteen could not officially be assigned to forced labor details,

17 Diary of Michael (Michal) Kraus, p. 54.

although in practice this regulation was seldom observed.[18] Those who did not or could not work found themselves continually at risk of deportation to a killing center in the frequent 'selections', which took place regularly in Auschwitz. Children proved especially vulnerable to these *selektsyes*, as prisoners called them, and several camps experienced genuine 'children's actions' aimed at culling young prisoners from the camp population. In the early fall just such an *Aktion* occurred in Birkenau; Kraus noted that sometime before the revolt of 7 October 1944, in which units of the camp's *Sonderkommando* succeeded in destroying Crematorium IV, physicians reviewed the boys. Those below a certain height were noted, as were those who were appeared ill or unfit for labor.[19] In the end a sympathetic *Rapportführer*—the SS official responsible for prisoner count at *Appell*—arranged for thirty boys to evade 'selection' and remain in Birkenau. A few weeks later a further selection and transport from Birkenau further decimated the ranks of Kraus's young friends from the former family camp.[20]

Youngsters who survived in Auschwitz needed an equal share of courage, stamina, and good fortune. Adolescents often did manage to mix in with the camps' adult population because of their fitness or ability to work, and many succeeded in enduring the harsh conditions and grueling labor through the help of adult prisoners.[21] In Birkenau, Kraus and his young comrades fell under the protection of the *Sonderkommando*, those prisoners whose responsibility it was to remove the bodies of victims from the gas chambers and to dispose of their remains in the crematoria. Because of the particularly grisly tasks assigned its members, *Sonderkommando* units at Auschwitz regularly received food of good quality and sufficient quantity. Thus Kraus and his young associates had better access to food and resources than did many Auschwitz prisoners; adult colleagues also taught the youngsters to pilfer food from the stores destined for the men's camp.[22] Other mature prisoners, such as Kraus's immediate block leader, appeared to watch over the boys and worked to thwart efforts to include the youngsters in selections or to remove them from the relative safety of their block. In the end, a fortunate constellation of forces—protective fellow prisoners, benign SS officials in their immediate sphere, and the resilience, initiative and pluck of the boys themselves, helped to facilitate their miraculous survival.

Kraus records that a light layer of snow covered the ground on the night of January 18, 1945—the evening on which Auschwitz officials received orders to evacuate the camp complex. The Red Army was approaching, and

18 Kubica, 'Children', p. 249.
19 Diary of Michael (Michal) Kraus, p. 60.
20 Ibid, p. 60.
21 Heberer, *Children during the Holocaust*, p.176.
22 Diary of Michael (Michal) Kraus, p.57.

Kraus and his fellow campmates in Birkenau made a hurried march across the frozen ground to Auschwitz I—the main camp [*Stammlager*]. In the early months of 1945, the fourteen-year-old endured a series of forced marches from Auschwitz to Gleiwitz concentration camp and further into the Reich interior through a series of Mauthausen sub-camps. He was severely ill with typhus when he was liberated by American forces at Gunskirchen *Lager* in Upper Austria on May 5, 1945.

Liberation did not end Michael Kraus's Holocaust odyssey. Alone and without resources, Kraus was bed-ridden and hundreds of miles away from his native Czechoslovakia. Like many child and adult survivors he now faced the daunting prospect of rebuilding his life after years of persecution. Where should he go and how should he accomplish this? After liberation, Jewish displaced persons often feared to return to their homes in view of the anti-Semitism which continued to persist in many regions of Europe. For others the inability to locate or discover the fate of family members made the journey back home a distressing prospect. Children who had lost their parents, or who had become separated from them in the course of the war, faced a number of difficult dilemmas. Should they attempt to make the arduous journey back to their place of origin, or should they remain in an orphanage or displaced persons' camp which could provide them with food and shelter? How was such a journey possible without adequate money or provisions? Would missing parents, siblings, or relatives be waiting for them on their return? Who would care for them if these were dead? Could one rebuild a new life and a new future beside one's old roots, in a place where one had perhaps been forgotten or forsaken by one's neighbors?[23]

After recovering in an American military hospital, Kraus and several other young Czech friends resolved that they would set off for Prague. The journey home was grueling; hungry and without sufficient funds, the boys made their way along the Danube River by boat and train, and walked nearly one hundred kilometers to reach Bratislava (today in Slovakia) where local rail lines fell into disrepair. The group reached the Czech capital on 28 June 1945. Here Michal stayed briefly with Vera Loewenbach, a close friend of Lotte Kraus. Loewenbach had accompanied her in June 1944 on a transport from Auschwitz to Stutthof concentration camp; and it was she who told the young boy of his mother's death there in January 1945. Learning that he was orphaned, Kraus lodged for a number of months with family friends and acquaintances in his home town of Nachod. It was at this time that he began a retrospective diary/memoir of his Holocaust experiences, which he completed in 1947 and dedicated to his deceased parents. In the summer of 1948, Michal's guardian arranged for him to join an orphans' transport to

23 Heberer, *Children during the Holocaust*, pp.400-401.

Canada, funded by the American Jewish Joint Distribution Committee. In 1951, the youth emigrated to the United States, where he enrolled in Columbia University's School of Architecture. After positions with architectural firms in London and Geneva, Kraus settled with his new wife Ilana in the Boston area, where he still lives today. Of Michael Kraus's extended family, only one aunt and one cousin survived the Holocaust.

Michael Kraus' survival as a child in Auschwitz is a marvel. The aspect which makes his story so compelling and which distinguishes his narrative from that of many other child survivors was his decision to record his experiences in a postwar 'diary'. Diaries written *in situ* in concentration camp settings are extremely rare, not least because of the physical difficulties that maintaining such a journal entailed. Kraus's diary/memoir, written in the immediate postwar, is a striking record of his experiences and captures the immediacy of events in a way that memoirs written decades later cannot. Kraus' testimony, as preserved through the journal, contributes to our knowledge of the Theresienstadt family camp. It is invaluable to our understanding of its children's block, an institution which enhanced the lives and hopes of so many of its young charges, but in the end left so few witnesses to tell us what it was like. His account relates the strange story of the 'Birkenau Boys'; spared for an unknown reason, these small 'runners' in Auschwitz demonstrate that a prisoner's survival in the killing center owed itself in large measure to luck and chance. Kraus's retelling of his painful return to Czechoslovakia is a useful corrective to a Holocaust history which ends with liberation. Filled with his remarkable drawings, Michal Kraus's diary adds to a wealth of source material concerning the lives and fates of child survivors, now our last living witnesses to the events of the Holocaust.

Bibliography

Archival Material

United States Holocaust Memorial Museum Archive, Acc. 2006.51 (Michael Kraus Collection), Diary of Michael (Michal) Kraus, 1945-1947.

Secondary Sources

I. Deutschkron, *Denn ihrer war die Hölle: Kinder in Gettos und Lagern,* Cologne, Verlag Wissenschaft und Politik, 1965.

J.-C. Favez, *The Red Cross and the Holocaust,* Cambridge, Cambridge University Press, 1999.

P. Heberer, *Children during the Holocaust,* Lanham, AltaMira, 2011.

N. Keren, 'The Family Camp', in Y. Gutman, M. Berenbaum (eds), *Anatomy of the Auschwitz Death Camp*, Bloomington, University of Indiana Press in association with the United States Holocaust Memorial Museum, 1994, pp. 428-40.

H. Kubica, 'Children', in Y. Gutman, M. Berenbaum (eds), *Anatomy of the Auschwitz Death Camp*, Bloomington, University of Indiana Press in association with the United States Holocaust Memorial Museum, 1994, pp. 412-27.

N. N. , 'Children and Adolescents in Auschwitz', in T. Iwasko, a. o., *Auschwitz, 1940-1945: Central Issues in the History of the Camp*, Oswiecim, Auschwitz-Birkenau State Museum, 2000, pp. 201-90, vol. II.

N. Stargardt, *Witnesses of War: Children's Lives under the Nazis*, New York, Alfred A. Knopf, 2006.

Zapruder, Alexandra, *Salvaged Pages: Young Writers' Diaries of the Holocaust*, New Haven, Yale University Press, 2002.

5   Oral Histories about the Daily Life Experiences of Children during World War II

Irina Rebrova

The history of childhood is an emerging theme in Russian historical research. A variety of documents, both of official and private origin, are now available as sources for the study of childhood. This paper discusses the results of a collaborative research project which aimed to collect, process, and systematize the oral histories of individual children's experiences of the Second World War. It was a regional research project and we have collected stories from the Northern Caucasus (the Stavropol and Kuban regions of Russia). Over a two-year period between 2007 and 2009, we gathered oral histories. In total, we conducted over fifty interviews, almost two thirds of which were with women. Almost all informants had undergone higher education and gone on to have relatively successful working careers. One third of our storytellers finished secondary school, and worked hard all their life. We did not aim to find our informants according to their gender and/or professional affiliation. Most informants were found through acquaintances, but there were few storytellers who were randomly selected in the villages and cities of Stavropol and Kuban regions. The main criterion of selection was the age of our potential informant. Most of our informants were over 60 years old at the time of interview, but during the war most of them were aged between 12 and 14 years.

Most interviews were conducted as a semi-structured interview in which the informant could respond to the main question about his or her remembrance of wartime in a free narrative. This method allows the storyteller to create their personal narrative and to speak about the moments of their life which they find personally significant. Follow-up questions were asked in the second part of the interview to specify and clarify any parts of the narrative that were not fully understood by the interviewee.

With the help of oral narratives about World War II a researcher can reconstruct models of children's behaviour, relations within the family, and the daily lives of children and their relatives during the war. We can also trace the channels of patriotic education, the formation of images of the enemy in children's consciousness, the links between individual and collective memories of events. The oral histories of wartime children provides the researcher with an opportunity to study how the images and impressions of an individual, or personal, war relate to the ideologically charged politics of state memorialisation and collective memory.

Although subjective, partial, and frequently fragmentary, memory is an excellent historical resource for social history and anthropology, shedding light on everyday life, and permitting psychological and gendered readings of the history of World War II. Even many years later, those who witnessed the war as children or teenagers can talk about aspects of wartime life that cannot be found in archival documents. According to Harald Welzer, the wartime stories of children are more emotional in their descriptions of what the storyteller saw or experienced than are those of adults. Furthermore,

> Neurological studies have shown that the old men have a more stable and clear memory of their distant past than of recent events in their life. The memory of the distant past is more static, it is beyond change or reflection.[1]

Most stories are filled with emotional description of family life during the occupation, relations between family members, and letters between them and relatives who were fighting at the front.[2] This paper is based on the analysis of such stories. Children's impressions of the war are quite complicated and usually consist of several fragmented stories. It can be explained by the age of informants at the time; they were too young to attempt to gain a holistic conception of the war they were experiencing.

The place of wartime children narratives in memory studies

Narratives about the war help researchers to study the problems of the dynamics of relationships that were set in the collective memory of the past and preserved by tradition or that became popular by changing social and political realities. In his study of 'collective memory' and 'individual memory', the American historian William Rosenberg has emphasised the peculiarities of social memory, which 'has a great analytical power to historians in understanding the concepts where the past experience makes sense through the narration'.[3] Oral stories of wartime children allow us to trace the ways

---

1   H. Welzer, 'Istorija, pamjat' i sovremennost' proshlogo: Pamjat' kak arena politicheskoj bor'by', *Pamjat' o vojne 60 let spustja. Rossija, Germanija, Evropa*, p. 56.
2   I. Rebrova, 'Individual'noeikollektivnoevpamjati "detejvojny"', *Obrazvojnirevoljucijvistoricheskojpamjati*, p. 389.
3   W. Rozenberg, 'Javljaetsjalisocial'najapamjat' "poleznojkategoriejistoricheskogoanaliza?" 'IstoricheskajapamjatʹiobshestvovRossijskojimperiiiSovetskomSojuze (konecXIX – nachaloXXveka)*, p.

in which the war was referred to within Soviet/Russian society and the mechanisms of remembering the war; to understand the differences in how the war is remembered by different generations. As Tamara Hareven argues,

> Oral history allows us not only to establish the sequence of events in people's lives, but also to see that various pieces of these lives can be added up to a certain picture, can be broken and folded back together; lose their meaning, change it, come and go in new configurations at different moments of the person's life.[4]

The impression of the war formed directly in childhood, differs greatly from the impression formed in the mind of the older generation. This happened because of the influence of state propaganda and existing of the state ideology about the war upon the ordinary peoples' consciousness. Nevertheless, the events fixed in children's memories significantly influence both the fate of the witnesses themselves and the mechanism by which an image of the war is formed in the collective representations of members of the social group.

Coming back to our sources it is important to allocate the main topic of children's narration we intend to study in this paper. Children are highly dependent on other people, in particular on their families. As they get older, this dependence and the associated relationships can weaken, and the person can form their own way of life. Oral histories of wartime childhood are full of the description of relationships with different people: family members, neighbours, friends, and enemies. The opposition between 'friend' and 'hostile' is the basis of all human relationships as well as of culture in general. The presence of 'hostiles' in the perception of the world, the contradiction between 'me' and 'a hostile' promotes objectively the internal consolidation and mobilization of any kind of social group. Indeed, it makes the internal differences and contradictions of the group less relevant in comparison with the differences and contradictions between the members of the group and 'hostiles'. Everybody who figures in the oral narratives of wartime children can be classified as 'friend' or 'hostile'. Yet, it is also possible to observe another category of people; the 'other'. The 'other' is not a 'friend', but at the same time he is not considered dangerous, as is a 'hostile'.[5] In this paper, we try to reconstruct the world of our informants – comprising 'friends', 'hostiles' and 'others' – through the rhetoric of their narration. We shall also try to trace how children were incorporated into the world of adults, to understand their place in the system of interpersonal relations during the war based on

225.

4   T. Hareven, 'Sem'jaipromyshlennost', in M.V. Loskutovoj (ed.), *Hrestomatija po ustnoj istorii*, pp. 172–173.

5   M. L. Dubossarskaja, 'Svoj-chuzhoj-drugoj: kpostanovkeproblemy', *VestnikStavropol'skogogosudarstvennogouniversiteta*, p. 171.

the analysis of interviews.

'In the circle of friends': children in the family and among their fellows

The child was a natural part of – and perhaps the main person in – any family. Before the war, families would be large with 5, 6 or more children; and children helped to form the team spirit of all family members. Children strongly depended on their parents yet they had to become self-supporting during the war. They were brought up in the spirit of the *Domostroj*[6], meaning that they were to respect and admire their parents, and obey them accordingly. Within this context, the child's world was strongly tied to the family unit. Many accounts of the wartime children we interviewed placed their parents in the story of the beginning and end of the war. One interviewee recounts;

> Mum began; she took a pair of scissors, paper, and glue that she had prepared by herself. And we glued crosses to the window. I also heard the word "war", but I didn't know this word. It meant absolutely nothing to me, but I realized that something had happened. My father and mother looked different from how they used to look. I didn't understand the reason of gluing the crosses. Later on, I understood everything. That is the way the war started for me. There were paper crosses on the windows so they wouldn't break.[7]

In this account, the storyteller connected the characteristics of the parents – 'dad and mum looked different from how they used to look' – with the beginning of the war. The emotional background becomes very important to the child. His parents couldn't hide their emotions at the beginning of the war, and the child felt this. The emotional relations with parents provides 'Friends' which are represented by the closest relatives to become his main defenders in extreme situations.

World War II as the extreme period of Soviet history strengthened the traditional model of the patriarchal family. This is outlined in the way of life as well as in the practice of the survival of Soviet people during the war on occupied territories. The main role in the patriarchal family belongs to the man. During the war, men left their family for the army or guerrilla groups and the oldest son thus took his place at the head of the family. He may not have been older than 10 years old but he became the head of the family and

---

6   A set of rules for the patriarchal governing of family life, dating from the 16th century. For discussion of the history of the *Domostroj*, see C. Johnston Pouncey, *The Domostroi: Rules for Russian Households in the Time of Ivan the Terrible*.

7   Interview with Victor Kovalenko, Kuban State Technological University Archive of Oral History, DV-08/IR02.

he took responsibility for all other family members: mother, younger brothers, and sisters. War-time correspondence shows that the father always asked his older son to take care of his mother and other children. Our male informants told us that they worked all day long to help their families to find food during the period of German occupation.

During the first half of the 20th century the family was the institution through which traditional gender identity was reproduced, and marriage itself became the powerful bastion of standards, feelings, and habits that bestowed privileges upon the man.[8] During the war these rules of family life were extended. The father of the family remained the head of the household and responsible for every person in his family, even at a distance when he arrived at the front. Victor Kovalenko recalls: 'In spring, 1942 dad wrote mum a letter. He told her to gather the children and move to the village where mother's sister lived. Mum did what my father told her.'[9]

The details in this account prove that the man in the patriarchal family was always the leader. The role of the executor of the man's choices was assigned to woman. In this account, the storyteller says that their life was not improved after moving to the village and moreover the family was subjected to fear during the combat near that village. But his mum wasn't able to override the decision of her husband.

The patriarchal model of family is based on economic relations. The elder boy took responsibility for all other members of the family when the head of the family was on the front-line. If there were no boys in the family the elder girls tried to carry it. The mother could also work, but often her work was domestic. The mother would for example make clothes and elder girls used to go to the other villages and towns to exchange clothes for food. The clear boundary between male public and female private spaces remained during the war period. According to Galina Olenskaya,

We bought the food. My mother and aunt made clothes from different material in the evenings. Then somehow, I remember, they bought a parachute somewhere. And they made beautiful dresses from it. Mother then went to the village somewhere near Krasnodar and there she exchanged clothes for flour and corn.[10]

In this situation, since her children were very young the woman assumed the man's role and combined private and public spaces in her activity. Teenagers participated in the commodity exchange; they obtained food. It was the way

---

8   N. Rimashevskajaetal., *Oknovchastnujuzhizn'. Supruzheskieparyv 1996*, p. 118.
9   Interview with Victor Kovalenko, DV-08/IR02.
10 Interview with Galina Olenskaya, KubSTU Archive of Oral History, DV-08/IR06.

they helped their mother, and thus they guarded her from public life. Another informant recalled:

> I was 11 or 12 years old, but exchanged the clothes myself. It was necessary to save the family. We were very hungry, we had nothing to eat. All people went to the villages and there they exchanged clothes for meals.[11]

Women could work or exchange clothes, remaining inside their space, on private land with neighbours, relatives, and familiar people. Only the head of the family, the father, could cross the border of public and private space. When he was at the front line, elder children could cross it. As Galina Strokoon recalls: 'My younger brother Vitya was born. We didn't have food. I was 11 years old at that time. I visited different cities and sold tobacco. We stayed alive during the war because I exchanged tobacco for food.'[12]

Children from 6–8 years old tried to help their family to find food. Sometimes children could find the food in places, where an adult could not. Galina Olenskaya recounts,

> I was sent to kindergarten before the occupation. Then the German army encamped at exactly that location. There was a German kitchen near the gates. The Germans threw out a lot of food into the big vats. And we children took everything in small pails. One day the Germans threw out a lot of tins of lentils. Some were opened, and some were closed. We immediately grabbed those tins and brought them home. And no one was poisoned, we ate them all.[13]

The work of every member of the family for all relatives is the main characteristic feature of traditional family relations. Children's stories about their contribution to the survival of the family during the period of occupation confirm this thesis. They also state the importance of this work for the family safety in the opinion of the storytellers. The strong bonds between family members were increased under the occupation, and without the head of family around, family members had to look out for each other. Lidia Tkachenko recalls the time when her mother disappeared:

> One Sunday a woman came, and she said: 'Go to the Sennoj Market and show them mother's passport, because your mother was caught in the round-up.' It was a real horror. My sister was 16 years old; she took mother's passport and went to the market. And I thought that they would seize my sister too and I

11 Interview with Galina Strokoon, , KubSTU Archive of Oral History, DV-08/IR01.
12 Ibid.
13 Interview with Galina Olenskaya, DV-08/IR06.

would be left alone. But soon my mother came back. I was very glad to see her. She asked where was my sister and I answered that she had gone to the market to look for her. The next moment my mother left, back to the market. It was very dangerous. Finally my mother and sister came back.[14]

The fear for their own life took second place to the fear of losing their relative. Each member of the family was ready to sacrifice himself to rescue the other. Just as her mother, the sister in this story might never have returned home. Yet, they thought about their relatives at the moment of making decisions. During the war and the occupation, the main problem for the family was the shortage of foodstuffs. Even during that time family members arranged special occasions, to continue family life. An informant remembered the birthday party of her elder brother:

We would give presents to each other. That time my brother's biggest wish was to eat a pot of maize porridge until he was full. I heard that mother asked every member of our family not to eat the porridge the next day. Next day mother brought the pot and she asked everybody to share in the meal. My father and brother refused, they said that they were full and they didn't want to eat. I said the same. So my brother ate all the porridge. And he felt ill.[15]

The informant was seven years old at that period. This case from her wartime childhood confirms the thesis that the family was considered to be a united association. In a family each member would be prepared to sacrifice everything he could for the happiness of others. During the war the elder brother dreamed of being full. All members of family sacrificed themselves to fulfil his request. They all forgot that eating a large meal after the many half-starved months could strongly affect the boy's health.

Family relations were very important to wartime children. Family members tried to be together in sorrow and in happiness. Often the concept of the family also included close friends and neighbours. Our storytellers considered their friends and peers to be 'friends' to them. Children remained children even during the war. They played different games, spent all day together, enjoyed having fun. The only thing was that the games were mostly military. Irina Manokchina recounts,

What to tell you about the bombs. The Russians bombed us mostly, the Germans didn't bomb us because they had their residence and Gestapo, or I don't know the correct name of the Germans' HQ, in the centre of the city

---

14 Interview with Lidia Tkachenko, KubSTU Archive of Oral History, DV-08/IR04.
15 Interview with GalinaOlenskaya, DV-08/IR06.

[Krasnodar]. So the Soviet Army bombed the central streets. And after that we ran to the street to watch the building burning. Our mother didn't let us go out on the streets, but we wanted to. Then we collected the burnt pieces of gas masks and the black canisters with coal inside. And then we played there. We weren't allowed to, because there could have been unexploded bombs.[16]

This female narrator did not specify what the children did with the trophies they had found. It seems that the game was about hunting for gas-mask canisters tins and fragments of bombs, as well as the opportunity of running away from her mother and spending time with friends.

It is interesting to note that all our informants talked about their relationships with friends during the war in relation to games. Asked to talk about children's entertainment during the war, our informants replied almost without hesitation, that they did not have games and that they only began playing games again after the war. Victor Kovalenko, for example, recounts: 'We had some kind of business, but not the real fun games. We played real games when the war was over'.[17] Nevertheless, informants mention games during the war. The only thing we need to mention here, is that these wartime games were very special and had a military character. One informant told us: 'We ate everything we could find, we tasted sparrows, frogs, crows. We ate everything because of the hunger and of curiosity as well.'[18] Of course children killed birds because they were hungry. At the same time the storyteller stressed that they killed the birds for curiosity. It is well known that the interest caused every kind of the game.

'Friends' were the people ready to help in every situation, with whom one could share one's life. One informant recalls the unity of children. When pupils were led into the shelter during a bombing attack, she recalls that older pupils read or told fairytales to the younger ones so that they would not to feel in danger.[19] 'Friends' helped children to adapt to wartime conditions. It was easier to a child to adapt to the war together with relatives and fellows. Family and friends became a bastion that protected them and helped them to become more responsible. Being cared for by their family, children themselves tried to protect their 'friends' at the same time as they worked, sought food, or looked after younger family members.

16 Interview with Irina Manokchina, KubSTU Archive of Oral History. DV-09/IR11.
17 Interview with Victor Kovalenko.
18 Ibid.
19 Interview with Lidia Tkachenko, DV-08/IR04.

Children and 'hostiles': the attitude towards the enemy

The trope 'friend-hostile' is most frequently manifested in the opposition 'us-them', 'ours-theirs'. The image of the Nazi soldier had been associated with the German enemy in Soviet mass consciousness for many years. In Soviet propaganda, the German enemy was considered to be an absolute measure of immorality and evil.[20] Recently, the enemy image has become associated only with Nazis, and has been dissociated from nationality of those who lost the Second World War.

The memories of soldiers and people who lived in the German-occupied territories offer a more complete picture of the image of the enemy, or 'hostile'. Official ideology and mass propaganda strongly influenced the making of this image.[21] According to Elena Zubkova, the psychological construction of 'us-them' exists in a clear form of mutual rejection only at war. The imperative of 'Kill him!' was the main principle of the 'science of hate' that most soldiers and witnesses of the war learned. 'They' were perceived as a dangerous community, who had nothing in common with 'us'. This mythological perception of the enemy's image can be founded in war memoirs, which are replete with emotional and negative descriptions of the enemy, such as 'monsters', 'Fritz', 'fascists', and 'looters'.[22]

The category of 'hostile' is often articulated in the oral narratives of wartime children, but its connotations do not always correspond to the opinions of adults. Lidia Tkachenko recalls: 'One day our teacher asked why the Germans all have names that start with the letter "G": *Gitler, Gimmler, Gebbels*. And one boy answered because all of them are bastards [*govnyuki*].'[23]

Usually a child doesn't reflect on his words. He learned from his elders who the 'hostile' was. Children were afraid of 'hostiles'. Based on their own experiences, 'hostiles' were always associated with pain and grief. Galina Strokoon recounts,

> Well, we went, of course, but we were afraid of them. We were teenagers. Once in winter we played with the other girls on the icy lake. We were afraid of the bombings, we were afraid of walking. And we were walking on the ice, and suddenly we heard the Germans coming. We tried to flee, and we were close

---

20 L. Gudkov, 'Ideologema "vraga": "Vragi" kakmassovyjsindromimehanizmsociokul'turnojintergracii', in L. Gudkov (ed.), *Obrazvraga*, p. 59.

21 E. M. Malysheva 'Sociojetnicheskiekomponentymassovogoobwestvennogosoznanija v godyVelikojOtechestvennojvojny: patriotizm, internacionalizmikollaboracionizm', *Informacionno-analiticheskijsbornik*, p. 166.

22 E. Zubkova, 'Obtchestvennajaatmosferaposlevojny (1945–1946)', *Svobodnajamysl'*, p. 6.

23 Interview with Lidia Tkachenko, DV-08/IR04.

to the home of one of the girls. We entered it, but the Germans caught one girl and beat her with a belt.[24]

In the memories of women who survived the war as teenagers, we can find stories about the fear of being raped by Germans. Parents often didn't let the girls go outside, they hid their daughters in cellars, coloured their faces with soot and dressed them in rags. The feeling of fear has stayed forever in the consciousness of the informants.

There were cases of voluntary collaborations of Soviet girls with the invaders. In such stories a women became a 'hostile' along with the enemy himself. Crossing the border of 'us-them' she became a 'hostile' to her former 'friends'. In the rhetoric of the informants, these women appear in a very negative way.

The existence of a 'hostile' itself threatens the existence of 'me' and 'us' in an individual or group's perception. For this reason, the only possible and justified response to a 'hostile' is the alienation and aggression in this kind of binary opposition. As a consequence, 'hostiles' must be defeated, humiliated, and morally or physically destroyed.[25] 'Hostile' delimits the borders of 'us', the limits of understanding and identity of the group. You can protect yourself from the enemy; you can hide from him, escape, or defeat him. But in any case the enemy is the important factor of mobilization for the whole community, who show solidarity and unity around the institutions or authorities that can guarantee their security.[26] In the oral narratives of wartime children much attention is given to the liberation of their town or village from invaders. In these stories, the happiness of meeting the liberators, 'us', and the expulsion of 'hostiles' becomes a kind of myth about the victory of good over evil.

The place of the 'other' in children's images of the war

In official historical discourse there is a tendency to represent the war as a simple confrontation between two blocs. According to this logic, the war – as well as children's war-games – is divided into 'us' – the Russians, Soviets, patriots, guerrillas, heroes, and so on – and 'them' – 'hostiles', Germans, invaders, fascists, Nazis, murderers, beasts, etc. In contrast to the narratives of official discourse with their stereotyped heroes and villains, the main characters of oral narratives are real human beings who behave in accordance with their own personality and under various circumstances.[27] This construction could be applied to the analysis of the oral histories of wartime children. Children's

---

24 Interview with Galina Strokoon, DV-08/IR01.
25 Dubossarskaja, 'Svoj-chuzhoj-drugoj', p. 168.
26 Gudkov, 'Ideologema "vraga"', p. 15.
27 Z. Kormina, S. Shtyrkov. 'Nikto ne zabyt, nichto ne zabyto. Istorija okkupacii v ustnyh svidetel'stvah', *Pamjat' o vojne 60 let spustja*, p. 223.

images of the war, because of their fragmentary and mosaic construction, are more complicated. The dichotomy of 'us-them' is endowed with more emotional colouring and has a distinct and personalized tone in the stories of wartime children. Moreover, the division between 'us' and 'hostiles' is complicated by the appearance in the stories of wartime children a new category of the 'other'.

The 'other' does not beget alienation and aggression as does the 'hostile', but is the object of interested attention.[28] The 'hostile' is never perceived as a real human being. He is considered to be a beast to which the normal laws of human society cannot be applied. The 'other' is without any doubt a man, but he differs greatly from 'us'.[29] The 'other' has a name and a personality. In narratives of wartime children there are frequently stories about invaders who helped the family survive. They call these people by name; there are notes of nostalgia and gratitude to these 'others' in the rhetoric of former children's narration. Michael Naumenko recalls,

> The German officer lived in our neighbour's house and our Hans worked as a driver for that officer. Hans was a Communist and said that he would never fight, and would not kill a single person. He was huge, about two meters high. He had a car, which later broke down. During the war there was anarchy in our region. We carried and brought in what was left from the fields. The boys took beetroots; he stopped them, offered them honey, and brought it round in the evening. He also set a Primus in the evening and we had a small iron pot and were heated by it. He washed his hands, treated us with honey, and brought us bread that was baked in 1938. He showed us his pictures. He had two daughters and a wife. He also had a summer cottage. He looked at the pictures and cried. He spoke very bad Russian. He said: "Why is the war going on? Stalin's down, Hitler's down, and Hans goes home". With this officer, we often fought with swords made from sunflowers. He was a cheerful, playful person, a good young man. He slept in the second room, which was not heated. He fed us. He was a good man.[30]

The informant considered Hans to be one of 'us'. He said that he helped the family survive, played with the kids because he had left his own family at home. The transformation of the role of a 'hostile', an enemy into 'ours', allows us to identify the category of the 'other' in the study of such stories of the wartime children.

Another example of a German helping a family can be found in an interview

28 Dubossarskaja, 'Svoj-chuzhoj-drugoj', p. 170.
29 Ibid, p. 171.
30 Interview with Michael Naumenko, KubSTU Archive of Oral History, DV-09/IR15.

with Irina Manokchina:

> Well, we did not have any electricity during the war. And the Germans had kerosene lamps in the room. We had many rooms and the largest one was selected by the Germans for the officer in our house. Once there was an accident. I ran into a large room, when the Germans were still arranging there. One of them hung the officer's uniform. I said: 'Oh, we also have a uniform.' And he asked who in our family could have a uniform. My dad. I showed them the pictures of my father. The families of Soviet senior officers had to be shot. First the Communists, Jews, and then the families of senior officers. But I showed them those pictures. The photos were in a small suitcase under the bed. The German officer asked my mum to come into his room in the evening and told her to hide the pictures because I had shown them to him already. Mum buried them in the garden, the suitcase with pictures and letters from the frontline, of course.[31]

The behaviour of the German officer, who lived with this informant's family, also draws him beyond the label 'hostile'. He helped the family. So he was considered to be 'other' of whom, and to whom the family was afraid and thankful at the same time. Galina Strokoon also recounts,

> There were good Germans as well. My mother gave birth to my brother during the war. She wanted to bathe the child, but we didn't have any soap. Once a German came in and said that war is bad for all people. Stalin and Hitler had quarreled with each other and all people suffer. And then he gave me some soap. All the other Germans usually only gave me a cuff round the ear.[32]

This storyteller didn't name the German who brought her the soap, but she opposed him to all the other 'hostiles' who would hit her. To expect help from the occupants seemed unnatural to a child. The episode with the soap stood out in the memory of the narrator because it was unusual. The attention of the 'other' brought a sense of gratitude.

Conclusion

The Second World War was a great test for every person individually and for the family institution as a whole. Here are the words of one of our storytellers: 'War was the main event in my life. War revealed to me the truth about people,

---

31 Interview with Iirina Manokchina, DV-09/IR11.
32 Interview with Galina Strokoon, DV-08/IR01.

the truth about life, the value of all things.'[33]

Psychological research into human memory shows that a child's memory is stable and emotional: a person can clearly remember events from their own childhood, just as they can find it difficult to remember events from their more recent past. Oral history shows the changes of people's evaluation of the events through ages. Traditions, stereotypes, fears, and hopes can all be revealed by means of oral history. These are the most valuable sources about the culture of society. The oral stories of war-time children demonstrate clearly, that the patriarchal model of the family was the only one possible during the Second World War. The war strengthened the family as the social institution. The family itself facilitated the survival of its members. Mutual aid was both economic and spiritual. At the local level the best features of patriarchal family life were manifested in the simple family relationships that has been fixed and carried in the memory of the wartime children throughout the years. In the circle of 'us' there is a place for friends, relatives and neighbours, whom children and adolescents spend most of the time with during the war. Children helped the adults, they worked and played, and believed that 'our people' would protect and help them to survive, would resist the 'hostile' at war and during the period of occupation.

Oral history reflects the personality of the storytellers, their cultural values, and the specific historical circumstances that formed their point of view. Oral history has the advantage of making it possible to reconstruct past events into a broader historical perspective. It also helps one to understand earlier events in the context of subsequent changes. Oral history thus presents new ways for understanding the forming of attitudes towards past events, correlating these events with changes in the views of the person at the same time.[34] This observation is especially important for analysis of the stories about wartime childhood. At the time of the interview, informants have a huge life experience behind them. The subject of their wartime childhood, as a rule, has previously remained outside of public attention, and that of their relatives and friends. Many informants stressed that their wartime experience cannot be compared with the life of real heroes; the defenders of the Motherland. Nevertheless, the description of the children's lives during the war opens up new avenues for understanding the Second World War.

33 Interview with Galina Olenskaya, DV-08/IR06.
34 Hareven, 'Sem'jaipromyshlennost', p. 172.

Bibliography

Primary Sources

Kuban State Technological University (KubSTU), Archive of Oral History, Interview with Galina Olenskaya, 2008. DV-08/IR06.

KubSTU, Archive of Oral History, Interview with Galina Strokoon. 2008. DV-08/IR01.

KubSTU, Archive of Oral History, Interview with Lidia Tkachenko. 2008. DV-08/IR04.

KubSTU, Archive of Oral History, Interview with Victor Kovalenko. 2008. DV-08/IR02.

KubSTU, Archive of Oral History, Interview with Michel Naumenko. 2009. DV-09/IR15.

KubSTU, Archive of Oral History, Interview with Irina Manokchina. 2009. DV-09/IR11.

Secondary Sources

M.L. Dubossarskaja, 'Svoj-chuzhoj-drugoj: k postanovkeproblemy', *VestnikStavropol'skogogosudarstvennogouniversiteta*, 2008, vol. 54.

L. Gudkov, 'Ideologema "vraga": "Vragi" kakmassovyjsindromimehanizmsociokul'turnojintergracii', in L. Gudkov (ed.), *Obrazvraga*, Moscow, OGI, 2005.

T. Hareven, 'Sem'jaipromyshlennost', in M.V.Loskutova (ed.), *Hrestomatijapoustnojistorii*, St. Petersburg, EU Publishing house, 2003.

Z. Kormina, S. Shtyrkov, 'Nikto ne zabyt, nichto ne zabyto: Istorijaokkupacii v ustnyhsvidetel'stvah', *Pamjat' o vojne 60 let spustja*, Moscow, NLO, 2005.

E.M. Malysheva, 'Sociojetnicheskiekomponentymassovogoobwestvennogosoznanija v godyVelikojOtechestvennojvojny: patriotizm, internacionalizmikollaboracionizm', *Informacionno-analiticheskijsbornik*, Adygejskijrespublikanskijinstitutgumanitarnyhissledovanij, Otdelistorii, Majkop, 2001, vol. 4.

I. Rebrova, 'Individual'noeikollektivnoe v pamjati "detejvojny"', *Obrazvojnirevoljucij v istoricheskojpamjati: mater. mezhdunar. Konf,* Pjatigorsk, Stavropol, Stavropol State University Publishing House, 2009.

N. Rimashevskaja et al., 'Okno v chastnujuzhizn', *Supruzheskiepary v 1996*, Moscow, Academia, 1999.

W. Rozenberg, 'Javljaetsja li social'najapamjat' "poleznojkategoriejistoricheskogoanaliza?"', *Istoricheskajapamjat' iobshestvo v RossijskojimperiiiSovetskomSojuze (konets XIX – nachalo XX veka). mezhdunar. kollokvium: nauch*, Saint Petersburg, Dokl, 2007.

H. Welzer, 'Istorija, pamjat' isovremennost' proshlogo: Pamjat' kak arena politicheskojbor'by', *Pamjat' o vojne 60 let spustja. Rossija, Germanija, Evropa*, Moscow, NLO, 2005.

E. Zubkova, 'Obtchestvennajaatmosferaposlevojny (1945–1946)', *Svobodnajamysl'*, 1992, vol. 6.

6   Polish Child Survivors and their Path to Legacy

Hanna. K. Ulatowska

"All that is necessary for the triumph of evil is that good men do nothing." –
Edmund Burke (1730-1797)

The lives of childhood survivors of WWII Concentration Camps progress
through distinctive stages. The initial trauma eventually ends in a legacy
for future generations. This progression begins with devastation, which
leads to silence. Survivors then begin to rebuild their lives. They begin by
understanding themselves. Finally, some construct their legacy through
testimonies, publications and/or social activism.

Initially, when a child experiences war, their world of love, human dignity
and protection is crushed. They have encountered a world of death. In

Fig. 6.1: 'People Did This to Other People', by 17-year old Łukasz
Bagnicki. (Exhibition: Youth Art Contest, Tychy, 2008)

Fig. 6.2: 'Where is my home – where is my city?' (Exhibition, 2005)

narratives of war experiences, family has been identified as a central theme.[1] 'In situations where all aspects of public and social life collapsed, family and home were the only social situations that symbolized the continuity of ordinary life.'[2] Family was a kind of asylum, an escape that was affected by the widespread destruction caused by the war. Family life was permanently threatened by the destruction of ties between family members.[3] Home was a safe place to hide, conspire, to operate an underground school and be together. The destruction of family ties often led to a loss of childhood, early maturity, and responsibility, but also to lasting trauma. In a sociological study of life in Auschwitz, Pawełczyńska describes how letters from family members outside the camp and the presence of other family members inside the camp could liberate dynamic heroic attitudes — even when family members were separated by subdivided camp space.[4] The prisoners developed a capacity for risk-taking in order to obtain food for a loved one and to seek help for that person. Camp reality was filled by sustained efforts to gain a glimpse of love, if only from a distance, and to gain information on how to help, all while concealing one's own suffering.

The children born in Auschwitz were doomed from the day of their birth. Stanisława Leszczyńska, a midwife in Auschwitz, delivered over 3000 babies with no deaths during delivery according to her own testimonies.[5] Of these

1   K. Kaźmierska, 'Narratives on World War II in Poland: When a life story is a family story', *History of Family*, 7, pp. 281-305.
2   P. Łukasiewicz, 'Funkcje domu w okupacji niemieckiej', *Kultura I Społeczeństwo*, 2, pp. 67-82.
3   P. Tobera, *Family in Polish war experiences: Elementary situations*, in M. Czyżewski, A. Piotrowski, A. Rokuszewska-Pawełek (eds), *Biografia a Tożsamość Narodowa*, pp. 123-135.
4   A. Pawełczyńska, *Values and Violence in Auschwitz: A Sociological Analysis*.
5   S. Leszczyńska, 'Raport', *Przegląd Lekarski*.

Fig. 6.3: The sculpture of Stanisława Leszczyńska in prison
uniform holding two newborn babies which is on the altar of one
of the churches in Warsaw. (Photo taken by the author.)

3000 babies born in the camp, 1500 were drowned and 1000 died of hunger.
She believed in the sanctity of newborn life with full awareness of their
awaiting death. Only 30 children survived the camps with their mothers. In
1970, the children and their mothers met with Leszczyńska. After her death,
Leszczyńska was commemorated for her heroic actions and a sculpture of her
in prison uniform holding babies in both hands was erected on the altar of one
of the churches in Warsaw. According to a report by Dr. Kempisty a total of
2,000,000 children died between 1939-1945 in Poland.[6] During the Warsaw
Uprising of August and September of 1944, 8,870 civilians were deported to
Auschwitz. Since most of them were families, there were also many children.

Immediately after the arrival of the civilian population from the Warsaw
Uprising in August and September of 1944, the adult prisoners in the camp
organized help, especially for the youngest children. Particularly those
prisoners who, because of their function in the camp had access to food,
clothing and medicine tried to provide help for the newcomers from Warsaw.
The Polish doctors were often involved in helping the sick children who were

6   C. Kempisty, *Spraw Norymbergi Ciag Dalszy.*

Fig. 6.4: A list of names copied in the camps which was used to pass information to family members outside the camps, and later used for compensation.

in the revir (hospital). Woman prisoners also tried to give some warmth and affection to the youngest children separated from their mothers and often made toys for them. The prisoners who were members of the underground movement in the camp, at an enormous risk to their lives, copied the lists of the Warsaw newcomers which were then smuggled outside the camp, usually during the night. Those lists provided important information for their families outside the camp and provided the basis for seeking compensation by the prisoners after the war.[7]

Some fathers who were imprisoned in Auschwitz did not forget their

7   *Pomoc Dzieciom w Czasie Wojny*, Fundacja Moje Wojenne Dzieciństwo.

children outside the camps. In 2010, a book was published by the Auschwitz-Birkenau State Museum. It was titled, *The Fables from Auschwitz* and subtitled *The Fables from a very Evil Place*. [8] Twenty-seven fathers wrote and illustrated these fables trying to build a pretense of normality at the risk of their lives, by giving the fables to their children and preserving their internal freedom. Fifty copies of these fables, inspired by books of fables brought into the camps illegally, were made in 1944 by the fathers still in the camp. Through their content, the fables fulfilled the aesthetic and spiritual needs of that group of prisoners locked behind barbed wire.

The story describing the transport of the population brought to the Auschwitz camp from the Warsaw Uprising in August of 1944 is based on the narratives elicited from 37 child survivors by the author.[9] Most children were between 12 and 14 when they arrived in the camp. The majority of prisoners had been in camp for 6 months before being evacuated to other camps in the Death March. The analysis of these 37 narratives focused on the effects that camp life had on the children brought to Auschwitz -- especially on the disruption of the family unit in the context of extreme conditions. These narratives reveal the common themes which indicated destruction of childhood and loss of innocence which remained as deep trauma throughout the lives of these child survivors. One of these themes is the separation from parents that caused feelings of abandonment, loss of protection, vulnerability, and even alienation:

Recollection of an 11-year old boy:
I had to experience the most tragic moment, separation from my mother. The trauma has remained with me up to now. Even after 28 years, every separation from her is horrible to me.

Recollection of a 10-year old girl:
I felt a horrible sense of loneliness and knew that my mother will never be able to defend me again.

Recollection of a 15-year old girl:
The concrete beside the cattle cars was glaringly illuminated by the searchlights and the nearby crematorium. The smoke and a strange acid stench were stifling and suffocated us while the searchlights blinded us. The faces of the Germans,

---

8 *The Fables from Auschwitz: The Fables from a very Evil Place*, Auschwitz, Auschwitz-Birkenau State Museum, 2008.
9 H.K. Ulatowska, M. Sadowska, D. Ka̧dzielawa, M. Polak, 'Mental Representation of Auschwitz Experiences: The Perspectives of Child and Adult Survivors', in D. Steinert, I. Weber-Newth (eds), *Conference Proceedings – Beyond Camps and Forced Labour: Current International Research on Survivors of Nazi Persecution*, pp. 664-672.

and the prisoners in striped uniforms, could not be seen. Only the tall military boots, the cuffs of the prisoners' pants, and the barking dogs were visible. My father helped us jump down from the cattle car. It was very high. They [the Germans] took him away immediately and I never saw him again.

Recollection of a 12-year old girl:
After returning from the camp I met my mother, but she seemed a completely different person to me so for a long time I addressed her by Mrs. and she would keep asking me "My poor darling. Will you ever call me *Mom* again?"

Recollection of a 14-year old boy:
I could not comprehend the world I was thrown into, and it has remained in my consciousness up to the present day.

Another theme expressed was helplessness and despair at seeing their parents and grandparents suffering:

Recollection of 12-year old girl:
The cruelty and tragedy of a 12 year old girl who never saw so many naked people and the shame of her grandma and mother who did not know how to cover themselves and hide.

Recollection of a 14-year old girl:
They beat my mother because she was not able to keep up with the work.

Recollection of a 9-year old girl:
I saw my grandmother sick and naked in the hospital bed and what I felt is impossible to describe.'

Recollection of a 12-year old girl:
'The scene of seeing my mother pulling a cart like a horse in horribly cold weather makes me terribly sad even now.

The theme of encountering death in childhood is another indication of loss of innocence and sanctity of life, as illustrated by the excerpts below:

A boy of 12 faces death for the first time:
Usually people face death at the end of their lives, but the children in the camp faced it at the beginning.

A 14-year old boy asked his mother about the flame from the crematorium

Fig. 6.5: 14-year old Józefa Glazowska, 'Children of War' Exhibition, 2001.

Fig. 6.6: Young Soldier of Warsaw, 'Children of War' Exhibition, 2001.

chimney upon entering the camp:
His mother's reply: 'Sonny, they are burning people.'

Recollection of a 13-year old girl:
Now, going down the road lined with corpses, I realized that they did not make any impression on me any longer. This realization was terrible to me.

Recollection of a 15-year old boy:
We were cleaning the crematorium and I saw notes written on the walls shortly before they died and I realized what death means.

Recollection of 12-year old boy:
They took a corpse like a sack and threw it on a pile. They were prisoners too. From that moment I felt a fear of death and that I would be buried only as a number.[10]

Having gone through such terrible events, children were discouraged from talking about them. Adult survivors also commonly rejected any attempt by children to discuss their wartime experiences, dismissing them as unimportant because the children would soon forget them. Moreover, they

10 Ulatowska, Sadowska, Ka̢dzielawa, Polak, *Mental Representation,* pp. 664-672.

were silenced by well-meaning people who did not want to listen and who said, 'It's over and you must put the past behind. Forget these terrible things and begin a new life.' Some children remained silent because they could not answer their own questions: 'How could human beings treat other human beings with such cruelty?' 'Why was I chosen to survive?' Some did not want to tell what cruelties human beings could commit, what they had suffered or what they had to do to survive. Some psychologists believe that shock leads to silence and that silence of the survivors was caused by a failure to cope with the burden of the past. The psychological mechanism of silence is related to too much knowledge and inability to mourn. After the war no support organizations existed to bring child survivors together, as evidenced by the fact that books about child survivors were mostly published decades later – specifically during and since the mid-1990s.

The Association of Child Survivors of Concentration Camps in Warsaw was started in 1989 and at that time had around 100 members. The president of the Association Dr. Bożena Krzywobłocka admitted around 800 child survivors who were displaced from their homes but were not prisoners of concentration camps. Out of this entire group, around 150 members remain at the present time. The attrition of membership is primarily related to the ageing of members and also the formation of other camp child survivor groups.

The trajectories of the child survivors' lives may be best understood as an attempt to generate a 'replacement world' in light of their lost childhoods. The legacy they leave is derived from responsibility to others. Those who leave a legacy are attempting to help others prevent similar crimes against humans, and to engage in various forms of social activism meant to improve the world. Brenner and Kestenberg note that although children suffered more than adults from chaotic conditions of the Holocaust, they also acquired 'premature' strength, resiliency, coping abilities, and the feeling of having become stronger and more understanding as a result of their experiences.[11] There is not one survivor who did not find support and help among fellow prisoners. No one could have survived on their own physical and mental strength alone.

A legacy surfaces in many different forms. As shown above, some survivors produce their legacy by giving testimonials. Others have published autobiographical books documenting their war experiences. After a remarkable sixty years of silence a book by one of the child survivors, Elżbieta Sobczyńska, was written and sent to the Auschwitz-Birkenau Archives in 2005. Sobczyńska is a member of the Child Survivor Association in Warsaw. She was deported to Auschwitz from the Warsaw Uprising when she was

11 I. Brenner, J. Kestenberg, 'Superego in young child survivors', *The Last Witness: the Child Survivor of the Holocaust*, p. 54.

ten. The book is titled *The Lost Childhood: Reminiscences and Reflections from years 1938-1954*, and is dedicated to her son and her grandsons.[12] What is remarkable about this testimonial is that it describes a history of one family over the period of the entire war, in addition to the very difficult period after the devastation of the war and the hardship of living under the communist regime. The testimonial contains an extremely detailed report of both the events of that period and a very insightful evaluation of them through both the perception of a child and through retrospection of a very knowledgeable adult. The book includes many valuable documents of the imprisonment of Sobczyńska's family from the Auschwitz Archives. It also includes photographs and documents of Sobczyńska's family over several decades. The book is a testimony to an exceptional memory that very few of us possess. The memories are stored and recorded in terms of the events and their reactions to those events. They are presented in a very detailed form. What is relevant to our discussion here, and our understanding of the silence of the survivors after the war, is documented in the following extract from the book:

> There was an urgent need to resolve the stress resulting from the recent tragic events that my mother, my brother and myself experienced in various places and situations, although in the same place, in Auschwitz. And each of us in a different moment underwent a traumatic shock. My brother during the expulsion from Warsaw when he saw a house in flames where his friend had lived. My mother on the train when she learned that our transport was destined for Auschwitz concentration camp. And I, in the camp sauna in Birkenau where they took my human dignity from me. Then thanks to my mother's intuition a spontaneous 'Silence Agreement' relating to the recent experiences was established between us.[13]

Continuing the moving descriptions of her early trauma in the camp Sobczyńska writes:

> During the same time I discovered that the stay in Auschwitz camp robbed me from any sensitivity. The loss of the basic faith in the positive behavior of humans resulted in my empathy for human plight to be numbed. The feelings of compassion and empathy were released only towards animals. And my camp experiences of loneliness were transformed into certainty that in life I can only depend on myself.[14]

12 E. Sobczyńska, *Utracone Dzieciństwo Wspomnienia i Refleksje z Lat 1938-1954.*
13 Sobczyńska, *Utracone.*
14 Sobczyńska, *Utracone.*

Fig. 6.7: The picture of the new home as drawn by
Wiesław Kępiński for his rescuers in 1949.

Bogdan Bartnikowski, born in 1932, published the book, *Childhood Behind Barbed Wire* in 1961.[15] His experiences in Auschwitz, where he was sent after the Warsaw Uprising, left an indelible mark on his memories. 'I wanted to discard them, to rid myself of them, forever. And so I began to write down my memories and those of the boys and girls I knew. I was hoping that if I wrote them down, they would leave me in peace. Unfortunately, this did not occur.'[16] His book had several editions; 1969, 1972, 1977 and 1989. In 2009, it was published again in both English and German. The book is unique in that Bartnikowski, as a writer and as a poet, was successful in conveying his and other children's experiences in Auschwitz through a child's perspective. The horrific existence of the camp is seen through the children's eyes and described in the language of a child. Bartnikowski expresses his legacy in the introduction of the book in the following words: 'That our children would not look at the world from behind barbed wires.'

Wiesław Kępiński, born in 1932, escaped mass execution during the

15 B. Bartnikowski, *Dziecinstwo za Drutami.*
16 Ibid.

Warsaw Uprising in 1944, in which his parents, siblings and other members of his family were killed. Five decades later, in 2006, he wrote a book, *"The Sixty First,"*[17] documenting his experiences. Here is his account of that execution.

> My father walked first. I, with my mother who carried Sylwuś (his little brother), was at the end of the march of those to be executed. Somewhere in the procession were my brother and his pregnant wife. She carried inside her body a baby that never saw the world. The voice of my mother who in despair repeated: 'They will kill us, they will kill us, they will kill us' I cannot hear today. How is it possible?[18]

The surviving boy, after the escape from execution, struggled through every adversity until 1947 when he was adopted by a prominent Polish writer called Jarosław Iwaszkiewicz. The writer provided Kępiński with home, family and most importantly with love and appreciation of the gifts of life, such as literature, art and travel. In his book he expresses 'gratitude to my rescuers for rendering help and for opening the new world for me.' The letters written to him from his adopted father shortly before his father's death acknowledges the rewards his father received as his rescuer: 'How important is your appearance in my life I have told you many times. You are my son and my closest friend. You are a flame of light in the last years of my life.'[19]

This story shows how the trauma of the encounter with death was overcome through the bond between the survivor and rescuer and led to the redemption and legacy of the survivor. At present, Kępiński has published another book containing hundreds of letters between him and his adopted father as his legacy of life that was lost and later regained. Kępiński also gives talks about his experiences and participates actively in the anniversaries of the executions during the Warsaw Uprising. Kępiński's path to legacy came through appreciation of the home and love he received and the love he gave to his rescuers.

Czesław Kempisty, born in 1925, was arrested and sent to Auschwitz when he was 15. It was many years later that he wrote about his experiences in the camp in the book, *To Live One Day*, published in 1989.[20] Since the book was written when Kempisty was already a practicing physician and a medical and social activist, it contains his reflections and deep humanistic concerns of creating a better world after a catastrophic collapse of the past. In the

---

17 W. Kępiński, *Sześćdziesiąty pierwszy.*
18 Kępiński, *Sześćdziesiąty pierwszy*, p. 28.
19 W. Kępiński, 'Moje Stawisko', in J. Termer, S. Nycza (eds), *Zostanie po mnie*, p. 155.
20 C. Kempisty, *Przeżyć Dzień.*

Fig. 6.8: Photograph published in *My Wartime Childhood*.

introduction to his book, Kempisty writes:

> The war was shock therapy for the nations. Many problems have been solved but many require further effort. But it is not sufficient to solve our own individual problems. We are given a great collective chance of understanding the nature of humanity, stopping forever the disastrous experiences of the world.[21]

The path to legacy of Kempisty consisted primarily of academic systematization and integration of the existing data through publication and research on child survivors of Auschwitz. As a medical researcher Kempisty participated in the Central Commission on Examination of Nazi Crimes. In 1975 he published a book, *After the Nuremberg Trials*, in which he describes his findings of socio-medical research on child survivors of concentration camps.[22] In 1977, Kempisty published an important study titled, '*Arteriosclerosis in Ageing and Mortality in Survivors of Concentration Camps*', in the Medical Journal of Auschwitz.[23] He also attended international peace conferences to share his research on survivors of concentration camps. Towards the end of

21 Kempisty, *Przeżyc Dzień*.
22 C. Kempisty, *Spraw Norymbergi Ciag Dalszy*.
23 C. Kempisty, 'Arterioskleroza w starości i śmiertelność u więzniów obozów koncentracyjnych' , *Medical Journal of Auschwitz*.

Fig. 6.9: Painting of an eleven year old girl's representations of war experiences.

his life, Kempisty, as a social activist, organized the *University of the Third Age* for seniors in Wroclaw, one of the first universities of this type in Poland. Kempisty's legacy can be best summarized in his own words given on the day he was awarded his medical degree: 'I saw with my mind's eye the image of the camp revir (hospital) in Auschwitz, many extended hands begging for help. I fulfilled my sad Auschwitz dream, to become a doctor and to take care of the survivors of the Nazi concentration camps. I became convinced that one can give one's life shape and sense.'[24]

The last child survivor, whose path to legacy will be discussed, is Eulalia Rudak. Born in 1932, Rudak was deported to Auschwitz from the Warsaw Uprising. Her path to legacy is social activism representing a wide range of different activities. Rudak adopted a motto from Georges Clemenceau, 'It is easier to understand the need to act than to act.' Rudak is the founder of the Wartime Childhood Foundation, established as a foundation of public benefit since 2004. The main goal of the Foundation is the documentation of recollections of World War II through publications of *My Wartime Childhood*. The Foundation also organizes exhibitions of children's representations of war experiences and photography of children in war. The Foundation also promotes Polish history, culture and national identity by publishing patriotic poetry, organizing photography exhibitions and films about Warsaw's history before and after the war, and taking care of the graves of war soldiers and war

24 Kempisty, 'Arterioskleroza'.

memorials. Finally, the Foundation promotes the welfare of war survivors by organizing symposia on post-traumatic syndrome, providing medical check-ups and health counseling and organizing a Christmas and Easter celebration for survivors and their families every year. In a personal interview, Rudak expressed her legacy as follows: 'My legacy comes not only from my survival, but also from the death of many innocent children in the wars.'[25]

When we reflect on the path taken by these child survivors to leave their legacy, we become aware of the intense feelings caused by the loss of their families and of the lonely walk they have taken in silence towards forgiveness and reconciliation. Bartnikowski, who suffered the loss of his father in the bombing during the Warsaw Uprising, became a writer, a poet and a pilot who could experience the freedom and beauty of soaring with the birds over the once bombarded city of Warsaw. He later described the experience in his book of poems, *Children behind Barbed Wire,* which was published in German to share his experiences with enemies of his past. Kępiński reached generational reconciliation that required integration of earlier traumas, allowing him to share his experiences with me (the author). He not only shared his books with me but also took me to the place of execution of his family and then through the path of his escape through the cemetery. Kempisty was invited to Germany for a conference on the Testament of the Victims of National Socialism in 1984 to give a lecture on child survivors of Auschwitz. There, he met a daughter of the Commandant of Ravensbrück Concentration Camp. Frantz Ratke, the daughter, was also a psychiatrist interested in the German concentration camps. During his discussion with her Kempisty stated: 'We have to overcome the past which divides us, the feeling of revenge or hatred is a feeling which for us Poles and especially the physicians is completely alien. One is not allowed to make the young generation guilty for the action of their fathers.' This statement given towards her, along with his life, summarizes Kempisty's mission and legacy.

Eulalia Rudak, the social activist working with young German volunteers to tidy up the deserted graves of war victims, then lighting candles to commemorate the victims, is the most meaningful symbol of transcendence and reconciliation. After discussing the legacy of child survivors, their trauma, vulnerability and years of silence, we will contrast it with the amazing rebirth from devastation of the adult survivors of Auschwitz. Thus to reflect on the long history of the legacy of Auschwitz survivors we will go back to the very beginning of that endeavor in 1947 when the Polish government created the Auschwitz-Birkenau State Museum on the site of the concentration camps. The plan to raze and plough the site, erasing it from the memory of all, went against the ideas of some. Years later historian Jacek Lachendro, working with

25 E. Rudak, Personal Interview with the author.

a descendant from the people from the surrounding village, documented the effort to erase the physical remnants of the site.[26] To the surprise of many, the period immediately following the establishment of the Auschwitz-Birkenau State Museum saw Auschwitz survivors returning to Auschwitz to secure and protect the remains of the camp as documentation of the Nazi crimes.

In 1947, Jerzy Adam Brandhuber, who was brought to Auschwitz in 1942, returned to the camp and started working as a historian in the State Museum. He was a painter and created a cycle of paintings called 'Forgotten Earth' in 1946, which conveys his memories of Auschwitz. Brandhuber decided to live in one of the buildings of Auschwitz in 1981, continuing his work and painting until the very end. One of the first directors of the Auschwitz Museum in 1947 is another survivor, Tadeusz Wąsowicz. The curator Tadeusz Szymański also comes there and lives on the camp premises and dies there. He was a curator from 1946-1951 and from 1956-1977. There are many other Auschwitz survivors, such as Władysław Siwek, Marian Kościelniak and Tadeusz Myszkowski, who helped organize the Museum in that early period.

Kazimierz Smoleń a prisoner of Auschwitz for four and a half years, who arrived when he was barely 20 years old, became the longest director of the Auschwitz-Birkenau State Museum, serving from 1955 to 1991. He lives on the premises of the camp and still, at the age of 91, comes daily to his office. Smoleń describes his return to the camp in a very moving way:

> In 1948 I came back to Auschwitz for the first time. I got out of the station and lost my way. I was frightened. Most of all I was frightened of the deafening silence. My memories were filled with noise from the prisoners.[27]

Smoleń has become a voice of the survivors. Over the years he has spoken with thousands of young people from many countries about the conditions and events of Auschwitz. Smoleń states:

> As ever I regard my work as a mission in the name of the many people who remained in Auschwitz. I am especially thankful for the many talks and meetings with young people, because these are the things that keep me alive.[28]

He wrote a book, *Auschwitz 1940-1945 Guide*, which was published through the Museum in 1981 and *History of KL-Auschwitz* in 1982. In an interview in the *Sunday Times* in 2003 Smoleń summarizes his feelings: 'I am

26 J. Lachendro, *German Places of Extermination in Poland, Auschwitz, Bełżec, Sobibór, Majdanek, Kulmohof Am Ner*.
27 K. Smoleń, 'History of KL-Auschwitz'.
28 Archive Article, *The Sunday Times*, Interview with Sue Fox, Jan. 26th 2003.

not interested in revenge, only justice. I don't feel bitterness. My feeling is of sorrow that it took my young years from me. But I gave a bigger perspective than my personal grief.' On his birthday in Auschwitz in 2010, Smoleń also stated, 'My work in the Museum is my mission, my duty on behalf of those who perished.'[29]

This journey through seven decades on the path to legacy may put in perspective the differences between the views of generations of child survivors and those of adult survivors. It shows the difference of legacy as immediate action by adult survivors, or action after decades of silence by child survivors. It also poses an important question: Will future generations continue to view legacy of the survivors, both children and adults, as an important lesson and warning? Or, will they do nothing?

Edmund Burke's admonishment is worth repeating:

All that is necessary for the triumph of evil is that good men do nothing.

Bibliography

B. Bartnikowski, *Dzieciństwo za Drutami. [Childhood behind the Barbed Wires]*, Warszawa, Nasza Ksiegarnia, 1961.

I. Brenner, J. Kestenberg, 'Superego in young child survivors', *The Last Witness: the Child Survivor of the Holocaust*, Washington D.C., American Psychiatric Press, 1996.

The Fables from Auschwitz: The Fables from a very Evil Place, Auschwitz, Auschwitz-Birkenau State Museum, 2008.

S. Fox, 'Interview with Sue Fox', *The Sunday Times*, Jan. 26th 2003.

K. Kaźmierska, 'Narratives on World War II in Poland: When a life story is a family story.' *History of Family*, 7, 2002, pp. 281-305.

C. Kempisty, *Przeżyc Dzień. [To Live One Day]*, Wrocław, Wydawnictwo Dolnoślaskie,1989.

Idem., *Spraw Norymbergi Ciąg Dalszy. [After the Nuremberg Trials]*, Warszawa, Panstwowe Wydawnictwo Naukowe, 1975.

Idem., 'Arterioskleroza w starości i śmiertelność u wiezniów obózow koncentracyjnych' [Artheriosclerosis in Aging and Mortality in Survivors of Concentration camps.], *Medical Journal of Auschwitz*, 1977.

W. Kępiński, *Sześćdziesiąty pierwszy [The Sixty First]*, Warszawa, Czytelnik, 2006.

Idem., 'Moje Stawisko' [My Stawisko], in J. Termer, S. Nyczaj (eds), *Zostanie po mnie [Left after Me]*, Warszawa, SEC Polskie Stowarzyszenie Kultury Europejskiej [Polish Association of European Culture], 2009.

29 Ibid.

J. Lachendro, *German Places of Extermination in Poland, Auschwitz, Belżec, Sobibór, Majdanek, Kulmohof Am Ner,* Parma Press, 2007.

S. Leszczyńska, 'Raport' [Report], *Przegląd Lekarski [Medical Review]* 1965, vol. 1.

P. Łukasiewicz, 'Funkcje domu w okupacji niemieckiej [Functions of home during German occupation]' *Kultura i Społeczeństwo,* 2, 1989, pp. 67-82.

A. Pawełczyńska, *Values and Violence in Auschwitz: A Sociological Analysis.* Berkley, University of California Press, 1979.

Pomoc Dzieciom w Czasie Wojny [Aid to children during the war] Symposium 2002. Fundacja Moje Wojenne Dzieciństwo.

E. Sobczyńska, *Utracone Dzieciństwo Wspomnienia i Refleksje z Lat 1938-1954 [Lost childhood: Reminiscences and Reflections from years 1938-1954.]* Unpublished manuscript. Warszawa, 2005.

K. Smoleń, *History of KL-Auschwitz,* Auschwitz-Birkenau State Museum, 1982.

P. Tobera, 'Family in Polish war experiences: Elementary situations', in M. Czyżewski, A. Piotrowski, A. Rokuszewska-Pawełek (eds), *Biografia a Tożsamość Narodowa [Biography and national identity],* Łódz, Wydawnictwo Katedry Socjologii Kultury UŁ., 1997.

H. K. Ulatowska, M. Sadowska, D. Ka,dzielawa , M. Polak, 'Mental Representation of Auschwitz Experiences: The Perspectives of Child and Adult Survivors', in D. Steinert , I. Weber-Newth (eds), *Conference Proceedings – Beyond Camps and Forced Labour: Current International Research on Survivors of Nazi Persecution,* Berlin, Körbel Stittung, 2005.

7   Fatherless Children of World War II in Germany: Persistent Psychosocial Impairment in Adulthood

Matthias Franz

In Germany, as in Austria, the trans-generational internalized models and inner images of the father are in many ways dysfunctional if not toxic. Over more than a hundred years, the picture of the father as an internal organizer of social role behavior ruled particularly over the aggressive tendencies of whole societies. Due to the trans-generational infection by such internalized models, we are still in touch with destructive parental delegations even decades later. Psychoanalysts, especially, within their transference oriented approach are in touch with and deal with these internalized, emotionally qualified interaction engrams acquired during childhood. They treat them as so called 'introjects', and are linked by them. Psychoanalysts are still in an anachronistic and unsettling contact with collective traumatic relicts within the infantile subconscious of their patients – and their own biographical imprints.

The genealogy of these dysfunctional paternal role models started hundred years ago, with the patriarchal father of the militaristic monarchies of Austria and Germany. This father was followed by the 'soldier father' of the Third Reich and Word War II, who was the carrier of maximal collective destruction and self-destruction. During and after this disastrous breakdown the dead father ruled the families for a further 25 years, followed by the contemporary absent father. The topic of this paper is the absent or dead father of World War II, and his biographical echo in the life of their children 50 or 60 years later.

A short overview of the role of the father in modern concepts of childhood development shall underline the long-lasting importance of father's presence during childhood.[1] In the first year of life the father is important for the validation of secure attachment, basic trust and self esteem of the baby. He has an own relation to the baby separated from the mother, and his quality and mode to play and interact with his child emphasizes motoric-impulsive and

---

1   M. Franz, 'Wenn der Vater fehlt. Die Folgen kriegsbedingter und heutiger Vaterlosigkeit für Kinder und Familien', *Psychoanalytische Familientherapie*, pp. 91-129.

separative aspects.[2] This separative function and his emotional presence are essential for the ongoing separation of the toddler and the encouragement of its autonomy in the second year. As the fascinating exponent of the outer world he can moderate the obligatory separation anxiety and frustration rage of the child under the maturation strain of the rapprochement-crisis at the end of the second year. His example demonstrates that dependency or independence from the mother is not an exclusive alternative and that separation is survivable and autonomy possible. This significant experience enables the child to explore the external field of triangular relation patterns beyond the maternal relation in the second and fourth years of life. Subsequently, he further plays a crucial role for the consolidation of the sexual identity of his boy, as well of his daughter. His role model and male self-esteem inspires the boy over how it could be to become a man in the future, and he also affirms and reinforces the daughter in her exploration of the female role within the phase of sexual role finding, approximately between the fourth and sixth year of life.[3] Finally, his way to cope with crises and conflicts is an unconscious reference for every man over the entire lifecycle. Altogether, father's presence, his empathic companionship, and his encouraging engagement have positive effects on the development of emotional, social and cognitive competences of his children, as well as on their educational and occupational success and well-being.[4]

So, father's presence or absence is crucial for the development of his child. We know from many epidemiological studies that the lack of the father during childhood, today mostly caused by separation or divorce, is one important risk factor for the development, health status and the social success of a child until adulthood.[5]

This in mind, here are presented some epidemiological findings and psycho-historical traces of the war-related absence of the father with a

2   A. Russel, J. Saebel, 'Mother-son, mother-daughter, father-son, and father-daughter. Are they distinct relationships?', *Dev Rev*, pp. 111–147.
3   M. Siegal, 'Are sons and daughters treated more differently by fathers than by mothers?', *Dev Rev*, pp. 183–209.
4   M. Franz, H. Lensche, N. Schmitz, 'Psychological distress and socioeconomic status in single mothers and their children in a German city', *Soc Psychiatry Psychiatr Epidemiol*, pp. 59–68; A. Sarkadi, R. Kristiansson, F. Oberklaid, S. Bremberg, 'Fathers' involvement and children's developmental outcomes: a systematic review of longitudinal studies', *Acta Paediatr.*, pp. 153-158.
5   H. Sadowski, et al., 'Early life family disadvantages and major depression in adulthood', *Br J Psychiatry*, pp. 112–120; P. R. Amato, 'Children of divorce in the 1990s: an update of the Amato and Keith (1991) meta-analysis', *J Fam Psychol*, pp. 355–370; G. R. Ringback Weitoft, A. Hjern, B. Haglund, M. Rosen, *Mortality, severe morbidity, and injury in children living with single parents in Sweden: a population-based study*, pp. 289–295; T. Huurre, H. Junkkari, H. Aro, 'Long-term psychosocial effects of parental divorce: a follow-up study from adolescence to adulthood', *Eur Arch Psychiatry Clin Neurosci*, pp. 256–263; Sarkadi, Kristiansson, Oberklaid, Bremberg, 'Fathers' involvement and children's developmental outcomes', pp. 153-158.

psychoanalytical understanding of his role. The data base of these findings is the Mannheim Cohort Study (MCS) on the Epidemiology of Psychogenic Disorders.[6] At the beginning of this study, a representative random sample of six hundred men and women was investigated. The sample was taken from the birth cohorts 1935, 1945 and 1955. They were examined from 1979 until 1993. Findings are reported from this interval. The subjects were investigated diagnostically by psychoanalytic interviews as well as by standardized psychometric instruments. The term 'psychogenic' disorders covers the group of mainly psychosocially and biographically induced and influenced psychic disorders, like neurotic spectrum disorders,[7] personality disorders, stress reactions, addictions or somatoform disorders. Beyond the common subjection of these disorders to the psycho-social biography of an individual, it seemed appropriate to focus on this group of disorders as a whole, because there is a well-known and considerable symptom shift and co-morbidity among these subgroups. The prevalence of this group of disorders in the German normal adult population is about 26 %.[8]

In 1979, the group around Heinz Schepank started this long-term investigation of the prevalence, natural history, and determinants of psychogenic disorders. The first survey, carried out between 1979 and 1982, studied the prevalence of psychogenic disorders.[9] In this cohort study, a representative sample of 600 German adults born in 1935, 1945, and 1955 was randomly selected from the urban population of Mannheim. Three years later, we re-evaluated 528 (88%) of the original subjects.[10] Between 1991 and 1993, further follow-up interviews were carried out on 333 of them. The mean time interval between t1 and t3 was 11.1 years (SD 0.8) with a minimum of 9 and a maximum of 14 years. Thirty-two subjects had accepted our offer of psychodynamic individual or group psychotherapy within a study on psychotherapy motivation,[11] thus the sample regarding the spontaneous course was reduced to 301 at t3 (50.2% of t1). The follow-up sample t1 → t3 (N = 301) was representative for the t1 sample (n = 600). With regard to social and clinical core variables, there were no significant differences between the t1 and the t3-follow-up samples at t1. Therefore, we were able to compare t1 and t3 for the follow-up sample without selection bias. The study methods have been reported in detail elsewhere.[12] After the subjects were provided with a

---

6 H. Schepank, *Epidemiology of psychogenic disorders*; Idem. (ed.), *Verläufe;* M. Franz, K. Lieberz, H. Schepank (eds), *Seelische Gesundheit und neurotisches Elend. Der Langzeitverlauf in der Bevölkerung.*
7 Mainly depression and anxiety.
8 Schepank, *Epidemiology of psychogenic disorders*; Idem. (ed.), *Verläufe.*
9 t1, Schepank, *Epidemiology of psychogenic disorders.*
10 t2, Schepank *Verläufe.*
11 M. Franz, *Der Weg in die Psychotherapeutische Beziehung.*
12 M. Franz, W. Tress, H. Schepank, 'Predicting extreme patterns of long-term course of psychogenic impairment – ten years later', *Soc Psychiatry Psychiatr Epidemiol,* pp. 243-251.

complete description of the study, written informed consent was obtained for the first study and each follow-up.

Personality characteristics and clinical and socio demographic variables were evaluated in each of the surveys. The degree of psychogenic impairment was assessed by psycho-dynamically trained and clinically experienced interviewers using the Impairment Score.[13] A symptom was assessed as psychogenic if there was no physical cause to be found. This was assured by anamnesis, with special attention given to earlier medical diagnostic procedures. Furthermore, a symptom-triggering psycho-social conflict had to be identified within the psychodynamic interview. Early childhood development conditions, reported at t1, were assessed by the interviewers using reference examples with regard to the absence and emotional distance of mother/father.[14] Similarly, the global burden during childhood development was assessed for those aged 1-6 and 7-12 years. Reference examples of traumatic influences[15] were used in this rating.[16] Personality traits (t1) were integrated in the statistical models using the Freiburger Persönlichkeitsinventar[17], a factor analytic, standardized and well-established German personality inventory.

Statistical tests of differences between t1 and t3 values of the t3 sample were performed two-tailed, using the Chi-Square test, Fisher's Exact Test, t-test or by analysis of variance for dependent samples. Intra-individual correlation coefficients (Spearman) between t1 and t3 were also performed two-tailed. Stepwise multiple regression analysis was used to examine the predictive contribution of gender, age, education, adverse burden and experiences in early childhood, clinical impairment and personality traits at t1 with respect to the clinical impairment at t3. Data were analyzed using SPSS (Statistical Package for the Social Sciences) for Windows, version 19.

This long-term study is unique in Germany because of its combination of psychoanalytical and epidemiological approaches. The MCS was able to find out psycho-historical traces of the missing father of World War II. They reach into the bodies and minds of the former children of war until today. Probably due to an unconscious preoccupation with trans-generational transferred collective traumatic residuals of World War II even our research team was impaired in realizing the severity of our findings immediately, and we hesitated for some years to publish them in German.[18] One could speculate

13 IS, German: BSS; H. Schepank *Der Beeinträchtigungsschwerescore (BSS). Ein Instrument zur Bestimmung der Schwere einer psychogenen Erkrankung*; Franz, Tress, Schepank, 'Predicting extreme patterns'.

14 Schepank, 1987

15 Such as loss of mother or father, broken home constellation, early experiences of aggressive assaults, emotional abuse, neglect or psychological ill parents.

16 Schepank, *Epidemiology of psychogenic disorders.*

17 J. Fahrenberg, H. Selg, R. Hampel, *Das Freiburger Persönlichkeitsinventar FPI. Handanweisung.*

18 M. Franz, K. Lieberz, N. Schmitz, H. Schepank, 'A decade of spontaneous long-term course of

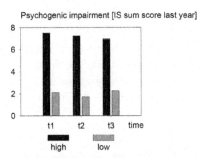

Adverse childhood experiences   Long term course of psychogenic impairment [IS]

	High (n=23)	Low (n=77)	Statistics
Psychological impaired mother	52,2%	20,3%	X² (df=1)=8.65, p<0.01
Missing mother (>6mo, 1ˢᵗ-6th year)	13,0%	9,2%	Fisher Test, ns
High maternal deficit	30,4%	13,0%	Fisher Test, (p<0.10)
Psychological impaired father	47,4%	13,8%	Fisher Test, p<0.01
Missing father (>6mo, 1ˢᵗ-6th year)	52,2%	33,3%	X²(df=1)=2.63, ns
High paternal deficit	52,2%	40,3%	X²(df=1)=1.03, ns
High global burden (1ˢᵗ-6th year)	82,6%	28,9%	X²(df=1)=20.96, p<0.0001
High global burden (7th-12th year)	91,3%	31,6%	X²(df=1)=25.40, p<0.0001

Fig. 7.1a: Association between stable high (black columns in the bar diagram) psychogenic impairment (IS sum score) over more than a decade and adverse childhood experiences: Psychological impaired mother or father, high global burden between the 1st and 6th and 7th and 12th year of life were more frequent in the group of chronically impaired probands. Probands with stable low psychogenic impairment are represented by grey columns. (Supplied by the author)

that this represents a late relict of the trauma driven neglect, which ruled the silence in millions of families and even the scientific discourse in post-war Germany, due to the defense against shame, guilt and the awareness of own familial losses. This perception bias may be an example for the interference of collective neglect and the influence of 'undigested' traumatic introjects. In Germany after World War II there was no place for decades to process one's own psychic pain, because the losses, the guilt and responsibility as an offending nation was overwhelming. This article is the first English communication on the connection between the war-related loss of the father

psychogenic impairment in a community population sample', *Soc Psychiatry Psychiatr Epidemiol*, pp. 651–656; Idem., 'The missing father. Epidemiological findings on the significance of early absence of the father for mental health in later life', *Z Psychosom Med Psychother*, pp. 113–127.

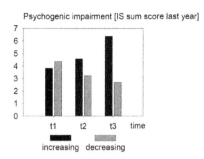

Psychogenic impairment [IS sum score last year]

t1   t2   t3   time

increasing decreasing

Adverse childhood experiences	Long term course of psychogenic impairment [IS]		
	Increasing (n=28)	Decreasing (n=28)	Statistics
Psychological impaired mother	37,0%	44,4%	X²(df=1)=0.31, ns
Missing mother (>6mo, 1st-6th year)	11,1%	3,6%	Fisher Test, ns
High maternal deficit	17,9%	25,0%	X²(df=1)=0.42, ns
Psychological impaired father	36,4%	34,8%	X²(df=1)=0.01, ns
Missing father (>6mo, 1st-6th year)	**69,2%**	**22,2%**	**X²(df=1)=11.81, p<0.01**
High paternal deficit	**71,4%**	**35,7%**	**X²(df=1)=7.18, p<0.05**
High global burden (1st-6th year)	50,0%	42,9%	X²(df=1)=0.29, ns
High global burden (7th-12th year)	75,0%	53,6%	X²(df=1)=2.80, ns

Fig. 7.1b: Association between constantly increasing (black columns in the bar diagram) psychogenic impairment (IS sum score) over more than a decade and adverse childhood experiences: Missing father (more than 6 months in the first 6 years of life) and a high paternal deficit (presence and availability) were more frequent in the group of probands who showed constantly increasing psychogenic impairment. Probands with constantly decreasing psychogenic impairment are represented by grey columns. (Supplied by the author)

and psychogenic impairment in later life of the German war children.

Besides the statistical analyses of the entire sample we carried out subgroup-analyses with respect to specific course patterns.[19] We compared very highly impaired subjects of the study sample suffering chronically from high psychic symptom loads at three measurement points over more than a decade,[20] to subjects with a constant low symptom load.[21] In addition to that we selected subjects who showed an increasing psychogenic impairment,[22] and compared them to subjects with a continuously better psychological adaptation, again

19 Franz, Lieberz, Schmitz, Schepank, 'A decade of spontaneous long-term course of psychogenic impairment', pp. 651–656; Idem., 'The missing father', pp. 113–127.
20 Figure 7.1a; black columns of the bar diagram.
21 Displayed in grey columns.
22 Again the black columns of the bar diagram of Figure 7.1b.

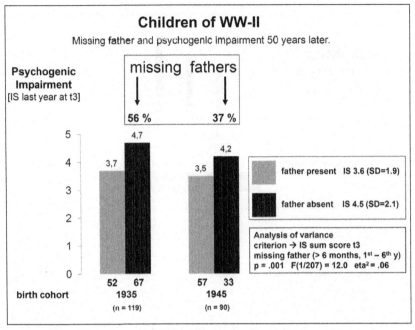

Fig. 7.2: Influence of father's presence/absence on psychogenic impairment (IS sum score at t3) of their children born 1935 and 1945 nearly 50 years later; black columns: probands grown up without fathers, absence at least 6 months during the first 6 years of life; grey columns: probands grown up with fathers. (Supplied by author)

over more than a decade.[23]

We looked for an association between the existing course differences and adverse childhood experiences. As expected, we found significant associations between high symptom load and adverse childhood experiences with both parents (figure 7.1a). A psychologically impaired mother or father, and global psychosocial burden during childhood, were more frequently associated with the chronically high impaired group. However, no maternal variable differed between the two other course-patterns (figure 7.1b). Surprisingly, we found that only variables related to a missing father or a paternal deficit (with respect to presence or availability) differed between the two course types with increasing or decreasing symptom loads. That means only the missing father was associated with the group of subjects who showed an increasing psychological mal-adaptation and symptom loads over more than a decade in later adulthood. Furthermore, we compared the fatherless grown up children

23 Grey columns.

Psychogenic impairment [IS sum score] t3 predicted by t1 and childhood variables	Stand. β	T-value	p-value
Psychogenic impairment [IS sum score] t1	0.387	5.74	.000
Global burden between age 7-12	0.196	3.20	.002
FPI scale „depression" t1	0.144	2.06	.040
Absent father between age 1-6	0.132	2.30	.023
FPI scale „openess" t1	0.127	2.04	.043

Fig. 7.3: Stepwise multiple regression of psychogenic impairment at t3 (IS) for the entire sample (Nt1=301) by socio demographic variables at t1 (age, sex, education), childhood variables (missing mother/father, global burden between age 1-6 and/or 7-12, psychological impairment of mother/father, deficient care by mother/father), clinical impairment at t1 (IS sum score last year, Goldberg-Cooper sum score), and personality characteristics at t1 (Freiburger Personality Inventory scales). Sample size t1 à t3 n=193, df = 5, F(5/187)=27.92, p<0.0001, R=.65, R^2=.43, adjusted R^2=.41. Age, sex and education could not qualify as predictive model variables. (Supplied by author)

with the group of children who lived together with the father; 'father yes/no', along the case threshold of the IS sum score, ≥5; 'case yes/no'. The odds ratio of the fatherless children to become and stay a case of psychogenic disorder at all three measurement points over more than a decade reached 2,6.[24] That was something unexpected.

The analyses of variance showed that the children of World War II born in 1935 and 1945 who missed their fathers during the first six years of life, had a significant enhanced psychogenic impairment even 50 years later, demonstrated by the black columns of Figure 7.2.

When performing these analyses, our research team was confronted with an incredible finding, when we found a missing father in 56% of the birth-cohort 1935 and still 37% of the birth-cohort 1945. Due to this extraordinarily high number of missing fathers, the association between the absent father and the psychogenic impairment of their children 50 years later was detectable by statistical methods.

As reported, we hesitated some years with the publication of these findings. The hidden reason of this hesitation was probably an emotional resistance against the detection of the paternal deficit in our own research, as a part of the collective defense against the war-related trauma of the guilt loaded German fatherlessness. Finally, in our analyses the absent father was manifest and predictive as an independent factor, for instance also in this regression model of psychogenic impairment (Figure 7.3).

24 95% CI 1,2 – 5,3.

Beside two clinically relevant personality characteristics ('depression' and 'openness') and one plausible clinical predictor of later psychogenic impairment in adulthood, the absent father was a strong biographical variable which could qualify within the regression model. Compared to clinical impairment at t1, 10 years ago, the relatively low transfer coefficient of the missing father within the model should be interpreted with respect to the very long time, (50 years ago), which has passed since childhood and t3.

The trauma of the German families due to the experiences of the war-related fatherlessness was denied and out of perception over decades, as defense against a mountain of loss and guilt. Nevertheless, the German children of war were also victims. Yet an empathic or even empirical view on their fate was not possible for a long time, because of the trauma related neglect. Only now, in the last fifteen years in Germany, are we confronted with a dam break of literature of contemporary witnesses, who as children survived the war also as victims without their fathers, and who want to finally demonstrate their lifelong suppressed grief as old men and women.[25]

The previous silence had objective reasons; since 1935 more than 2,000 German soldiers – sons, brothers and of course fathers too – died every single day for nearly six years. Fatherlessness during World War II was a very common family occurrence, because nearly 90% of all young and middle aged men were soldiers in Germany and Austria over the six years. Over 4.3 million of them were killed in action or missing during World War II. After the war, 11 million were prisoners of war and the returning fathers were often traumatised and not able to get into close emotional relations with their children. The divorce rate in Germany after the war was enormous. All in all 25% of all German children grew up without fathers after World War II, and often with an emotionally absent, depressive and demanding mother who also was not able to cope with this emotional disaster. It seems the only way for the German population to cope with this was to neglect it over decades. The loyalty to the damaged parental objects inhibited the view to this epochal trauma in the German as well as in the Austrian population. For a long time after the war, the enduring and ruling silence of the active offender generation forced the public emotional neglect of these historical facts. The underestimated role of the father in traditional psychoanalysis also contributed to the delayed discovery of the war-related fatherlessness; even in research. The withdrawal of the collective denial of the long lasting effects of the war, and the war related fatherlessness in the last decade, was promoted by the psychoanalytical research on holocaust victimization, the detection of lifelong lasting consequences of psycho-traumatic events and the growing

---

25 H. Radebold, *Abwesende Väter;* Idem. (ed.), *Kindheiten im II. Weltkrieg und ihre Folgen;* L. Janus (ed.), *Geboren im Krieg,* I. Fooken, J. Zinnecker (eds), *Trauma und Resilienz.*

Fig. 7.4: Düsseldorf, April 1945: Hypervigilant toddler and
his broken mother at the side of the road when the first tank
platoon rolled into the destroyed city. (© Cogis)

public acceptance of the fact of an enduring impact of adverse childhood
experiences.

In the experience of the child the loss of the father very often is mediated
and aggravated by a depressed mother. Due to her own demanding state and
due to her impaired empathic maternal functions, a depressed mother is often
unable to support the separative wishes and impulses of her child. The child
than suppresses his or her own needs and feelings in reference and loyalty
to their most important caregiver and her needs. The strategic goal of this
behavior is to reintegrate the caregiver into a functional state, because the
caregiver's health and stability is crucial for the security and the survival of
every child. When children try to help their depressed mother, they necessarily
refrain in the long run from the development of their own autonomy, and they
are in danger of becoming 'infected' by the depression of the mother.[26] Under

26 Franz, Lensche, Schmitz, 'Psychological distress', pp. 59–68; T. Trapolini, C. A. McMahon,
   J. A. Ungerer, 'The effect of maternal depression and marital adjustment on young children's
   internalizing and externalizing behaviour problems', *Child Care Health Dev*, pp. 794-803;
   S. B. Ashman, G. Dawson, H. Panagiotides, 'Trajectories of maternal depression over 7
   years: relations with child psychophysiology and behavior and role of contextual risks', *Dev
   Psychopathol*, pp. 55-77; C. J. Foster, J. Garber, J.A. Durlak, 'Current and past maternal

this dyadic condition even normal separation needs of the child lead directly into guilt, self-accusation and finally depression.

To give an example of this 'parentification' process; my home university town Düsseldorf suffered heavily under the World War II bombing attacks since 1940, because Düsseldorf was an important center of war industry. There were a total of 240 bombing attacks until 1945. Thousands of civil victims died under these military strikes and urban buildings and infrastructure were largely destroyed by the time US troops occupied the city on 7 April 1945. When the head of the first tank platoon drove into the town the commander of the first tank took a heart breaking picture. See Figure 7.4.

In a prototypic way one can see a little boy of perhaps four years standing in a very soldierly way beside his despairing mother, who is sitting completely sunk down at the pavement. Confronted with the thundering tank platoon after weeks of bombing she is not able to protect her little son. Instead, she clings to her son without any eye contact, reminiscent of the primitive Moro-reflex of a frightened baby. While the mother is dissociated and absent in a regressive state, the son takes over the management of the dangerous situation. Due to her desperation and traumatic state the adaptation to the threatening situation is delegated to the little toddler. In fact he looks like a protective father or a combat-ready soldier directly into the camera of the tank commander, ready to defend his mother. But it is clear: he will be completely overcharged in the long run, particularly when the real father is missing permanently in future. This paradigmatic picture represents the lack of maternal empathy, emotional mirroring and protection and the lack of the male role model which was the ongoing situation for millions of World War II children in Germany and Austria.

As pointed out, the consequences for the child were very often feelings of guilt related to the enduring depression of the mother, followed by role reversal and parentification of the child which finally internalized their mother's depression like a socially mediated infection. The developmental consequences of this effected in many cases an incomplete dyadic separation of the child from the demanding mother, an unstable male identity of boys covered by a forced development of pseudo-autonomy (to relieve the mother) and impaired affect regulation competences, e.g. resulting in an impaired ability to feel and express own grief. For these children, and especially for

depression, maternal interaction behaviors, and children's externalizing and internalizing symptoms', *J Abnorm Child Psychol*, pp. 527-37; A. W. Riley et al., 'Mental health of children of low-income depressed mothers: influences of parenting, family environment, and raters', *Psychiatr Serv*, pp. 329-336; S. H. Goodman et al., 'Maternal depression and child psychopathology: a meta-analytic review', *Clin Child Fam Psychol Rev. doi*: 10.1007/s10567-010-0080-1; C. D. Kouros, J. Garber, 'Dynamic associations between maternal depressive symptoms and adolescents' depressive and externalizing symptoms', *J Abnorm Child Psychol*, pp. 1069-1081.

Impact of WW-II on German war children:

depression and anxiety 60 years later

SCL-27	absent father (n = 169) $\bar{x}$ (SD)	present father (n = 702) $\bar{x}$ (SD)	significance	p
DEP: **depressive symptoms**	0,56 (0,72)	0,38 (0,53)	$t_{216} = 3,16$	.002
DYS: dysthymic symptoms	0,64 (0,74)	0,52 (0,61)	$t_{288} = 1,94$	.061
VEG: vegetative symptoms	0,43 (0,59)	0,34 (0,48)	$t_{225} = 1,98$	.048
AGO: agoraphobic symptoms	0,34 (0,60)	0,25 (0,47	$t_{221} = 1,84$	.054
SOP: **sociophobic symptoms**	0,52 (0,70)	0,31 (0,50)	$t_{210} = 2,68$	< .001
MIS: **symptoms of mistrust**	0,75 (0,77)	0,49 (0,58)	$t_{216} = 4,06$	< .001

Fig. 7.5: Long-term impact on mental health of the war-related absent father in a representative German random sample of former war children 60 years after the war.

the boys, as young adults a pseudo-normal operative functioning within work and achievement was possible in many cases after the war. This was probably one powerful reason of the German 'Wirtschaftswunder' after World War II, under the support of the Marshall Plan: 'Mom, you should cry never again, therefore I build for you a new home, a new car and a new economy.' However, dealing and coping with emotional conflicts within close relations was often difficult or even impossible for these men, because as former children of war they could not develop their own emotional competences in contact with an emotional responsive caregiver. In short, they succeeded in business but they often failed within close emotional relations.

Maybe because our findings seemed so incredible and were touching the painfully untouchable, they were criticized and neglected at first again.[27] That was the challenge for us to carry out a large epidemiological replication study.[28] We investigated a random sample of 883 men and women, who were

27 Franz, Lieberz, Schmitz, Schepank, 'A decade of spontaneous long-term course of psychogenic impairment', pp. 651–656; Idem., 'The missing father', pp. 113–127.
28 M. Franz, J. Hardt, E. Brähler, 'Fatherless: Long-term sequelae in German children of World War II', *Z Psychosom Med Psychother*, pp. 216–227.

Impact of WW-II on German war children:

Global psychic symptom load 60 years later

SCL-27 GSI - symptom load	men	women	total
father present	0,33 (0,41)	0,41 (0,46)	**0,37** (0,44)
	(n=319)	(n=382)	(n=701)
father absent	0,50 (0,59)	0,55 (0,55)	**0,52** (0,57)
	(n=79)	(n=90)	(n=169)
total	0,36 (0,46)	0,44 (0,48)	0,40 (0,47)
	(n=398)	(n=472)	(n=870)

Fig. 7.6: Psychological symptom load in men and women grown
up as children during World War II dependent from absence
or presence of father in childhood. Mean values (SD)

representative for the German population born before 1946. Subjects were asked at an average age of 68 years about psychological symptom load,[29] loss of fathers and adverse childhood experiences during the war. Of them, 171 (19.4 %) of the participants reported that they grew up with their mother alone. What we found was a complete replication of the MCS-findings; see Figure 7.5. Again, compared to the children who grew up with a present father the fatherless children showed enhanced psychological impairment as adults – but this time it was 60 years later. Within regression models this association was controlled and independent from other adverse war related experiences.

We did not find any effects of gender. Men and women showed no significant differences of psychological impairment dependent on family status. The SCL-index of the global psychic symptom load (GSI) shows the

29 SCL-27; J. Hardt, H.U. Gerbershagen, 'Cross-validation of the SCL-27: A short psychometric screening instrument for chronic pain patients', *Eur J Pain*, vol. 5, 2001, pp. 187–197.

same finding; see Figure 7.6. That means that not only the sons but also the daughters are suffering from the war-related absence of their fathers, even 60 years later.

Depression, mistrust and social phobia anxiety were significantly enhanced in the adult children of war whose fathers were absent. Exactly these symptoms may indicate a deeply grounded insecurity of these children within close relations. These clinical signs might be a biographical echo of a childhood, which allowed no internal separation from the mother. So, the child still as an adult or old aged man or woman stays occupied and impaired by the internalized depression of the mother and an incomplete development of autonomy caused by the missing father. This may be reflected by findings of psychological mal-adaptation in fatherless children of war in the MCS and our replication study. The psychological long-term consequences of the war related lack of paternal protection, and probably the associated lack of maternal empathy, is still detectable as an enhanced psychological impairment in our epidemiological research two generations later. These findings demonstrate the enormous biographical outreach of the war related loss of the father.

Finally, our research findings were only detectable because we have lived without war in Europe for more than 60 years.

Bibliography

P. R. Amato, 'Children of divorce in the 1990s: an update of the Amato and Keith (1991) meta-analysis', *Journal of Family Psychology*, vol. 15, 3, 2001, pp. 355–370.

S. B. Ashman, G. Dawson, H. Panagiotides, 'Trajectories of maternal depression over 7 years: relations with child psychophysiology and behavior and role of contextual risks', *Development and Psychopathology*, vol. 20, 1, 2008, pp. 55-77.

J. Fahrenberg, H. Selg, R. Hampel, *Das Freiburger Persönlichkeitsinventar FPI. Handanweisung*, Göttingen, Hogrefe, 1978.

I. Fooken, J. Zinnecker (eds), *Trauma und Resilienz*, Weinheim, Juventa, 2009.

C. J. Foster, J. Garber, J.A. Durlak, 'Current and past maternal depression, maternal interaction behaviors, and children's externalizing and internalizing symptoms', *Journal of Abnormal Child Psychology*, vol. 36, 4, 2008, pp. 527-37.

M. Franz, *Der Weg in die Psychotherapeutische Beziehung*, Göttingen, Vandenhoeck und Ruprecht, 1997.

Idem, 'Wenn der Vater fehlt. Die Folgen kriegsbedingter und heutiger Vaterlosigkeit für Kinder und Familien', *Psychoanalytische Familientherapie*, vol. 20/21, 2010, pp. 91-129.

M. Franz, J. Hardt, E. Brähler, 'Fatherless: Long-term sequelae in German children of World War II', *Zeitschrift für Psychosomatische Medizin und Psychotherapie*, vol. 53, 3, 2007, pp. 216–227.

M. Franz, K. Lieberz, N. Schmitz, H. Schepank, 'A decade of spontaneous long-term course of psychogenic impairment in a community population sample', *Social Psychiatry and Psychiatric Epidemiology*, vol. 34, 1999, pp. 651–656.

Idem, 'The missing father. Epidemiological findings on the significance of early absence of the father for mental health in later life', *Zeitschrift für Psychosomatische Medizin und Psychotherapie*, vol. 45, 1999, pp. 113–127.

M. Franz, K. Lieberz, H. Schepank (eds), *Seelische Gesundheit und neurotisches Elend. Der Langzeitverlauf in der Bevölkerung*, Wien, Springer, 2000.

M. Franz, H. Lensche, N. Schmitz, 'Psychological distress and socioeconomic status in single mothers and their children in a German city', *Social Psychiatry and Psychiatric Epidemiology*, vol. 38, 2003, pp. 59–68.

M. Franz, W. Tress, H. Schepank, 'Predicting extreme patterns of long-term course of psychogenic impairment – ten years later', *Social Psychiatry and Psychiatric Epidemiology*, vol. 33, 1998, pp. 243-251.

S. H. Goodman et al., 'Maternal depression and child psychopathology: a meta-analytic review', *Clinical Child and Family Psychology Review*. doi: 10.1007/s10567-010-0080-1, 2010.

J. Hardt, H.U. Gerbershagen, 'Cross-validation of the SCL-27: A short psychometric screening instrument for chronic pain patients', *European Journal of Pain*, vol. 5, 2001, pp. 187–197.

T. Huurre, H. Junkkari, H. Aro, 'Long-term psychosocial effects of parental divorce: a follow-up study from adolescence to adulthood', *European Archives of Psychiatry and Clinical Neuroscience*, vol. 256, 4, 2006, pp. 256–263.

L. Janus (ed.), *Geboren im Krieg*, Gießen, Psychosozial-Verlag, 2006.

C. D. Kouros, J. Garber, 'Dynamic associations between maternal depressive symptoms and adolescents' depressive and externalizing symptoms', *Journal of Abnormal Child Psychology*, vol. 38, 8, 2010, pp. 1069-1081.

H. Radebold, *Abwesende Väter,* Göttingen, Vandenhoeck & Ruprecht, 2000.

Idem (ed.), *Kindheiten im II. Weltkrieg und ihre Folgen*, Gießen, Psychosozial-Verlag, 2004.

A. W. Riley et al., 'Mental health of children of low-income depressed mothers: influences of parenting, family environment, and raters', *Psychiatric Services*, vol. 60, 3, 2009, pp. 329-336.

G. R. Ringback Weitoft, A. Hjern, B. Haglund, M. Rosen, 'Mortality, severe morbidity, and injury in children living with single parents in Sweden: a population-based study', *Lancet* 361, 2003, pp. 289–295.

A. Russel, J. Saebel, 'Mother-son, mother-daughter, father-son, and father-daughter. Are they distinct relationships?', *The Development Review*, vol.

17, 1997, pp. 111–147.

H. Sadowski, et al., 'Early life family disadvantages and major depression in adulthood', *British Journal of Psychiatry*, vol. 174, 1999, pp. 112–120.

A. Sarkadi, R. Kristiansson, F. Oberklaid, S. Bremberg, 'Fathers' involvement and children's developmental outcomes: a systematic review of longitudinal studies', *Acta Paediatrica*, vol. 97, 2, 2008, pp. 153-158.

H. Schepank, *Der Beeinträchtigungsschwerescore (BSS). Ein Instrument zur Bestimmung der Schwere einer psychogenen Erkrankung*, Göttingen, Beltz, 1995.

Idem, *Epidemiology of psychogenic disorders*, Berlin, Heidelberg, New York, Springer, 1987.

Idem (ed.), *Verläufe*, Heidelberg, Springer, 1990.

M. Siegal, 'Are sons and daughters treated more differently by fathers than by mothers?', *The Development Review*, vol. 7, 1987, pp. 183–209.

T. Trapolini, C. A. McMahon, J. A. Ungerer, 'The effect of maternal depression and marital adjustment on young children's internalizing and externalizing behaviour problems', *Child Care Health and Development*, vol. 33, 6, 2007, pp. 794-803.

Part Two   **Representations of Children in War**

---

8   German War Literature for Children, 1914-1918

Carolyn Kay

How did German children – in particular, middle-class boys and girls between the ages of four and twelve – imagine the battlefields of World War One during the war years? What ideas did authors emphasize in war literature for children and why? These are central questions of my current research, part of a broader investigation into the parental values and societal ideals prescribed for children in Imperial Germany.[1] Some clues as to the connections between German children and World War One are to be found in the enormous literature for boys and girls created during the war years. Young readers and their parents had a wide variety of war literature to choose from, including picture books, fairy tales, adventure stories, almanacs of poems and songs, histories, collections of letters from the Front, and pamphlets appealing for patriotic support.[2] Moreover, by the time of the war books were the predominant avenue of children's culture. During the nineteenth century children's books had become more commonplace and popular in Germany, especially among the middle classes; technological advances allowed book publishers to print more copies of books, reduce prices and include illustrations of better quality. The result was a dramatic increase

---

1   See C. Kay, 'How Should We Raise Our Son Benjamin? Advice Literature for Mothers in Early Twentieth-Century Germany', *Raising Citizens in the Century of the Child*, ed. Dirk Schumann, *105-121*. See also M. Gebhardt, *Die Angst vor dem kindlichen Tyrannen* and G. F. Budde, *Auf dem Weg ins Bürgerleben. Kindheit und Erziehung in deutschen und englischen Bürgerfamilien 1840-1914.* The subject of child-rearing in Germany's *Kaiserreich* has also been explored cinematically in an intriguing film by Michael Haneke, entitled *The White Ribbon / Das weisse Band – eine deutsche Kindergeschichte*, Berlin 2009.
2   A selection of wartime literature for children, excluding titles discussed in this article, includes W. Planck, *Haltet aus im Sturmgebraus. Bilder aus dem großen Kriege 1914-15*; W. Kotzde, *Die Musik kommt! Bilder aus dem Soldatenleben*; *Patriotisches Bilderbuch*; K. Hachez, *Kriegs-ABC*; J. Ermler, *Märchen in Feldgrau*; C. Grünebaum, *Aus der Kriegszeit: Märchen und Erzählungen*; R. Kleinecke, *Spitzel, der Kriegshund und andere Kriegsgeschichten*; G. Schlipköter (ed.), *Fürs teure Vaterland. Ein Kriegslesebuch für die deutsche Jugend*; W. Müller-Rüdersdorf, *Deutschland über alles! 1914-15 Kriegslesebuch für Schule und Haus*; H. Werdenfels, *Unsere Feldgrauen in Feindesland*; G. Dennler, *Mein Vaterland. Aus Sturm und Drang ein Hochgesang*; O.Seeler, *Germania und ihre Kinder*; A. Herbert-Cronau, *Was sollen unsere Knaben und Mädchen durch den Krieg lernen?*

in the number of children reading books or being exposed to picture books by the turn of the century onwards.[3] For the historian, then, this aspect of family culture is of great interest.

As historian Andrew Donson has noted in his study of German youth in the war, German war literature was tremendously popular after 1914, and it emphasized such concepts as nationalism, militarism, sacrifice, heroism, adventure, and (for boys) manhood.[4] Girls were also expected to support their nation and its troops; literature for girls often extolled self-sacrifice, with literary heroines marrying wounded soldiers and promising to tend to them forever.[5] These books were written by authors eager to mobilize support for the war from young Germans, and they tended to depict the war in very romantic terms, with little reference to the actual conditions at the front, or to the appalling loss of life. War here became a kind of "holy" struggle, with all Germans coming together to participate and thus to defend the Fatherland.[6] What is striking is how such ideas were not only directed at teenage boys and girls, but also at very young children. Picture books and stories for children under twelve imagined the war in ways that would have been powerful, seductive and accessible for a child: war was depicted as a glorious adventure, even for the very young. Heroic self-sacrifice, societal unity, and respect for ones parents and for the national leaders were all held up as essential qualities of any good child. Furthermore, the nationalism expressed in these books directed the child to think of himself or herself as one important part of a greater whole, gloriously struggling to defend the Fatherland.

Before considering this war literature, we should remember that the child's world changed dramatically in Germany after 1914: families were torn apart as fathers, uncles and brothers went off to war and mothers took on wartime employment or took over family businesses and farms. Along with the excitement evoked by the changes during the early stages of the war children came to witness their mothers struggling with illness, worry, sadness, and sometimes depression.[7] It was not uncommon for children to be placed with other family members while mothers worked, a wrenching experience for some girls and boys. School life was affected too, as teachers signed up for the army and were then replaced by older instructors. By the latter years of

---

3   G. Wilkending, 'Vom letzten Drittel des 19. Jahrhunderts bis zum Ersten Weltkrieg', in R. Wild (ed.), *Geschichte der deutschen Kinder-und Jugendliteratur*, pp. 173-174.
4   A. Donson, *Youth In the Fatherless Land: War Pedagogy, Nationalism and Authority in Germany 1914-1918*, p. 91.
5   See G. Wilkending, *Mädchenliteratur der Kaiserzeit*, pp. 280-297; G. Wilkending, 'Geschichtserzählende Literatur für Mädchen bis zum Ende der Weimarer Republik', in C. Pohlmann, R. Steinlein (eds), the exhibition catalogue *Geschichtsbilder. Historischer Jugendbücher aus vier Jahrhunderten*, pp. 133-149.
6   Donson, *Youth In the Fatherless Land*, p. 91.
7   R. Whalen, *Bitter Wounds: German Victims of the Great War, 1914-1939*, pp. 77-78.

Fig. 8.1: Arpad Schmidhammer, *Die Geschichte vom General Hindenburg*.

the war, deaths of loved ones and the scarcity of food and fuel because of the Allied blockade created great hardships, and the glamour of war surely faded. Despite all of these tough conditions most children's books were produced in the early years of the war, and there is plenty of evidence to show that boys, in particular, were thrilled by what they saw as the adventure of combat: boys of ten and up became obsessed with military weaponry and the violent nature of war; they also tended to identify strongly with fathers and brothers in action.[8]

If we turn to the subject of books for young children, the glorious nature of war is a constant theme. One of the most popular picture books from the war years was Arpad Schmidhammer's *The Story of General Hindenburg* (1915),[9] a book recommended to parents by teachers.[10] This text was created as a patriotic book for small children, depicting the famous war general as a smiling leader of skill, strength and purpose – a protector against the enemy.

---

8   Ibid., pp. 79-80.
9   A. Schmidhammer, *Die Geschichte vom General Hindenburg*.
10 Schmidhammer's book was contained in several lists of recommended texts in the *Jugendschriften-Warte* for 1914 and 1916 – a journal produced by educational reformers in the Vereinigte Prüfungsausschüsse. This publication encouraged parents and teachers to expose Germany's children to good literature, rather than poorly-written, immoral, or war-mongering pulp fiction. The leading figure in this battle for children's literature was Heinrich Wolgast.

The story shows Hindenburg leading the German troops in a hilarious game of tricking and then tripping the Russian enemy and sending him flying into muck and water. War here literally becomes child's play. Schmidhammer was a prolific illustrator of children's books and a satirist of German society who had often contributed to the well-known satirical periodical based in Munich, *Jugend*. He wrote several children's books during the war, such as *Beloved Fatherland Have No Fear* (1914) and *Hans and Pierre: A Comical Story from the Trenches* (1916).[11] The art in these picture books is skilful, funny, appealing, and yet firmly nationalistic (see figure 8.1). There is no hint of anti-war sentiment here.

The Story of General Hindenburg introduces children to Hindenburg and the victories of the German army in late August 1914 at the battle of Tannenberg in East Prussia. Thousands of Russian soldiers were effectively surrounded in the area of the Masurian Lakes, with some units driven into the swamps by German forces under Hindenburg's command. An enormous number were also taken prisoner. This was a glorious early victory for the Germans, and one of the most extraordinary campaigns of the war, transforming Hindenburg into a national hero. Hindenburg, in fact, had not played a leading role in the military planning of this offensive, but the subsequent reporting of the victory elevated him to a lofty position within the pantheon of First World War heroes. For most Germans, concerned about Russia's invasion of East Prussia at the start of the war, such a triumph over the "barbaric" Russians brought enormous relief and joy. And the celebration of Hindenburg – as a stolid, confident and resolute leader – knew few bounds.[12] (For the Russians, there was no such glory; indeed, General Samsonov shot himself after 90,000 Russians were taken prisoner by the Germans.)[13]

Hindenburg became the most popular figure of the war, seen as the German giant who had brought down the Russian bear. His military leadership caught the imagination of the public, who embraced him and venerated his achievements, perhaps from a desire for a hero to succeed Bismarck or who could evoke the past glories of Prussia.[14] Hindenburg also appealed to every German – to Protestants and Catholics, rural dwellers and urbanites, conservatives and Social Democrats; his image soon appeared on glasses, cups, plates, card games, cigars, and soldiers' mouth organs.[15] Photographs and drawings of the great leader were placed on walls, replacing images of the Kaiser and hanging next to religious icons. And in the most remarkable

11 A. Schmidhammer, *Lieb Vaterland magst ruhig sein! Ein Kriegsbilderbuch mit Knüttelversen*; Idem., *Hans und Pierre. Eine lustige Schützengrabengeschichte*.
12 A. von der Goltz, *The Hindenburg Myth*, pp. 14-42.
13 C. Falls, *The Great War*, p. 56.
14 von der Goltz, *The Hindenburg Myth*, p. 25.
15 Ibid., pp. 22-23, 26.

Fig. 8.2: Arpad Schmidhammer, *Die Geschichte vom General Hindenburg.*

example of hero-worship, an enormous "Iron Hindenburg" nailing statue was placed in front of Berlin's victory column in September 1915, whereby citizens could donate to a widows' and orphans' war fund, climb a scaffold, and hammer a nail into the statue's coat, uniform and sword.[16] 20,000 did so on the first day of its opening.[17] Other nailing statues were soon erected in towns throughout the nation. A month later, a father wrote to his local newspaper about the Hindenburg phenomenon's effect on his son:

> One has to imagine, when the little boy wakes up in the morning, the first thing he sees is a framed etching of the Field Marshal, who looks at him admonishingly. Then the frightened boy frantically demands his morning milk. Naturally, the porcelain mug is decorated with the full body image of Hindenburg. Next to the bed, a real-size Hindenburg is keeping guard. From the cover of a picture book the Liberator of East Prussia smiles at him....Even on the plate the boy uses for his porridge, Hindenburg's characteristic head can be found....When my son wants to play with tin soldiers, he has at least an entire battalion of Hindenburgs in all imaginable sizes at his disposal.... [It is] not surprising that the boy is a proper Hindenburg-maniac.[18]

As Anna von der Goltz concludes, Hindenburg "became Germany's major symbol of victory against the enemy and of unity at home" representing such

16 Ibid., p. 27, 30.
17 Ibid., p. 31.
18 von der Goltz, *The Hindenburg Myth*, p. 26.

Fig. 8.3: Arpad Schmidhammer, *Die Geschichte vom General Hindenburg.*

qualities as self-sacrifice, loyalty to the fatherland, courage, military prowess, steely nerves, and quiet confidence.[19] "Hindenburg will sort it out," became a common expression, revealing the popular belief that trusting in Hindenburg would bring victory.[20]

Arpad Schmidhammer celebrates Hindenburg in the picture book (perhaps the one referred to in the newspaper letter above) as a supreme strategist and leader, and as a father-figure who smiles and watches over the troops defeating the Russians. He is drawn with a large head and formidable moustache, atop a robust and yet corpulent body [Figure 8.2]. His contemporary, the poet Wilhelm von Scholz, described the actual Hindenburg as a "heavy, mighty ... General with a square head."[21] Thus, as Anna von der Goltz notes he "embodied a specific type of masculinity; he was no youthful or athletic warrior, but symbolized virile gravitas through his rectangular features and broad frame."[22] This is decidedly the image that Schmidhammer presents to the children. Hindenburg is the large, sturdy, determined figure on each page. Sometimes he wears a top hat, at other points a military cap; he is shown in the field but also in his quarters, dressed in slippers and fez or in a long military coat. In all the depictions Hindenburg becomes familiar, accessible and an object of beloved authority: the leader and the people's man who would

19 Ibid., p. 23, 25.
20 Ibid., p. 25.
21 Ibid., p. 20.
22 Ibid.

Fig. 8.4: Arpad Schmidhammer, *Die Geschichte vom General Hindenburg.*

stand firm as a rock in the face of the enemy.

Furthermore, what's striking about this book is the breezy way in which the war is presented, as child's play between good boy-soldiers and dumb bullies. The German soldiers appear boy-like, with twinkling eyes and a cheeky smile. They never show fear or worry; instead they are prepared – with Hindenburg's help – to trick and defeat the Russians [Figure 8.3]. This they do by beckoning the Russians to come into a field with several ponds, setting down a plank for them to walk upon (Hindenburg's positioning of troops between the lakes) and then pulling up the plank – like a slapstick comedy – to topple the Russians into the water and mud [Figure 8.4]. The Russian soldiers are also boyish, but bigger and with long, unruly hair. In one image of the book, as they are pummeled with snowballs, their faces are grotesque and threatening. Here they are definitely drawn as bullies.

What's also noticeable is what's missing here in the depiction of war. There is no mention of trenches or machinery (the soldiers carry rifles, but not machine guns), gas or grenades. This is the kind of war where a hero can be celebrated, and where the worse punishment, for the loser, is falling into a muddy puddle or being pelted with snowballs. Clearly, the intent of this book was to celebrate Hindenburg's victories, praise the German troops, and evoke nationalism: the final page reads "Deutschland, Deutschland über alles, über alles in the world! / Long live General Hindenburg the great German hero / He has saved our Fatherland from distress and danger / And the eagle of victory soars over a world of enemies."[23]

In her analysis of Hindenburg, historian Anna von der Goltz emphasizes that ordinary people were instrumental in the creation of the Hindenburg myth; that men and women throughout the nation embraced the songs, poems, photographs, and newspaper reports that extolled Hindenburg as the greatest war hero and looked forward to a glorious German victory. They also eagerly purchased for their children the toys and miniature statues of the victor of Tannenburg. [24] The people helped to make Hindenburg a German giant, an image of glory that would continue into the Weimar years. In Schmidhammer's book we see this hero worship communicated to small children; boys and girls are encouraged to adore the smiling general and to emulate the bourgeois qualities he encapsulates: determination, obedience, gentlemanly chivalry, loyalty to the Fatherland, calm strength, and fighting skill.[25] The book also encourages unity in the nation behind the German struggle, as expressed in the final stanza of the book. And it shows war as an uneven struggle between the smart German soldiers – well organized, ready for a tussle – and the stupid Russian soldiers – easily tricked, stupid oafs. Implicit in this story is the notion that the civilized Germans are miles apart from the backward Russians (and cannot fall to their treachery). Children reading Schmidhammer's book would thus learn the following: that Hindenburg was a great and glorious leader; that the war was winnable and a question of strategy; that the Russians were very different from the Germans and lacked German brilliance and power; and that service to the Fatherland was the highest achievement any German could fulfill.

Such nationalistic sentiment, glorifying Hindenburg, is echoed in another story for children aged 5 to 8 by Else Ury, a popular German-Jewish writer of girls' literature and author of the famous Nesthäkchen series, including *Nesthäkchen and the World War*.[26] She wrote a short story for the 1917 edition of *Meidingers Kinder-Kalendar*, entitled "Little Hans' Ride to Hindenburg"[27] In this story, one small boy's separation from his father on the eastern front is solved at Christmas time, when he decides to ride a magical horse to Hindenburg, on Christmas eve, and ask for his father to come home on leave. Says Hans:

Dear Herr Hindenburg. You are truly so good and you have driven away all

23 Schmidhammer, *Die Geschichte vom General Hindenburg*, final page.
24 Ibid., p. 25.
25 Ibid..
26 E. Ury, *Nesthäkchen und der Weltkrieg*; see also B. Asper, H. Kempin, B. Münchmeyer-Schöneberg, *Wiedersehen mit Nesthäkchen. Else Ury aus heutiger Sicht.*
27 E. Ury, 'Hänschens Ritt zu Hindenburg', in *Meidingers Kinder-Kalender für das Jahr 1917*, pp. 18-27.

the terrible Russians. And my Uncle Max says that if you only knew how much our father would be missed on this holy night then surely you would grant him leave.

Calling Hans a "brave boy" who would also be a fine soldier, Hindenburg grants the request. Father and son tearfully reunite, mount the magical horse, and return home. The next day Hans wakes up to find his father sitting next to his bedside, his mother overwhelmed by the surprising turn of events. Here the child is the rescuer in wartime, playing a heroic part in reuniting the family – surely every child's wish. Ury celebrates Hans as brave, daring, heroic, and loving, and connects him with his hero – depicting Hindenburg as strong, compassionate, and wise. She also makes clear that the German cause in the war is just and true.

While children's literature from the war routinely carried a strong nationalistic message and praised Hindenburg (far more than the Kaiser), these books also extolled societal unity in Germany, showing this togetherness as a positive development of the war.[28] The emphasis on societal unity was joined with stereotypical views of the enemy (such as the Russian savage), sometimes incorporating racist depictions. For example, Rudolf Prebster's *Father's in the War. A Picturebook for Children* (1915) – a book aimed at readers from ages 6-10 – introduces young readers to "the Russian prisoners" captured by Hindenburg's forces at Tannenburg, and shows images of brutish, coarse-looking men in heavy coats and hats.[29] The text reads:

> What kind of trait is this?
> Only the devil can understand it!
> Silly hats, tall hats
> Wide braid, silver braid
> Shabby coats, without buttons
> Bony Mongolian heads
> Hollow eyes, flat noses[30]

In another popular book of the war, *The Greater the Danger the Greater the Honour* (1916), the Allied soldiers are drawn as racially different and characterized as either brutally threatening or pathetically comic.[31] The

28 An excellent example of this is the story 'Die jungen Feinde' by Max Karl Böttcher-Chemnitz in *Meidingers Kinder-Kalender für das Jahr 1917*, 61-72. Two boys from the same village, enemies because of their feuding families, enter the war and become best friends when they are faced with gunfire and possible capture by the French.
29 R. Prebster, *Vater ist im Kriege. Ein Bilderbuch für Kinder.*
30 Ibid., unpaginated.
31 *Viel Feind, viel Ehr! 1914-1916,* no author is listed.

Fig. 8.5: *Viel Feind, viel Ehr! 1914–1916*

Fig. 8.6: *Viel Feind, viel Ehr! 1914–1916*

Russians – "Wladimir" and "Nikolauski" – are brutal hooligans, burning down German homes and pillaging the countryside. [Figure 8.5] The British are effete numbskulls with bad teeth. The French are decrepit old soldiers. And on one page of the text an exotic assortment of prisoners of war – indigenous peoples, Africans and Indians – are compared to animals in a zoo by a child. [Figure 8.6] Such images were intended to draw laughter from the young reader and to reinforce the notion that the Germans constituted a distinct and superior civilization, now threatened by inferior races. The last page of this book presents the German soldiers as glorious victors, holding the French, British and Russians as prisoners. The top caption reads: "Be proud that you are a German!" Clearly, then, nationalist and racist ideas were closely intertwined in some of the war literature for children.

Notably, some wartime texts were specifically directed at younger girls between the ages of 5 and 10, including Paul Telemann's *How Our Small Housemothers Must Be Industrious During the War*.[32] In this beautifully illustrated book of 1915 flags fly high, Hindenburg's victories are celebrated and young girls are encouraged to be useful in wartime Berlin. Three girls – Marie, Greta and Lotte – make themselves busy by knitting leg warmers, arranging care packages for their father, and even by collecting money for the Red Cross. In one scene little Greta and her dog Puck join a wartime celebration in Berlin to ask for spare coins. Wartime responsibilities are expected of boys and girls, and Telemann makes clear in a humorous way that the girls have much to do. At the start of the book their mother encourages them to make themselves useful, and thus to help their men-folk, telling the girls that they must keep busy and be mindful of the sacrifices made for them. The author writes about their "feminine" talents – and thus emphasizes the traditional gender divide in the home, with girls taking charge of domestic tasks and skills. Girls are urged in the book to give of their talents generously to the men at the front – who will be comforted by their efforts. There is even a song, with musical score, celebrating the girls' knitting skills. Once again, such books made clear that every German had a part to play in the war, with the nation coming together to support the war effort. For young girls or boys these appeals were powerful.

Finally, two of the most popular and well-written wartime books for young children were *What Little Heini Will Saw and Heard in the World War* by Ernst Lorenzen, and Luise Glass's *Hansemann Mobilizes For War*.[33] Both books appeared in 1915 and are thoughtful and engaging stories for children aged 8-12. *Heini* is the story of a ten-year-old boy in Hagen, whose world is transformed

32 P. Telemann, *Wie uns're kleinen Hausmütterlein im Kriege müssen fleißig sein.*
33 E. Lorenzen, *Was der kleine Heini Will vom Weltkrieg sah und hörte*; L. Glass, *Hansemann macht mobil. Feldgraue Kindergeschichten.*

by the war. He wakes up one night in early August 1914 to the sounds of men singing *Deutschland über Alles*; by the next day crowds have assembled in the town square: women, men, children, soldiers, the commanders of the troops, officers on horses, the mayor. To Heini the outbreak of war is a grand celebration, punctuated by music. Singing constantly breaks out – "A Mighty Fortress is our God"; "Hail to Thee in Victor's Crown." There are hurrahs and hugs, handkerchiefs and swooning girls. The soldiers are heroes before even departing by train for Belgium. The youth long to enlist: Heini thinks – "if I were only six years older, I know exactly what I would do!"[34] The town is soon emptied of able-bodied men, and the women take over work in shops and in the local school. A short time later, when news breaks out of Hindenburg's success at Tannenburg, the town's church bells ring out, and crowds gather to read the newspaper headlines; at a coffeehouse customers sing "The Watch on the Rhine." People say to each other "Yes, Hindenburg is a fine fellow!" – and his portrait soon hangs in all the windows.[35]

In *Hansemann Mobilizes for War*, scenes of celebration and excitement at the war's outbreak are also described in detail; Hansemann is eight and, like Heini, wants to take part! He asks a woman in his village, "Does it hurt much when a soldier is shot dead?"[36] She replies, "of course!" but then tries to make things sound a bit better by saying that soldiers who are wounded can go to hospital and be given chocolate by friendly nurses. Hansemann begs his mother to let him go to war; when she warns him that he might become wounded, he retorts that he could then go to a *Lazarett* and eat *Schokolade*. And if he is severely wounded? "Then I will grin and bear it!"[37] To Hansemann, the soldiers are inspiring; he had played with toy soldiers on many occasions, but now real soldiers were gathering in his village and he saw them as "masters of the world."[38]

Not all is glorious in these two war stories, though. Both books do offer some mention of death and suffering in the war, depicted with skill and sensitivity by the authors. For example, Hansemann's friend Liselotte loses her father in the first year of the war. Although her father has won the Iron Cross and Liselotte's mother says he has gone to heaven as a hero, the young girl still begs God to bring back her father at Xmas.[39] This poignant scene makes clear the sacrifices of war. In Lorenzen's book the town where Heini lives contains a war hospital, and when a young soldier dies there a solemn funeral is held; Heini then thinks about the grieving parents of soldiers who

34 Lorenzen, *Was der kleine Heini Will*, p. 13.
35 Ibid., pp. 14-16.
36 Glass, *Hansemann macht mobil*, p. 12.
37 Ibid., p. 33.
38 Ibid., p. 21.
39 Ibid., pp. 99-105.

Fig. 8.7: Ernst Lorenzen, *Was der kleine Heini Will vom Weltkrieg sah und hörte.*

will die on the battlefront in unmarked graves.[40] Later in the story he meets a wounded soldier who describes the formidable conditions of the trenches – the mud, the water, the shelling – and describes the trench as a kind of grave.[41] Despite these thoughtful scenes addressing the human cost of war, neither Heini nor Hansemann reject the war. They accept Germany's effort as essential and are enthusiastic supporters of the army and its troops.

Ultimately, in both of these books the war begins as a marvellous kind of adventure; to the children, war is spectacle, movement (as the soldiers gather to board trains), celebration, and – of course – something out of the ordinary. School is suspended and everyone assembles in the town's centre to hear speeches and profess their loyalty to the nation and the Kaiser. The songs, the crowds that gather, the soldiers that stand tall – all impress upon the children how important the war is and how glorious, exciting and heroic the struggle will be. And in the opening year of the war each German victory is celebrated with church bells and ice cream. School is also let out for the day. Hindenburg is acclaimed as the greatest German leader. For the historian this depiction of the war makes clear the tremendous sense of excitement and purpose as the war first breaks out; it also emphasizes Germans' sense of their just cause and their dedication to the nation. Children are swept up in the euphoria – and indeed in the nationalism and the rejection of the enemy -- in a particularly powerful way (even incorporating racist ideas). They observe the changes of the time with awe and anticipation, as war becomes an epic struggle of good

40 Lorenzen, *Was der kleine Heini Will*, pp. 51-52.
41 Lorenzen, *Was der kleine Heini Will*, pp. 76-78.

versus bad, of the innocent versus bullies. They also play at war – either as soldiers of the Reich battling the enemies or as spies within enemy territory helping the German cause. [Figure 8.7]

These children's stories give a deeper sense of the war's effect upon German society – and thus upon the future adults of the post-war era. It becomes evident that the war was seen as just, important and winnable; that the soldiers of the Reich, led by Hindenburg, were glorious heroes who defended the nation by their bravery and sacrifice; that the Allies were perceived as inferior to the German people and German civilization – depicted as jealous, spiteful, and greedy competitors who sought to limit and indeed weaken the young German nation; and that many writers believed God was on Germany's side. The children's books on war also offer us a clear, fascinating and yet heartbreaking portrait of life in Germany at the very beginning of the struggle – when so much seemed possible. It is impossible to read these books without reflecting on the terrible suffering that the war would bring to the lives of these children after the songs, the speeches, and the celebrations were over.

ক

The author would like to thank Carola Pohlmann of the Kinder-und Jugendbuchabteilung in Berlin's Staatsbibliothek, along with Trent University, for support in writing this article.

Bibliography:

B. Asper, H. Kempin, B. Münchmeyer-Schöneberg, *Wiedersehen mit Nesthäkchen. Else Ury aus heutiger Sicht*, Berlin, Text Verlag, 2007.

M. K. Böttcher-Chemnitz, 'Die jungen Feinde', in *Meidingers Kinder-Kalender für das Jahr 1917*, pp. 61-72.

G. F. Budde, *Auf dem Weg ins Bürgerleben. Kindheit und Erziehung in deutschen und englischen Bürgerfamilien 1840-1914*, Göttingen, Vandenhoeck & Ruprecht, 1994.

A. Donson, *Youth In the Fatherless Land: War Pedagogy, Nationalism and Authority in Germany 1914-1918*, Cambridge, Harvard University Press, 2010.

C. Falls, *The Great War*, New York, Capricorn Books, 1961.

M. Gebhardt, *Die Angst vor dem kindlichen Tyrannen*, München, Deutsche Verlags-Anstalt, 2009.

L. Glass, *Hansemann macht mobil. Feldgraue Kindergeschichten*, Heilbronn, Eugen Salzer, 1915.

A. von der Goltz, *The Hindenburg Myth*, Oxford, Oxford University Press, 2009.

C. Kay, 'How Should We Raise Our Son Benjamin? Advice Literature for Mothers in Early Twentieth-Century Germany', *Raising Citizens in the Century of the Child*, ed. Dirk Schumann, New York, Berghahn Books, 2010, pp. 105-121.

E. Lorenzen, *Was der kleine Heini Will vom Weltkrieg sah und hörte*, Leipzig, Dürr'schen Buchhandlung, 1915.

C. Pohlmann, R. Steinlein (eds), *Geschichtsbilder. Historischer Jugendbücher aus vier Jahrhunderten*, Berlin, Staatsbibliothek zu Berlin, 2000.

R. Prebster, *Vater ist im Kriege. Ein Bilderbuch für Kinder*, Berlin, Hermann Hillger Verlag, 1915.

A. Schmidhammer, *Die Geschichte vom General Hindenburg*, Mainz, Scholz Verlag, 1915.

Idem., *Hans und Pierre. Eine lustige Schützengrabengeschichte*, Mainz, Scholz Verlag, 1916.

Idem., *Lieb Vaterland magst ruhig sein! Ein Kriegsbilderbuch mit Knüttelversen*, Mainz, Scholz Verlag, 1914.

P. Telemann, W*ie uns're kleinen Hausmütterlein im Kriege müssen fleißig sein*, Berlin, Hermann Michel, 1915.

E. Ury, 'Hänschens Ritt zu Hindenburg', *Meidingers Kinder-Kalender für das Jahr 1917*, Berlin, Meidingers Jugendschriften Verlag, 1917, pp. 18-27.

Idem., *Nesthäkchen und der Weltkrieg*, Berlin, Meidingers Jugendschriften Verlag, 1922.

Viel Feind, viel Ehr! 1914-1916, Duisburg, J.A. Steinkamp, 1916.

R. Whalen, *Bitter Wounds: German Victims of the Great War, 1914-1939*, Ithaca, Cornell U. Press, 1984.

R. Wild (ed.), *Geschichte der deutschen Kinder-und Jugendliteratur*, Stuttgart, Verlag J.B. Metzler, 2008.

G. Wilkending, 'Geschichtserzählende Literatur für Mädchen bis zum Ende der Weimarer Republik', in C. Pohlmann, R. Steinlein (eds), the exhibition catalogue *Geschichtsbilder. Historischer Jugendbücher aus vier Jahrhunderten*, Berlin, Staatsbibliothek zu Berlin, 2000, pp. 133-149.

Idem., *Mädchenliteratur der Kaiserzeit*, Stuttgart, J.B. Metzler, 2003.

Idem., 'Vom letzten Drittel des 19. Jahrhunderts bis zum Ersten Weltkrieg', in R. Wild (ed.), *Geschichte der deutschen Kinder-und Jugendliteratur*, Stuttgart, Verlag J.B. Metzler, 2008, pp. 173-174.

Yvonne Kozlovsky Golan

Children have always represented the future of humanity. Each society has its own unique attitude to its nation's sociocultural life. Civilized societies consider children as young adults deserving of care and supervision to grow up to continue their parents' legacy and nation's customs. Since the early 1940s, images of child victims and survivors of World War II in Europe have captured the imagination of filmmakers as a reliable reflection of the horrors of war. Major films made from 1945 to the present show broad common denominators in their portrayal of children and teenagers during World War II.

The present article examines two major issues:

First, do the historical representations of Jewish children in world cinema reflect a commonly accepted cultural perception of the Holocaust? Second, is the narrative of their life, survival and/or death onscreen fair and truthful in terms of how the filmmaker's home country dealt with the Holocaust and its visual materials?

Some American scholars of history and cinema have stated that the Holocaust has taken up a disproportionate share of the cultural discourse in the USA. Peter Novick stated that Holocaust constitutes a relatively large portion of the American public discourse, emphasizing memory instead of research.[1] We shall explore whether he is correct about the representation of children during the Holocaust in American cinema.

Identity, identification and justification

The Hollywood genre of the 'Holocaust film' reworked the reasons for the country's having entered World War II, and explored the endeavor of rebuilding the 'new Europe'. One of the first films on the subject was Fred

---

1   P. Novick, *The Holocaust and Collective Memory: The American* Experience.

Zinnemann's *The Search*,[2] portraying UNRRA soldiers' encounter with a young survivor whom they help to search for his mother.[3] Its depiction of soldiers in 'Franconia', West Germany, sent a covert propaganda message emphasizing the common humanity of liberators and liberated to justify America's entering the war.[4]

The Diary of Anne Frank was made in 1959 by George Stevens, Sr., one of the first to film the liberation of the concentration and death camps in Western Europe.[5] He decided not to recreate the horrors on film, so as not to unsettle the public, but instead to concentrate on Anne's character: she is optimistic in a world full of hatred and fear.[6] Anne's story inspired numerous versions in several media,[7] including a one-of-a-kind series, screened among other Sunday programs such as *Me and the Colonel* (1958) aimed at limited special-interest groups, for example Jewish children, science fiction fans, and other genres.[8]

The young Jewish Dutch girl seems to be part of an "All-American family," but it is important to remember that this film appeared during the postwar period when there was still no consensus on the look of children during the Holocaust in film. Filmmakers made a conscious choice neither to feature children as the main characters, nor to portray the Holocaust for children in order to avoid shocking the audience.

The theme of universal lessons from history was presented to the public in *The Sound of Music* in a fitting way for its time and place, billed as a film for the entire family.[9] Children were on the center stage, but their designated role could not contain the behind-the-scenes story of the Holocaust since it was a broader narrative than could be presented in the plot.

The function of the children was to show the dangers of Nazism, and hint

---

2   1948, from a play by Ivan Jandl.
3   L. Baron, *Projecting the Holocaust into the Present: The Changing Focus of Contemporary Holocaust Cinema* , Chapter Two: Picturing the Holocaust in the Past.
4   R. J. Berger, *Fathoming the Holocaust: A Social Problems Approach*, pp. 143-146.
5   Y. Kozlovsky Golan, 'The Shaping of the Holocaust Visual Conscience by the Nuremberg Trials. Birth of the Holocaust in Hollywood-Style Motion Pictures: The Impact of the Movie "Nazi Concentration Camps"', *Search and Research;* pp. 6-50. See also L. Douglas, *The Memory of Judgment: Making Law and History at the Trials of the Holocaust*, pp. 22-27.
6   The director's interview with George Stevens, Jr., in the film, *Imaginary Witness: Hollywood and the Holocaust,* Dir. Daniel Anker (USA, 2004).
7   The film and the play of 'The Diary of Anne Frank' were staged in innumerable versions, beginning with the film by George Stevens, Sr. in the USA and other films in Europe Scandinavia and the Far East, including *Anne no nikki*, (Dir. Akinori Nagaoka), an anime adaptation of the Diary (Japan, 1995). As Judith E. Doneson states, Anne Frank became the first image in the west to represent events that took place during Nazi domination of Europe and the first to be reflected in American culture as such. See J. E. Doneson, 'The American History of Anne Frank's *Diary*', *Holocaust Genocide Studies*, p. 2.
8   Baron, *Projecting the Holocaust*, p. 172.
9   Filmed in 1965 and directed by Robert Wise.

at what would have happened had it not been stopped in time. The young Nazi Ralf is the polar opposite of the Von Trapp children, who were educated by their anti-Nazi father, the Captain. The film characters, based on the real family, are intended to show that Austrians and Germans who opposed Nazism also suffered. The teenagers enchanted by Nazism represent the loss of childhood, while children in general represent the next generation. Postwar America wanted to bury the memory of the past so that Europe could rebuild itself. The sweet, innocent Von Trapp children are messengers of hope for the new era. As in many family films, *The Sound of Music* also shows the limitations of the era in which it was made.[10]

Not many American films used images of children to transmit the narrative of the Shoah, but rather as allegory. The absence of children as major protagonists during this decade may be contrasted to their role in the later expanded cinematic discourse on the Holocaust. In 1960, director Otto Preminger confronted the events of the Holocaust directly, in his monumental feature film, *Exodus*, entirely focused on the 'illegal' immigration to Mandatory Palestine. One of the main characters is a young Holocaust survivor who joins the struggle of the native-born Jews,[11] the core being the narrative of rising from the ashes. The young man, with an Eastern European look and dark features ('very Jewish-looking'), finds his way to the immigrant ship *Exodus* and joins the Jewish underground to break into Acre prison. As the representative of the millions killed in Europe, he is the film's *raison d'être*, a 'New Jew' whose spirit cannot be broken, fighting for a Jewish state.

The television series *Holocaust*, a significant milestone in bringing Holocaust memory to the world's consciousness, portrays children as the seismograph of wartime horrors.[12] This miniseries was an excellent way for the American viewer to learn which values the USA was defending by entering the war: family values, individualism and the pursuit of happiness in the USA and in Europe.

The similarity begins with the depiction of the child's family. Most of the onscreen family scenes take place around the dinner table as the most common location of the family's social and cultural encounters. Mixed marriages and assimilated families constituted an integral part of the life of the society, culture and economy of Germany, as well as a reflection of many American families in postwar USA.

Furthermore, children become the critical marker creating the dichotomy between Good and Evil – 'us' vs. 'them'. The daughter goes to her death in the gas chamber with other Jewish children, while the son escapes to join the

---

10 V. Lebeau, *Childhood and Cinema*, p. 148.
11 They are called *'sabras'*.
12 Directed in 1978 by Martin Chomsky.

partisans, becomes a hero – another obvious American element, and finally realizes his dream to reach the Land of Israel. The actors' fame, accents and looks help create similarities and identification between the two societies.

Children play an important role in Steven Spielberg's film, *Schindler's List*, becoming integral to the adults' narrative.[13] The outstanding, unforgettable image of children in the film is the girl in the red coat, alone and lost in a crowd.[14] It is one of the most impressive and memorable sequences in the entire film because of the double take on the situation: the personal viewpoint of the lost girl, turning outward to a world collapsing around her and the wordless cinematic viewpoint describing the little girl as a victim whom no country tried to save.

The futility of 'race' and futility of the difference

Children became the guiding motif of common values because they are the younger generation who were saved and sought refuge in the USA. They were depicted as different-looking from their parents to pacify American viewers whose sons fought for the 'right people', and who wanted to make sure that the refugees into the USA are similar to the 'real Americans' in skin color and values. The children on film look 'All-American', fair-haired with light-colored eyes, hardworking, courageous, with initiative, young people who take their fate into their own hands. Thus, for example, the boy in Zinnemann's *The Search* has 'Aryan' looks, testifying that children's suffering is universal, with no relation to religion or ethnicity. In this way, the Jewish children's suffering is assimilated into the general suffering.[15]

Despite the 12-year gap between *The Sound of Music* and *The Search*, there is no great change in the approach to the Holocaust and its young victims. More is concealed than revealed. When *Schindler's List* came out 33 years later, children were portrayed differently, although there was still a great deal missing. Viewers became accustomed to ignoring the childish aspect of children, often seeing them as icons of adults bearing their troubles as mature

---

13 Filmed in 1993.
14 The figure of the girl in red is drawn from the testimony of Martin Paldi at the Eichmann Trial. His testimony was integrated into Nathan Mansfeld's film, *Gideon Hausner: And I shall speak on their behalf* (Israel Broadcasting Authority, 2005), in which Gavriel Bach, the junior prosecutor in the Eichmann Trial, soon to become Justice Bach, described the intensity of the storm aroused by Paldi's story of how he succeeded in tracking his wife and daughter in the noisy crowd on the ramp 'only thanks to' the little girl's red coat. In Daniel Anker's interview with Spielberg, in his film *Imaginary Witness: Hollywood and the Holocaust* (2004), Spielberg explains how he was influenced by the trial. One of the reasons for making his film in black and white was to symbolize the partial blindness of the nations of the world to the genocide of the Jews. Having the girl in red was intended to make this stand out even more.
15 S. Sand, *Cinema as History: Imagining and directing the 20th Century*, p. 227.

human beings. A closer look at some films reveals portrayals of childhood similar to icons of Jesus as an infant with the face of an adult. For example, *Sophie's Choice*,[16] has the shocking scene in which Sophie is forced to choose which of her children will live and which will die.[17] Nevertheless, the question remains as to why, in the modern age, as Susan Sontag states in her book *On Photography*, when viewers 'prefer representation over reality', has the issue of abuse of children not been raised explicitly in cinema.[18] After all, photographs have the power 'to determine our relationship to reality', and the photograph of a child being killed could be useful when the goal is to portray cruelty towards children in the camps and specific acts between aggressor and victim.

One possible reason is the filmmakers' desire to preserve the survivors' dignity and avoid damaging the memory of the dead, proceeding cautiously so as not to descend into banality which would change the context from an historical event into a cheap pornography of death. Perhaps they felt a sense of responsibility or a desire to expose the ugliness of human behavior without antagonizing an audience seeking to be entertained. After all, the director navigates between terror and wonder, between knowledge and entertainment.

For all these reasons and more, American filmmakers prefer to portray evil taking place elsewhere around the world, such as the Shoah in Europe and the genocide of the Armenians, instead of engaging in internal issues, such as slavery in America's past, or Vietnam.[19] In Sontag's opinion, America feels that its tragic past is incompatible with its patriotic consensus that the USA stands always at the frontier of progress.

An additional important response is found in the film footage taken by the Americans as they liberated Europe in 1945. These films did not comprise footage of children, except for William Wyler's full-length produced in 1945 *Die Todesmühlen/Death Mills*, based on various materials not necessarily filmed by the Americans. It depicts children marching in a row between barbed wire, displaying tattooed numbers on their arms. Documentary films' depiction of children differed from feature films because the camps in Western Europe liberated by the Americans contained mostly male slave laborers. Jewish children, considered unproductive to the Third Reich, had been transported to the death camps in the East, mainly Poland, where most were sent to the gas chambers immediately. The Soviets filmed some child survivors, but there

---

16 Filmed in 1982.
17 Despite the case that in this specific film Sophie, the boy's mother, was Catholic, the viewer's first association is with Jewish children.
18 S. Sontag, *On Photography*.
19 Quoted by A. Mintz, *Popular Culture and the Shaping of Holocaust Memory*, who emphasizes the different understanding of events in different cultures, based on their social outlooks. For example, the memory of the Shoah is different in countries such as Israel, Poland, Germany, France, and the United States, due to earlier pre-war cultural perceptions.

are much fewer visual materials in their archives than the images that reached the West.

These films seem to reject Novick's thesis. More than serving allegedly Jewish interests, they served the American society which was looking for answers about what happened in Europe, what the GIs saw and what they had to cope with. The films touched upon their courage and contribution to saving Europe, but did not turn their eye on the domestic setting. Stephen J. Whitfield, in responding to Novick, stated that America feels it is important to teach the world a lesson, to remember the past so as not to be doomed to repeat it, with the hope of forming universal memory.[20]

Children in European cinema

Ever since the end of the war, the European film industry chose childhood as the prism through which to address the recent Holocaust. France and Italy were the major cinematic arenas for the representation of the Holocaust through children. Showing similar characteristics, French and Italian films often compare the image of the Jewish child to the biblical Binding of Isaac, offered up in sacrifice by his father Abraham. Alternatively, the Holocaust was 'Christianized', with the Jewish child iconized as a suffering Christ figure.[21]

Roberto Benigni's film produced in Italy in 1997, *Life is Beautiful,* is entirely focused on the point of view of the young boy Joshua-Giosué, who joins his father on his journey into the unknown. The model Benigni chooses is essentially a Scriptural model; he gives biblical names to his characters, but with role-reversal. Here, the father consecrates his life to the son and gives him the gift of life, as Jesus did in the New Testament, sacrificing himself for the sins of his 'children'. European viewers understand and identify well with this motif.[22]

Father and son arrive at a concentration camp. It is a world within a world, standing alone with its own codes, command and thinking, understandable only to those in control. The adult world is even more distorted as the father breaks down reality into concepts the boy can accept and understand: it is a 'quiet contest' of hide-and-seek, with a grand prize. Their game is taken from the mythology of Scripture – commandments and obeisance to powers stronger than themselves who control their fate. The boy's world is formed parallel to the adults' world which coexists within it. In contrast to other

20 S. J. Whitfield, 'Reflections on Peter Novick's Holocaust in American Life: Two Perspectives', *Judaism*, pp. 484 – 492. See also: J. D. Popkin, 'Holocaust Memory: Bad for the Jews?', *Judaism*, pp. 112-117.

21 An expanded discussion on Holocaust survivors and the link to Christianity may be found in E. Meir, *Toward an Active Memory: Society, Man and God after Auschwitz*, pp. 73-77.

22 L. Baron, 'Holocaust Film', *Encyclopedia Judaica*, pp. 437-446.

Holocaust films, the uniqueness of *Life is Beautiful* lies not in telling but in showing the boy's world.[23]

The camera takes the viewpoint of the child who sees his father live and die. The film opens with the adult narrator's description of his sublime happiness as a boy in the company of his mother, and his father's death as part of the game which he will explain later in the film. Critics stated, perhaps correctly, that the film was insufficiently descriptive and lacked the minimum number of elements expected in a film attempting to portray a forced labor camp, such as for example, relations between kapos and prisoners, or scenes of hunger, which are missing.

Nevertheless, although the film strives to achieve an adult level of description of the camp, it is the partial memory of the child that Benigni portrays, intensifying the boundless sadness. Even the father's jests seem to be an allegory for the Jewish prisoners who, to the last moment, were unable to believe that anything bad would befall them as long as they fulfilled their guards' strange and impossible demands. In this case, the viewers' 'sorrow and pity' is increased, and the images from the film persist long after it is over.

An additional characteristic of children during the Holocaust in European cinema is the image of the child survivor as brave, talented and resourceful, yet simultaneously similar to the European icon of Jesus suffering on the cross, entreating, "Why have You forsaken me?". Jo, the likeable boy from the Weismann Family in the film *La Rafle* has these qualities.[24] He initiates his escape from the detention camp to make his way to the Free French territory. The boy in *The Island on Bird Street*,[25] learns to survive in inhuman conditions among the ruins of homes, and the hero of the film based on Martin Grey's autobiography, *Au Nom de Tous les Miens/Martin Grey*, 1983, steals from the 'Aryan' side of the ghetto to support his family. All are fair-haired with light-colored eyes, and would not be taken for Jewish were it not for the Yellow Star sewn onto their clothing.

European cinema after Auschwitz shows clearly it is not interested in Jewish identity as something separate from it, nor is it interested in recognizing Jewish suffering as distinct from Europe's suffering. The Jewish identity represented onscreen is not determined only by racist anti-Semitism, which strives to rid the world of Jews, but is associated with humanization,

---

23 See also K. Niv, *Life is Beautiful – but not for Jews: Another look at Benigni's film*. Niv attacks Benigni's film harshly but convincingly. Yet he totally ignores the child's gaze while delving into technical questions of cinematic gaze: the art aspect of the scenery and props, the model of the father's car, and more. His critique would be entirely acceptable but for the simple fact that the inaccuracies and seeming 'bloopers' in the film are actually the result of childhood memory.

24 *La Rafle* [The Roundup] was filmed in 2010.

25 A film produced in 1997.

the major foundation value of humanity.[26] The films create the impression that the children were formed culturally and socially entirely as Europeans, which rules out any stereotypical religious markers which would depict them as different or exceptional.

What is interesting is that in most of the films made around the 1980s, this paradigm is repeated, both in the USA and European cinema. In earlier decades, children and adolescents such as Anne Frank in the film of that name from 1959, or Nicole in Pontecorvo's film *Kapo*[27] were brunettes, their appearance faithfully reflecting the ethnic origins of the heroines they represent. The cinematic choice of these figures was essentially intended to link the plot to the period and visually illustrate the differences in color and race between the Jewish 'other' and the Europeans. Nicole's Christian friends in the concentration camp had light hair and a 'Nordic' appearance. In Cavani's film produced in 1976, *The Night Porter*, the protagonist is dark-haired, although not Jewish. The identification made by the director between coloring (dark) and persecution of the 'other' by Fascist society, is now directed to the persecution of Socialists and Communists who were imprisoned just like the Jews. Thus the dark-featured characters are the persecuted, and the persecutors are the fair-haired ones.

Since 1978, with the screening of the TV miniseries Shoah in the USA, a huge change took place in ratings of film and television programs on the Holocaust, and the subject now became dramatically open for discussion.[28] However, consciously or unconsciously, filmmakers now began to represent the young protagonists of such films as 'the children next door', in order to make the Shoah and its victims universal rather than focusing on the particular, the ethnic and sectorial.[29] The Jewish children on film now began to be represented as not too different,[30] not too stereotypical,[31] but as normal as American kids.[32] The change resulted in casting most of the actors playing the role of Jewish children with blond or very light brown hair and blue eyes, as if all of the directors wished to challenge the issue of race from its aesthetic viewpoint, thus showing how it is erroneous.

Director Istvan Szabo created three thought-provoking films on the two world wars: *Mephisto (1981)*, *Colonel Redl (1984)* and *Hanussen (1988)*, followed by *Sunshine (1999)*, in which the root family tree is represented by the males,

26 Meir, *Toward an Active Memory*, pp. 86-87.
27 Filmed in 1959.
28 Most scholars of this subject refer to 1978 as the watershed year, with *Shoah*'s first US screening. See Sand, *Cinema as History*, pp. 218-259.
29 The way that the process began with the 'naturalization' of Anne Frank by Stevens.
30 To show that there was no concrete 'reason' to persecute them.
31 To break the tendency to think associatively about Jewish children as wearing skullcaps and having sidelocks and traditional black clothing.
32 To identify with the hero and create empathy for the child's adventures.

all played by one actor – Ralph Fiennes, with William Hurt as his brother, neither of whom look very Eastern European. Szabo's success derives from his ability to isolate the cinematic gaze and contemplate the innermost (and tortured) souls of his protagonists.

In *Au Revoir, mes enfants*,[33] the Jewish boy is indistinguishable from his French classmates, with no signs defining 'otherness'. In *La Rafle*, Joseph's 'Nordic' looks help him escape. This trend also stands out in Italian films such as *The Garden of the Finzi-Continis*, filmed in 1970, by Vittorio de Sica. Austrian actor Helmut Berger, who one year earlier had played a degenerate Nazi in Visconti's *The Damned* from the year 1969, was cast as the Jewish brother. Discomfort is inevitable at seeing Berger in a major role in both films, but, more important is the clear association between the figures, concluding that Jewish children are like other children and cannot be identified by external appearance only. However their parents were openly or covertly represented as stereotypically Jewish, such as the actor Gad Almaliah in the role of the father in *La Rafle*.

Even in Tarantino's *Inglourious Basterds*, the Jewish Shoshanna is none other than a lovely blonde, although this time he uses the insight of color/race to make racial theory ridiculous.[34] In the final scene, he juxtaposes the crowds of Nazis who have come to watch the film with the image of the heroine. She is fair and projects warmth,[35] while they are all dark like dark angels, in black uniforms, dark-haired, against a dark background of the auditorium, like the image of Hell from whence they came and to which they will return in the end.

It is interesting in contrast that in Agniecka Holland's film *Europa, Europa* (1990), the young Solomon Perel has dark hair but meets the 'classical Aryan' definition and tells his interrogators 'that his ancestors mixed with Nordics'. The director places his protagonist in several interesting situations that will convince the viewer as it convinced the Nazis of this truth– which is what happened in real life. All believed in the lie that was disguised as the truth of the aesthetic racial theory.

Expressions of Jewish morality are re-validated in extreme situations of survival. In *The Old Man and the Boy*, a film produced in 1957, the boy contradicts the old man's grotesque description of Jews. He tells the old man that he fits the criteria and so must be Jewish. In *The Boy in the Striped Pajamas*,[36] the Jewish boy teaches his friend, son of the camp commandant, what friendship is, and about the humanistic values of love and family, even

---

33 Filmed in 1987.
34 *Inglourious Basterds*, Dir. Quentin Tarantino, USA/ Germany, 2009.
35 She has blonde hair, is dressed in a red dress and lights a fire to burn the Nazis.
36 Filmed in 2008.

though he is the enemy.

Another theme referring to the depiction of Jewish children in postwar films is their geographical space and sense of belonging to the country in which they were born and raised. Their essential civilian identity lies in being French or German or Italian, with a homeland 'Heimat' – and a fatherland – 'Vaterland'.[37] They speak the same language and live the culture of their country through its institutions. This is why the filmmakers usually take time to show the child's school and classroom. The essence of their social and religious identity is emphasized, with no external features such as skullcap or ritual fringes to mark them out as Jewish and Jews.

The choice to focus on the portrayal of children in their own habitat seems to be natural, although later the films show that this is a means of keeping certain evidence secret. Most, if not all earlier European films excluded the drama from distinctly hellish settings such as ghettos, camps and the like. They chose, instead, to depict neutral areas such as streets and houses. As the plots unfolded, they became almost a game between Jew-hunters and fleeing Jews. However, unlike 'cops and robbers', viewers are aware of the real-life deadly consequences. Children as film heroes were usually the only survivors of big families, or two children joined together as a substitute family due to the force of circumstances.[38] Their alternative family was represented by the public space bounded by the ghetto walls, in the Aryan section or in a secret hiding place. In most of the films, it is usually a Gentile with a conscience who comes to the aid of the children; a non-Jew who bears the risk of saving a Jewish child. The major theme of such films is almost always the child's rescue, which becomes the rescuer's salvation. The children in these films serve as models through which the filmmaker deconstructs racist Nazi thinking about Jewish children to show how impossible and absurd it is. Furthermore, heaps of corpses are not normally portrayed, nor are children torn from their mothers' arms only to be sent to a certain death – the actual horrific reality of the Holocaust. If the children were not saved by the end of the film, the conclusions tended to be open-ended, along the unwritten lines of '...and their fate was unknown', instead of specific closure.

---

37 J. Améry, *Beyond Guilt and Atonement: The Attempts of Defeated Man to overcome Defeat*, p. 9

38 In his important article on child survivor testimonies, Boaz Cohen wrote that the vast majority of child survivors were survivors of death marches, ghettos and camps. This fact was not emphasized in the European films. B. Cohen, 'Representing Children's Holocaust: Children's Survivor testimonies published in Fun Lezten Hurban, Munich 1946-1949', in A. J. Patt, M. Berkowitz (eds), *We are Here: New Approaches to Jewish Displaced Persons in Postwar Germany*, p. 84. The writer also notes on page 81 that a majority of children who survived were found with at least one relative, a parent, a cousin or the like. The European films do not reflect this at all, and usually portray a boy, alone against the world. Further testimonies appear in B. Cohen, 'The Children's Voice: Post-War Collection of Testimonies from Children Survivors of the Holocaust', *Holocaust and Genocide Studies*, pp.74-95.

Space considerations allow us only a brief mention of the central theme shared by children's films. The broad common denominator in the above films as well as *Démanty noci*,[39] is their didactic tone and similar structure. At the beginning of each film, the non-Jewish rescuers are portrayed as racist boors, while others are simply indifferent to Jews, especially if they are 'out of sight, out of mind', believing that the Jews would be much better off after being deported to 'their new home'.

In the second stage of the plot, circumstances bring rescuers together with their wards, even if unwillingly. Some of them are aware of the children's condition and extend assistance as if they have no choice. Others become the children's protectors in their role as religious or educational leaders, or due to their status, which enables them to protect the children without conscious knowledge of their ethnic and religious origin. In the third stage of such plots, the rescuers get to know the children emotionally and cognitively, and become close to them through bonds of love and responsibility, they grow so close as to endanger their own lives. Finally, the rescuers are frequently transformed, divesting themselves of their prejudices through the children. They could not have learned their lesson had the plot centered on the rescue of adults.

It is usually the lone child, mostly a boy saved by a non-Jew, who is seen by the viewer as a *tabula rasa* on which the 'New Europe' could be built. The child is the future, while his parents, who represent the past, no longer exist. Through the child survivor, there is new life for Europe. However, up to the new millennium, hardly any of the films present an explicit portrayal of the children's final fate. They seem to take place in a continuous past of childhood which is abruptly stopped. Their past lies at the margins of the cinematic discourse, seen only to orient the viewer to the children's national geographic space and religious affiliation, except for a very few films, such as *The Night Porter*, filmed in 1974, and *Kapo*.

Liliana Cavani's scandalous *Night Porter* tells the story of a young woman who becomes the sex slave of the camp commandant,[40] focusing on her presence as an adult woman. Pontecorvo's *Kapo* is about a Jewish woman who pretends to be a political prisoner and takes on the standing of a *prominente* after being sexually used by the camp guards – and how she finds her death during the camp uprising, which purifies her from all guilt.

The conclusion is clear: the memory of the Holocaust became the source of melodramatic, sentimental cinematic entertainment, disguised as a revelation of 'the truth of the past', attempting the grand didactic task of teaching us 'what really happened'. The European films were a mix of historical simplification

39 *Diamonds of the Night*, directed by Jan Nemec in Czecheslovakia in 1964.
40 She is the daughter of a non-Jewish Socialist political prisoner.

and cinematic guile, breaking through directly and boldly, presenting itself as righteous, but entirely lacking in ideological awareness. The portrayal on film of the survival of Jewish children provides a slight, selective peek at the wartime years in Europe, as if to show that 'at least we tried'. However, it is as if the wartime years of occupation, collaboration, resistance is still an open wound in Europe's consciousness, especially for France and Italy. Very few films have dared to address that period of history; those which made the attempt show hesitance and avoidance.

The change in the portrayal of the children's fate takes place in the new century in films such as *La Rafle,* where it is only hinted at, and in *The Boy in the Striped Pajamas;* crudely but in a clear way. Both children – the Jewish boy and the German son of the camp commandant, enter the gas chamber together and go to their death. The death of the Jewish boy seems trivial by comparison, seemingly required by the circumstances of this distorted story, while the death of the German boy is seen and felt as needless and unfair. The film dictates emotions of identification not with the boy prisoner, the one wearing the striped uniform, but with the son of the man who gave the order to operate the machinery of death. From there, the conclusion is that the death of one little Jewish boy, like millions of others, is unimportant and unworthy of cinematic discussion.

In the film *La Rafle*, as in Spielberg's *Schindler's List*, the stages of hunting down Jews, rounding them up and herding them into the Vélodrome – the large stadium – are covered one by one. The hunger, thirst and illness also receive film treatment that had not been seen before in films on children. Furthermore, the film pays intense attention to the character of the boy Joseph and young Noah, named Nono, portraying them properly as children. They make innocent mistakes that give them away to their hunters, and their final words, which can apply to all of the captured children in their neighborhood, are summed up by Nono's statement, 'I don't understand a thing.' The world of the children is in incomprehensible chaos, and the grown-ups' statement, 'All of us, all of us believed that they wouldn't hurt us,' only adds to the feeling of loss and confusion.

One of the most shocking scenes in the film is when the children find out that they will soon be 'sent to their parents'.[41] Only 3-year-old Nono runs from the clinic to the military truck waiting to take him to his death. The boy, barely a meter tall, stands between the two rows of Vichy collaborators, tall and strong, dressed in spotless uniforms, standing on guard to take the rag-clad little boy to his death. Some of the gendarmes seem embarrassed but continue to follow orders. The sharp contrast to the helpless boy, ending with his being swallowed up into the maw of the open truck, expresses the full horror of the

---

41 They were already killed "in the East".

Holocaust. At these moments the viewer's breath is caught – which is the film's great achievement. *La Rafle* dialogues with *Schindler's List*, which describes a similar situation in Eastern Europe. Both are based on authentic situations and historical research; both have a plot and a message that may be found mostly in documentaries. The difference between the films remains however. *Schindler's List* did not whitewash the German conscience through the figure of Schindler, but addressed the historical event as a traumatic experience, and was consistent with reality. *La Rafle* attempted in a slightly twisted manner to reflect all of France's forces striving for freedom. The film tries to show that the majority of the French were part of the resistance, which is patently false.

In 2006, the BBC screened *Holocaust*, its dramatic historical miniseries, creating a film that is almost a docudrama.[42] It describes events with horrific detail including individual photographs of children from the Drancy transit camp who were shipped to the gas chambers of Auschwitz. The adults who accompanied the children to their death and the camp guard give their unambiguous testimonies in interviews. Clear, unambiguous statements describe their arrival in Auschwitz, the guards' treatment of the children and how they felt they were dolls in a game who had to be disassembled, i.e., killed and 'finished up'.[43]

As detailed but slightly different is Lajos Koltai's film produced in 2005 *Fateless*, based on Nobel prizewinner Imre Kertész's autobiography of the same name. The plot combines the narrative aesthetic of classical European cinema with the literary narrative of American movies to capture the story of the camps through the eyes of the boy. *Fateless* is very sensitive to its subject. It explains the essence of the boy's existence and survival, without going into great detail about the enigmatic operations of the camp. Based on a profound understanding of the nature of suffering and its adaptation into cinema, the showpiece of the concentration and death camp is replaced by seemingly minor, but strong elements drawn from the experience of childhood. The director shows events through the innocent, childish gaze of young prisoners who are starving. In an extremely chilling scene, the director intelligently used a long, extended look by a young prisoner gazing directly at a German guard chewing his flaky sausage roll with a hearty appetite. The starving boy imitates the motions of the German's jaw and mimics his frenzied chewing

---

42 *Auschwitz: The Nazi 'Final Solution,' Part 3,* Dir. Laurence Rees, UK, 2006.
43 In the documentary *Einzatzgruppen: Les Commandos de la mort,* Dir. Michael Prazan, for France 2 and Planète, produced with the support of the Region of Ile de France (France, 2009), an ex-soldier was asked why they killed the children – while a hidden camera filmed the answer. 'After all', the filmmaker asked, 'they didn't do anything to you'. The soldier responded, 'True, the children were not to blame, but their Jewish parents were considered dangerous and had to be destroyed.' The children symbolized future danger, which is why they had to be killed when young.

while imagining that he is the one consuming the meal, but then he finds that his saliva has dried up. The boy's miserable look is captured in a close-up shot which the director closes on his face to preserve the definition of 'hunger' in the collective memory of all who view this scene. The lad's hungry gaze is many times more powerful than any scene that could be filmed of a starving adult.

Even in Germany, children during the Holocaust constituted a major narrative in the cinematic discourse, but the choice was different. They were not Jewish or survivors, but the heroes of German films were Germans portrayed as German victims. The aggressors were the ones wearing the black uniforms. German cinema chose to subdivide the world into Nazis, the villains, and regular Germans, the 'good ones'. The Nazis were the ones in uniform, and the simple citizens were civilians who fought the phenomenon. In *NAPOLA* (*Before the Fall,* 2005) a German boy is recruited against his parents' will and sent to the school for cadets where he finds Nazism and the Nazis lacking in content, threatening and dangerous.

A very important figure who is repeatedly seen onscreen in postwar films concentrating on Nazi Germany is Sophie Scholl of Munich, a young student who joined the White Rose underground with her brother. They distributed broadsheets intended to arouse popular resistance, but were captured, interrogated by the Gestapo, and executed on the guillotine. Sophie is a model figure in German society, commemorated in many mediums, such as stamps, and numerous made-for-TV movies and feature films. *Sophie Scholl: The Final Days*, directed in 2005 by Marc Rothemund, responds to the earlier 1982 film by Michael Verhoeven, *Die Weiße Rose*. Set in 1933-1945, the heroes are the children of the 'good Germans', and the villains are the Nazis in uniform. Jewish youth and their history is utterly lacking in these films, although one may think that the goal of the filmmakers is to show that there was a German opposition, which, had it succeeded in overthrowing the regime, would obviously also have succeeded in saving Germany's Jews.

Even when it is obvious that the German cinema is ripe for coping with the issue, once again, in the film *The Nasty Girl*, filmed in 1990, it is a young woman in postwar Germany who is seeking answers to what went on in her town during the war years. She is the only one who can look her family and community straight in the eye and say out loud, 'J'accuse'.

The film produced in 2008 based on Bernhard Schlink's book *The Reader* also arouses an uncomfortable feeling. There is an evident absence of Jewish peers after the war and an even more discordant lack of the victims in the Nazi lover's past, which clearly show director's choice of narrative. This is a film about Germany and a German boy of the generation of the 'New Germany', the 'other' Germany, coping with his country's past, embodied by an 'Aryan' beauty. She is the victim, while the narrative and the physiological embodiment of the boy makes him the historian protecting his country's ignorance in the present and its evil in the past. This means that the younger generation is protecting the parents' generation of evildoers.

About one year later, the film *Berlin 36*, produced in 2009, was screened in cinemas and art movie houses. It centers on Gretel Bergmann, a young Jewish athlete, considered the greatest high jumper of her time. Her participation in the Berlin 1936 Olympics became an international affair. The Americans made her participation in the Olympics a condition of their participation, after the International Olympics Committee made Jewish participation a condition of Germany holding the Olympics. The Germans in uniform agree because they have no choice. Gretel participates, but numerous obstacles are placed in her path by her teammates and managers. Then a strange German, Marie Ketteler, joins the team. Marie is a top athlete, and is meant to defeat Gretel in the championship team and keep her out of the Olympics. But Marie is actually a boy who was forced by Nazi officials to disguise himself as a girl. The viewer's tendency to side with the young people is now divided between the Jewish victim and the lad made a prisoner of his own body. The friendship between the two turns into romance, but is this realistic? Gretel, of course, has light reddish hair, like the Finzi-Continis, while her parents, especially the mother, are depicted as Eastern Europeans in behavior and looks. The 'villains', the Nazis, are the ones in uniform, while those in authority in civilian clothes (the coach), are the good and the fair.[44] However, the film has its moments: the protagonist of a German film is Jewish for a change, a representation not seen in previous films. The end is foreseen: Gretel succeeds in leaving with her family for New York. A happy end …

In Holland, Belgium and Luxembourg, there were very few popular films dealing with children in the Holocaust or childhood during World War II. The only slight exception in this context is the 2002 film *Twin Sisters*,[45] a story of twin girls born into a 'mixed marriage' of Catholic and Protestant late in the Nazi occupation of Holland. When the girls' parents die and they are separated, one is given to the Catholic side of the family – a family of ignorant and primitive farmers, who abuse the girl and cause her to be sterile. The second goes to the Protestant relatives. She grows up happily under good conditions. Their struggle for survival during the war years is the major subject of the film. Through their eyes the true face of European 'propriety' is revealed. The Catholic farmers' display crudeness and cruelty to themselves and their relatives and certainly to outsiders, and the Protestants' 'pious fairness' means that they are willing to inform on Jews in the name of 'law and order', and steal food from their own relatives, not caring if they

---

44 They represent German civilians.
45 The film was directed by Ben Sombogaart.

starve to death.

Conclusion

An analysis of postwar world cinema leads us to conclude that films engaged in the depiction of war in all its aspects have created and structured a cinematic consensus in which moods and the spirit of the time are expressed, as well as the spirit of social and cultural events associated with wars. In Europe, children in the Holocaust are represented as the sole litmus test of what Europe is 'supposed' to feel for its murdered children, but the results are slightly distorted.

Through the cinematic representation of Jewish children during the Holocaust, a process of 'Christianization' and 'iconization' makes it easier for viewers to see and identify with the persecuted Jewish child. The Jewish children are very energetic, with great initiative and resourcefulness, which makes them especially liked, and provides the justification for saving them or wishing them to survive. Their representation as Europeans who are dissimilar to the common Jewish stereotype makes it easier to identify with the children, who look like 'the kids next door', or the viewer's co-religionists. They usually look very European – fair-haired with light eyes. They are portrayed as moral lovers of justice, which arouses empathy towards them. There are not many scenes of ghettos or concentration camps.[46] There is always one good person in the worst situations – a non-Jew who saves the Jewish child – and shares his fate. Usually, the fate of the children is 'unknown', and the viewer is spared dealing with the direct knowledge of their murder, again, except for the later films, some of which prefer to portray the non-Jewish murder victim instead of the murdered Jewish child.

Suggested Reading

Imre Kertész, *Fateless*, 1992.

Bibliography

J. Améry, *Beyond Guilt and Atonement: The Attempts of Defeated Man to Overcome Defeat*, Tel Aviv, Am Oved, 2000.
L. Baron, *Projecting the Holocaust into the Present: The Changing Focus of Contemporary Holocaust Cinema*, San Diego, San Diego State University, 2004.
Idem., 'Holocaust Film', *Encyclopedia Judaica*, Detroit, Thomson-Gale, 2006,

---

46 Except for the newer films after 2000.

vol. 9.

R. J. Berger, *Fathoming the Holocaust: A Social Problems Approach*, New York, de Gruyter, 2002.

J. E. Doneson, 'The American History of Anne Frank's Diary', *Holocaust Genocide Studies*, 1987, pp.149-160.

B. Cohen, 'Representing Children's Holocaust: Children's Survivor testimonies published in Fun Lezten Hurban, Munich 1946-1949', in A. J. Patt, M. Berkowitz (eds), *We are Here: New Approaches to Jewish Displaced Persons in Postwar Germany*, Detroit, Wayne State University Press, 2010.

Idem., 'The Children's Voice: Post-War Collection of Testimonies from Children Survivors of the Holocaust', *Holocaust and Genocide Studies*, 2007, pp.73-95.

L. Douglas, *The Memory of Judgment: Making Law and History at the Trials of the Holocaust*, New Haven, Yale University Press, 2001.

Y. Kozlovsky Golan, 'The Shaping of the Holocaust Visual Conscience by the Nuremberg Trials. Birth of the Holocaust in Hollywood-Style Motion Pictures: The Impact of the Movie "Nazi Concentration Camps"', *Search and Research: Lectures and Papers*. International Institute for Holocaust Research, Yad Vashem, Jerusalem, 2006, vol. 9.

V. Lebeau, *Childhood and Cinema*. London, Reaktion Books, 2008.

E. Meir, *Toward an Active Memory. Society, Man and God after Auschwitz*, Tel Aviv, Resling, 2006.

A. Mintz, *Popular Culture and the Shaping of Holocaust Memory*, Seattle, University of Washington Press, 2001.

K. Niv, *Life is Beautiful – but not for Jews: Another look at Benigni's film*, Tel Aviv, N.B. Books, 2000.

P. Novick, *The Holocaust and Collective Memory: The American Experience*. London, Bloomsbury, 2000.

J. D. Popkin, 'Holocaust Memory: Bad for the Jews?', *Judaism*, 2001, pp.49-84.

S. Sand, *Cinema as History: Imagining and directing the 20th Century*, Tel Aviv, Am Oved, 2002.

S. Sontag, *On Photography*, New York, Farrar, Straus & Giroux, 1977.

S. J. Whitfield, 'Reflections on Peter Novick's Holocaust in American Life: Two Perspectives', *Judaism*, 2000, pp.484-492.

10   Girls at War: Historical Perspectives and Representations

Jane Rice

Introduction

Child soldiers and girl soldiers have gained increased attention in recent years, particularly in light of the many brutal post-colonialist civil wars in Africa and Latin America but also because of the role of children in the so-called War on Terror in Afghanistan and Iraq. This new attention, however, masks the fact that children have always been part of war. Well-known examples including accounts of boy soldiers taking part in the American War of Independence and World War I.[1] However even when children do not take part in direct action, they are still deeply involved. Children cannot be separated and isolated from the consequences of conflict because modern warfare is interpersonal in nature, entering the home, school and other locations that children frequent. Their parents, older siblings, neighbours and friends may be involved in the conflict and may become victims of the conflict. Children also experience the causes of the war in their daily lives, manifested in instances of economic, social and political discrimination. In addition there are hundreds of accounts where children participate in war, be that formally as combatants in armed groups (both state and non-state) or informally or indirectly by carrying out ancillary roles for armed groups.

The current discourse of humanitarian agencies, supported by governments, casts children solely as victims. This discourse emphasises the need for children to be protected, separated and sheltered from war and proclaims that children may gain nothing positive from conflict and may have no influence except perhaps in programmes which pay lip service to their role in 'peace building'. However, rather than trying to separate children from war, this chapter will argue that children should be recognised for the ways in which war affects them, not only negatively but positively. Children participate in war not only because they are coerced or for reasons of revenge; their reasons

1   See D. Rosen, *Armies of the Young: Child Soldiers in War and Terrorism*.

are complex and contradictory but often rational as well. By ignoring their experiences and agency in war and dismissing them as victims, children are done a great disservice. Children suffer great political and social injustice from governments, and unequal social structures supported by rich elites and may join non-state armed groups because they see them as the only actors trying to change these inequalities. When we dismiss child soldiers as victims of immoral, illegitimate armed groups their experiences and struggles for justice are ignored and political, social and economic inequalities go unchanged.

This chapter will argue that that the representation of female child soldiers as passive victims of meaningless wars is a way for governments, NGOs and other interested parties to discredit their opponents, in this case armed groups, and gain unarguable moral authority for their own regimes, *casus belli* or missions. In addition, the image of a vulnerable girl with no political agency who is a victim of so-called brutal non-state armed groups conceals the social, economic and political realities which may be the reasons for the war and the reasons why girls join in the first place. Governments and humanitarian organisations have a get-out clause: they can focus on helping these victims of child exploitation rather than solving the social injustices which plague their country.

Examining how girl soldiers have been represented before and after they became a target of international humanitarian agencies, the paper focuses on three examples: the independence war in Mozambique in the 1960s, the recent civil war in Sierra Leone and the on-going Colombian civil war. For each conflict, the paper will show how female child soldiers have been characterised and how these characterisations are designed to legitimise stakeholders. It will show that the consequences of characterisations which present female child soldiers as one-dimensional victims can have a negative effect on female child soldiers, as it denies their political agency and experiences of social, economic and political injustice.

Rather than being one dimensional, agency-less victims and sex slaves, as they are more often than not represented by the humanitarian world and by governments, this paper argues that a far more constructive and productive representation is one which is complex and multi-layered, while at the same time not diminishing the effects of war or glamorizing those who fight. It is important, therefore, to examine girls' individual decisions, motivations, and experiences in armed conflict and to place these narratives within the political, economic and social realm, analysing the larger societal injustices and how these influence children and girls. These structural causes of armed conflict, which lead girls to fight, can only be solved by deep system-level change.

I will first examine the origins of this representation and will then demonstrate with evidence from the war of independence in Mozambique that this representation has not always existed. Comparing this older representation to more recent representations of girl soldiers in the newer conflicts of the civil wars in Colombia and Sierra Leone, it can be demonstrated that there are political purposes behind them. The paper will conclude with a look at the consequences for girls and at ways of constructing positive routes out of conflict for them. Challenging and changing the social injustices of society, especially those which led to the conflict should lie at the heart of conflict resolution, but this is often drowned out by calls to delegitimize armed groups because, among other immoral acts, they use child soldiers.

The humanitarian conception of childhood

The current conception of childhood used by western stakeholders in many conflicts such as NGOs and governments can be described as 'the straight-18 position'.[2] This refers to the idea that childhood and all the rights, responsibilities and capabilities that come with it, ends on the eighteenth birthday. This definition of a 'child' is problematic as in many societies childhood does not begin when one is born nor end on one's eighteenth birthday.[3] The straight-18 position ignores local understandings of the capabilities and capacities of young people and denies the possibility that children may gain skills, competencies and coping mechanisms at younger ages than children in the west. The straight-18 position together with theories of staged development (such as Jean Piaget's stages of cognitive development) were devised in the West, coming out of the Enlightenment period with the creation of formal schooling, the end of child labour and the emergency of the concept of childhood innocence.[4] This notion of childhood is regularly exported and projected onto non-western societies, all the time ignoring the cultural, social, economic and political context which creates a different experience for children.

An example of this process is the use of the straight-18 position in the United Nations Convention on the Rights on the Child (CRC) defining a specific group who can be protected by certain rights.[5] This is now the definition used by humanitarian agencies and governments around the world.

Although this convention affirms the special rights of everyone under the age of 18 (which is a huge number of people in the world), it also implies that they should be treated the same, no matter whether they are five years old or nearly 18. This treatment denies their agency and any kind of political interest

2   Rosen, *Armies of the Young*.
3   J. Hart, 'Displaced children's participation in political violence: Towards greater understanding of mobilisation', *Conflict, Security & Development*, pp. 277-293; Rosen, *Armies of the Young*.
4   Rosen, *Armies of the Young*.
5   Ibid.

they may have in conflict. Instead, they are all seen as victims.

Popular representations of child soldiers

Popular conceptions and representations of child soldiers in the global literature are, it can be argued, a collection of assumptions, misconceptions and oversimplifications. The common image in NGO literature is often one of a lost looking boy clutching an AK-47. Denov argues that in these portrayals of child soldiers, children are exoticized and taken out of any political context and thus essentialised.[6] These representations of the innocent victim are present in popular memoirs of child soldiers such as Ishmael Beah's *A Long Way Gone* (2007) and *War Child: A Boy Soldier's Story* by Emmanuel Jal (2009). The child soldiers in these accounts show no political agency and very little political knowledge about the conflict they have been forced into fighting for. The image presented by the media and Northern states is very often one of evil, violent, unrepentant, sociopathic youth. They are still apolitical though, and have been so damaged and corrupted by war that they can never be rehabilitated.[7] These children are so pathologically violent that they are dangerous to the rest of society, especially after conflict. These portrayals feed into theories of young men (especially from the global South) as a major security threat to the global North.[8] Child soldiering is shown to be a violation of childhood innocence; any notion that children may have agency and they are using that agency to fight for something they want to change being completely ignored.[9]

A major problem with this portrayal is that it focuses on boys, although it uses the gender neutral term 'child soldier'. Indeed, most popular portrayals of child soldiers appear to be gender neutral when they actually are focusing on boys.[10] The emphasis on boys has been partly due to the patriarchal nature of the societies combined with a concern during post-conflict security about the reintegration of male combatants rather than female members of armed groups, usually regarded as only undertaking ancillary roles rather than combat roles.[11] In recent years girls have come to be recognised as taking

---

6   M. Denov, *Child Soldiers. Sierra Leone's Revolutionary United Front*, p. 19.
7   Ibid.
8   Ibid.
9   Hart, 'Displaced children's participation in political violence', pp. 277-293.
10 M. Denov, R. Maclure, R. Maclure, 'Engaging the Voices of Girls in the Aftermath of Sierra Leone's Conflict: Experiences and Perspectives in a Culture of Violence', *Anthropologica*, pp. 73-85; M. G. Wessells, *The Recruitment and Use of Girls in Armed Forces and Groups in Angola: Implications for Ethical Research and Reintegration*, Working Paper, Ford Institute for Human Security.
11 Wessells, *The Recruitment and Use of Girls*, pp. 2-3.

part in war and a huge number of articles reflect this.[12] Nevertheless, authors rarely explain their reasons for joining as political and continue to relegate them to involuntary sexual or domestic roles. Many authors simply state the finding that girls are participating in conflict and fail to go into deeper analysis of their involvement. The refocus on girls is more helpful for those stakeholders who want an easy way to discredit non-state armed groups. Girls can be victimised more easily than boys who, as described above, can often be characterised as violent, politicised youth. Women and girls' motivations for joining armed groups and their experiences can easily be derailed and dismissed as exploitation, due partly to women's perceived role in society.

Girls are often represented as having been kidnapped in order to serve the male commanders as 'wives' or sex slaves. If girls are portrayed as having joined 'freely' then it is usually to protect a family member.[13] Representations of female soldiers are also often highly sexualised.[14] Following this, Sjoberg and Gentry argue that women who take part in political violence have often been portrayed as filling one of three roles – a 'mother' who is satisfying a

12 See for example: R. Brett, *Girl Soldiers: Challenging Assumptions*; C. Coulter, M. Persson, M. Utas, *Young Female Fighters in African Wars Conflict and Its Consequences*; M. Denov, 'Wartime Sexual Violence: Assessing a Human Security Response to War-Affected Girls in Sierra Leone', *Security Dialogue*; M. Denov, *Girls in fighting Forces: Moving Beyond Victimhood*, A Summary of the Research Findings on Girls and Armed Conflict from CIDA's Child Protection Research Fund; M. Denov, 'Girl Soldiers and Human Rights: Lessons from Angola, Mozambique, Sierra Leone and Northern Uganda', *The International Journal of Human Rights*; M. Denov, C. Gervais, 'Negotiating (In)Security: Agency, Resistance, and Resourcefulness among Girls Formerly Associated with Sierra Leone's Revolutionary United Front', *Signs: Journal of Women in Culture and Society*; M. Denov, R. Maclure, *Girls and Small Arms in Sierra Leone: Victimization, Participation, and Resistance*, Paper presented for the International Studies Association Conference; Denov, Maclure, Maclure, 'Engaging the Voices of Girls'; M. Fox, 'Girl Soldiers: Human Security and Gendered Insecurity', *Security Dialogue*; Y. E. Keairns, *The Voices of Girl Child Soldiers: Summary*; T. Lyons, *Guns and Guerrilla Girls: Women in the Zimbabwean Liberation Struggle*; D. Mazurana, K. Carlson, *From Combat to Community: Women and Girls of Sierra Leone*; D. E. Mazurana, S. McKay, K.C. Carlson, J. C. Kasper, 'Girls in Fighting Forces and Groups: Their Recruitment, Participation, Demobilization, and Reintegration', *Peace and Conflict: Journal of Peace Psychology*; S. McKay, 'The Effects of Armed Conflict on Girls and Women', *Peace and Conflict: Journal of Peace Psychology*; S. McKay, 'Reconstructing fragile lives: girls' social reintegration in northern Uganda and Sierra Leone', *Gender and Development*; S. McKay, 'Girls as "Weapons of Terror" in Northern Uganda and Sierra Leonean Rebel Fighting Forces', *Studies in Conflict & Terrorism*; S. McKay, D. E. Mazurana, *Where are the Girls? Girls in Fighting Forces in Northern Uganda, Sierra Leone, and Mozambique: Their Lives During and After War*; C. Nordstrom, *Girls and Warzones: Troubling Questions*; E. Paez, *Girls in the Colombian Armed Forces: a diagnosis*; S. Shepler, 'Les filles-soldats: trajectories d'apres-guerre en Sierra Leone', *Politique Africaine*; M. Utas, 'Agency of Victims: Young women in the Liberian civil war', in F. Honwana, F. de Boeck, (eds.), *Makers and Breakers: Children and Youth in Postcolonial Africa*; Wessells, *The Recruitment and Use of Girls*; H. G. West, 'Girls with Guns: Narrating the Experience of war of FRELIMO's 'Female Detachment', in J. Boyden, J. De Berry, (eds.), *Children and Youth on the Front Line: Ethnography, Armed Conflict and Displacement.*

13 Phillips, 'A Soldier Returns', *Developments Magazine.*

14 C. Coulter, 'Female fighters in the Sierra Leone war: challenging the assumptions', *Feminist Review*, pp. 54-73.

biological urge to avenge the death of a loved one or to protect loved ones, a 'monster' who is obviously psychologically ill or a 'whore' who is participating in political violence because of sexual dependence on men.[15]

Although Sjoberg and Gentry do not examine the representation of girl soldiers, their central thesis is that women are depoliticized because of their gender. I would add that girl soldiers are depoliticized because of both their age and their gender. As illustrated above, children are perceived as having no political agency or identity and that the only possible explanation for their participation is biological, sexual, psychological or the fault of others, not because of any rational decision making on their own part. For Nordstrom, girls were often 'considered only as silent victims of (sexual) violence – devoid of agency, moral conscience, economic potential or political awareness'.[16] These portrayals ignore the complexities of girls' recruitment and deny the fact that girls may suffer great political, social and economic inequalities that they want to change by joining armed groups.

The humanitarian community has bought into these portrayals partly because the nature of humanitarian work demands the presentation of people in conflicts as depoliticized and traumatised, not as exhibiting any kind of agency. It is this imagery which gains donations and support.[17] Lenz argues that complex portrayals of child soldiers, where their agency is emphasised, also complicate the legitimate narrative of war and may create an entirely new one, which can also have severe political implications.[18] When children talk about their experiences of conflict their capacity for agency and for managing their own survival is ignored. Vanessa Pupavac contends that humanitarian programmes always reflect western donor interests rather than the interests and needs of the society whose children they are trying to help.[19]

Women and children in armed groups present a challenge for state armies who have to obey international human rights norms and cultural and social norms.[20] Thus states that are fighting irregular forces that use girl soldiers (for example the Colombian state fighting the FARC) portray those groups as immoral and the girls within them as victims of sexual and physical abuse. State armies gain legitimacy and moral authority for themselves by condemning the immorality of the opposite side and thus, indirectly

---

15 L. Sjoberg, C. E. Gentry, *Mothers, Monsters, Whores: Women's violence in global politics.*
16 Nordstrom, *Girls and Warzones: Troubling Questions*, p. 36.
17 L. Edmundson, 'Marketing Trauma and the Theatre of War in Northern Uganda', *Theatre Journal.*
18 Ibid, p. 469.
19 V. Pupavac, 'Misanthropy without Borders: The International Children's Rights Regime'.
20 N. Herrera, D. Porch, '"Like going to a fiesta" – the role of female fighters in Colombia's FARC-EP', *Small Wars & Insurgencies*; M. Trawick, *Enemy Lines: Warfare, Childhood and Play in Batticaloa.*

emphasising the morality, innocence and pureness of motive of their fight.[21] However by taking these positions on child soldiers, NGOs and governments not only negate the strength and resilience child soldiers have shown in being able to survive, but also negate the legitimacy of political injustices these girls may have suffered from the state.

Girls, I argue, are misrepresented twice over; firstly because they are children and are seen as apolitical with no active role; and secondly, they are female and seen as only capable of filling nurturing, caring and sexual roles and being of a lower status than men or boys in society. Girls in armed groups challenge the received traditional notion that war is a place for men who go off to fight for the protection of women and children. This stereotype emphasises both women and children's apolitical nature and the fact that they are unaffected and disinterested by politics and war; that this is a man's realm.

Historic representations

Girl soldiers have not always been portrayed in this way. In the Mozambique war of independence, women played a significant role in the greater war effort but especially in combat. FRELIMO (*Frente de Libertação de Moçambique*– Liberation Front of Mozambique) was the socialist independence movement fighting against Portuguese colonial occupation.[22] FRELIMO actively encouraged girls to join as it furthered the morality and legitimacy of their socialist cause.[23] Freedom for Mozambique, FRELIMO claimed, also meant the emancipation of women. Their representation in the west followed their self-proclaimed reasons for girls recruitment – their most famous soldier, Graça Machel now leading the global campaign against the use of child soldiers, has defended her role in the war of independence.

In Mozambique, girls have been portrayed as joining up freely to fight for a moral political ideology, in this case the independence of Mozambique from its cruel colonial oppressors. As was the case in many of the independence wars in Africa, many women and girls participated in the war in Mozambique through roles not dissimilar to those they undertook in the household.[24] Girls in Mozambique however also took part in combat as part of the DF

---

21 A. McIntyre, 'Introduction', in A. McIntyre (ed.), *Invisible Stakeholders: The Impact of Children on War*, p. 1.
22 Although FRELIMO later became a government force, I only examine its time during the independence war period when it was a non-state armed group.
23 West, 'Girls with Guns'.
24 S. Arnfred, 'Women in Mozambique: Gender Struggle and Gender Politics', *Review of African Political Economy*; C. Bop,'Women in Conflicts, their gains and their losses', in S. Meintjes, A. Pillay, M. Turshen (eds.), *The Aftermath: Women in Post-Conflict Transformation*; West, 'Girls with Guns'.

(*DestacamentoFeminino*– Female Detachment) movement.[25]

Women and girls were fully engaged and a played a key role in this conflict. Comparing this participation and the attitude towards them with the current representations it becomes clear that a fundamental shift has taken place. This change is, I argue, due mainly to the change in the nature of conflicts but also a change in how these conflicts are fought.

The characterisation of new wars

The old conflicts are the independence wars of Africa and Cold War proxy wars. These wars are characterised as having a clear political and moral motive. They were either for the purposes of over-throwing colonial rulers or were a fight against capitalism or communism. The groups fighting had legitimate claims to power as they were defending or liberating themselves or others against an often external threat, be that colonial rule or a 'foreign' political ideology. The focus was entirely on political goals.

In comparison the modern conflicts, dubbed by Mary Kaldor the 'new wars' are post-independence, internal conflicts which are motivated very often by identity, ethnic struggles, competition over economic resources, power and state formation and aim to control the population rather than territory.[26]

These new post-cold war conflicts are often portrayed as having unclear political motives or political motives obscured and corrupted by the armed groups taking illegitimate actions such as the trade of 'blood diamonds', drugs and human trafficking. Indeed the use of child soldiers is another action that has caused them to be deemed immoral and has delegitimised their political claims. In addition to obscuring their political demands, this view also draws attention to non-state armed groups' motivation for control of natural resources, be they drugs or diamonds or minerals, rather than 'pure' political ideology. A further problem with the depiction of these new wars is that the non-state armed groups are often irregular armies which blur the distinction between civilian and combatant, making the situation of children who participate in these wars even more complex. In summary, the new wars can be described as complex, corrupt, brutal and excessively violent and as utilising unjust means. All of these obscure and legitimise the political purposes of the conflict and the social, political and economic injustices which have caused them.

The recent civil war in Sierra Leone and the current civil conflict in Colombia are both examples of these new wars. Both the RUF (Revolutionary United Front) in Sierra Leone and the FARC (*Fuerzas Armadas Revolucionarias de Colombia – Ejércitodel Pueblo* – Revolutionary Armed Forces of Colombia –

---

25 West, 'Girls with Guns'.
26 M. Kaldor, *New and Old Wars: Organized Violence in a Global Era*.

People's Army) are examples of non-state armed groups that have used girl soldiers. However, the ways in which these groups have been talked and written about differ hugely from the way FRELIMO was ever represented. The FARC, like FRELIMO, is a left-wing Marxist non-state armed group based on a socialist ideology. Like FRELIMO, the recruitment of women and girls has been part of its emancipatory ideology. However contrary to FRELIMO, they have been criticised harshly for their use of combatants under the age of 18. In addition, the FARC is perhaps most famous for its role in the illegal drugs trade, particularly cocaine trafficking. It has regularly kidnapped politicians (including, infamously, the presidential candidate Ingrid Betancourt, who was held captive for six and a half years), wealthy individuals and soldiers for both political and financial reasons. Due to these illegitimate acts of war, the FARC has completely lost any political authenticity, leverage and morality. Its political demands have become obscured by its actions, which are not accepted actions in war. Although the FARC is not the only belligerent in the Colombian civil war engaged in these kinds of activities, it has, more than any other group in the Colombian Civil War, become synonymous with these perceived deplorable and immoral acts of war. The FARC has engaged in deplorable acts of war and should of course be criticised for these, but it should not be singled out as the only belligerent in the Colombian civil war that is engaging in these acts. FRELIMO did not knowingly participate in similar acts, partly due to the nature of the war it was participating in and partly due to receiving funding and support from sympathetic allies. Therefore it did not need to engage in criminal acts such as kidnapping or drug dealing to raise funds.

Girls' experiences in non-state armed groups

Non-state armed groups are not only criticised for the fact that they use children in war, but also for the way in which they use them. Non-state armed groups' use of girl soldiers is often reduced down to girls' existence as sex objects. Girls in non-state armed groups are sex slaves or are only in the armed group for sexual reasons (see analysis of Sjoberg and Gentry, above). Both the FARC and RUF have been criticised for their use of rape and sexual abuse of girl recruits.

Both the Colombian and US governments have been particularly vocal in their criticism of the FARC's use of women and girls and claims that they cannot be anything other than victims and sex slaves of a brutal organisation.[27] "'Communities that are so isolated, such as the FARC camps, have a need for

27 Herrera, Porch, "'Like going to a fiesta'".

women', insists Sergio Jaramillo, Colombian Deputy Minister of Defense".[28] Others add that when female combatants become pregnant they are forced to have abortions, which sometimes occur late and in unfit conditions.[29]

However, what is ignored in the case of the FARC, are their own rules around relationships between soldiers. A study by Human Rights Watch states:

> Although rape and overt sexual harassment are not tolerated, many male commanders use their power to form sexual liaisons with under-age girls. Girls as young as twelve are required to use contraception, and must have abortions if they get pregnant.[30]

Likewise, Herrera and Porch's research on female recruits in the FARC found that if a man wants to have sexual relations with a girl, the girl must consent.[31]

Many girls in the RUF have also reportedly suffered from severe sexual and physical abuses.[32] Although there is no similar evidence of strict rules around relationships and pregnancy in the RUF, girls have also used sexual relations with men for their own advantage. Girls have been reported having sex with senior commanders in order to gain food, security and relief from hard labour.[33] Similarly, girls in the FARC and the RUF would 'marry' a senior commander in order protect themselves from sexual abuse by other male soldiers. It would also gain them higher status as they would often share the status of their husband.[34]

In FRELIMO, on the other hand, there were very few reports of sexual and physical abuse of young female combatants during the independence struggle.[35] This is partly due to the nature of the wars – the conflicts in Colombia and Sierra Leone have been precisely about controlling people and girls may only be used in these groups for sexual purposes. In Mozambique, however, the FRELIMO leadership was concerned that its soldiers not be a threat to civilians because Mozambicans were not the enemy and were depended on for support.[36]

28 Ibid, p. 610.
29 Ibid.
30 S. Brett, *"You'll Learn Not to Cry": Child Combatants in Colombia*, p. 10.
31 Herrera, Porch, '"Like going to a fiesta"'.
32 Coulter, 'Female fighters in the Sierra Leone war'.
33 Ibid.
34 L. Cortes, M. J. Buchanan, 'The experience of Colombian Child Soldiers from a resilience perspective', *International Journal for the Advancement of Counselling*; Denov, Gervais, 'Negotiating (In)Security'; Herrera, Porch, '"Like going to a fiesta"'.
35 Fox, 'Girl Soldiers'.
36 West, 'Girls with Guns'.

As well as using their gender and sexuality in order to maintain their own security, girls have also been known to use other weapons of war for this purpose. Denov and Gervais found that girls who were willing to perpetuate violence often gained respect from commanders, more food, raised their profile and sometimes gained promotion.[37] Adopting 'masculine' traits also protected girls more from abuse compared to girls who only performed ancillary roles.[38] Being able to quickly adapt to new situations and engage with violence had the effect of reducing soldiers' feelings of victimisation and left soldiers less emotionally and mentally damaged.[39] More practically, girls in the RUF reported that having a gun also offered them protection against abuse and violence directed towards them and decreased their feelings of victimization. At the same time, a gun gave them feelings of authority, status, control, self confidence and a sense of belonging and supremacy, particularly over civilians.[40] Within the context of the armed group, girls felt a sense of relief from their victim status and managed to have some control over their lives and experiences.

Modern portrayals of child soldiers are an important part of portrayals and dismissals of the political aims of non-state armed groups. This is evidenced in the wording of Article 4 of the Optional Protocol to the Convention on the Rights of the Child, which states that no child under 18 should participate in a non-state armed group, in contrast to state armed forces for which the minimum age for voluntary recruitment is 15 years.[41] This is an obvious example of the reaffirmation of state forces as the only location for political violence with all other groups being illegal.

Far from being passive and often sexual victims of non-state armed groups, the reality is far more complex and nuanced. There have been cases of rape and sexual violence in the FARC and RUF but the current discourse is one which gives unfair emphasis to girl soldiers as victims rather than as political actors who enter armed groups for their own purposes.

Politics as lived experience and motivation

The shift in portrayal from the old wars to the new is, as stated above, a way for state governments to delegitimise non-state armed groups and reclaim their

---

37 Denov, Gervais, 'Negotiating (In)Security'.
38 A. Twum-Danso, *Africa's Young Soldiers: The Co-option of Childhood,* pp. 41-42.
39 Cortes, Buchanan, 'The experience of Colombian Child Soldiers'; Denov, Gervais, 'Negotiating (In)Security'.
40 Coulter, 'Female fighters in the Sierra Leone war', p. 60; Coulter, Persson, Utas, *Young Female Fighters in African Wars Conflict,* p. 15; Denov, Gervais, 'Negotiating (In)Security, p. 895; Twum-Danso, *Africa's Young* Soldiers, p. 38.
41 United Nations 'Convention on the Rights of the Child'; United Nations 'Optional Protocol to the Convention on the Rights of the Child on the involvement of children in armed conflict'.

monopoly on the legitimate use of physical force.[42] However, humanitarian organisations also have an interest in these portrayals. In order to function, humanitarian organisations need passive victims. In order to create these passive victims, Northern conceptions of childhood are imposed onto the global South in order to create passive victims who can receive aid without problems.

Rather than attempting 'Band Aid' humanitarianism by calling for the international abolition of the use of children in conflict, humanitarian organisations and governments should be examining the reasons why children are participating in armed groups. What must be understood is that children also suffer the consequences of structural inequalities and children are also political and attempting to change these inequalities through the only means available to them. Children who come from ethnic groups, regions or communities which have suffered prolonged political injustices learn about this through being socialised and by living through the continued political injustices they experience everyday:

> The experience of growing up in situations where profoundly asymmetrical power relations give rise to systematic oppression may lead to the early development of 'political' understanding.[43]

When children have grown up in an environment of political instability, violence or have experienced persecution, injustice and unequal treatment on political grounds, this may sow the seeds for political violence as a solution.

This idea of politics as a lived experience should not be confused with the indoctrination of children. Many authors argue that children are indoctrinated into joining armed groups, suggesting that children were previously unaffected politically and joined against their will.[44] This denies the daily experiences in which children may experience gross political inequalities and that these children may have themselves been victims of discrimination and are acting in the only way they see possible to actively change their political situation.

Girls join armed groups in order to fight for greater societal female

---

42 M. Weber, *The Vocation Lectures: "Science as a Vocation, Politics as a Vocation"*.
43 Hart, 'Displaced children's participation in political violence', p. 277.
44 M. Denov, 'Wartime Sexual Violence'; Denov, Gervais, 'Negotiating (In)Security'; M. Denov, R. Maclure, 'Turnings and Epiphanies: Militarization, Life Histories and the Making and Unmaking of Two Child Soldiers in Sierra Leone', *Journal of Youth Studies*; J. Leatherman, N. Griffin, *Runaway Norms and Complex Political Victimhood: Child Soldier and Challenges for Peace Processes*, Paper presented at the annual meeting of the ISA's 50th Annual Convention "Exploring the past, anticipating the future"; J. Tabak, *The Voices of the Returning Children: Critical Reflections on the Disarmament, Demobilization and Reintegration of Former Child Soldiers*, Paper presented at the annual meeting of the ISA's 50th Annual Convention "Exploring the past, anticipating the future".

emancipation, to gain equality within armed groups or for their own personal emancipation and freedom. In Mozambique, girls were portrayed as joining up freely with the motivation to fight for a moral political ideology. FRELIMO actively encouraged girls to join as it furthered the morality and legitimacy of their socialist cause.[45] Freedom for Mozambique, FRELIMO claimed, also meant the emancipation of women. Similar reasons for the recruitment of female combatants have been found in the FARC which also has a left-wing Marxist agenda. Girls here have joined up in order to escape the gender inequalities they face at home. As in FRELIMO, female recruitment is also compatible with the FARC's ideological goals.[46]

As well as joining to fight for equality at the societal level, girls also join because the armed groups treat them equally. Girls are given access to training, education and routes to power similar to that of boys that they would not have access to in ordinary society. As well as gaining gender equality within armed groups, girls also gained age equality in the FARC: 'Once you are a guerrilla, you are treated like everyone else regardless of age.'[47] However, in Sierra Leone, women and girls did not fight in order to improve the position of females in Sierra Leone as a group, but rather fought for their own survival. However, girls did experience empowerment through their roles and experiences in the Sierra Leonean war in a similar way to females in FRELIMO and the FARC.[48]

Girls also join armed groups in order to escape from abuse and violence. This has particularly been the case in the post-independence wars such as the civil wars in Sierra Leone and Colombia. Brett and Specht argue that girls recruited into armed groups in these wars stated they joined in order ' ... to escape domestic violence, abuse, and poverty'.[49] The FARC also provides women and girls with a sense of autonomy, sexual freedom and an opportunity to prove their worth as well as skills, a vocation, a way of escaping rural poverty and a chance to feel important in their life. Women and girls in Colombia have joined the FARC for ideological as well as for reasons of family solidarity, a sense of adventure and for friendship.[50]

Economic circumstances also give personal and political reasons for joining armed groups. Armed groups provide food, shelter, and company. If children and young people become separated from their families and communities during conflict, armed groups provide a place to go for this.[51] In a situation

45 West, 'Girls with Guns'.
46 Herrera, Porch, '"Like going to a fiesta"'.
47 Felipe, a former FARC company commander, cited in ibid, p. 622.
48 Coulter, 'Female fighters in the Sierra Leone war', p. 60.
49 Cited in Coulter, Persson, Utas, *Young Female Fighters in African Wars Conflict*.
50 Herrera, Porch, '"Like going to a fiesta"'.
51 J. Boyden, 'Children's Experience of Conflict Related Emergencies: Some Implications for

of conflict where the economy is most likely failing, armed groups provide situations where resources are often available.

The economic inequalities which provoke girls to join armed groups are intrinsically part of political inequalities. Inability to access economic opportunities because of gender, class or ethnicity, may prompt a girl to join an armed group in order to fight for improved access and a fairer society or it may be that the armed group provides opportunities such as training, education and a wage.[52] Lack of economic opportunities and lack of access to education may be a cause of war which in turn can have a devastating effect on a country's economy.[53]

Girls, because of their position in society, may not be prioritised at home and may miss out on food or education. Many girls who join armed groups are from poor, rural backgrounds without access to education, employment opportunities or social mobility. This has especially been the case of girls in the FARC and FRELIMO, where they have joined armed forces in order to gain training, education or social mobility that they would not have been able to access otherwise.[54]

Closely linked to economic circumstances are social and cultural reasons for joining armed conflict. As argued above, it is not easy to separate out individual and societal motivations for joining armed groups as personal motivations are often rooted in social forces. We cannot be sure if girls are joining in order to change the position of females in society or if they are joining armed groups only for their own individual freedom and equality, but it is important to examine all these reasons. Girls may face sexual or physical abuse at home which the state cannot or will not prevent because of a lack of social services. In this way, the armed group may become the service provider and provide care and support that is lacking in the girl's home. For example, a reason regularly cited for recruitment of girls into the FARC has been escape from domestic abuse.[55]

Girls may join in order to follow family members.[56] Girls, particularly those who have been orphaned or separated from their family, may also join armed groups in order to find a place in society where they are treated equally and can have some chance of obtaining success and authority.[57] An

Relief Policy and Practice', *Disasters*.

52 Herrera, Porch, "'Like going to a fiesta'"; McKay, 'Girls as "Weapons of Terror"'; K. Peters, *Re-examining Voluntarism: Youth Combatants in Sierra Leone*; West, 'Girls with Guns '.

53 Peters, *Re-examining Voluntarism*; M. Denov, R. Maclure, 'Turnings and Epiphanies'.

54 Herrera, Porch, "'Like going to a fiesta'"; West, 'Girls with Guns'.

55 Brett, *"You'll Learn Not to Cry"*; R. Brett, I. Specht, *Young soldiers: Why they choose to fight*; Herrera, Porch, "'Like going to a fiesta'".

56 Herrera, Porch, "'Like going to a fiesta'"; McKay, 'Girls as "Weapons of Terror"'.

57 Herrera, Porch, "'Like going to a fiesta'"; Watchlist on Children and Armed Conflict, 2003, cited in S. Kenyon Lischer, *War, Displacement, and the Recruitment of Child Soldiers*, Working

armed group may provide a girl with a sense of importance and give her life a different purpose and meaning, something which would not happen if she stayed in her rural, poor community. Armed groups provide a route to social mobility, albeit social mobility within the context of a militarised illegitimate insurgency group, the consequences of which are usually not positive.

The recruitment and involvement of children and young people in armed conflict can also be viewed as an extension of 'normal' society. For example, Shepler found that recruitment in Sierra Leone followed cultural practices about how children and young people were socialised and educated.[58] She found that practices in normal daily life such as fostering, apprenticeship, child labour and initiation into secret societies were also used as ways of recruiting children. Thus recruitment was not something alien to Sierra Leoneans, but rather was something that fitted into everyday cultural practices. Shepler's study show that recruitment of children and young people can often follow cultural practices that the received belief that children are kidnapped or coerced into armed groups may ignore.

In Sierra Leone, young people who joined the RUF in Sierra Leone were not brainwashed into committing violent acts. He argues these were intelligent people that joined the RUF because they saw it as a way to change or improve their current social and economic circumstances. The war in Sierra Leone initially started as a youth movement. Young people were angry with the government over corruption and lack of employment opportunities but they were also angry because of the way decisions were made.

In some [African] countries more than 50% of the population is below 18. Democracy, based on the principle that the majority of the people decide, has another meaning in this context. Here, a minority (above 18 years) of the population decides for the majority (below 18 years).[59]

Decision-making still took place in traditional ways that left out young people. Young people were being discriminated against because of their age.[60] Because of this, young people joined the RUF in an attempt to overturn these traditional age hierarchies. This was similar to recruitment of young people in FRELIMO where young people were especially targeted to join in order to overturn age hierarchies and fight against traditional society.

It is imperative not to ignore the political aspect of girls' decisions. In doing so, we may be denying the political and social inequalities they have experienced. Girls not only join armed groups for broader ideological reasons but also to find a way out of rural poverty and to find a place in society through

Paper, Ford Institute for Human Security.
58 S. Shepler, *The Social and Cultural Context of Child Soldiering in Sierra Leone*, Paper for the PRIO sponsored workshop on Techniques of Violence in Civil War.
59 Peters, *Re-examining Voluntarism*, p. 25.
60 Ibid.

the skills and education provided by armed groups. In ignoring the political motivations of girls we fail to acknowledge the political injustices they have experienced and more broadly ignore any legitimate political reasons for the armed group.

Conclusion

As long as war continues, girls will continue to be implicated and involved in some way. Girls cannot be excluded from the effects of war and conflict and often cannot be stopped from taking part in armed groups and forces.

This chapter has argued that, rather than always being the exploited victims of illegitimate non-state armed groups; children, both boys and girls, are political actors, who make decisions to join armed groups because of political as well as social and economic inequalities. Girls who experience political inequalities everyday may be driven into joining armed groups in order to escape from these inequalities, or to change them. Conflict creates displacement and separation from carers, which may mean that armed groups can be 'safe' places for girls to be. However, conflict also exacerbates social and economic inequalities and armed groups often provide basic needs such as shelter, food and care, which may be unavailable elsewhere. Armed groups may also provide 'safe' places for girls to be in, protecting them from violence and sexual abuse. All of these should be guaranteed by governments and the fact states cannot or refuse to protect children from having to join armed groups is in itself political.

The literature too often represents girls as passive victims lacking in agency and political awareness. When girls do take part in armed groups they are only thought to take on sexual roles as forced wives or sexual slaves. Due to the perception and place of women and girls in western society, the roles that women and girls have in armed groups and in armed conflict can only ever be seen as exploitative and damaging in the eyes of the West, as this chapter has shown. These representations are beneficial to western states, who are the chief donors to humanitarian organisations, as they can use them to discredit and delegitimize the political goals of these armed groups and further their own political goals. Moreover, they are also beneficial to humanitarian organisations, which use these representations in order to justify their work and raise money.

However these representations may not benefit the girls in question, as they ignore their political demands and the political, economic and social injustices that they have been fighting over. Instead, girls are treated as apolitical victims only of a brutal military and not as the victims of larger structural injustices. The idea that children are political actors who may have actively perpetrated violence complicates the humanitarian ideal of the depoliticised, ahistorical, universal humanitarian subject.[61] This subject is someone who does not get in the way of the goals of fundraising and provision of neutral and impartial aid. A child that expresses political agency and perpetrates violence is not an ideal victim and ceases to be deserving of aid and humanitarian protection when they act outside what our conception of both a child is and what an ideal humanitarian subject is.

Humanitarian agencies also maintain the dominant political and moral ideology of the West and impose their cultural beliefs of who is a child by stating children should not take part in war. In doing so, the West, and state governments, gain legitimacy and reinforce the state as the only legitimate perpetrator of violence, thus rendering children again as depoliticized victims who are denied access to political participation.

Instead, states and humanitarian organisations should adopt a more nuanced approach to how conflict and the people affected by conflict are represented and promote a more realistic view of conflict, one in which those who take part are represented more three-dimensionally and not simply as victims or perpetrators. This broader view could be reflected in funding and programming from donors and governments and humanitarian NGOs. Programming could include improved DDR (Disarmament, Demobilisation and Reintegration) programmes to bring girls into democratic political fields where girls have a distinctive, recognisable voice which is taken seriously. In these arenas, girls must have the opportunity to articulate their demands for equality and have a meaningful role in this process, where proper justice can be achieved. In addition to actual political participation, girls also need access to economic activity and proper education and training so they can provide for themselves and obtain the qualifications and skills for fulfilling employment, which provides enough compensation for themselves and their families. However, both of these, the provision of democratic spheres where girls can have a voice and sufficient economic and educational opportunities, can only successfully be brought about by significant structural change which cannot be achieved quickly or simply.

This chapter has focused on one aspect of how girls in the global South are exploited by the global capitalist system. Girls are used and manipulated (to much the same extent that many male soldiers are in armed groups fighting in the new wars) to fight for what they believe will be political, economic, and social justice when in actual fact armed groups such as the FARC and the RUF tend to be corrupt and elitist. However, as Reynolds states

Concentration on the role of children in armed conflict should not obscure our

---

61 L. Malkki, 'Speechless Emissaries: Refugees, humanitarianism and dehistoricisation', *Cultural Anthropology*.

analysis of the way in which powerful forces (global and national), including progress in the industry of war, exploit and oppress the young.[62]

Rather than promoting 'Band Aid' humanitarianism, which aims to protect people from war and conflict, we should rather be focusing our attention on eliminating the poverty, social injustice and structural violence which cause conflicts.

Bibliography

S. Arnfred, 'Women in Mozambique: Gender Struggle and Gender Politics', *Review of African Political Economy*, 1988, 15, 41, pp. 5–16.

I. Beah, *A Long Way Gone: Memoirs of a Boy Soldier*, New York, Farrar Straus and Giroux, 2007.

C. Bop, 'Women in Conflicts, their gains and their losses', in S. Meintjes, A.Pillay, M. Turshen(eds), *The Aftermath: Women in Post-Conflict Transformation*, London and New York, Zed Books, 2001.

J. Boyden, 'Children's Experience of Conflict Related Emergencies: Some Implications for Relief Policy and Practice', *Disasters*, 1994, 18, 3, pp. 254-267.

R. Brett, *Girl Soldiers: Challenging Assumptions*, New York, Geneva, Quaker United Nations Office, 2002.

R. Brett, I. Specht, *Young soldiers: Why they choose to fight*, London, Lynne Rienner Publishers, 2004.

S. Brett, *"You'll Learn Not to Cry": Child Combatants in Colombia*, New York, Washington, London, Brussels, Human Rights Watch, 2003.

C. Coulter, 'Female fighters in the Sierra Leone war: challenging the assumptions?', *Feminist Review*, 2008, 88, pp. 54– 73.

C. Coulter, M. Persson, M. Utas, *Young Female Fighters in African Wars Conflict and Its Consequences*, Uppsala, NordiskaAfrikainstitutet, 2008.

L. Cortes, M. J. Buchanan, 'The experience of Colombian Child Soldiers from a resilience perspective', *International Journal for the Advancement of Counselling*, 2007, 29, 1, pp. 43-55.

M. Denov, 'Wartime Sexual Violence: Assessing a Human Security Response to War-Affected Girls in Sierra Leone', *Security Dialogue*, 2006, 37, 3, pp. 319-42.

M. Denov, *Girls in fighting Forces: Moving Beyond Victimhood*, A Summary of the Research Findings on Girls and Armed Conflict from CIDA's Child

---

62 P. Reynolds, '"Where wings take dream": On Children in the Work of War and the War of Work', in J. Boyden, J. De Berry (eds.), *Children and Youth on the Front Line: Ethnography, Armed Conflict and Displacement*, p. 266.

Protection Research Fund, 2007.

M. Denov, 'Girl Soldiers and Human Rights: Lessons from Angola, Mozambique, Sierra Leone and Northern Uganda', *The International Journal of Human Rights*, 2008, 12, 5, pp. 813-836.

M. Denov, *Child Soldiers Sierra Leone's Revolutionary United Front*, Cambridge, Cambridge University Press, 2012.

M. Denov, C. Gervais, 'Negotiating (In)Security: Agency, Resistance, and Resourcefulness among Girls Formerly Associated with Sierra Leone's Revolutionary United Front', *Signs: Journal of Women in Culture and Society*, 2007, 32, 4, pp. 885-910.

M. Denov, R. Maclure, *Girls and Small Arms in Sierra Leone: Victimization, Participation, and Resistance*, Paper presented for the International Studies Association Conference, Honolulu, Hawaii, 2005.

M. Denov, M. Maclure, R. Maclure, 'Engaging the Voices of Girls in the Aftermath of Sierra Leone's Conflict: Experiences and Perspectives in a Culture of Violence', *Anthropologica*, 2006, 48, 1, pp. 73-85.

M. Denov, R. Maclure, 'Turnings and Epiphanies: Militarization, Life Histories and the Making and Unmaking of Two Child Soldiers in Sierra Leone', *Journal of Youth Studies*, 2007, 10, 2, pp. 243-261.

L. Edmundson, 'Marketing Trauma and the Theatre of War in Northern Uganda', *Theatre Journal*, 2005,57, 3, pp. 451–474.

M. Fox, 'Girl Soldiers: Human Security and Gendered Insecurity', *Security Dialogue*, 2004, 35, 4, pp. 465–479.

J. Hart, 'Displaced children's participation in political violence: Towards greater understanding of mobilisation', *Conflict, Security & Development*, 2008, 8, 3, pp. 277-293.

N. Herrera, D. Porch, '"Like going to a fiesta" – the role of female fighters in Colombia's FARC-EP', *Small Wars & Insurgencies*, 2008,19, 4, pp. 609 – 634.

E. Jal, *War Child: A Boy Soldier's Story*, London, Little, Brown, 2009.

M. Kaldor, *New and Old Wars: Organized Violence in a Global Era*, Cambridge, Polity, 2001.

Y. E. Keairns, *The Voices of Girl Child Soldiers: Summary*, New York, Geneva, Quaker United Nations Office, 2002.

S. Kenyon Lischer, *War, Displacement, and the Recruitment of Child Soldiers*, Working Paper, Ford Institute for Human Security, University of Pittsburgh, PA, 2006.

J. Leatherman, N. Griffin, *Runaway Norms and Complex Political Victimhood: Child Soldier and Challenges for Peace Processes*, Paper presented at the annual meeting of the ISA's 50th Annual Convention "Exploring the past, anticipating the future", New York Marriott Marquis, New York, 2009.

T. Lyons, *Guns and Guerilla Girls: Women in the Zimbabwean Liberation*

Struggle, Asmara, Eritrea, Africa World Press, 2004.

L. Malkki, 'Speechless Emissaries: Refugees, humanitarianism and dehistoricisation', *Cultural Anthropology*, 1996, 11, 3, pp. 377-404.

D. Mazurana, K. Carlson, *From Combat to Community: Women and Girls of Sierra Leone*, Washington DC, Women Waging Peace Policy Commission, 2004.

D. E. Mazurana, S. McKay, K.C. Carlson, J. C. Kasper, 'Girls in Fighting Forces and Groups: Their Recruitment, Participation, Demobilization, and Reintegration', *Peace and Conflict: Journal of Peace Psychology*, 2002,8, 2, pp. 97-123.

A.McIntyre, 'Introduction', in A. McIntyre (ed.), *Invisible Stakeholders: The Impact of Children on War* Pretoria, ISS, 2004.

S. McKay, 'The Effects of Armed Conflict on Girls and Women', *Peace and Conflict: Journal of Peace Psychology*, 1998,4, 4, pp. 381-392.

Idem, 'Reconstructing fragile lives: girls' social reintegration in northern Uganda and Sierra Leone', *Gender and Development*, 2004, 12, 3, 19-30.

Idem, 'Girls as "Weapons of Terror" in Northern Uganda and Sierra Leonean Rebel Fighting Forces', *Studies in Conflict & Terrorism*, 2005, 28, 5, pp. 385–397.

S. McKay, D. E. Mazurana, *Where are the Girls? Girls in Fighting Forces in Northern Uganda, Sierra Leone, and Mozambique: Their Lives During and After War,* Montreal, International Centre for Human Rights and Democratic Development, 2004.

C.Nordstrom, *Girls and Warzones: Troubling Questions,* Uppsala, Sweden, Life & Peace Institute, 1997.

E. Paez, *Girls in the Colombian Armed Forces: a diagnosis*, Osnabruck, Terre des Hommes, 2001.

K. Peters, *Re-examining Voluntarism: Youth Combatants in Sierra Leone,* Institute for Security Studies Monograph series, no. 100, South Africa, 2004.

J. Phillips, 'A Soldier Returns', *Developments Magazine* 31, 2005. Online. Available HTTP: http://www.developments.org.uk/articles/a-soldier-returns/, (accessed 11. January 2011).

V. Pupavac, 'Misanthropy Without Borders: The International Children's Rights Regime', *Disasters*, 2001, 25, 2, pp. 95–112.

P. Reynolds, '"Where wings take dream": On Children in the Work of War and the War of Work', in J. Boyden, J. de Berry (eds), *Children and Youth on the Front Line: Ethnography, Armed Conflict and Displacement,* New York, Oxford, Berghahn Books, 2004.

D.Rosen, *Armies of the Young: Child Soldiers In War and Terrorism,* New Jersey, London, Rutgers University Press, 2005.

S. Shepler, 'Les filles-soldats: trajectories d'apres-guerre en Sierra Leone',

Politique Africaine, 2002,88, pp. 49-62.

Idem, *The Social and Cultural Context of Child Soldiering in Sierra Leone,* Paper for the PRIO sponsored workshop on Techniques of Violence in Civil War, Oslo, 2004.

L. Sjoberg, C. E. Gentry, *Mothers, Monsters, Whores: Women's violence in global politics,* London, Zed Books, 2007.

J. Tabak, *The Voices of the Returning Children: Critical Reflections on the Disarmament, Demobilization and Reintegration of Former Child Soldiers,* Paper presented at the annual meeting of the ISA's 50th Annual Convention "Exploring the past, anticipating the future", New York, 2009.

M. Trawick, *Enemy Lines: Warfare, Childhood and Play in Batticaloa,* Berkeley, London, University of California Press, 2007.

A.Twum-Danso, *Africa's Young Soldiers: The Co-option of Childhood,* Institute for Security Studies Monograph series, no. 82, South Africa, 2003.

United Nations 'Convention on the Rights of the Child' 1989. Online. Available http://www.unhchr.ch/html/menu3/b/k2crc.htm, (accessed 10. January 2011).

United Nations 'Optional Protocol to the Convention on the Rights of the Child on the involvement of children in armed conflict', 2002. Online. Available   http://www.unhchr.ch/html/menu2/6/protocolchild.htm (accessed 10. January 2011).

M. Utas, 'Agency of Victims: Young women in the Liberian civil war', in A. Honwana, F. de Boeck, (eds), *Makers and Breakers: Children and Youth in Postcolonial Africa,* Trenton, Africa World Press, 2005.

M. Weber, *The Vocation Lectures: "Science as a Vocation, Politics as a Vocation",* Hackett Publishing Co, Inc, 2004.

M. G. Wessells, *The Recruitment and Use of Girls in Armed Forces and Groups in Angola: Implications for Ethical Research and Reintegration,* Working Paper, Ford Institute for Human Security, University of Pittsburgh, 2007.

H. G. West, 'Girls with Guns: Narrating the Experience of war of FRELIMO's 'Female Detachment', in J. Boyden, J. De Berry, (eds), *Children and Youth on the Front Line: Ethnography, Armed Conflict and Displacement,* New York, Oxford, Berghahn Books, 2004.

11   Too Extreme to be True: Unshared Images of Soldiers in Sub-Sahara Africa

Hideyuki Okano

Introduction

This article examines three images (representations) of soldiers which can be seen in the studies of armed conflicts in Sub-Sahara Africa (thereafter 'Africa'). Since the 1990s, armed conflicts have attracted the public attentions and the studies of armed conflicts have also accumulated.

In such 'armed-conflict studies', various scholars participated. Their interests and their objectives are diverse. Some scholars explore armed conflicts in order to clarify "what happens" (I call them simply 'reality') and "why it happens". Among such scholars, the disciplines are different. Econometrics, anthropology and political science are the main disciplines for armed-conflict studies. In addition, some scholars discuss armed conflict aiming at conflict resolution.[1] These scholars publish articles on the practices of peacebuilding in order to find better ways to resolve or relieve armed conflicts.

These scholars show their interpretations of armed conflicts in their respective researches. From such interpretation, images of armed conflicts and images of soldiers are produced and reproduced. Some scholars might consciously employ these images, while some might unconsciously use specific images.

This article examines three images of soldiers in African conflicts. These images are popular among scholars. They represent the ways of thinking by specific groups of scholars. In this sense, these images are the reflection of what scholars envision.

Although these images are widely shared, they are too extreme to be true. They are one-sided and biased if aiming to provide an explanation of

---

1   For example, see R. Paris, T. D. Sisk (eds), *The Dilemmas of Statebuilding: Confronting the contradictions of Postwar Peace Operations*; E. Newman, R. Paris, O. P. Richmond (eds), *New Perspective on Liberal Peacebuiding*; C. A. Crocker, F. O. Hampson, P. Aall (eds), *Leashing the Dogs of War: Conflict Management in a Divided World*.

what really happens in armed conflicts. These images cannot explain "what happens" and "why it happens" on their own. Thus, the images I discuss are ambiguous: even though widely shared among scholars, they cannot explain the actual situation. In this article, I analyze why such ambiguous images are constructed.

For the purpose of simplification, I concentrate on images of male soldiers. Readers might criticize my lack of gender perspective, but this has a reason. This article deals with images of soldiers shared by previous researchers. The majority of previous research deals with male soldiers.[2] For this reason, I concentrate on images of male soldiers in the discussion.

The objective of this research is to shed light on a problem in armed-conflict studies. As we have seen, armed-conflict studies is an arena of discussion in which scholars of various disciplines participate. What is a problem in the current armed-conflict studies? Why do the problems arise? Through the discussion of three images, I tackle these questions.

In the exploration of three images, I reveal the process in which new concepts and frameworks become deviated in the course of discussions. This process shows that attempts at portraying the reality are easily impaired. In conclusion, I claim that such deviations are brought about by mutual incomprehension among various participators of armed-conflict studies.

Image One: Innocent Child Soldiers

The first image is 'innocent child soldiers'. This image is applied to specific categories of soldiers. Those in the category are soldiers who fit into a clear-cut definition of under 18-years-old. Those who are defined as 'innocent child soldiers' are regarded as victims of abuse and of exploitation by adults.[3] The image is prevalent since the 1990s because it is used by media, NGOs and international organizations.[4] Some scholars also adopt this image in their works.[5]

---

2   Recently, several works mainly deal with female soldiers. See M. Utas, 'Agency of victims: young women's survival strategies in the Liberian civil war', in F. De Boeck, A. Honwana (eds), *Makers and Breakers: Children and Youth as Emerging Categories in Postcolonial Africa*, pp. 53-80; C. Coulter, *Bush Wives and Girl Soldiers: Women Lives through War and Peace in Sierra Leone*.

3   The majority of advocates of an international legal ban on child soldiers seeks to prevent the recruitment and use of any person under 18 years old. This delineation of age stems from the UN convention on the Right of Children (1989), which defines children as "every human being below the age of eighteen years." In actual international laws, the definitions are different from 15 to 18 years old, but, 18 years old is considered to be ideal.

4   J. Hart, 'The politics of "child soldiers"', *Brown Journal of World Affairs*, pp. 217-226.

5   For examples, see Human Right Watch, *Easy to Prey: Child Soldiers in Liberia*; United Nations Security Council Resolution 1539, S-RES-1539 (2004); R. Brett, I. Specht, *Young Soldiers: Why They Choose to Fight*; R. Brett, M. McCallin, *Children: the Invisible Soldiers*; A. Honwana, *Child Soldiers in Africa*; M. Denov, *Child Soldiers: Sierra Leone's Revolutionary United Front*.

In this image, soldiers are regarded only as 'innocent victims', no matter what they did. Even though they engaged in senseless murders, tortures or lootings, their malicious behaviors are regarded as the results of brainwashing or an unavoidable choice for survival. Thus, child soldiers can be innocent regardless of their misdeeds.

In the majority of cases, a patterned story is adopted when the image of child soldiers is used. This story is typically full of calamity and hardship which includes the process of forced recruitment, indoctrination, hard life as soldiers and unsuccessful reintegration into his society;

> When a village is attacked by a rebel, a child is abducted from a village along with other children. After he is brought to a military camp, he was indoctrinated or brainwashed by adult commanders. Then, one day, he was commanded to kill a captured man. He cannot refuse, because the commander tells him that if he fails, he will be killed. So, he killed a man. After he first kills, he gradually adapts to the rebel's culture. He works for the rebels engaging in military combat, looting civilians and murders. At first, he is tormented by remorse, but gradually become insensible. When the war ends, he was sent back to his home after undergoing a disarmament program. However, he was not accepted by people in his home village. In addition to his life of loneliness, he is traumatized from his experience during the soldier's days. Thus, he was plagued even after the war ends.

Such a typical story is prevalent in media, NGO reports and even academics.[6]

Recently, several scholars have argued the fallacy of this concept.[7] Such criticism can be summarized into two points. First, they concern over-emphasis of the victimhood. As I point out, the image of 'innocent child soldier' treats child soldiers as victims of abuse and exploitation. Critics raise doubts about this image. According to them, it contradicts images from narratives of civilian victims who suffered the misdeeds by child soldiers. Second, critics concern the uniformity of childhood. They criticize the single universal understanding of child soldiers. According to them, the notion of 'children' is different among various cultures and should be discussed along with social and cultural contexts. They claim a necessity to understand the diversity of child soldiers. For them, child soldiers are culturally codified and

---

6   On publicly shared images, see I. Beah, *A Long Way Gone: Memoirs of a Boy Soldier*. On NGO report, see Brett, McCallin, *Children*. On academic studies, see A. Honawa, *Child Soldiers in Africa*, and Denov, *Child Soldiers*.

7   D. M. Rosen, *Armies of the Young: Child Soldiers in War and Terrorism*. See also introduction of Denov, *Child Soldiers*.

defined not only by age, but also by ethnicity, gender, history and locations.[8] Thus, the critics call in question the existing image of child soldiers. For them, it is too universal and too victimized to be true.

I agree with the critics in the sense that the image does not reflect the reality. However, the extremity is relevant when considering the original purpose of the image. Considering the original purpose, the criticism above is irrelevant. Originally, the image of innocent child soldier is not for describing the actual situation. The concept is intended to be used for the other purpose. The victimhood and blanket definition are indispensable for the original purpose. This purpose is to advocate the right of the child.

The concept of child soldier has developed in parallel with universalization of the concept of *childhood*.[9] In this concept, children are vulnerable and should be protected. It was during the first half of the 20th century that this notion was established as human rights, for example the Geneva Declaration of the Rights of the Children, which was adopted by the League of Nations in 1924, provides that:

> The child that is hungry must be fed; the child that is sick must be nursed; the child that is backward must be helped; the delinquent child must be reclaimed; and the orphan and the waif must be sheltered and succored.

This declaration is prompted by concerns over young people affected by conflict in the Balkans. In this declaration, physical needs and aspects of protection are emphasized.[10] What is distinctive in this declaration is its exclusive focus on children. On the other hand, the later international laws deal with the rights of children in the context of human rights which are applicable to all human beings. The Declaration of the Rights of the Child, adopted by the General Assembly of the United Nations in 1959, sees the rights of the child in the context of universal human rights. The rights of children in this declaration are basically the same as human rights for adults. This declaration states how universal human rights should be guaranteed for children who need special attention.

The status of children is also provided in the context of wars. The First Additional Protocol to the Geneva Convention in 1977 provides that:

> The Parties to the conflict shall take all feasible measures in order that children who have not attained the age of fifteen years do not take a direct part in

---

8   D. Rosen, 'Child soldiers, international humanitarian law, and the globalization of childhood', *American Anthropologist*, pp. 296-306.
9   Ibid.
10 J. Herbst, *International laws of war and the African child: norms, compliance, and sovereignty.*

hostilities and, in particular, they shall refrain from recruiting them into their armed forces.

As seen so far, international laws on the rights of the child have accumulated since the early 20th century. The United Nations Convention on the Rights of the Child in 1989 is a landmark for international laws on the rights of the child. The convention set the international norm for a child's inherent right to life, survival, development, and freedom of thought, regardless of race, religion and gender. 191 of 193 countries in the world have ratified the convention (except for the United States and Somalia).[11] Thus, the rights of the child have been spread as norms since the former part of the 20th century. In this norm, children are regarded as vulnerable and should be protected.

The image of the child soldier has become popular since the mid-1980s, responding to the increase of civil unrest mainly in Africa. The rise of the image has been parallel to that of the rights of the child in the context of armed conflict.[12] This trend was further enhanced after the promulgation of the United Nations Convention on the Right of the Child in 1989.[13] In the 1990s, tremendous grassroots efforts by international Non-Governmental Organizations (NGOs) to advocate protection of children in armed conflicts can be observed. In the advocating activities, the image of the child soldier is highly visible.

This concurrent development of the two concepts (childhood and child soldiers) indicates that the concept of the child soldier is a byproduct of the universally designed concept of *childhood*. In the concept of universal childhood, children are subjects who should be protected by adults. On the other hand, the concept of child soldiers emphasizes that they are not protected, but they are exploited and abused.

Considering the contrast, the concept of the child soldier works as a tool that makes the gap between the ideal and the real stand out. Ideally, the rights of children should be firmly guaranteed, however, in the real world, children are exploited and abused as soldiers. By emphasizing the gap, the concept of child soldiers owes a role to advocate the rights of the child. The concept of the child soldier can be regarded as a part of a 'project' which establishes and familiarizes the norm that children should be protected by adults and humanitarian laws.

For this 'project', the universality and victimhood of child soldiers are quite useful. The users of the concept in humanitarian organizations intentionally emphasize the two components. For example, a research report jointly

11 Honwana, *Child Soldiers in Africa*, p. 35.
12 Ibid.
13 Hart, 'The Politics of "Child Soldiers"'.

published by NGOs and the UN sub-organizations, *Children: The Invisible Soldiers*, declares their intentional disregard of specific contexts in each case. Authors confidently claim that they should disregard the contexts and specific events in which child soldiers suffered in order to emphasize the universality for children's suffering.[14] For humanitarian organizations such as NGOs and international organizations, it is quite reasonable to use the image of child soldiers, even though it is too extreme to be true. Thus, for humanitarian organizations, the concept of the child soldier is not to describe the reality impartially. Rather, this concept is a tool for sensitization.

Confusion on the image child soldier arises because it is detached from the 'project'. Being disembodied from the 'project', they are mistakenly embraced as the tool of impartial description. Consequently, the discussion of child soldiers becomes strayed in two ways.

In the first way, one-sided victimhood of child soldiers is accepted as impartial description. Some users of the concepts follow the same descriptive methods which emphasize universality and victimhood. They do not have an intention of advocating the rights of children, but continue to use the same method. They just believe that their description is impartial. In the text of such authors, child soldiers are reduced to victims without any purpose.[15]

The second way is the attempt of modification. Some scholars attempt to modify this biased concept into a concept for impartial description. These scholars are aware of the bias. They try to make the concept a descriptive tool by modifying the already-established biased image. For example, Rosen deconstructs the image of victimhood by describing the aspect of actively participating child soldiers.[16]

Endeavors of such scholars are important in the sense that they shed light on the fallacy of child soldiers. However, it is impossible to describe soldiers impartially as far as the concept of the child soldier is used. The description of child soldiers cannot escape from the over-emphasized victimhood and universality. Several authors attempted to break free from them, but they never succeeded. For example, Myriam Denov sets her research objective as "to explore the lives and realities of... former child soldiers".[17] Even though she shows her intention to describe positive aspects in child soldiers along with the aspect of victimhood, she fails to achieve her attempt. Her description of positive aspects still evokes a victimized image.

The reason of her failure is in her descriptive techniques. She uses techniques which are used in the traditional concept of child soldiers. These techniques are

14 Brett, McCallin, *Children*.
15 For example, see Honwana, *Child Soldiers in Africa*.
16 Rosen, *Armies of the Young*.
17 Denov, *Child Soldiers*, p. 1.

used for the purpose of emphasizing universality and victimhood. Ironically, Denov uses such techniques unconsciously.

First, in the literature of child soldiers, monologues are frequently used. We, contemporary humans, are conditioned to evoke hardship from monologues. A monologue often comes along with hardship or tragic stories in movies, TV drama and novels. Main stories that are full of hardship and tragedies come after monologues which consist of introductory parts. In addition, monologues evoke in the reader an image of a child who narrates his experience with detached tones (as written sentences are usually in a detached tone). Thus, the use of monologue emphasizes the victimhood of child soldiers.

Second, the author gives impunity to child soldiers by shifting their responsibility to others. Her description is limited exclusively to soldiers under 18 years old. Soldiers above that age are excluded from the research focus. She never shows voices of adult commanders, cadres and older soldiers. When they appear, they are pictured as callous and selfish exploiters of 'children'. This method of description puts the blame of misdeed by children on adult exploiters. Crimes and misdeeds perpetrated by children are either described as behaviors enforced by adult's survival strategies for children (otherwise, children have no choice but to be killed). Thus, the author unintentionally emphasizes victimhood.

Third, children's narratives are not cross-checked with historical courses of wars or with others' testimonies. The narratives of children are not embedded in specific settings. Due to the lack of contexts, the description encourages universality of the victimhood.

Some scholars try to describe the experience of child soldiers along with their specific contexts and specific events. However, most of these works fail to embed children's experience into the context, for the majority of such attempts only introduce the overview of social and economic situations, or the course of wars in their targeted countries. It is huge gap between a panoramic view of an armed conflict and personal experiences of individuals.

One of the methods for describing the context is to present several voices of those who experience a same event (for example, a bullet exchange or a massacre in a village). Readers can grasp a whole picture if narratives from various people are presented. For example, voices of adult soldiers, other child soldiers, commanders and civilians involved in the event can help to grasp the situation. However, most of the works on child soldiers use monologue. Normally, voices of others who experience the same event are not presented.[18]

Such lack of context is justified by excuses. For example, the following excuses are used to justify their lack of contexts: "children are ignorant of their surrounding situations", "it is impossible to reach out to those who experience

18 See Denov, *Child Soldiers*; Rosen, *Armies of the Young*; Honwana, *Child Soldiers in Africa*.

the same event", "researchers are careful in their interviews not to confuse traumatized children". By using such justification, a personal experience is accepted without any critical examination. Thus, experiences of child soldiers are not contextualized.

The fourth, and last, delineation of 18 years old picks up a distorted portion of a society. This partition is groundless, because the roles and social status of soldiers are not based on chronological age. It means that scholars use a definition which is not applicable for a society. In the West, the delineation of 18 years old might be embedded in a society through rights to vote and regulations on cigarettes or alcohol. However, in countries of armed conflict, this delineation is not embedded in the people's lives.

As seen so far, four techniques are used along with the concept of child soldiers. Scholars who try to describe the reality by using the concept of child soldiers unintentionally use such techniques.

The concept of the child soldier is not to describe the reality at birth, but the concept began being wrongly used for a description of reality. This concept was originally intended to show the tragedy of victimization of 'children' in armed conflicts around the world aiming at advocating the rights of the child. The descriptive techniques of the child soldier are designed to emphasize the aspects of victimhood and to decontextualize child soldiers' experiences.

The concept of the child soldier has been recently criticized with its biased image. However, this criticism comes from misunderstandings. The concept of the child soldier is to advocate the rights of a child, and the biased image is useful for the purpose. The problem of child soldiers arises because the concept is recklessly used to describe the reality.

Image Two: Rational Thugs

The second image assumes soldiers as actors who choose their own behavior rationally for their personal interest. I call this image 'rational thugs'. In this image, soldiers are actors who pursue material interest by rational calculation. They are assumed to use violence and ferocity aiming at gaining material interest.

The most outstanding example is seen in the study of David Keen (1998).[19] His work, *The Economic Functions of Violence in Civil Wars*, attempts to explain armed conflicts by economic factors. According to him, "'traditional' analyses portray civil wars as primarily political or military struggles". Because of their limited perspective, Keen claims that the economic aspect of civil war is overlooked.[20] He further mentions that "civil wars persist partly because of

19 D. Keen, *The Economic Functions of Violence in Civil Wars*.
20 Ibid, p. 15.

rational economic calculations".[21]

Based on this assumption, he categorizes violence in armed conflicts into two categories. One is 'Top-down violence'. Top-down violence is violence mobilized by political leaders in order to gain economic benefit. According to him, there are several means to gain economic interest in armed conflicts such as pillage, trade, looting and labor exploitations. Political leaders exploit economic benefit by using such means. The second category is 'Bottom-up violence'. Bottom-up violence is violence embraced by low-rank soldiers and ordinary people. According to Keen, they also follow their economic agenda and try to benefit from armed conflicts. Thus, Keen considers that each actor behaves by seeking their own interest in armed conflicts. [22]

Low-rank soldiers in Keen's argument hold true to the image of 'rational thugs'. According to Keen, ordinary people join armed factions on their rational calculation.[23] They perpetrate top-down violence for the sake of political leaders if it is beneficial for them too. Keen also claims that bottom-up violence is frequently seen in armed groups which lack discipline. The soldiers in such groups seek their immediate reward through violence toward unarmed civilians.[24]

This understanding more or less grasps actual soldiers' behaviors, but his assumption emphasizes the economic perspective to the extreme. In his assumption, the purpose of an armed group is material gain; cadres always fight for economic benefit. With this assumption, he reduces all actors of armed conflict into rational actors who pursues economic objectives.

However, the understanding of 'rational thugs' is too extreme to be true. Although Keen claims in his introduction that civil wars persist PARTLY because of rational economic calculations, his argument excludes other aspects. In his argument, he carries out the discussion as if economic factors can explain everything.

Why does Keen discuss the topic in such a way? Behind Keen's discussion, there is a genealogy of rational choice theory. The image of rational thugs also stems from the genealogy. The image of 'rational thugs' resembles the concept of 'rational economic man (*homo economicus*)'. This concept defines humans as "rational and narrowly self-interested actors who seeks one's own subjectively defined purpose by choosing the best behavior for achieving the one". Needless to say, human behavior cannot be so coherently consistent.[25] The concept of

21 Ibid, p. 11.
22 Ibid, p.46.
23 Ibid, p. 51.
24 Ibid, p. 52.
25 In the study of market economy, the limitation of rational economic man is also argued. See C. Cramer, 'Homo economicus goes to war: methodological individualism, rational choice and the political economy of war', *World Development*, pp. 1845-1864.

rational economic man does not indicate actual human behaviors.

The significance of this unrealistic concept is in explaining a phenomenon. The concept of rational economic man exclusively picks up on a particular segment of specific human traits. The reason why only specific segments of human behavior are picked up is for the purpose of explaining a specific phenomenon. Some works of political science attempt to explain various political phenomena by reducing related actors into rational economic man. According to economist Fritz Machlup, rational economic man has fictitious characteristics, but the concept is significant when it is used for the interpretation of specific phenomena. What he emphasizes is that the concept is a tool for explaining phenomenon, not for describing a reality by the concept itself.[26] For example, Mancur Olson explains chronological organizational change of a labor union.[27] Robert H. Bates illuminates the mechanism of economic failure in African states. He points out that economically irrational policies are adopted because they are politically rational for politicians.[28] In these works, related actors such as members of a labor union and politicians are reduced to rational economic men.

Actually, one of the origins of the image of 'rational thugs' stems from explanations regarding a specific phenomenon: how armed conflicts break out. One of the scholars, who clearly illuminates the mechanism of armed conflict by using the rational economic man, is Shin'ichi Takeuchi.[29] Similar explanations are shared among political scientists who study armed conflicts.[30]

Takeuchi explains an outbreak of an armed conflict from the collapse of informally constructed ruling systems. In order to show the ruling system, Takeuchi employs the concept of 'patron-client relation'. Patron-client relation is:

> ... an exchange relationship between roles, which is defined as dyadic (two-person) ties involving a largely instrumental friendship in which individuals of higher socioeconomic status (patron) uses his own influence and resources to provide protection or benefit, or both, for a person of lower status (client) who, for his part, reciprocates by offering general support and assistance, including personal services, to the patron.31

26 F. Machlup, *Methodologies of Economics and Social Science*, pp. 267-277.
27 M. Olson, *The Logic of Collective Action: Public Goods and Theory of Groups.*
28 R. H. Bates, *Market and States in Tropical Africa: The Political Basis of Agricultural Policies.*
29 S. Takeuchi, 'Afurilka no hunsou: sono kon'nichiteki tokushitsu ni tuite no kousatsu', in S. Takeuchi (ed.) *Gendai Afrika no Hunsou: Rekishi to Shutai*, pp. 3-52.
30 For example, W. Reno, 'Reinvention of an African patrimonial state: Charles Taylor's Liberia', *Third World Quarterly*, pp.109-120; Idem, *Warlord Politics and African States*; J-F Bayart, *The State in Africa: the Politics of the Belly*; P. Chabal, J-P. Daloz, *African Works: Disorder as Political Instrument.*
31 J. Scott, 'Patron-client politics and political change in Southeast Asia', *American Political Science*

To put it simply, the patron-client relation is the interdependency between the superior (patron) and the inferior (client). In this concept, a patron needs clients' compliance of requirements and obedience in order to maintain their authority. On the other hand, a client needs protection and support from the patron for their own survival and well-being.

Patron-client relations vertically connect person to person in sequence. The relation is pervasive through countless chains of patron-client relations (I call this the 'patron-client network'). As a patron usually holds more than one client, this network can be visualized as pyramidal structure (Figure 11.1). In this network, a sole ruler of a state stands on the top, ordinary people are at the bottom, while several levels of authorities are located in the middle-level, such as political elites in the capital (politicians and bureaucrats), business elites and local authorities.[32]

The ruler of the state, who exclusively controls political resources, governs the state by providing political resources to their clients.[33] This rule is maintained by sequences of patron-client relations, in which each patron controls their own clients. The distribution of political resources along with patron-client network is the principle of rule and control of a state.

According to Takeuchi, armed conflicts break out by splitting the network into several factions. When the state is faced with a power struggle (such as elections or the fall of the ruler), political elites, who had once been in obedience to the ruler, compete with each other for control of political resources. This makes the pyramidal network split into several networks. Political elites may compete in political arenas at first, but soon the competition expands to ordinary people through the patron-client networks. A political struggle easily turns into a conflict among several networks. When politicians arm their clients, this conflict turns into an armed conflict (Figure 11.2).

In this explanation, Takeuchi reduces people in patron-client networks

---

Review, pp. 91-113.

32 It is argued that while the rule of patron-client networks brings personalization of politics and institutionalized corruption, it also functions to integrate a state. In such discussions, various social groups such as ethnic groups or classes are considered to be integrated into a 'nation' through patron-client networks. For detail, See R. H. Jackson, C. G. Rosberg, *Personal Rule in Africa: Prince, Autocrat, Prophet, Tyrant*; R. Lemarchand, 'Political clientelism and ethnicity in tropical Africa: competing solidarities in nation-building', *American Political Science Review*, pp. 68-90.

33 Resources provided through patron-client relation are different among client's status. For example, in rural communities, village authorities (patrons) provide peasants (clients) with protection, security, land and support when in trouble. On the other hand, in the higher level (especially inside political institutions), employment, promotion, licensing and permits are provided to clients. In this case, as politicians and administrators violate the formal norms of public conduct for providing rewards to clients, corruption is mundane. For details, see Scott, 'Patron-client politics and political change'.

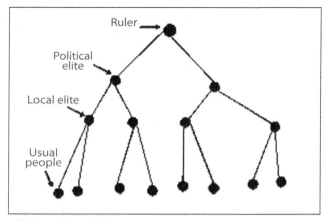

Fig. 11.1: Takeuchi's model – patron-client network with pyramidal structure.

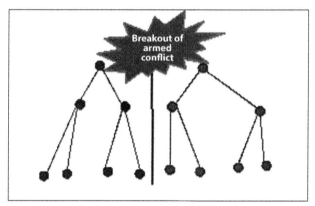

Fig. 11.2: Takeuchi's model – the split of patron-client network.

into rational economic men.[34] Actual human relations might not be simple

---

34 The relation between patron and clients is analyzed by Szefel. Szefel shows three ways for
patrons to mobilize clients; (1) coercive mobilization, (2) mobilization by politicized identity
and (3) the one by reciprocal relations. Among the three, Takeuchi choose (3) for simplifying
the relation between patron and client. This choice is appropriate for the following reasons. First,
coercive relations are possible when clients depend on patrons for their access to income and for
their lives. Otherwise, they can exit from the relationship. Second, Takeuchi regards the split of
patron-client networks as a cause of politicization of ethnicity, not the other way around. In his
explanation, ethnicity is politicized for easy mobilization within a faction. In this explanation, as
patron-client relations are often constructed along ethnic lines, a faction tends to have ethnically
homogenous members. With this background, ethnicity is used for mobilization after the
factional conflict arises. Thus, in Takeuchi's explanation, mobilization by ethnicity comes after
factional conflict. With these two reasons, it is reasonable for Takeuchi to choose the reciprocal
relation for simplification. For details, see M. Szefel, 'Clientelism, corruption and catastrophe',
Review of African Political Economy, pp. 427-441.

as what Takeuchi explains. However, this simplification works for explaining breakouts of armed conflicts. The image of rational thugs stems from such an explanation.

The problem in Keen's discussion is to detach this economic man assumption from the explanation. Keen uses the concept of the rational economic man not for explaining a phenomenon, but for describing actors *per se*. In Takeuchi's explanation, rational economic man is an assumption for the explanation, but in Keen's study, rational economic man is a concept which describes actual soldiers' behavior. Rational economic man is too extreme to be true.

Image Three: Marginalized Youth

The third image regards soldiers as political actors who take up arms because of their economic and political status. I call this image 'marginalized youth'. In this image, soldiers are one of the conspicuous examples of young people who have few choices for survival. Global markets, economic crisis, authoritarian rule, and local social structures are considered as factors which oppress young people and drive them to be soldiers.

Similar to the child soldier, this image also has the image of victimhood. While child soldiers are considered to be victims of adults, this image considers soldiers as victims of socio/political/economic situations. However, contrary to the image of the child soldier, they are neither passive nor vulnerable entities. They are possible actors who attempt to change their surrounding situations.

This concept is the counter-argument of the concept of child soldier in two senses. First, the rigidity of definition is different. The image of the child soldier is defined clearly by chronological age. The criterion is universally set. Whether the person is under 18-years-old or not is the only criterion of child soldiers. On the other hand, the concept of 'youth' is equivocal. It denotes those who are not considered as children anymore, and who cannot obtain the social status of adulthood in their own societies. For example, Weiss defines the youth as "anyone between the ages of 15 and 35, and occasionally people over 35 who are not married or financially independent."[35] Thus, youth are prescribed by the social contexts they are encompassed by. Second, youth implies power. In the image of youth, they are active agencies who try to change the surrounding environment and to improve their own status, even under harsh situations. Sometime, youth are considered a security threat.[36]

Initially, the image of youth developed in anthropological researches on

---

35 T. Weiss, *Perpetrating Power: Small Arms in Post-Conflict Sierra Leone and Liberia*, Pretoria, Institute for Security Studies, p. 43.
36 Ibid, p. 43.

resistance against apartheid in South Africa and on urban lives in Sub-Sahara Africa.[37] Then, the concept was applied to the study of armed conflicts and soldiers. One of the pioneers is Paul Richards. He interprets the rebel group in Sierra Leone, the Revolutionary United Front (RUF), as an uprising of socially marginalized youth.[38] He regards RUF soldiers as victims of harsh social surroundings, as well as active political actors that aim at overthrowing the government. After Richards's discussion, research of youth in armed conflicts became one of the trends in anthropology[39].

The extreme image of youth can be seen in the work by Krijin Peters.[40] In his doctoral thesis, he describes lives and narratives of ex-soldiers of the RUF. In common with Paul Richards, he strongly claims that the war is a revolutionary project by youth who are marginalized in the society.[41] Even though his work is not published, scholars of the Sierra Leonean civil war have widely referred to his doctoral thesis. His work is excellent in the detail description of lives in the RUF based on his anthropological field work and collection of narratives.

What he emphasizes in his work are aspects of 'revolution' and social change in the RUF. The RUF is infamous for ill-discipline and diamond smuggling, but he tries to elucidate the other aspect of the RUF: its ideology and their revolutionary views. For example, he introduces a narrative by a cadre, who embraces a vision of 'revolution' but cannot achieve this because of a failure to discipline soldiers. Peters also introduces another cadre who established an NGO in post-conflict Sierra Leone for achieving his ideological view. For Peters, the cadre is a revolutionist who once failed in armed struggle, but attempts to change Sierra Leone through NGO activities.

He looks at the RUF too favorably. The RUF is notorious for brutal murders, senseless atrocities, lacks of discipline and a war economy ('blood diamonds'). However he does not discuss these issues. Peters' description exclusively focuses on the aspects of the revolutionist. This aspect might be true, and his work is significant as he shows ideological aspects of the RUF. However, his description is too extreme to be true because he only introduces the positive aspects. He does not discuss negative aspects of the RUF.

One of his problems is his uncritical acceptance of narratives. It seems that he describes what ex-soldiers claim to him without any consideration. He does

37 F. De Boeck, A. Honwana, 'Introduction: Children and Youth in Africa', in A. Honwana, F. De Boeck (eds), *Makers and Breakers: Children and Youth in Postcolonial Africa*, pp. 1-18.

38 Paul Richards, *Fighting For The Rain Forest: War, Youth and Resources in Sierra Leone*.

39 Honwana, De Boeck (eds), *Makers and Breakers;* M. Bøås, K. C. Dunn (eds), *African Guerrillas: Raging against the Machine;* J. Abbink, I. van Kessel (eds) *Vanguard or Vandals: Youth, Politics and Conflict in Africa;* M. Utas, *Sweet Battlefield: Youth and Liberian Civil War.*

40 K. Peters, *Footpath to Reintegration: Armed Conflict, Youth and the Rural Crisis in Sierra Leone.*

41 Krijin Peters is an advisee of Paul Richards.

not cross-check the narratives he collects with existing written materials such as fact-finding reports published by NGOs, international organizations, the Sierra Leone Special Court and the Truth and Reconciliation Commission. He might dare not to refer to these materials in order to focus on what soldiers say. He fails to understand how the negative aspects (such as atrocities, lootings and lack of discipline) and the positive aspects which he describes are interrelated. As a result, his discussion becomes one-sided.

Another problem is in his literature review. In his literature review, he exhaustively presents previous works on the RUF and Sierra Leone conflict regardless of academic disciplines. However, he criticizes other disciplines with his own logic. He does not consider why they provide such understandings.[42] The one-sidedness of his arguments partly stems from his lack of argument on how his understandings are interrelated to previous understandings.

One of the examples is his criticism toward Paul Collier.[43] As an econometrician, Collier has attempted to find out the factors of armed conflicts by statistical analysis. His interest is in predicting which societies might be the most prone to civil wars. He does not have interest in a specific conflict, and his research objective is to explore tendencies of all armed conflicts in the world since the end of World War II. In his conclusion, he states:

> The risk of civil war has been systematically related to a few economic conditions, such as dependence upon primary commodity exports and low national income ... I argue that this is because civil wars occur where rebel organizations are financially viable.[44]

Thus, Collier finds a correlation between dependence upon primary commodity and exports low national income on one hand, and the risk of civil war on the other hand. As one of the examples, Collier presents the case of Sierra Leone:

> Sierra Leone is......a major exporter of diamonds, and there was considerable evidence that the rebel organization [RUF] was involved in this business on a large scale.[45]

Thus, Collier used the case of Sierra Leone as one of the examples. However, Peters just refers to the sentences in which Collier mentions Sierra Leone.

42 Peters, *Footpath to Reintegration*, pp. 5-8, 102-110.
43 P. Collier, 'Economic causes of civil conflict and their implications for policy', in C. A. Crocker, F. O. Hampson, P. Aall, *Turbulent Peace: the Challenges of Managing International Conflict*, pp. 143-162.
44 Ibid, p. 143.
45 Ibid, p. 146.

Peters criticize Collier as follows:

> What needs to be noted here…is that the evidence in Sierra Leone is highly ambiguous. The war was fought for several years without major diamond income.[46]

Thus, Peters criticizes only a part of Collier's argument which is related to Sierra Leone. Peters' interest is only on Sierra Leone even though Collier's object is to find out which societies might be the most prone to civil wars.

Peter does not argue with Collier's main findings: the correlation between risk of civil war and dependence upon primary commodity exports and low national income. It holds true to Sierra Leone. Collier is wrong in his interpretation of Sierra Leone but the correlation he finds is still worthy to examine, but Peters only picks up Collier's argument on Sierra Leone.

As can be seen in this example, Peters criticizes other disciplines with his own logic. In his literature review, he fails to "stand on the shoulders of giants." He cannot learn findings of other disciplines. Peters' work is admirable in describing high-minded commanders and soldiers inside ill-disciplined rebel groups, but, his description is too extreme to be true by not arguing the other aspect.[47]

Conclusion

We have examined three images of soldiers. These three images are popular as representations, but they are too extreme to be true. The objective of this article is to elucidate the problem of armed conflict studies. This article sets two questions: "What are the problems in existing armed conflict studies?" and "Why do these problems arise?"

For the answer to the first question, I conclude that exclusive acceptance of one image makes the understanding deviate. Each image cannot escape from one-sidedness. Every image captures one aspect of soldiers, but it cannot capture the whole picture. Thus, one image is not enough, but it is possible to approach a more reasonable explanation by accumulating several images. A scholar might provide only one specific image in one article. If a scholar examines interrelation between his interpretation and previous interpretations of soldiers, one can come close to a more appropriate interpretation. However, if a scholar only claims one's own interpretation without examining the consistency with previous research, what the scholar provides would be too

---

46 Peters, *Footpath to Reintegration*, p. 7.
47 These aspects are explored by the following works: D. Keen, *Conflict and Collusion in Sierra Leone*; L. Gberie, *A Dirty War in West Africa: The RUF and the Destruction of Sierra Leone*.

extreme to be true.

The second question is "Why does the problem arise?" Here, I present two reasons why images of soldiers are unpalatable.

First, images evolve to extremes as discussions proceed. As we have seen, images have objectives. For example, that of child soldiers is to advocate the rights of the child. The image of rational thugs is to explain a phenomenon. These images are tools for achieving specific objectives. In order to achieve objectives, specific aspects are picked up. As the picked-up portions are too limited, it is often too extreme to be true. These extreme images have significance because they have objectives. However, these images are detached from objectives. As the result, they lose reasons why specific aspects are exclusively picked up. As the result, the images lose *raison d'être*. These images are too extreme to be compatible.

Second, the participation of a broad range of disciplines in armed-conflict studies prevents scholars from understanding the other disciplines. In the discussion of armed-conflict studies, scholars of various disciplines have provided various understandings. Scholars in a specific discipline often have limited understanding toward other disciplines. Sometimes, scholars criticize other disciplines with their own logic. Peters' arguments hold true to the case. I present another example. Paul Collier, econometrician, criticizes the approach of political science in order to justify his econometric approach. Collier argues as follows:

Political science offers an account of conflict in terms of motive: rebellion occurs when grievances are sufficiently acute that people want to engage in violent protest. In marked contrast, a small economic theory literature... models rebellion as an industry that generates profits from looting, so that 'the insurgents are indistinguishable from bandits or pirates'. ...the incidence of rebellion is not explained by motive, but by the atypical circumstances that generate profitable opportunities.[48]

Thus, he justifies the econometric approach by criticizing political science with his own logic. But, to put his claim another way, econometricians do not have any choice but to regard insurgents as bandits or pirates because their analytical tool is only appropriate for economic factors. Thus, scholars in one discipline reject other disciplines to justify their own approaches. As Collier's rejection of political science and Peters' adherence to the image of 'marginalized youth' show, scholars fail to "stand on the shoulder of giants". Thus, the two reasons make images unpalatable.

There are two lessons we can learn from the discussion in order to surmount the problem. First, we should not pay attention exclusively to individual specific theories and concepts. We have to consider objectives and

---

48 P. Collier, A. Hoeffler, 'Greed and grievance in civil war', *Oxford Economic Papers*, pp. 563-595.

raison d'etre behind the theory and the concept. Second, it is necessary to understand other disciplines which explore the same phenomenon. We have to evaluate previous literatures in order to "stand on the shoulder of giants" (or to draw lessons from previous research). As armed conflict is a complex phenomenon, it is impossible to grasp the whole picture by one specific discipline. Due to the complexity of the phenomenon, analyses from various aspects are needed. In addition, the integration of various understandings is also essential to understand armed conflicts. Therefore, scholars have to understand what the other disciplines explore, how they tackle the issue, and how these understandings are related to his/her own findings. Without open-minded critical examination, the study of armed conflicts would not develop.

Bibliography

J. Abbink, I. van Kessel (eds), *Vanguard or Vandals: Youth, Politics and Conflict in Africa*, Leiden, Boston, Brill, 2005.

R. H. Bates, *Markets and States in Tropical Africa: The Political Basis of Agricultural Policies*, Berkley, University of California Press, 1984.

J.- F. Bayart, *The State in Africa: the Politics of the Belly*, London, New York, 1993.

I. Beah, *A Long Way Gone: Memoirs of a Boy Soldier*, New York, Farrar, Straus and Giroux, 2007.

M. Bøås, K. C. Dunn (eds), *African Guerrillas: Raging against the Machine*, Boulder, Lynne Rienner, 2007.

R. Brett, M. McCallin, *Children: the Invisible Soldiers*, Stockholm, Rädda Barnen, 1996.

R. Brett, I. Specht, *Young Soldiers: Why They Choose to Fight*, London, Lynne Rienner, 2004.

P. Chabal, J-P. Daloz, *African Works: Disorder as Political Instrument*, London, International African Institute in association with James Currey, 1999.

P. Collier, 'Economic causes of civil conflict and their implications for policy', in C. A. Crocker, F. O. Hampson, P. Aall, *Turbulent Peace: the Challenges of Managing International Conflict*, Washington D.C., United States Institute of Peace Press, 2001, pp. 143-162.

P. Collier, A. Hoeffler, 'Greed and grievance in civil war', *Oxford Economic Papers*, 2004, vol. 56, no. 4, pp. 563-595.

C. Coulter, *Bush Wives and Girl Soldiers: Women Lives through War and Peace in Sierra Leone*, Ithaca, Cornell University Press, 2009.

C. Cramer, 'Homo economicus goes to war: methodological individualism, rational choice and the political economy of war', *World Development*, 2002, vol. 30, no. 11, pp. 1845-1864.

C. A. Crocker, F. O. Hampson, P. Aall (eds), *Leashing the Dogs of War: Conflict*

Management in a Divided World, Washington D.C., United State Institute of Peace Press, 2007.

M. Denov, *Child Soldiers: Sierra Leone's Revolutionary United Front*, Cambridge, Cambridge University Press, 2010.

L. Gberie, *A Dirty War in West Africa: The RUF and the Destruction of Sierra Leone*, Bloomington, Indiana University Press, 2005.

J. Hart, 'The politics of "child soldiers"', *Brown Journal of World Affairs*, 2006, vol. 13, pp. 217-226.

J. Herbst, *International laws of war and the African child: norms, compliance, and sovereignty*, Working Paper #00-02, Center for Research on Child Wellbeing, Princeton University, 2000.

D. Hoffman, *War Machine: Young Men and Violence in Sierra Leone and Liberia*, Durham, Duke University Press, 2011.

A. Honwana, *Child Soldiers in Africa*, Philadelphia, University of Pennsylvania Press, 2006.

A. Honwana, F. De Boeck (eds), *Makers and Breakers: Children and Youth in Postcolonial Africa*, Trenton, Oxford, Africa World Press, James Currey, 2005.

Human Right Watch, *Easy to Prey: Child Soldiers in Liberia*, New York, Human Rights Watch, 1996.

R. H. Jackson, C. G. Rosberg, *Personal Rule in Africa: Prince, Autocrat, Prophet, Tyrany*, Berkley, Los Angeles, London, University of California Press, 1982.

D. Keen, *Conflict and Collusion in Sierra Leone*, New York, Oxford, James Currey, New York, Palgrave, 2005.

Idem, *The Economic Functions of Violence in Civil Wars*, Adelphi Paper 320, Oxford, Oxford University Press for the International Institute for Strategic Studies, 1998.

R. Lemarchand, 'Political clientelism and ethnicity in tropical Africa: competing solidarities in nation-building', *American Political Science Review*, 1972, vol. 66, no. 1, pp. 68-90.

F. Machulup, *Methodologies of Economics and Social Science*, London, Academic Press Inc., 1978.

E. Newman, R. Paris, O. P. Richmond (eds), *New Perspective on Liberal Peacebuiding*, Tokyo, United Nations University Press, 2009.

M. Olson, *The Logic of Collective Action: Public Goods and Theory of Groups*, New York, Schoclen Books, 1968.

R. Paris, T. D. Sisk (eds), *The Dilemmas of Statebuilding: Confronting the contradictions of Postwar Peace Operations*, London, New York, Routledge, 2009.

K. Peters, *Footpath to Reintegration: Armed Conflict, Youth and the Rural Crisis in Sierra Leone*, Unpublished Dissertation, Wageningen University, 2006.

W. Reno, *Warlord Politics and African States*, Boulder, Lynne Rienner Publisher,

1998.

Idem, 'Reinvention of an African patrimonial state: Charles Taylor's Liberia', *Third World Quarterly*, 1995, vol. 16, no.1, pp.109-120.

D. M. Rosen, 'Child soldiers, international humanitarian law, and the globalization of childhood', *American Anthropologist*, 2007, vol. 109, pp. 296-306.

D. M. Rosen, *Armies of the Young: Child Soldiers in War and Terrorism*, The Rutgers Series in Childhood Studies, New Brunswick, Rutgers University Press, 2005.

J. Scott, 'Patron-client politics and political change in Southeast Asia', *American Political Science Review*, 1972, vol. 66, no. 1, pp. 91-113.

M. Szefel, 'Clientelism, corruption and catastrophe', *Review of African Political Economy*, 2000, vol. 27, no. 85, pp. 427-441.

S. Takeuchi, 'Afurilka no hunsou: sono kon'nichiteki tokushitsu ni tuite no kousatsu' (Armed conflicts in Africa: analysis of the contemporary characteristics), in S. Takeuchi Shin'ichi (ed.), *Gendai Afrika no Hunsou: Rekishi to Shutai*, (Contemporary Conflicts in Africa: its History and Actors), Tokyo, Institute of Developing Economies, 2000, pp. 3-52.

United Nations Security Council Resolution 1539, S-RES-1539 (2004).

M. Utas, 'Agency of victims: young women's survival strategies in the Liberian civil war', in F. De Boeck, A. Honwana (eds), *Makers and Breakers: Children and Youth as Emerging Categories in Postcolonial Africa*, Oxford, James Currey, 2005, pp. 53-80.

M. Utas, *Sweet Battlefield: Youth and Liberian Civil War*, PhD Thesis, Department of Cultural Anthropology, Uppsala University Dissertations in Cultural Anthropology, 2003.

T. Weiss, *Perpetrating Power: Small Arms in Post-Conflict Sierra Leone and Liberia*, Pretoria, Institute for Security Studies, 2005.

Part Three   **Children in War: An Institutional Perspective**

12 Raising the 'future of the nation': Child welfare in Spain and Greece during the civil wars (1936-39, 1946-49)

Loukianos I. Hassiotis

Introduction

Concepts of child welfare changed profoundly during the 20th century, due to the political and social upheavals that the world experienced. The process of change was already underway from the end of the 19th century, as a result of the growing interest of the governmental elites in decreasing infant mortality, and in improving children's living standards and intellectual capacities. This was also part of their aim to create a strong and healthy race, capable of confronting growing national and imperialistic antagonism. This policy derived from the belief that children represented the nation's most valuable asset and needed to be treated as such, or the country would fall into decline and degeneration. Thus, as in other areas of welfare, state intervention assumed an increasingly prominent role in the protection and upbringing of children; sometimes replacing the more traditional forms of individual charity or the philanthropic work of non-governmental institutions (like the Church, the Red Cross and other benevolent societies), but more often working alongside them.[1] State interventionism and political considerations regarding the protection of childhood acquired a new meaning during the age of total war. Doubtless this was partly a consequence of the unprecedented embroilment of children in the conflicts: as victims of starvation, bombardment, atrocities, executions and, indeed, genocide; as actual participants in the military effort, especially in the revolutionary movements and in the Resistance during the Second World War; and, last but not least, as tools of propaganda and social control by governments and political parties. Moreover, children became part of the 'meaning' of war, as societies used them as symbols of virtue, sacrifice

---

1   F. Ewald, *L'Etat providence*, p. 53; H. Hendrick, *Child Welfare*, pp. 19-86; H. Cunningham, *Children and Childhood in Western Society*, pp. 137-8, and Ibid., *The Invention of Childhood*, pp. 15-6, 178-88, 208.

213

and patriotism.[2]

The experience of Spanish and Greek minors during the respective civil wars in the two countries was shaped, more or less, by the same factors. A few children participated actively in the struggle, to make good the shortfall in adult belligerents. Tens of thousands were killed in bombardments, 'liquidations' or died of starvation and epidemics. Many more were orphaned or were separated from their parents and were relocated either inside their country or abroad, 'for their safety'. The camps involved in the conflicts soon realized that children should be 'saved' both for humanitarian reasons and for the success of their own struggle, as the 'protection' of the minors became a matter of prestige and propaganda. The measures they took varied according to their military and economic potentials, as well as their political aspirations. This paper attempts to examine these measures and the ideas behind them, focusing on the policies and the conceptions of the victorious sides; that is, the Spanish and the Greek nationalists and anti-communists. In my approach I have used archives of the relevant relief organisations, their official publications, articles of the Spanish and Greek Press of the period under consideration, as well as contemporary historiography.

The historical context

The Spanish and the Greek Civil Wars of the 20th century have been broadly discussed in contemporary historiography – indeed the Spanish case has been proved to be one of the most favourite themes of historians. Thus, this article will only present a very general description of both events, in order to help the reader better understand the following narrative.

The Spanish Civil War began on July 1936, after a *coup d'etát* by a group of generals against the elected government of the 'Popular Front'. The rebel coup was supported by a number of conservative, monarchist and fascist groups, which were soon to be merged in 1937 into the Falange Española Tradicionalista y de las Juntas de Ofensiva Nacional-Syndicalista, headed by general Francisco Franco, who took the title of 'Caudillo', leader.[3] The Republican side was supported by the participants of the 'Popular Front'; that is, centrist liberals, socialists, communists, trotskyists, as well as the conservative Basque and the more left-orientated Catalan autonomists. The strong anarchist movement, although not part of the 'Popular Front', also sided with the Republicans. Since the coup did not manage to gain immediate control of Spain, the country was militarily and politically divided in two

2   E. Simonsen, 'Children in Danger', pp. 271-2; P. N. Stearns, *Childhood in World History*, pp. 110-2; J. Marten, 'Introduction', pp. 4-8, and N. Stargardt, *Witnesses of War*, pp. 7, 56-79.
3   FET y de las JONS

zones, where bloody purges occurred against political adversaries and their families. General Franco began a protracted war of attrition against the Republicans, assisted by Nazi Germany, Fascist Italy as well as neighbouring Portugal. Meanwhile the Soviet Union, Mexico and left-wing volunteers of the International Brigades intervened in support of the Republican side. The war ended in April 1939 with the victory of the nationalist or 'Francoist' side, the overthrow of the Second Spanish Republic, the exile of tens of thousands of Republican Spaniards and the imprisonment or execution of many others. Franco established an authoritarian regime, which shared many common aspects with Nazi Germany and Fascist Italy, although after the end of the Second World War it largely eliminated its fascist credentials, replacing them with more traditional authoritarian ones. Nevertheless, Spain remained a dictatorship until Franco's death in 1975.[4]

The Greek Civil War started ten years after the beginning of the Spanish conflict, as a consequence of a highly polarised struggle between leftists and rightists that had already begun during the Axis occupation of the country (1941-1944). During that period, the royalist Greek government remained in exile, unable to influence the situation at home, where various resistance groups of differing political affiliations emerged, the dominant one being the leftist National Liberation Front,[5] controlled effectively by the Greek Communist Party.[6] Political antagonism remained alive after the liberation and, indeed, led to an open British military intervention, in December 1944, in favour of the royalist government. Many leftists were imprisoned by the authorities or persecuted and killed by right-wing bands, while KKE decided to boycott the elections of 1946. From then on, KKE increasingly turned its focus to an armed struggle, supporting the emergence of a newly formed guerrilla army that was named Democratic Army of Greece,[7] and which for the next three years would fight against the National Army controlled by the government and the King. Although the communist guerrillas managed to establish their positions in the mountainous areas of rural Greece, they never solved the problems they faced around small numbers of recruits and inefficient supplies, neither did they gain control over a significant part of the country. Eventually, increased American aid to the anti-communist camp and the side-effects of the Stalin-Tito Split led to victory for the government forces. As a result of the civil war, the Greek Communist Party was outlawed and tens of thousands of its supporters were imprisoned or exiled. Although

---

4   As already mentioned, the literature on the Spanish Civil War is vast. Indicatively, see H. Thomas, *The Spanish Civil War*; A. Beevor, *The Battle for Spain*, and P. Preston, *The Spanish Civil War*.

5   *Ethniko Apeleftherotiko Metopo*, EAM.

6   *Kommunistiko Komma Elladas*, KKE.

7   *Dimokratikos Stratos tis Elladas*.

Greece remained a parliamentary monarchy in the post-war years, the regime remained largely under control of non-democratic institutions, like the Army and the Palace, while left-wing opinion was semi-censored and political prisoners were not freed until the late 1950s and early 1960s. Even then, democratisation of the regime was halted by a *coup d'etât* and a military dictatorship that was supported by the United States, and lasted until 1974.[8]

The 'Children's Question' in wartime Spain and Greece

In Spain, the Republicans initially decided to create special 'colonies' for all refugee children from the Nationalist Zone, and from their own cities that faced constant bombardment. When this proved impossible, as the unfortunate refugee children were too numerous, they turned to the notion of expatriating more than 35,000 Spanish minors to several European countries, mostly France, Britain, Belgium and the Soviet Union, as well as to Mexico. This was a tough decision for parents and children alike; it was in line, however, with both the demand to 'save the children' and to the need to free fathers and mothers from their parental duties, so that they could serve the Republic. The expatriation of children could also be used for propaganda purposes in the countries where the refugee minors were moved.[9]

Almost ten years later, at the beginning of 1948, the Democratic Army of Greece decided to evacuate approximately 25,000 children mainly from the northern provinces of the country, where the main strongholds of the guerrillas were situated, to the neighbouring 'People's Republics'. The official argument put forward was that in this way children were saved from bombardment by governmental forces, and from starvation and hardship. Although this claim should not be understood solely as an act of propaganda, we do know that the enterprise's main aim was to encourage the recruitment of (the children's) mothers to the guerrilla's army. The Greek government denounced KKE's evacuation enterprise as treacherous, claiming that it was part of a Soviet plan to re-habilitate Greek youngsters and transform them

---

8   L. Baerentzen, J. O. Iatrides, O. L. Smith (eds), *Studies in the History of the Greek Civil War, 1945-1949.*; D. Close (ed.), *The Greek civil war 1943-1950*, and A. Nachmani, *International intervention in the Greek Civil War.*

9   On the republican 'colonias infantiles' and 'colonias escolares' see R. Crego Navarro, 'Las colonias escolares durante la guerra civil (1936-1939)', *Historia Contemporánea*, pp. 299-328; C. Ruiz Rodrigo, *Política y educación en la II República*, pp. 131-70; A. Alted Vigil, E. Nicolás Marín, R. González Martell, *Los niños de la guerra de España en la Unión Soviética*, pp. 30-1, and E. Pons Prades, *Los niños republicanos en la Guerra de España*, pp. 36-8, 60-1. On the evacuation enterprise and the experiences of the Spanish refugee children abroad see indicatively: D. Legarreta, *The Guernica Generation*; Alted Vigil, Marín, González Martell, *Los niños de la guerra de España*; D. Kowalsky, *Stalin and the Spanish Civil War*, and E. Pons Prades, *Los niños republicanos.*

into enemies of their homeland. The same argument was made concerning the Republicans, by the Spanish Nationalists ten years earlier.[10] Yet, if we consider the living conditions in the Republican zone in Spain and in the guerrillas' zone in Greece, a temporary –as it was then considered– expatriation of some thousands of children seemed to offer the best relief they could get.

The Francoist side in Spain and the anti-communist camp in Greece had many more opportunities to follow a coherent and systematic relief programme for war-handicapped children. In military terms, they were significantly more powerful and their territories were rarely challenged. Moreover, they had many more supplies, since they controlled the most productive and prosperous areas in the respective countries, notwithstanding the help they received from abroad (especially in the Greek case).[11] Crucially, they were the sides that actually won the war, which enabled them to implement and consolidate their welfare policy in the following decades. In Spain, the initiative for children's relief was taken by the party of *Falange*, which in the very first stages of the war created *Auxilio Social*.[12] In Greece, it was the Queen herself, who had recently returned with her husband from self-exile following a controversial plebiscite, who insisted on the establishment of *Eranos tis Vassilissas*, 'Queen's Fund', aimed to help Greek war-handicapped children.

During the Spanish Civil War, the first collection fund in the zone controlled by the Nationalists was organised in the autumn of 1936. It was aimed to help those who had been wounded in the fighting or suffered in other ways. Known as *Auxilio de Invierno*, Winter Relief, the fund soon turned its focus to orphans and abandoned children. This organisation was established through the initiative of two members of the FET y de las JONS, namely Mercedes Sanz Bachiller[13] and Javier Martínez de Bedoya, another member of the JONS, and followed the model of the respective Nazi organisation *Winterhilfe*. In 1937, its name was changed to *Auxilio Social*. *Auxilio Social*

---

10 L. Baerentzen, 'The "Paidomazoma" and the Queen's Camps', in L. Baerentzen, J. Iatrides, O. Smith (eds), *Studies, in the History*, pp. 127-55; E. Lagani, *The 'paidomazoma' and Greek-Yugoslav Relations*, pp. 13-32; H. Jones, 'A New Kind of War', p. 140; T. Vervenioti, 'Charity and Nationalism: The Greek Civil War and the Entrance of Right-Wing Women into Politics', in P. Baccheta, M. Power (eds), *Right-wing Women*, pp. 115-26, and M. Ristović, 'Children as Refugees: Greek Children in Yugoslavia, 1948-1960', in S. Naumović, M. Jovanović (eds), *Childhood in South East Europe*, pp. 215-34.

11 These advantages have been extensively discussed by contemporary historiography. Indicatively only see: For the Spanish case, Beevor, *The Battle for Spain*; Preston, *The Spanish Civil War*, p. 135, and J. Tusell, *Historia de España en el siglo XX*, pp. 288-404. For the Greek case: L. S. Witner, *American Intervention in Greece*, pp. 70-102, 167; D. Close, T. Veremis, 'The Military Struggle, 1945-49', in D. Close (ed.), *The Greek Civil War*, pp. 97-128, and G. Margaritis, *History of the Greek Civil War*, pp. 127-52, 174-212.

12 It means Social Relief.

13 The widow of Onésimo Redondo Ortega, a syndicalist leader of the JONS who was killed in the first weeks of the hostilities.

organised numerous messes and relief centres for mothers and children, and, increasingly, closed institutions, the *hogares*, for minors – mainly orphans, destitute children, and the sons and daughters of political prisoners and exiles. The organisation's intention was to replace the crumbling traditional welfare system and thus become the only relief agency of Franco's *Falange*.[14] It gradually became an official institution –always under the party's control– and obtained wide responsibilities and several privileges, due to its political and ideological role, although it was not fully integrated into the state welfare system until the late 1960's.[15]

On the other hand, the birth of the Queen's Fund,[16] during the Greek Civil War ten years later, claimed to be a response to a real humanitarian disaster that the country's youth faced: A report of the time by the newly formed UNESCO estimated that there were more than 340,000 war-handicapped children in post-war Greece, who could not be assisted by the state's relief services.[17] So, much like in the Spanish example, a semi-official organisation was formed, under the auspices of Queen Frederica. It involved the participation of men and women loyal to the monarchy and to the Queen herself, government departments, the Hellenic Red Cross, the Orthodox Church and some Christian and charity associations. The National Army and other security forces cooperated closely too, at least until the end of hostilities. The creation of *paidopoleis* or child-towns for war-handicapped children was considered the organisation's main work. The role of the *paidopoleis* gained new momentum in the first months of 1948, when the guerrillas initiated their enterprise of evacuating children to the neighbouring Balkan countries: The Greek authorities initiated a race to gather as many children as possible to the institutions run by the Queen's Fund, in order to 'save' them from 'abduction'. Additionally, the communist 'evacuation' policy justified the children's relocation policy followed by the government and the Queen's Fund. Thus, in the Greek civil war the so called 'children's issue' was used as a part of the war strategy, as a diplomatic tactic and,[18] finally, as a tool for propaganda that gained much significance, especially in the post-war anti-

---

14 On the formation and the function of *Auxilio Social* see M. Orduña Prada, *El Auxilio Social (1936-1940)*, and Á. Cenarro, *La sonrisa de Falange*. Paul Preston offers a biography of Mercedes Sanz Bachiller in *Doves of War*, pp. 205-93.

15 Orduña Prada, *El Auxilio Social*, pp. 27-126, and P. Carasa, 'La revolución nacional-asistencial durante el primer franquismo (1936-1940)', *Historia Contemporánea*, pp. 104-19.

16 Officially: Fund for the Welfare of the Northern Provinces of Greece or *Eranos Vorion Eparhion Ellados*.

17 On the problems that orphan and destitute children were facing in post-war Greece see the report by T. Brosse in hers, *War-handicapped Children*, pp. 22-6.

18 Since it was internationalised by the Greek government, and was discussed in the UN General Assembly in the context of the so-called 'Greek Question'.

communist rhetoric.[19]

Structure and functional issues of Auxilio Social and Eranos

Both the *Auxilio Social* and *Eranos* had pyramid-like, centralised and strictly hierarchical structures, based on a militarized pattern. Their staffs were supposed to be selected on the basis of two criteria: affiliation to the *Falange/* Greek monarchy respectively, and professional profile. Heading the *Auxilio Social* was its National Representative[20], who represented the organisation in the National Council of the *Falange*, Consejo Nacional de FET y de las JONS. Next to the National Representative were the Technical Secretary, Secretario Técnico, and the National Expert Advisory Office, Asesoría Técnica Nacional. Under these stood the Regional Representatives and below them the Local Representatives, Delegados Provinciales, Locales, as well as the administration of the organisation's institutions, which included the director, teachers, falangist instructors, nurses, guards, cooks and other staff. Every member of this network had to adhere to the strict hierarchy and rules, which were generally defined by the National Representative, the Expert-Secretary and the National Expert Advisory Office. *Auxilio Social's* structure was further interwoven with other party and state services, like the *Sección Femenina*,[21] *Servicio Social*,[22] and, last but not least, the –nationalists'– Ministry of Interior.[23]

Accordingly, at the top of the Queen's Fund hierarchy was Queen Frederica herself, followed by her trustees, the so-called 'commissioned ladies', who were upper class volunteers, and the executive committee.[24] The executive committee was responsible for the general administrative and managerial control of *Eranos*, and issued the operational rules of the child-towns, whereas the commissioned ladies were supposed to have an advisory role and to mediate between the executive committee and the supervisory committees of the child-towns. In contrast to the *Auxilio Social*, the structure of *Eranos* was largely based on the scout pattern. At the head was the general chief, or director, after him/her the deputy commander, then the community leader, and finally the group leader. Teachers, nurses, guards, cooks and others

19 On the creation of the Queen's Fund: Baerentzen, 'The "Paidomazoma" and the Queen's Camps', pp. 148-50, and L. Hassiotis, 'Relocating Children during the Greek Civil War (1946-1949), in J. Reinisch, E. White (eds) *The Disentanglement of Populations*, pp. 271-88.
20 Delegado Nacional, a position initially assigned to Mercedes Sanz Bachiller.
21 The female organisation of Falange.
22 An obligatory service for unmarried women, which was enacted in 1937 and lasted until the end of Franco's dictatorship.
23 Orduña Prada, *El Auxilio Social*, pp. 129-176, Carasa, 'La revolución nacional-asistencial', pp. 103-5, and Cenarro, *La sonrisa*, pp. 87-9 ff.
24 The equivalent of the Spanish National Expert Advisory Office.

were also included in the personnel of the *paidopoleis*. Furthermore, the Greek government established in the spring of 1948 the Committee for the Coordination of Rescue and Relief of the Greek Children,[25] and its executive branch, the Special Service for the Relief of Greek Children,[26] in order to coordinate the enterprise of 'saving' the children of the northern provinces from 'abduction' by the communist guerrillas, and to shelter them in the *paidopoleis* – whose number grew rapidly during the next year.[27]

Soon, however, the intricate nature of both *Auxilio Social* and *Eranos*, arising from the special status they enjoyed, proved to be a source of tension, competition and overlapping responsibilities.[28] These frictions usually reflected personal or fractional antagonisms within the respective regimes, but occasionally indicated ideological differences and strife too. To give an example, the much discussed conflict between Mercedes Sanz Bachiller and Pilar Primo de Rivera,[29] began when the former was granted permission by Franco to recruit young Spanish women for the activities of her organisation. This meant that in practice the majority of the members of *Sección Femenina* were placed under the orders of Mercedes Sanz, a development that obviously disturbed Pilar Primo.[30] At the same time, the tension between them also reflected their differing views regarding the role of women in the public sphere: Pilar was strongly distrustful of Mercedes' initiative to place women in responsible positions, as in her words, 'family and children are the only goal that women can achieve in life'.[31] To this we should also add the struggle for dominance in the party between the old *Jonsistas*, with whom Mercedes was associated, and the so-called *legalistas*, who were supposed to express the dogma of pre-war *Falange* and its founder José Antonio.[32]

In Greece, the Queen's Fund faced similar competition with other state

---

25 *Epitropi Sintonismou, Diasosis kai Perithalpseos Ellinopedon*, ESDPE.

26 *Idiki Ypiresia Perithalpseos Ellinopedon*, EYPE.

27 The structure of the organisation is discussed in L. Hassiotis, *Children of the Civil War*.

28 It should be noted that, although both organisations were independent of the state mechanism, they received state's financial support and logistics. Furthermore, they held the exclusive right to raise money for the benefit of the war-handicapped population. On the money collections of *Auxilio Social* see Orduña Prada, *El Auxilio Social*, pp. 211-230; Carasa, 'La revolución nacional-asistencial', 109-11, and Cenarro, *La sonrisa*, pp. 47-50. On the equivalent privilege of *Eranos* see *Efimeris tis Kiverniseos tou Vassiliou tis Ellados* (Gazette of the Government of the Greek Kingdom), 11 July 1947, and Hellenic Literary and Historical Archive (HLHA)/Royal Welfare: Alexandra Mela, *The Chronicle*, pp. 283, 292, vol. 140. For an early critique of the Queen's Fund financing and institutional status see J. Meynaud, *Les forces politiques en Grèce*, pp. 277-8.

29 Chief of *Sección Femenina*, daughter of ex-dictator Miguel Primo de Rivera, and sister of José Antonio, leader of the pre-war fascist *Falange Española*, who became a 'martyr' of the nationalist camp after being jailed and eventually executed by the republicans.

30 Cenarro, *La sonrisa*, pp. 73-109.

31 St. G. Payne, *Fascism in Spain*, p. 323.

32 Preston, *Doves*, pp. 247-8, 256-7, 281-3; J. Maria Thomàs, *La Falange de Franco*, pp. 137-9, and Cenarro, *La sonrisa*, pp. 63-5.

relief agencies and military men, who participated in the enterprise of gathering children from the Northern provinces into the child-towns. The primary cause of their disagreement related to the management and control of the newly formed institutions: Officials of ESDPE and EYPE were discontented with what they considered as Fund's interference in their work. There was also disagreement regarding the role played by the Queen's commissioned ladies: military officers and other officials, including members of the *Eranos'* executive committee, seemed dissatisfied with the broad powers that Frederica's trustees assumed.[33]

Disagreements over the role of women in the activities of both organisations prove the prominent status they acquired in this type of mobilization of the population. In fact, in both Spain and Greece, relief work offered at that time the only possibility for women to participate in right-wing politics. Conservative women in both societies faced not only the traditional patriarchal characteristics of their respective country, but also the contradiction between their personal ambitions and their political camp's view regarding the role of women. The most famous women of the francoist camp in Spain were Mercedes Sanz and Pilar Primo, both involved in social work of the new regime. Accordingly, in the anti-communist side in Greece the most distinguished figure was Queen Frederica, who was proclaimed 'mother of the army and the people' and 'Goddess of Providence', having saved Greek children from starvation or abduction by the communists. Other women, who later rose to the hierarchy of the Greek post-war government had also served in the *Eranos* or in other relief activities – it is no coincidence that Lina Tsaldari, the first woman to obtain a ministerial portfolio in Greece, was a former executive of the organisation.[34]

The ideological factor of child-welfare in Spain and Greece: Similarities and differences

The ideological orientation of the two relief organisations corresponded to the

---

33 On the dispute between the Queen's Fund and other state services, as well as between the male and female members of the Fund see indicatively, General State Archives (GSA), Central Service/Archive of Ex Royal Palaces /1222: L. Zarifi, F. Hartoulari (commissioned ladies) to the executive committee of the Queen's Fund, Alexandroupoli, 15 August 1947; GSA Central Service/Archive of Ex Royal Palaces/1214: M. Pesmazoglou to the Committee for the Coordination of Rescue and Relief of the Greek Children (ESDPE), Athens, 14 July 1948; GSA, Central Service/Archive of Ex Royal Palaces/1228: Memorandum of the executive committee of the Queen's Fund, Athens, 28 February 1949; and GSA, Central Service/Archive of Ex Royal Palaces/1233: Special session of the Committee of the Commissioned Ladies, Athens, 30 March 1949.

34 V. L. Enders: "'And we Ate Up the World": Memories of the *Sección Femenina*', in Baccheta, Power (eds), *Right-wing Women*, pp. 87-9; in the same volume, Vervenioti, 'Charity and Nationalism', pp. 118-21; see also Carasa, 'La revolución nacional-asistencial', pp. 94-102.

general characteristics of the sides they represented and, therefore, differed significantly. *Auxilio Social* was considered an organic part of the *Falange*, which combined traditional Spanish conservatism with fascist doctrines under the principles of national-syndicalism and national-Catholicism. This explains the impact of the totalitarian welfare schemes of Nazi Germany and Fascist Italy to Social Relief's theoretical approaches, as well as the increasing influence of the Catholic Church on the organisation. *Auxilio Social's* leadership believed in the creation of a united and powerful national community, without class or regional divisions. In their declarations, *Auxilio Social* spoke about fulfilling the ideals of the 'Spanish race' and the creation of a 'New Spain', which would be faithful to Catholicism, disciplined, hierarchically structured, purified from socialist and liberal ideas, and capable of following its 'imperial historic mission of the nation'. The radical change brought about by *Auxilio Social* in the practice of charity in Spain consisted of replacing the individual, as a benefactor and beneficiary, with the nation. According to the organic and national-syndicalist principles of the organisation, the care of children, mothers and the population as a whole represented a national project of national and state reconstruction; in this project the nation *en masse* had to participate as an organic whole, integrating the various social groups it consisted of.[35]

For its part, *Eranos* followed the ideology of *ethnikofrosyni*, national-mindedness, which became dominant in the post-war political regime in Greece. It was a conservative ideology based on anti-communism, nationalism, adherence to the Greek Orthodox Church and the traditional social order. For the rulers of the organisation the main aims of child-towns were to prepare the younger generation for the reconstruction of the country and to promote the ideals of *Hellino-Christianikos politismos*, Greek-Orthodox Christian civilization, namely patriotism, loyalty to the monarchy and to the political and social system as a whole. Despite *Eranos'* declarations in favour of establishing a 'new welfare system in rural Greece', it was actually, more or less, a continuation of existing welfare politics: *Eranos* was largely based on the existing network of the traditional charitable activities, sponsored by the Church and of several benevolent societies, and it never became part of a wider social policy of the Greek state. Indeed, its most significant new feature was the monarchical paternalism it promoted, which was achieved through the exaltation of the Queen's, or the King's, role in the nation's 'regeneration', and, especially, in the 'salvation of the Greek children'.[36]

35 On *Auxilio Social's* main principles see M. Sanz Bachiller, *La mujer y la educación de los niños*, pp. 42-55, and FET y de las JONS, *Auxilio Social desde el punto de vista religioso y moral*, pp. 12-24.

36 GSA, Central Service/Archive of Ex Royal Palaces/1232, 15 (1950-54): Speech by N. Siniosoglou on the Queen's Fund, January 1951, and HLHA/Eirini Kalliga's Archive: Alexandra Mela, 'What Royal Welfare is and what offers to the Greek people', Athens 1967. See

This was quite different from the totalitarian ideology of *Auxilio Social*, and was more in line with the political and ideological atmosphere of the beginning of the Cold War. Nevertheless, both organisations had several ideological characteristics in common, which allow us to better understand the continuity of conservative ideas before and after the Second World War. Among these common ideological features, anti-communism was probably the most important factor that bridged the chronological and geographical gap between the two examples. Religious faith was another. Nationalism and ethnocentrism did too, as well as a sense of the nation's historic mission. Last but not least, both organisations adopted socio-biological theories that had wide appeal during the interwar period but had been largely repudiated after the Nazi experience. In the Spanish case, anti-Fascist attitudes were diagnosed as manifestations of delinquent or deficient minds, in need of education, control and correction. The eugenicist and military doctor Antonio Vallejo-Nágera believed that *Auxilio Social* was able to 'combat the degenerative trend that boys and girls, nurtured in the republican environment, had acquired', because it could guarantee 'the uplift of the bio-psychological racial capacities and the extinction of the environmental factors that had led them to degeneration.'[37]

In Greece, the new generation was often conceived as a sick body that needed treatment, 'for the very survival of our suffering Race'.[38] Kleanthis Boulalas, a retired general, appointed as director of EYPE, claimed that his task was not only confined to the relief of children in danger, but extended to the 'recovery' of those who had 'imbibed communist teachings'; in other words, the terminology he used to describe the inmates of the child-towns was similar to that used to describe the left-wing political prisoners of the same period. Indeed, at the end of his service as director, he argued that 'the children [of *paidopoleis*] had been sufficiently enriched with the Greek moral values of love and devotion to Religion, Homeland, King and family'.[39] It is worth noting, that both organisations referred to the 'communist virus' that had infected the bodies and souls of part of the population, which subsequently had to be 'cured'. Programmes aimed at children and women of the opposite

also L. Hassiotis, 'Ethnikofrosyni and anticommunism in the juvenile press', *Histor*, pp. 277-84.

37 Auxilio Social, *Normas y orientaciones para delegados*, pp. 34-8, and A. Vallejo-Nágera, *Ninos y jovenes anormales*, pp. 257-65.

38 P. Hippolytos, 'In order to save the children', *Empros*, 24 December 1947.

39 GSA, Central Service/Archive of Ex Royal Palaces/1214: Proceedings of the 52nd session of ESDPE, Athens, 23 June 1949. Cf. K. Ericsson, 'Introduction', in K. Ericsson, E. Simonsen (eds), *Children of World War II*, pp. 9-10. For the biopolitical aspects of *Eranos* views see also EYPE, *Annual Report of the Procceedings of EYPE*, p. 3; A. Metaxas, 'Save the child', *Empros*, 30 December 1948; GSA, Central Service/Archive of Ex Royal Palaces/1231: Boulalas to all child-towns, Athens, 26 July 1948, and Ibid., Executive committee to all child-towns, Athens, 24 December 1949.

camp were largely motivated by an interpretation of certain political attitudes as manifestation of mental pathology – especially in the Spanish case.[40]

A new type of social welfare?

Life inside the closed institutions of the two organisations was semi-militarised: staff and inmates alike had to observe hierarchy and discipline; children were dressed in uniform, gathered for review or inspection, slept in squad rooms and performed their duties. Every aspect of daily life was strictly regularized: the daily schedule, the educational programme and process, leisure activities, diet and so on were all regulated and determined by central administration circulars. In practice, however, the implementation of such circulars depended on the resources of each institution, as well as on the willingness of the director and other staff. When discipline was breached, inmates were subjected to a penal micro system that conforms to the foucauldian theoretical model of 'docile bodies', which included corporal punishment, additional duties or the deprivation of a meal.[41] Priests, nuns and members of Christian societies were usually responsible for the religious, moral and political indoctrination of the children (as it has been noted, in the Spanish case this role was partly played by the falangist educator). Members of religious organisations were deeply involved in the running of *hogares* and *paidopoleis*, although their position and power was more institutionalized in *Auxilio Social*.[42]

Perhaps the most significant element of both *Auxilio Social* and *Eranos'* perception of relief related to the creation of an established relationship of dependency between the giver and the receiver, or the 'patron' and the 'protégés'. In other words, 'children's salvation' from orphan-hood, starvation, maladies, hardship or 'abduction' (in the Greek case) called for a kind of reciprocity or 'payback'. Once they graduated from their respective institutions, inmates of the Spanish *hogares* or the Greek *paidopoleis* were supposed to commit themselves to the nation's regeneration, on the principles, of course, of the

40 Ericsson, 'Introduction', pp. 9-10.
41 M. Foucault, *Discipline and Punish*, pp. 177-8.
42 For the Spanish case: Cenarro, *La sonrisa*, pp. 145-74; Fr. González de Tena, *El papel de la Iglesia*, pp. 35-119; L. Sánchez Blanco, J. L. Hernández Huerta, 'La educación política de los Hogares de Auxilio Social en el franquismo', in M. R. Berruezo Albéniz, S. Conejero López (eds), *El largo camino hacia una educación inclusiva*, pp. 427-8. Cf. the autobiographical comic stories by Carlos Giménez, especially in *Paracuellos 4*, pp. 23-44. For the Greek case: C. Yannaras, *Shelter of Ideas*, pp. 84-6; M. Dalianis, M. Mazower, 'Children in Turmoil during the Civil War: Today's Adults', in Mazower (ed.), *After the War was Over*, pp. 98-9. For information regarding the regulations of the *paidopoleis*, and the policy of normalization followed by the organisation's executive committee in HLHA/Archive of Royal Welfare Fund: *First Congress of the Chiefs of Child-Towns*, Athens 1956, pp. 17, 23, 59, 86, 106-7.

post-war regime.[43] For Spanish falangists, these children represented 'the flower of the Empire... the unity, the potential and the glory of the unique Homeland', as claimed in an article of the official party's newspaper *Arriba*.[44] Children had the right to receive care and treatment not only as individuals, but as an organic part of society and within the framework of the totalitarian state. As Carmen de Icaza, an executive member of *Auxilio Social*, underlined in one of her speeches;

> Every child born in Spain ... belongs to Spain ... We do not want unruly and early corrupted creatures. We want children who are happy with the principles of spirituality and camaraderie, of work and discipline, principles we inculcate in their minds through games... Children that know how to say 'Holy Father' and happily hold our flag. Spaniards conscious of and worthy of the great tomorrow.[45]

Similarly, for a commissioned lady of the Greek Queen, '*Eranos* has never forgotten to cultivate in these children [the inmates of the child-towns] the feeling that they were born Greeks, and as Greeks it is their fate to fight alongside with the defenders of the land of their fathers, with the rifle in their hands'.[46] Furthermore, according to the anticommunist and pro-monarchic arguments of that time, Queen Frederica substituted the maternal care that the inmates had lost, as a result of forced separation from or loss of their birth mothers. The personnel of the child-towns never ceased to remind the children that the Queen was their mother and that they should be grateful to her.[47] The inmates themselves expressed their gratitude in various ways, through their presence in public meetings during the Queen's official visits to the *paidopoleis* or even through writing collective or personal letters to Frederica. In one such letter of an inmate we can read, inter alia:

> I am one of the many Greek children who your loving Greek heart made sure that he would be removed from the destruction and the sword of the Bulgarians.[48] If I had stayed in my favourite village who knows in which village of Bulgaria I would be now, and what I would have suffered for not denying my

43 E. Voutira, A. Brouskou, ' "Borrowed children" in the Greek civil war', in C. Panter-Brick, M. T. Smith (eds), *Abandoned Children*, pp. 93, 104-5, and Simonsen, 'Children in Danger', pp. 269-86.
44 'Veraneos de niños', *Arriba*, 5 July 1937.
45 F. del Olmo Rodríguez, 'La vida cotidiana de los niños y niñas en las instituciones de Auxilio Social', p. 4.
46 GSA, Central Service/Archive of Ex Royal Palaces/1232, 15 (1950-54): Speech by N. Siniosoglou on the Queen's Fund, January 1951.
47 Dalianis, Mazower, 'Children in Turmoil', pp. 99-100.
48 Greek guerrillas were presented by the anti-communist rhetoric as agents of the Slavs, and especially of Bulgarians, the 'perennial enemies' of Hellenism.

faith and our Greece. But now thanks to your care, my great Mother, I stand well and secure ... I owe to you all my gratitude, and the only way to prove it to you is to fight for Greece not once but a hundred times, to shed my blood for her, all my blood, in order to secure her honour and her freedom ... Let's my voice get there and let it be heard by those who steal and burn our villages. I, together with the other children of the child-town, we swear revenge and we declare that we are ready to show to those that want to drown Greece in blood that we will win, because Greece has by her side Jesus Christ, and because Greece never dies.[49]

The above communication is an example of the relationship of dependence and loyalty that was cultivated between Frederica and her 'protégés' during the civil war and in following years. In other words, children's relief and welfare was not considered as their social right but as an 'offer' of her majesty's magnanimity. This reflects a kind of paternalism, typical of both the traditional conservative view of the monarchy and of the role assumed by the Greek post-war regime. Both versions of paternalistic relations cultivated by the respective organisations were only partially successful, although neither had a lasting impact.[50]

Child welfare as a tool of propaganda and social control

Both organisations undertook to protect and educate children regardless of their parents' political affiliation, although priority was given to children, whose fathers had died for the nationalist cause. Their attitude towards the 'children of reds' was, however, inconsistent: intense propaganda and explicit political indoctrination sometimes had an effect opposite to that desired. That was especially pertinent in the Spanish case. According to contemporary accounts of ex-inmates of the *hogares*, whose family background was anti-francoist, the staff's severe attitude towards them preserved rather than undermined their undesirable identity.[51] In others words, the experience at the *hogares* of children with a republican or left-wing background affected the beliefs they developed in a direction opposite to the expectations of the executives of *Auxilio Social*. An ex-inmate comments today:

---

49 GSA, Central Service/Archive of Ex Royal Palaces//1222: N.P. to Queen Frederica, Mytilene 14 June 1949.
50 See K. Vergopoulos, 'The Emergence of the New Bourgeois, 1944-1952', in J. O. Iatrides (ed.), *Greece in the 1940s*, p. 301, and, in the same volume, C. Tsoucalas, 'The Ideological Impact of the Civil War', pp. 321-31.
51 Á. Cenarro, *Los niños del Auxilio Social*, pp. 138-239, and Ibid., 'Memories of Repression and Resistance. Narratives of Children Institutionalized by Auxilio Social in Postwar Spain', *History & Memory*, pp. 39-59. Cf. Fr. González de Tena, *Niños invisibles en el cuarto oscuro*, p. 51.

They didn't just kill my father, they also wanted to defuse his potential continuity, in case we ended up thinking like him. In fact that is exactly what happened: my sisters Suzy, Margarita, just like me, continue to think like my father. Ultimately, that is, they were right and we are bad seeds, aren't we?[52]

Indeed, political indoctrination and punishment in the *hogares* remained immutable long after the end of the war, whereas in the *paidopoleis* political propaganda inside the institutions was relatively reduced during the late 1950's and early 1960's. Nevertheless, even in the less totalitarian spirit of the Greek child-towns, the children of left-wing families, whose parents had been killed, executed, imprisoned or had disappeared during that turbulent period, retained at least a vague sense of their distinct identity. This was because they knew that their relatives were treated as 'bandits'; accused of committing a multitude of crimes, especially the 'ignoble paidomazoma', something that understandably particularly touched their feelings. Those who later rejoined their parents or other relatives were able to work through their experiences and challenge or renegotiate what they had heard in the institutions, a process that was probably particularly stressful. It is likely that the social environment of their later life played a key role in shaping their political attitudes and identities, and therefore confirmed or undermined the political upbringing they had previously received in the child-towns.[53]

The propagandistic role of the two relief organisations was not confined to the political indoctrination of inmates. Indeed, the very existence of *Auxilio Social, Eranos* and their associated institutions became an important tool for propaganda both for Spanish and Greek Nationalists. The former functioned literally as a rearguard of the nationalist army, since, from the summer of 1937 onwards, its members followed the nationalist troops on every city or region they captured. In this way, *Auxilio's* activities could show to the Spanish population that *Falange* was ready to undertake the task of the country's reconstruction. At home they could attract volunteers for the creation of a 'new national community'; abroad, they could improve the Nationalists' reputation and gain friends for Franco's 'Crusade'. Moreover, *Auxilio Social's* work involved thousands of men, women and children, both those who offered help and those that received it, at a time when mass mobilization was considered a decisive factor for victory.[54]

---

52 R. Vinyes, M. Armengou, R. Belis, *Los niños perdidos del franquismo*, p. 145.

53 Dalianis, Mazower, 'Children in Turmoil', pp. 97-100, and Hassiotis, 'Ethnikofrosyni', p. 286. Cf. the autobiographical novel by Y. Atzakas, *Muddy Bottom*, pp. 153-5. The question of the political indoctrination in the two institutions is discussed in Hassiotis, *Children of the Civil War*.

54 M. Seidman, *Republic of Egos*, p. 95; A. Jarne, 'Niños "vergonzantes" y "pequeños rojos". La población marginal infantil en la cataluña interior del primer franquismo', *Hispania Nova. Revista de Historia Contemporánea*, (20 November 2010), pp. 25-42; Orduña Prada, *El Auxilio*

Eranos' political role was equally important: its relief activities strengthened the monarchy's prestige both at home and abroad during the crucial period of the civil war. The Greek authorities named the enterprise of gathering children in the child-towns *paidofylagma*, child-guardianship, in contrast to the guerrillas' *paidomazoma*, child-abduction.[55] This terminology reflected the familiar argument that the Communist Party fought against the Greek nation itself. Indeed, both terms became basic components of the ideology of *ethnikofrosyni*: they demonstrated to society the crucial role that monarchy played in the struggle for the salvation of the new generation, the 'future of the race', from hunger, disease, orphan hood, abduction and 'denationalization'. Child-towns became symbols of this anti-communist struggle both during and after the Civil War, while their inmates were actively involved in official propaganda activities, expressing publicly their gratitude to Queen Frederica, King Paul and the National Army. *Eranos*, too, created a wide network of people and families that depended on its assistance and that were expected to be loyal and grateful to the Queen and the post-war political establishment in general.[56]

Conclusion

In sum, being the product of civil war, *Auxilio Social* and the *Eranos tis Vassilissas* represented two types of militarized welfare. The former was strongly influenced by contemporary fascist doctrines as well as Spanish nationalist ideas, and constituted an organic part of a party with totalitarian aspirations. The latter was founded by a Queen who wanted to consolidate the monarchy's position in her country, and was inspired by early Cold-War anti-communism and traditional Greek conservatism. Both organisations claimed to bring revolutionary changes to the existing welfare system, by mobilizing the population and by monopolising relief for war-handicapped children. Their paternalistic and reciprocating concepts of relief, however, did not challenge the fundamental principles of traditional charity, nor did they promote evolution towards the welfare state. As such, the creation of a new welfare bureaucracy contributed to the development of a culture of dependence, which in turn became a cornerstone of the reconstruction of power relationships in both post-war Spain and Greece.

Social, pp. 172-6, 239-54, and Carasa, 'La revolución nacional-asistencial', pp. 132-4. See also Falange's publication in English, FET de las JONS, *Auxilio Social: Social Help*.

55 In Greek the term *paidomazoma* refers to the 'devshirme' practice (15th-18th Century), that is the forced gathering of boys from Christian families by the Ottomans, their forced conversion to Islam and their conscription to the janissary corps.

56 Baerentzen, 'The "Paidomazoma" and the Queen's Camps', pp. 128-9; Vervenioti, 'Charity and Nationalism', p. 118, and Hassiotis, 'Relocating Children', pp. 275-6.

Bibliography

Archival Material

Hellenic Literary and Historical Archive (HLHA)/Royal Welfare
HLHA/Eirini Kalliga's Archive
General State Archives (GSA), Central Service/Archive of Ex Royal
    Palaces/1214, 1222, 1228, 1231, 1232, 1233

Newspapers

Arriba, 5 July 1937.
Empros, 30 December 1948.
Efimeris tis Kiverniseos tou Vassiliou tis Ellados (Gazette of the Government of
    the Greek Kingdom), n. 140, 11 July 1947.

Secondary Sources

A. Alted Vigil, E. Nicolás Marín, R. González Martell, *Los niños de la guerra
    de España en la Unión Soviética. De la evacuación al retorno (1937-1999)*,
    Madrid, Fundación F. Largo Caballero, 1999.
Y. Atzakas, *Muddy Bottom*, Athens, Agra, 2007.
Auxilio Social, *Normas y orientaciones para delegados. II Congreso Nacional, 16-
    23 octubre 1938*, Valladolid, 1939, vol. II.
L. Baerentzen, J. O. Iatrides, O. L. Smith (eds), *Studies in the History of the
    Greek Civil War, 1945-1949*, Copenhagen, Museum Tusculanum Press,
    1987.
L. Baerentzen, 'The "Paidomazoma" and the Queen's Camps' in L. Baerentzen
    and others (eds), *Studies in the History of the Greek Civil War, 1945-1949*,
    Copenhagen, Museum Tusculanum Press, 1987, pp. 127-55.
A. Beevor, *The Battle for Spain: The Spanish Civil War 1936–1939*, London,
    Weidenfeld and Nicolson, 2006.
T. Brosse, *War-handicapped Children. Report on the European Situation*, Paris,
    UNESCO, 1950.
P. Carasa, 'La revolución nacional-asistencial durante el primer franquismo
    (1936-1940)', *Historia Contemporánea*, 1997, pp. 89-140, vol. 16.
Á. Cenarro, *La sonrisa de Falange. Auxilio Social en la guerra civil y en la
    posguerra*, Barcelona, Crítica, 2006.
Idem, *Los niños del Auxilio Social*, Madrid, Espasa, 2009.
Idem, 'Memories of Repression and Resistance. Narratives of Children
    Institutionalized by Auxilio Social in Postwar Spain', *History & Memory*,
    2008, pp. 39-59, vol. 20, 2.

D. Close (ed.), *The Greek civil war 1943-1950: Studies of Polarization*, New York, Routledge, 1993.

D. Close, T. Veremis, 'The Military Struggle, 1945-49', in D. Close (ed.), *The Greek Civil War, 1943-1950: Studies of Polarization*, New York, Routledge, 1993, pp. 97-128.

R. Crego Navarro, 'Las colonias escolares durante la guerra civil (1936-1939)', *Espacio, Tiempo y Forma, Serie V, Historia Contemporánea*, 1989, pp. 299-328, vol. 2.

H. Cunningham, *Children and Childhood in Western Society since 1500*, London, Pearson, 2005.

Idem, *The Invention of Childhood*, London, BBC Books, 2006.

M. Dalianis, M. Mazower, 'Children in Turmoil during the Civil War: Today's Adults', in M. Mazower (ed.), *After the War was Over. Reconstructing the Family, Nation and State in Greece, 1943-1960*, Princeton, Princeton University Press, 2000, pp. 91-104.

F. González de Tena, *El papel de la Iglesia en Auxilio Social*, Málaga, Sepha, 2009.

Idem, *Niños invisibles en el cuarto oscuro. Experiencias en el Auxilio Social del franquismo*, Madrid, Tébar, 2009.

V. L. Enders, '"And we Ate Up the World": Memories of the *Sección Femenina*', in P. Baccheta, M. Power (eds), *Right-wing Women. From Conservatives to Extremists Around the World*, New York-London, Routledge, 2002, pp. 85-98.

F. Ewald, *L'Etat providence*, Paris, Bernard Grasset, 1986.

EYPE, *Annual Report of the Proccedings of EYPE from its establishment to the end of June of 1949*, Athens 1949.

F. del Olmo Rodríguez, 'La vida cotidiana de los niños y niñas en las instituciones de auxilio social, Madrid, 1939-1950'. Online. Available HTTP: http://www.ahistcon.org/docs/Santiago/pdfs/s4h.pdf (accessed 5 June 2012), p. 4.

FET de las JONS, *Auxilio Social: Social Help*, Valladolid, 1938.

Idem, *Auxilio Social desde el punto de vista religioso y moral*, Madrid, Ayala, 1940.

M. Foucault, *Discipline and Punish: The Birth of the Prison*, London, Penguin, 1991.

C. Giménez, *Paracuellos 4*, Barcelona, Glénat, 2001.

L. Hassiotis, '*Ethnikofrosyni* and anticommunism in the juvenile press: the example of the *Paidopolis* magazine, 1950-51', *History*, 2009, vol. 15. pp. 277-84.

Idem, 'Relocating Children during the Greek Civil War (1946-1949): State Strategies and Propaganda', in J. Reinisch, E. White (eds) *The Disentanglement of Populations: Migration, Expulsion and Displacement in Post-War Europe, 1944-1949*, New York, Palgrave Macmillan, 2011, pp. 271-88.

Idem, *Children of the Civil War. From Franco's Social Relief to Frederica's Fund, 1936-1950*, Athens, Estia, 2012.

H. Hendrick, *Child Welfare. Historical Dimensions, Contemporary Debate*, Bristol, The Policy Press, 2003.

A. Jarne, 'Niños "vergonzantes" y "pequeños rojos". La población marginal infantil en la cataluña interior del primer franquismo', *Hispania Nova. Revista de Historia Contemporánea*, 2004. Online. Available HTTP: http://hispanianova.rediris.es (accessed 5 June 2012), pp. 25-42, vol. 4.

H. Jones, *'A New Kind of War': America's Strategy and the Truman Doctrine in Greece*, Oxford, Oxford University Press, 1997.

D. Kowalsky, *Stalin and the Spanish Civil War*, e-book, New York, Columbia University Press, 2004. Online. Available HTTP: http://www.gutenberg-e. org/kod01/frames/fkod07.html: 'The evacuation of Spanish Children to the Soviet Union' (accessed 5 June 2012).

E. Lagani, *The 'paidomazoma' and Greek-Yugoslav Relations, 1949-1953. A Critical Approach*, Athens, Sideris, 1996.

D. Legarreta, *The Guernica Generation. Basque Refugee Children of the Spanish Civil War*, Reno, University of Nevada Press, 1984.

G. Margaritis, *History of the Greek Civil War, 1946-1949*, Athens, Vivliorama, 2005, vol. II.

J. Maria Thomàs, *La Falange de Franco. Fascismo y fascistización en el régimen franquista (1937-1945)*, Barcelona, Plaza Janés, 2001.

J. Marten, 'Introduction', in Idem (ed.), *Children and War. A Historical Anthology*, New York, New York University Press, 2002, pp. 1-10.

J. Meynaud, *Les forces politiques en Grèce*, Lausanne, Bellanger, 1965.

A. Nachmani, *International intervention in the Greek Civil War*, New York, Praeger, 1990.

M. Orduña Prada, *El Auxilio Social (1936-1940). La etapa fundacional y los primeros* años, Madrid, Escuela Libre, 1996.

S. G. Payne, *Fascism in Spain, 1923-1977*, Madison Wisconsin, University of Wisconsin Press, 1999.

E. Pons Prades, *Los niños republicanos en la Guerra de España*, Madrid, Oberon, 2004.

Idem, *Los niños republicanos. El exilio*, Madrid, Oberon, 2005.

P. Preston, *Doves of War. Four Women of Spain*, London, Harper Collins, 2002.

Idem, *The Spanish Civil War: Reaction, Revolution, and Revenge*, New York, W. W. Norton and Company, 2006.

M. Ristović, 'Children as Refugees: Greek Children in Yugoslavia, 1948-1960', in S. Naumović, M. Jovanović (eds), *Childhood in South East Europe: Historical Perspectives on Growing Up in the 19th and 20th Century*, Belgrade a. Graz, List Verlag, 2004, pp. 215-34.

C. Ruiz Rodrigo, *Política y educación en la II República (Valencia, 1931-1936)*, Valencia, Universidad de Valencia, 1993.

L. Sánchez Blanco, J. L. Hernández Huerta, 'La educación política de los Hogares de Auxilio Social en el franquismo', in M. R. Berruezo Albéniz, S. Conejero López (eds), *El largo camino hacia una educación inclusiva: La educación especial y social del siglo XIX a nuestros días: XV Coloquio de Historia de la Educación*, Pamplona, 2009, pp. 427-38, vol. II.

M. Sanz Bachiller, *La mujer y la educación de los niños*, Madrid, ediciones Auxilio Social, 1939.

M. Seidman, *Republic of Egos. A Social History of the Spanish Civil War*, Madison Wisconsin, University of Wisconsin Press, 2002.

E. Simonsen, 'Children in Danger: Dangerous Children', in K. Ericsson, E. Simonsen (eds), *Children of World War II. The Hidden Enemy Legacy*, Oxford a. New York, Berg, 2005, pp. 269-86.

N. Stargardt, *Witnesses of War. Children's Lives Under the Nazis*, London, Pimlico, 2006.

P. N. Stearns, *Childhood in World History*, New York, Routledge, 2006.

H. Thomas, *The Spanish Civil War*. London, Penguin, 1961.

C. Tsoucalas, 'The Ideological Impact of the Civil War', in J. O. Iatrides (ed.), *Greece in the 1940s. A Nation in Crisis*, Hanover N.H., University Press of New England, 1981, pp. 319-42.

J. Tusell, *Historia de España en el siglo XX, La crisis de los años treinta: República y Guerra Civil*, Madrid, Taurus, 2007, vol. II.

A. Vallejo-Nágera, *Ninos y jovenes anormales*, Madrid, Sociedad de Educacion 'Atenas', 1941.

K. Vergopoulos, 'The Emergence of the New Bourgeois, 1944-1952', in J. O. Iatrides (ed.), *Greece in the 1940s. A Nation in Crisis*, Hanover N.H., University Press of New England, 1981, pp. 298-318.

T. Vervenioti, 'Charity and Nationalism: The Greek Civil War and the Entrance of Right-Wing Women into Politics', in P. Baccheta, M. Power (eds), *Right-wing Women. From Conservatives to Extremists Around the World*, New York-London, Routledge, 2002, pp. 115-26.

R. Vinyes, M. Armengou, R. Belis, *Los niños perdidos del franquismo*, Barcelona, Debols, 2003.

E. Voutira, A. Brouskou, ' "Borrowed children" in the Greek civil war', in C. Panter-Brick, M. T. Smith (eds), *Abandoned Children*, Cambridge, Cambridge University Press, 2000, pp. 92-110.

L. S. Witner, *American Intervention in Greece, 1943-1949*, New York, Columbia University Press, 1982.

C. Yannaras, *Shelter of Ideas*, Athens, Domos, 1994.

13   Polish children in exile 1939-1950. War experiences, deportation and repatriation

Janusz Wróbel

During the global conflict that was World War II, massive migrations took place, mostly mandatory. Even the end of the war, first in Europe, and later in Asia, did not mean the end of migrations, and further movement continued because of the changes in country borders and the confrontation between the communist East and the democratic West. Poland was the first country in Europe beset by open military aggression in the war and which precipitated the obligatory migrations. In September 1939 millions of people found themselves running from the German forces. After the defeat of Poland, its territory was divided in half by the two totalitarian superpowers, the Nazi Third Reich and the communist Soviet Union.

In order to strengthen their power over the annexed Polish territories, the Nazis and Soviets carried out massive resettlements of Poles and Jews, which were very similar to ethnic purges. The Nazis resettled Poles to make room for Germans, who were to colonize the new territories, while the Soviets transported Poles to Siberia and Kazakhstan. A common characteristic of these resettlements during the 1939-1941 was the massive scale, the brutality with which they were carried out and that they were perpetrated against whole families, from infants to elders and the disabled.

Until mid-1941, hundreds of thousands of Poles were forced to leave their homes, and in the later years of the war the exodus continued. Most of the resettled people were sent to forced labor in Germany. Altogether, during the war, several million Poles found themselves outside their homeland, against their will. It is impossible to deal with such a big issue in such a short paper, so I will concentrate on just one fragment of the problem, which shows the drama of exiled Polish children during World War II and what ensued after the war.

During the four big deportations of Poles by the Soviets from 1939 to 1941 about 325, 000 people were resettled to Siberia and Kazakhstan.[1] About 1/3

---

1   A. Głowacki, *Sowieci wobec Polaków na ziemiach wschodnich II Rzeczypospolitej 1939-1941*, p. 622.

of them were children under the age of 14. Wiesław Adamczyk, after many years, remembered his family's deportation. He wrote in his book:

On the night May 14, 1940, we went to sleep anticipating the next day's celebration of Zosia's name day. In the middle of the night, however, we were awakened by heavy pounding on the front and back doors. Jurek, Zosia, and I jumped out of our beds to see what the commotion was about. It was 2:00 A.M. We came out of our rooms to see Mother standing in the middle of our guestroom, trembling. Her face was ashen, her black hair tumbling in disarray over her white nightgown. Her feet were bare and her hands were clasped together as though in prayer. She stood frozen, looking toward us as we ran up to her. I had never seen Mother like this before. Her usual smile was gone, her eyes were distant and filled with fear, and her lips were open as if she were trying to tell us something.[2]

Wiesław's mother was frightened of what was waiting for them; because she knew of the conditions Poles deported to Siberia were forced to endure. Of course, her children did not know this, but they also sensed their childhood was over.

Bożena Masojada, the daughter of a teacher from Brest on the Bug River, who was scared of being arrested and fled to the German side, remembers the deportation as a big trauma. On 19 June 1941 Soviet soldiers entered their house; her mother was convinced that they would be deported to Siberia. The frightened children were crying and they became more terrified when they were brought to a train station and put in freight cars, which were tightly sealed.[3]

Many Polish children died in such transports on the way to the Soviet Union, most of them in the winter of 1940. The youngsters, in particular the infants, who were stuffed into those cattle cars during the winter, had little chance of surviving the ordeal. Even in June, when Wiesław's family was deported, the days were miserably hot and people died because of lack of water.

Poles were sent to territories where the conditions were very hard, even for healthy men. For children these harsh conditions were deadly. In Siberia and Kazakhstan there were no roads. The houses and the barracks where families lived were very primitive. Łucia Skałka, who now lives in the USA, remembers the house her family was located in. She wrote in her book:

It was to one of these simple houses that our family and two other families were

2   W. Adamczyk, *When God Looked the Other Way. An Odyssey of War, Exile, and Redemption*, p. 26.
3   *Dziennik Bożeny Masojady*, pp. 6-7.

assigned. The house contained three small rooms. Other than having a stove in each room, it was totally bare of furniture. My father built a bed, a small table, and benches for us. My parents slept on the bed, while we children huddled on the floor beside the door ... the only available space.[4]

The adults were sent to hard labor, cutting down woods or in the farms. Children were sent to Russian schools, if they were nearby. The wages were so low that there was not enough money even for food. Most of the Poles starved. In the summer months, when it was easier to get food, the children looked for mushrooms, wild fruit and went fishing, but during winter the situation was much worse. Because of the hunger, many diseases became widespread, and the lack of health care meant a dramatic rise in the death rate. Many of the children who survived this horror remember the death of their parents, brothers and sisters. Łucja Skałka remembers the loss of her close ones.

The adults realized that my mother's life was fast coming to an end. That last night my uncle Joseph came to visit. My mother asked him to help her turn on her other side. Because of his own weakened condition, my father was unable to do this for her. As my uncle was helping my mother, my father turned to me and said. 'Go child. Go and get some rest.' I left and went to lie down. Tired and anxious, I fell into deep sleep. Later that night, my father came and woke me up. My mother had died! I was numb! I woke my brothers, Francis and Louis. Together with my father we gathered around our mother, sharing our sorrow and praying for her eternal happiness [...]. Ten days after my mother's death, my baby brother, Walter, died. No doctor, no medical care, nothing. That was December 10, 1940.[5]

In 1941, when the Germans invaded the Soviet Union, there was hope that the situation of Poles would change. Indeed, Moscow did alter its approach to the Poles and diplomatic relations were resumed with the Polish government in exile located in London. In July of 1941 a treaty was signed, in which the Russians were to free all Poles from prisons and from forced labor camps and to create a Polish Army in the Soviet Union. The Polish ambassador was sent to Moscow, and he started building a relief system for the polish civilians. He especially wanted to help the children. In the vast land of the Soviet Union, representations of the embassy were established. They tried to give material help, especially food and clothing. Help from the American and Polish Red Cross and other humanitarian organizations was also very important.

Unfortunately, it was all too little. Hunger and disease weakened all of the

---

4   M. I. Petrykowski (ed.), *Lucia's Journey. The Life Story of Sister Mary Lucia Skalka, C.S.S.F.*, p. 25.
5   Petrykowski (ed.), *Lucia's Journey*, pp. 28-9.

deportees. In this situation, Poles saw the Polish Army created in the Soviet Union as the only hope to improve their conditions. Masses of desperate Polish deportees followed the army, gathering around it for protection and hoping to share its food supplies. Their most fervent wish was that the Polish Army would lead them out of the Soviet Union to freedom. With the coming of spring and then summer of 1942, the civilians in particular suffered from the desert heat. Sanitation was lacking, medical care was poor or nonexistent, and food was scarce. Contagious diseases started to spread, with people dying in such numbers that they had to be buried in mass graves.

According to the report of a Polish army field doctor, Lieutenant Doctor Polkowski, from 6 March of 1942: '3,000 Polish civilians which resided near the army quarter are on the rock bottom of material misery, mostly in old run down clothes, starving and often dying of weakness and hunger.'[6] Equally tragic news came from reports of the Polish delegation of the embassy located in Samarkand. The embassy reached two Soviet republics of Uzbekistan and Tajikistan in which there were about 90,000 Polish citizens. The Polish delegation organized 20 Polish orphanages for 4,400 children and 45 sites with food for the children, but the situation was still very tragic. In the Samarkand region in the spring of 1942, because of famine and sickness, 1,632 Polish citizens died and the situation was getting worse.[7]

In the middle of 1942, the Soviets, British and Poles agreed that the Polish Army would serve much more effectively by fighting the Germans in Africa and southern Europe.[...] General Anders, the Commander of Polish Armed Forces in the Soviet Union, was pleased with the agreement because he knew that this would be the only way to get as many Polish civilians as possible out of the USSR. In July of 1942, during his talks with the Soviet authorities, the ambassador of Poland in Samara raised the problem of the evacuation of Polish children. He communicated to the Russians that the government in exile had held talks with Great Britain, the United States, Canada and South Africa and had been promised that 50,000 Polish children would be taken and protected. The Polish government optimistically expected that in the future they could find asylum for more children, who were to be evacuated from the Soviet Union. The needs were great, because it was estimated that about 160,000 Polish children resided in the Soviet Union.[8]

The Polish government in exile did not, in fact, actually have any firm

6   W. Essigman, 'Kompania sanitarna 6 Dywizji Piechoty i 5-ty Ewakuacyjny Szpital Polowy Wojsk Polskich w ZSRR, na Bliskim Wschodzie i we Włoszech (1941-1946) Wspomnienia osobiste', *Archiwum Historii i Filozofii Medycyny*, p. 233.

7   Hoover Institution on War, Revolution and Peace, Stanford, Ca., (HI), Ambasada RP w Związku Sowieckim, box 31, Report of the Polish consul in Samarkand, 12 VI 1942.

8   HI, Ambasada RP w Związku Sowieckim, box 125, Note prepared for a meeting with A. Wyszyński, 1 VI 1942.

assurances from other countries to take the Polish children. Neither the Americans, nor the governments of British dominions were eager to change their strict immigration policies and to let the Polish civilians enter their territories. The British were also reluctant to go ahead with this plan; the Allies already had huge problems managing the war and were concentrated on the fighting and thus humanitarian problems were not their top priority.

Polish diplomats acted because of greater necessity. In order to save the Polish children from a sure death, they were ready to present their western allies with a *fait accompli*, believing that when the Polish children left the Soviet Union, they would not refuse their help. The efforts of the Polish authorities to evacuate the Polish children were only partly successful. The Soviet deputy commissioner of foreign affairs, Andrzej Wyszynski, during his talks with the Polish ambassador Stanisław Kot, denied that the situation of the Polish children was tragic. He also thought that the plan to evacuate 50,000 of them was 'extravagant and unrealistic'.[9] Ultimately the Poles were able to get acceptance from Stalin to evacuate the whole Polish Army and their families, but the other Poles had to stay in the Soviet Union.

During the spring and summer of 1942 about 116,000 Polish soldiers and civilians, of whom 20,000 were children, left the Soviet Central Asia (now Turkmenistan) through the Caspian Sea headed for Iran. The evacuation on Russian ships was hasty and took place in terrible conditions.[10] An eyewitness of the evacuation in July of 1942 wrote that the ship on which he sailed from Krasnovodsk to Pahlevi was old and decrepit. Soldiers and civilians leaving the Soviet Union were packed on and below the deck and suffered due to excessive heat. The sanitary conditions were 'dreadful' and the food supply scarce.[11] Starved people ate large amounts of food on the shores of Iran, which also did not help their health.

In Iran the British forces, Polish Mission in Tehran and the Iranian government helped the Polish refugees. The British colonel Alexander Ross, who organized the help, was terrified by what he saw. In his report to London he wrote:

> Due to very poor living conditions in prisons, labor and concentration camps [...] the general physical and mental state of the refugees upon their arrival in Teheran was very bad. The most widespread diseases were dysentery, diarrhea, prolonged malnutrition – related diseases, various types of malaria brought from Russia and typhus. One visit to a hospital during the first or second stage

9   K. Zamorski, *Dwa tajne biura 2 Korpusu*, pp. 221-222.
10 HI, Ministerstwo Spraw Zagranicznych, box 187, A. Ross, *Report on Polish Refugees in Persia. April 1942 to December 1943*; J. Wróbel, *Uchodźcy polscy ze Związku Sowieckiego 1942-1950*, p. 41.
11 Essigman, 'Kompania sanitarna', p. 151.

of the evacuation was enough to get an indelible picture of undeserved poverty and physical suffering. General Anders said after his arrival from Russia that he expected 25% of the refugees to die when they reach Persia. Actually, by the end of 1943 the number of deaths reached 2,119 i.e. slightly less than 5%. This alone testifies to the vitality of the Polish nation and to the efforts of those who contributed to their regaining heath.[12]

Even though the living conditions improved in Iran, many children were still under a lot of physical and emotional stress. The death rate was still very high, mainly because of contagious diseases. Almost all of the children suffered from malaria. Today the only remaining physical evidence of these hard times is the big Polish cemetery in Teheran, in which lie many children.

The traumatic war experiences of these Polish children in 1939 and later due to the deportation to Russia, started their lives in poverty and constant fear of death. Such experiences marked their psyche. Welfare workers of the Polish government in exile and teachers of Polish schools, which took care of children which were evacuated from Iran, saw this problem. While looking at their notebooks and diaries they saw that the subjects of their texts were different from the ones of their prewar contemporaries. The twelve and thirteen year olds had departed from the world of fun and child fantasies. Their minds were still absorbed by the tragic experiences from the Soviet Union, where they got to know hunger, sickness and death. Particularly hard psychologically was the situation of orphans and children who had lost their parents. They took their parting with parents especially hard and often called the names of their parents at night; the efforts of educators to direct their thoughts onto other routes proved ineffective. A thirteen-year-old Władysław Wojewoda was a good example of this. The personnel of his orphanage had many problems with his behavior; he was stubborn, insubordinate and disobedient. But despite all of this he was a very vulnerable boy. His most prized possession was a notebook in which he wrote poems dedicated to his mother, whom he lost in the Soviet Union.[13]

In the spring of 1944, almost two years after the evacuation from the Soviet Union, a Polish representative from Tehran, Karol Bader, had a similar impression while visiting the Polish child camp in Esfahan. He thought the educators and teachers could not free themselves from the tragic memories from the years of 1939 – 1942. Most of the teachers had also been in the Soviet Union. The diplomat thought that there was an atmosphere 'of spiritual

---

12 HI, Ministerstwo Spraw Zagranicznych, box 187, A. Ross, *Report on Polish Refugees in Persia. April 1942 to December 1943*, p. 41.
13 HI, Ambasada RP w Związku Sowieckim, box 33, Recall of Irene Wasilewska, referent from the Department of Guardianship of the Polish Embassy in USSR from visiting an orphanage in Mashhad.

captivity to Russia' which led to 'the impossibility of a vital and fruitful contact with the Western world and its ideas.[14]

The first stop of the refugees evacuated with Gen. Anders' army was Iran, where they found temporary quarters in large temporary camps initially located in Pahlevi and Mashhad, and later in Tehran and Ahvaz. While General Anders' troops were subsequently transferred to Palestine and Iraq, and then to Italy, the civilians remained in Iran. Their stay, however, was cut short because of the hostility of the Soviet Army units occupying northern Iran and because of the threat of the German armies which had reached the Caucasus in the summer of 1942. The problem of finding a place for the civilian refugees from the Soviet Union was very complicated. There was, after all, a war going on that embraced almost the entire world. The German armies had already conquered almost all of Europe and were threatening the Middle East from the west and north while the Japanese also threatened it from the east. It became imperative, therefore, to find a place where the people could spend the remainder of the war years in tolerable and safe conditions.

The Polish government in exile, with help from its allies, the United States, Great Britain and other countries, found a resolution to this problem. By the end of 1943, 33,000 refugees had been transferred from Iran to others countries. Great Britain played the decisive role in resolving the problem of Polish civilians evacuated from the Soviet Union. The British felt liability towards the Poles because the Polish Armed Forces fought under British command and provided great services to the British Empire during the very hard first period of the war. During a conversation between the Polish prime minister, General Władysław Sikorski, and Winston Churchill on 30 August 1942 at Chequers, the British prime minister guaranteed that he would welcome the refugees to British colonies in Africa.[15]

In Palestine, camps for over 5,000 refugees who were transferred there were located in Jerusalem, Nazareth, Rehavot, Ain-Karem, and Barbara. By the end of 1945, another 4,300 were evacuated to Lebanon; by 1946 that number rose to 6,000. The same exiles also found asylum in India, in temporary camps set up near Karachi. But more stable settlements also emerged such as those in Balachadi, near the city Jamnagar, and in Valivade, near Kolhapur. Balachadi became a refuge for some 1,000 Polish children. Valivade housed 5,000 Polish refugees. Africa provided another safe harbor for the Poles. In 1944 East Africa hosted over 13,000 Polish citizens. They settled in stationary camps in

---

14 HI, Ministerstwo Spraw Zagranicznych, box 194, Report of a Polish deputy in Teheran Karol Bader from a visit to Polish camps in Esfahan, 21 IV 1944.

15 'Rozmowa gen. Władysława Sikorskiego z premierem Winstonem Churchillem w Chequers 30 VIII 1942 r', in M. Zgórniak, W. Rojek, A. Suchcitz (eds), *Protokoły posiedzeń Rady Mistrów Rzeczypospolitej Polskiej, grudzień 1941-sierpień 1942*, Kraków, Oficyna Wydawniczo-Drukarska "Secesja", p. 422.

the British colonies of Uganda, Kenya, and Tanganyika (now Tanzania). In Uganda, the camps were located in Masindi and Koja on Lake Victoria. In Tanganika, the largest settlement was Tengeru (4,000 refugees) and smaller camps were located in Kigoma, Kidugala, Ifunda, Kondoa i Morogoro. In Kenya they were located in Rongai, Manira, Makindu, Nairobi, and Nyali near Mombasa.

South Africa, North Rhodesia (now Zambia), and South Rhodesia (now Zimbabwe) also became home to Poles. The largest of those settlements were: in South Africa – Oudtshoorn; in North Rhodesia – Abercorn, Bwana M'Kubwa, Fort Jameston, Livingstone, and Lusaka; in South Rhodesia – Digglefold, Marandellas, Rusape, and Gatooma.[16] Overall, in the British colonies in eastern and southern Africa by the end of 1944, there were about 18,000 Poles, of which 80% were children and women and, along with the Italian captives, they were the biggest group from Europe. In mid 1946, a year after the war ended, the number of Poles in British possessions in Africa was still at a high number of 17,000 people.[17]

The coordinated action of the Polish, American and British governments also embraced Mexico, whose government showed a great deal of understanding in regard to the difficult situation of the Poles and expressed willingness to allow a certain number of them to come into the country. As a result, in two voyages aboard the American ship *USS Hermitage* over 1,400 Poles arrived in the city of Leon, located in central Mexico. Near it lay the hacienda of Santa Rosa, which the Mexican government allowed the refugees to use during the time of war.[18] New Zealand also came to the rescue, its government offering asylum to 700 Polish orphans, guaranteeing them full care. On 1 November of 1944 Peter Fraser, the Prime Minister of New Zealand and the Polish Consul Kazimierz Wodzicki welcomed the children to New Zealand in Wellington. The same day, the last part of the long journey was completed by two special trains from Wellington to the Polish Children's Camp in Pahiatua.[19]

Most of the settlers in the Polish refugee camps who spread from the Middle East to South Africa and from Lebanon to Mexico were children and teenagers. With the help of local authorities, the Polish government in exile

16 T. Piotrowski (ed.), *The Polish Deportees of Word War II. Recollections of Removal to the Soviet Union and Dispersal Throughout the Word*, p. 11.
17 The National Archives (London) (NA), Treasury , 236/1376, Polish refugees in the Colonies, Draft Memorandum on Refugees, Displaced Persons and Evacuees in Colonial Territories, 1946; K. Sword, N. Davies, J. Ciechanowski, *The Formation of the Polish Community in Great Britain 1939-1950*, pp. 71, 459; J. Wróbel, 'Polacy w Afryce Wschodniej i Południowej 1941-1950', *Zeszyty Historyczne*, pp. 85-91.
18 HI, Ambasada RP w Waszyngtonie, box 84, Report from a Polish deputy in Mexico M. Marchlewski about the ressetelment of Poles from Asia to Mexico, 14 I 1943.
19 'The Polish Children's Camp in Pahiatua', in *New Zealand's First Refugees: Pahiatua's Polish Children*, pp. 24-26.

built a care system with orphanages, kindergartens and primary and middle schools. After some initial problems they were equipped with textbooks and other resources, including staffing. The Polish authorities, who organized the welfare and educational systems in refugee camps were aware that it was very important for the children to forget their traumatic experiences from the Soviet Union in order to be able to function normally in their future lives. A Polish representative in Teheran thought that the 'systematic contact with the world [...] especially by the written word' would help to achieve this goal. In a report to the Polish government in London he wrote 'we need a large and steady inflow of books'.[20]

The request was taken into consideration. After these initial problems, Polish schools and libraries in the refugee camps were supplied with Polish books printed in Great Britain, the United States and in the Middle East (Palestine) and even from India. Larger settlements had their own periodicals, with some dedicated to children. In the Iranian city of Esfahan there was a magazine printed for the youth called 'My' [We], whilst in Tehran there was a gazette called 'Demawend'. A special addition for the children was printed with the magazine 'Polak w Indiach' [Poles in India]. The Polish scouts even printed their own newspapers. In the camp in Valivade there was a journal called 'Młodzi' [Jouth]. In Africa it was very similar and in Oudtshoorn a magazine called 'Southern Cross' was printed.[21] There were also after-school programs. Common rooms and sport clubs were created and tourism also developed. Polish youths in Tanganyika climbed Kilimanjaro, the biggest mountain in Africa, many times, and their colleagues from Koja in Uganda sailed Lake Victoria. The teenagers in Mexico went to Mexico City and Guadalajara.

The humanitarian aid started mainly from the United States. The National Catholic Welfare Conference (NCWC) and Polish War Relief sent mostly clothes, but also equipment for schools and common rooms. By the end of the war, the living conditions in the Polish refugee camps were very good, much better than their counterparts in Europe devastated by the war. A journalist from a Polish Gazette, who in 1944 was for a couple of months in Polish camps in Africa, was greatly impressed by the amount of work which had been done. While in such exotic places as Tengeru by the mountain Meru or Camp Koja by Lake Victoria, he felt the 'atmosphere of a Polish village' for the first time since he had to flee the country four years ago.[22]

---

20 HI, Ministerstwo Spraw Zagranicznych, box 194, Report from Polish deputy in Tehran Karol Bader from his visitation of Polish camps in Esfahan, 21 IV 1944.

21 E. Wróbel, J. Wróbel, *Rozproszeni po świecie. Obozy i osiedla uchodźców polskich ze Związku Sowieckiego 1942-1950*, pp. 88, 127-28, 198.

22 A. Skąpski, 'Na tułaczach szlakach: Polacy w Afryce Wschodniej', *Polska Walcząca-Żołnierz Polski na Obczyźnie*, pp. 4-5.

The great material improvement in the lives of Polish children in refugee camps and the development of Polish schools had a great effect in helping them to recover the mental balance after their experiences in the Soviet Union. In the case of the orphans, individual work by the teachers was equally important, as the educators took a lot of time talking to the children. Irene Dalgiewicz, a representative of the NCWC working with the Polish refugees in Santa Rosa in Mexico said:

> Listening is a therapy to them. I cannot give them any of the things they want, but hearing them out is sometimes the only therapy I can make available to them. I see it as corrective for the impersonal cruelty they have known in the past years. They have been part of anonymous mass in the Soviet Union, thrust about and never listened to, much less consulted. That is over.[23]

A similar role was played by the essays about the life in Russia, which the children had to write as homework. About 2,300 Polish children wrote about their recollections. Today they are a great historical source, but then they helped the children to free themselves from the 'Russian' trauma.[24]

The accounts of former refugees, currently living in different countries all over the world are, for the most part, consistent with the view that the huge efforts of the adults to let them regain their physical strength and mental stability were successful. Irene Beaupre-Stankiewicz highlights the role of Polish schools in Iran, which not only started them on the path to future studies and getting good jobs, but also widened their horizons, and 'awakened them from mental apathy from the years spent in Russia, where the only content of life was survival [...] on a strictly physical basis.'[25] Also, the former refugees from Oudtshoorn highlight in a book printed on the 50th anniversary of their arrival in South Africa, that the guardians did everything they could to prepare them for living in an independent Poland, and when this became impossible they prepared for a life of emigration.[26]

It would be a mistake to say that the life of Polish youths who lived in camps all over the world was idyllic. The teenagers were full of energy, and female personnel had a hard time dealing with young boys. We must remember that most of them were orphans and half-orphans. Some of them

23 E. Egan, *For Whom There Is No Room. Scenes from the Refugee Word*, pp. 48-49.
24 Zamorski, *Dwa tajne biura 2 Korpusu*, p. 223.
25 I. Beaupre-Stankiewicz, D. Waszczuk-Kamieniecka, J. Lewicka-Howells (eds), *Isfahan. Miasto polskich dzieci*, p. 211.
26 'Today, we can see clearly the sound merit of these educators. It is thanks to their efforts that so many young people matriculated, that some even graduated from universities and occupied prominent positions in the social and economic life of South Africa.' quoted from J. Jaworski, *Przetrwaliśmy. We have Survived*, p. 24.

had parents, but they were serving in the army in Europe, and their time in the Soviet Union left many emotional scars. The delegate from the Ministry of Education, Szczepański, pointed out that in the Polish camps, among the adults, there were demoralized people (prostitutes, thieves, brawlers) who had a very bad influence on the children and teenagers. The Polish consul from Rhodesia, I. Ziętkiewicza agreed with this. In a very interesting report to the Ministry of Foreign Affairs in London, he pointed out that the reasons for trouble with the youths were much more complex. In his opinion, life and continuous inactivity in camps, isolated from the outside world, made for an unhealthy atmosphere which was especially adverse for the young. This atmosphere was increased by other elements, like the prolonged life in refugee camps, personal tragic experiences, impaired nervous systems, the constant worry about close ones left in Poland or Russia and about the soldiers fighting in the war. To some extent the climate, to which Europeans were not used, did its part.

From his observations, consul Ziętkiewicz has drawn the conclusion that the stay in the camps should be treated as a necessity, and it would be best to give the Poles a normal life outside the camps. This applied also to the children and teenagers. As a good example, the consul pointed to the Polish women's boarding high school in Digglefold, Polish volunteers from the Women's Auxiliary Air Force, and the Polish nurses form a hospital in Salisbury. Polish girls were glad they could get out of the camps, to study, work and earn money. They were so happy that even their free time was spent mainly outside the camps. In Ziętkiewicz's opinion, the girls were also satisfied that they could work as an equal with the British, thanks to which any inferiority was dissipated. Cooperation with people from different countries gave them greater ambitions and they tried to exceed their counterparts in studies and work.[27]

Not all Polish officials responsible for the protection of young Poles had the same views as the consul from Salisbury. Many of them concentrated on enlargement of the camps, isolating them from the outside world, and neglected the teaching of English. In part this was a result of the demands from local authorities. The British and South Africans were against contacts between the Polish youth and the local tribes as they thought it would undermine the positions of the white people. The impact on the local economy was also a lingering issue; local jobs were scarce and finding a job outside of the camps was very difficult.

Issues of education continued to occur even after the beginning of functioning of the settlements. Bohdan Szmejko, a delegate of the MPiOS in

27 HI, Ministerstwo Spraw Zagranicznych, box 189, Letter from Polish Consul General in Salisbury I. Ziętkiewicz to the Ministry of Foreign Affairs in London, 23 IX 1944.

Mexico, said that in the Polish settlement in Santa Rosa there was too much tolerance for drunkenness and crime, which demoralized the Polish youth, and only hard educational and organizational work helped the situation.[28] In the fall of 1946, three years after the arrival of Polish refugees in eastern Africa, during a conference of British directors of refugees and their Polish advisers, it was decided that a disciplinary commission should be created in every Polish settlement.[29]

Sometimes, the local authorities were helpless against the excesses of the Polish youth. For example, in the town of Oudtshoorn in South Africa, where a Polish orphanage was built, the deputy sheriff wrote to his internal affairs minister:

> Sir, I beg to advise you that the boys of the local Polish camp have become a disgrace to the town of Oudtshoorn. They go about the town practically every night and get into everybody's gardens and simply play havoc with every bit of fruit they can get hold of.

None of the reprimands helped, because the superintendent of the camp did not react. The deputy had to take drastic actions:

> Superintendent simply ignored my letter and about a week later we caught three of those boys in my garden, they were taken to the charge office and the Magistrate warned them and gave them eight cuts each.

A similar thing happened in Rusape, where the English commandant of the camp was very upset by the pranks of Polish boys and he imposed corporal punishment on them. The Polish consul in Southern Rhodesia thought the punishment was just, and that corporal punishment was a good method to control the youth. Not all Polish teachers had the same idea, and corporal punishment was used rarely.[30]

The end of the war in Europe, which came in May 1945, was to end the migration of Polish youth, and they hoped to return to a free country. Unfortunately for the Poles in refugee camps in Africa, the Middle East and India, it was not the end of their drama. Poland was now controlled by the Soviets and governed by the Polish communists. For those who remembered the life in Siberia, coming back to a communist country was not an option. Asked by the British refugee commissioner in Tanganyika why he would not

---

28 Archiwum Akt Nowych (Warsaw), Poselstwo RP w Meksyku, 182, Letter from Bohdan Szmejko to the Ministry of Work and Welfare in London, 6 IX 1944.
29 *Głos Polski*, 6 X 1946.
30 HI, Ministerstwo Spraw Zagranicznych, box 189, Letter from Polish Consul General in Salisbury I. Ziętkiewicz to the Ministry of Foreign Affairs in London, 23 IX 1944.

return to Poland, one of the refugees said:

> I am ready to go back to a free Poland and work as a peasant or a labourer
> to help rebuild my country; but if Poland is to be the XVIII Republic in the
> U.S.S.R., I would sooner cut my throat on the spot than go back there.[31]

Polish youth had a dilemma – should they stay in foreign countries or go back to their homeland? Both decisions were hard and risky. Great Britain and other countries, which took care of young Poles, did not force them to go back, but it was hard for them to fully understand what they were going through. The local governments thought it would be best if Polish teens quickly assimilated with their peers. The actions of the South African Union are a good example. The local administration in Pretoria wanted to resolve the problem of Polish children as quickly as possible. A couple of solutions were considered. It was thought that some of the Poles would go back to the communist Poland. Those who wanted to stay in Africa were to be integrated with the local white communities. On 19 September 1946 in Cape Town a group of Polish boys attending a local school took part in a hearing during which they were asked if they wanted to stay in South Africa or go back to their home country. The hearing was held by a special government commission, the guardian of the boys and a social worker, and all of them assured the boys that they should answer freely and that they could change their mind after they thought the problem out.

Out of thirty boys attending the hearing, seven of them wanted to leave South Africa in the near future. Only three of them wanted to go back to Poland, the rest of them wanted to reunite with their families in other countries. Ten of the boys wanted to legalize their stay in the Union of South Africa. The biggest group of thirteen boys said that they would like to stay in South Africa until the living conditions in Poland improved. The officials were impressed by how mature the young Poles were. A closing report stated that the Polish youth was deeply patriotic, and that it would be 'unwise' to speed up their assimilation process.[32]

Only about 20% of Poles who had been to the Soviet Union returned to Poland after the war; the rest of them emigrated to different countries. In the first years after the war, most went to Great Britain, as part of a program to reunite families with the former soldiers of the Polish Army. Later it was made easier to emigrate to the United States of America, Argentina,

---

31 NA, Foreign Office, 371/51183, Refugees 1945, Letter from A.L. Pennington to Foreign Office, 22 I 1945.
32 National Archives of South Africa, Polish Camp Oudtshoorn, SW 432, vol. 2, Report from a hearing of 30 Polish boys in Cape Town, 19 IX 1946.

Australia and Canada.[33] Few stayed in the countries they lived in during the war. This emigration meant that families would be torn apart indefinitely, which brought about more drama. For example, Ala Kuchcińska-Sussens who, during the war lived in Northern Rhodesia, wrote in her memoirs:

> It came as a shock to us when we were informed that the British government was going to close all their refugee camps in Africa. They offered us a choice of going to Canada, Australia or of returning to Poland. Neither Canada nor Australia appealed to us and we were still fearful of the influence of communism in Poland. Mother would rather have died than experience the communist regime again.[34]

After the refugee camp was closed, Ala and her mother stayed in Africa, while her father lived in communist Poland, which he could not leave. They reunited after several years.

The case of Polish orphans in South Africa, India, Mexico and New Zealand was the most complicated. The Polish government, dominated by communists, wanted a mandatory repatriation of the children, in accordance with international law. This was opposed by the determined objections of the still functioning Polish Government in Exile, the children themselves, and from their guardians. For a few years after the war a fierce battle for the future of these children was fought. The British government did not agree to a mass repatriation, allowing only individual repatriations, and only with the consent of the children. Finally, the main role in resolving this problem was played by committees registered in courts by Poles and prominent citizens of countries in which the children were staying. They decided the future of the orphans. Polish children from a big orphanage in Tengeru found refuge in Canada, where they were taken care of by Catholic priests. Orphans from India and Mexico made their way to the United States of America, where they were put in Polish orphanages and schools. Polish children from New Zealand were allowed to stay there.

33 Countries which gave asylum to the Poles often thought they would be good citizens. Dr J. B. Mathieson, who was recruiting in Polish camps in Africa to go to Australia, wrote in his report: 'They are a very fine type and, am sure, will make good New Australians. The children are remarkably healthy and fine, intelligent, physical types.' M. Allbrook, H. Cattalini, *The General Langfitt Story. Polish Refugees Recount their Experiences of Exile, Dispersal and Resettlement.*
34 A. Kuchcinska-Sussens, J. Duff, *Ala's Story. A Window full of Elephant. A Life Journey from Poland through Siberia and Iran to the wilderness of Africa,* p. 32.

Conclusion

Polish children were treated very brutally by the war. In 1939 their lives were in danger because of military actions against civilians. Later they were deported to Siberia, where they suffered from hunger, disease and humiliation. In almost all of their families they were witness to deaths of their close ones. The evacuation from the Soviet Union in 1942 freed the children from hunger and diseases, but did not end all of their problems. Families were broken and they had to adapt to a different way of life in Africa or India. After the war, they could not return to communist Poland.

The physical and emotional stress was enormous, and had negative influences on their whole lives, but to the astonishment of historians, most of the Poles who suffered such harsh times were very successful later in life. They became good citizens of their new homelands, and maintained contact with Poland, its language and culture. All of this would not be possible without the help of people from different countries and nationalities in the countries in which the Poles found.

Bibliography

Archival Material

Archiwum Akt Nowych (Warsaw)
Poselstwo Polskie w Meksyku [Polish Legation in Mexico], folder 182.
Hoover Institution on War, Revolution and Peace, (Stanford, Ca.)
Ambasada RP w Waszyngtonie [Polish Embassy in Washington], box 84.
Ambasada RP w Związku Sowieckim[Polish Embassy in Soviet Union] , box 31, 33, 125.
Ministerstwo Spraw Zagranicznych [Polish Ministry of Foreign Affairs], box 187, 189, 194.
National Archives of South Africa (Pretoria)
Polish Camp Oudtshoorn, folder SW 432.
The National Archives (London)
Treasury, folder 236/1376.
Foreign Office, folder 371/51183.

Books and articles

W. Adamczyk, *When God Looked the Other Way. An Odyssey of War, Exile, and Redemption*, Chicago, University of Chicago Press, 2004.
M. Allbrook, H. Cattalini, *The General Langfitt Story. Polish Refugees Recount their Experiences of Exile, Dispersal and Resettlement*. Online.

Available   HTTP: http://onlinebooks.library.upenn.edu/webbin/book/lookupid?key=olbp10476, (accessed 5 September 2012).

I. Beaupre-Stankiewicz, D. Waszczuk-Kamieniecka, J. Lewicka-Howells (eds), *Isfahan. Miasto polskich dzieci,* London, 1987.

Dziennik Bożeny Masojady, [a copy is in authors possession], Esfahan, 1943.

E. Egan, *For Whom There Is No Room. Scenes from the Refugee Word,* New York, Mahwah, Paulist Press, 1995.

W. Essigman, 'Kompania sanitarna 6 Dywizji Piechoty i 5-ty Ewakuacyjny Szpital Polowy Wojsk Polskich w ZSRR, na Bliskim Wschodzie i we Włoszech (1941-1946). Wspomnienia osobiste', *Archiwum Historii i Filozofii Medycyny,* 1997, vol. 62.

Głos Polski, 1946.

A. Głowacki, *Sowieci wobec Polaków na ziemiach wschodnich II Rzeczypospolitej 1939-1941,* Łódź, Wydawnictwo Uniwersytetu Łódzkiego, 1998.

J. Jaworski, *Przetrwaliśmy. We have Survived,* Johannesburg, 1993.

A. Kuchcinska-Sussens, J. Duff, *Ala's Story. A Window full of Elephant. A Life Journey from Poland through Siberia and Iran to the wilderness of Africa,* Hoedspruit, 2007.

New Zealand's First Refugees: Pahiatua's Polish Children, Wellington, Polish Children's Reunion Committee, 2004.

M. I. Petrykowski, *Lucia's Journey. The Life Story of Sister Mary Lucia Skalka, C.S.S.F.,* Chicago, LifeStories LLC, 2003.

T. Piotrowski (ed.), *The Polish Deportees of Word War II. Recollections of Removal to the Soviet Union and Dispersal Throughout the Word,* Jefferson a. London, McFarland&Company, Inc., 2004.

A. Skąpski, 'Na tułaczach szlakach: Polacy w Afryce Wschodniej', *Polska Walcząca-Żołnierz Polski na Obczyźnie,* 1944, vol. 27.

K. Sword, N. Davies, J. Ciechanowski, *The Formation of the Polish Community in Great Britain 1939-1950,* London, University of London, 1989.

E. Wróbel, J. Wróbel, *Rozproszeni po świecie. Obozy i osiedla uchodźców polskich ze Związku Sowieckiego 1942-1950,* Chicago, Panorama Publishing Co, 1992.

J. Wróbel, 'Polacy w Afryce Wschodniej i Południowej 1941-1950', *Zeszyty Historyczne,* Paris, 1996, vol. 115.

K. Zamorski, *Dwa tajne biura 2 Korpusu,* London, Poets and Painters Press, 1990.

M. Zgórniak, W. Rojek, A. Suchcitz (eds), *Protokoły posiedzeń Rady Ministrów Rzeczypospolitej Polskiej, grudzień 1941-sierpień 1942,* Kraków, Oficyna Wydawniczo-Drukarska "Secesja", 1998, vol. IV.

14   An Investigation into the NGOs who Assist Child Soldiers in Southern Sudan

Christine Ryan

Introduction

In considering children's role in war, child soldiers have a complex position of victim and perpetrator, and contested levels of agency.[1] This chapter presents and examines research focused on the Non Governmental Organisations (NGO) responsible for the former child soldiers of the Sudan People's Liberation Army (SPLA) in Southern Sudan. Specifically, their approach and interaction with the child soldiers will be explored. This chapter will identify the weaknesses of the NGOs' approach and include recommendations as to how to better serve children as a research subject.

This chapter is drawing on thirty-three face-to-face interviews with NGO workers in Southern Sudan, in which the research parameters extended to all organisations that were engaged in working on the issue of former child soldiers.[2] The NGOs represented a wide range of social, political and religious interests. They included organisations directly engaged in humanitarian work, but also academics and those involved in the policy forming process.

In collecting the interviews I aimed to obtain as large and varied of a pool of interviewees as possible. Accordingly, I sought all avenues available to me and would draw on both pre-scheduled and ad hoc interviews as opportunities arose. The interviews conducted with NGO workers were largely made by appointment after establishing the key organisations, and individuals within them, working on the topic of child soldiers.

---

1   The age of a 'child soldier' is defined by the Optional Protocol of the CRC. It did not extend to those who may have served in the Northern Sudanese government forces since child soldiers were used on both sides during the Second Civil War.
2   Interviews were conducted from Sep 2007 to June 2008 in Southern Sudan. Although not addressed in this chapter, the research in its entirety also involved seventy-six face-to-face interviews with former child soldiers which provided the basis of comparison. All participants in the interviews were over the age of 18 and were thus reflecting on their childhood experience additionally, my research parameters were limited to individuals who had been members of the SPLA in the Second Southern Sudanese Civil War.

Interviewees were not just chosen for their experience or engagement with child soldiers, but also for their responsibility within any given NGO to represent or investigate the topic. The distinction is highlighted because it was not always the case that NGO workers' responsibility matched their field experience, as some at manager level did not have any contact with child soldiers. The range of interviewees includes groups such as UNICEF to the Diocese of Rumbek and the University of Juba, however for the purposes of simplification will be referred to as NGOs. From the pool of NGO workers interviewed, sixteen were not from Sudan, and seventeen were natives.[3]

The interviews conducted were semi-structured, where set questions were provided whilst at the same time interviewees were allowed to emphasise exactly which issues they felt most pressing. Background information including extent of experience in the field, length of time in Sudan, degree of exposure to child soldiers, and familiarity with the Southern Sudan case study were all collected. Some had been in Sudan for two weeks at the time of the interview, while others had been there for over 40 years.

Empirical data was also drawn from outside the recorded interviews. Observations were made as to how NGO workers conducted themselves in their daily lives; including how they travelled within the city and to what extent they intermingled with natives outside of their organisation. In addition, prior to each interview I explained the perspective my research took and that I was also conducting interviews with former child soldiers. Their reaction to me as an academic researcher as well as someone who valued the input of child soldiers, proved valuable in further assessing their attitudes and beliefs.

Southern Sudan Case Study

After nearly half a century of civil war, only interrupted by 11 years of suspended conflict from 1972-83 with the Addis Ababa Agreement, Southern Sudan signed the Comprehensive Peace Agreement (CPA) on 9th January 2005, which brought an end to Africa's longest running civil war and granted Southern Sudan a large degree of autonomy, with a referendum for secession that took place in January 2011.[4] The CPA came to an end in 1983 whilst at the same time the Sudan Peoples' Liberation Movement and Army (SPLM/A) was formed by Colonel John Garang in July 1983, forming one side to the second civil war against the central government.[5]

---

3   Only eight out of the seventeen natives were also child soldiers in the SPLA, five of whom were stationed outside of Juba and four occupied a role that only a native was allowed to, such as the Southern Sudan DDR Commission. One interviewee overlaps in these categories.
4   A. M. Lesch, *The Sudan – Contested National Identities*, pp. 51-52.
5   Ibid., p. 88.

The Second Civil War's underlying causes and the grounds for its length are not easily explained and debated within the literature. Although Collins argues the main areas of contention are largely historic and cultural, he claims that the start of the Second Civil War was due to the introduction of Shari'a law along with the treatment of the Southern government. Others have claimed that,

> Underlying the South-North conflict therefore are two broad and opposing political principles: that of the absolute national uniformity demanded by the Muslim-Arabicised elite and that of a democratically decentralised government, reflecting the diversity of the country, held primarily by Southerners.[6]

All the factors mentioned above attributed to fuelling the Second Civil War to varying extents.

Deng argues that the racial divide between the north and south of Sudan is based largely on identity rather than bloodline considering how racially mixed the country is.[7] An alternative view to divisions of Arab versus African and Muslim versus non-Muslim is suggested by Wenger; 'It is because these ethnic and religious cleavages often coincide with the divide between rich and poor, powerful and weak, that they become explosive.'[8]

Combining racial tensions as well as economic positioning, in 1995 slavery and abduction were reported to be in operation by the Northern government and is believed to currently be in operation today.[9]

The Sudanese central government's relationship with aid agencies increased in tension as its mistrust and control over aid agencies grew. The International Committee of the Red Cross (ICRC) were ousted from Southern Sudan in 1992, as well as many NGOs, all accused of assisting the SPLA.[10] It was not until 2005 that aid agencies were allowed a significant role in state reconstruction and development.

---

6   E. N. Wakoson, 'The Politics of Southern Sudan 1972-83', in M. W. Daly, A. A. Sikainga (eds), *Civil War in the Sudan*, p. 29.

7   "The conventional emphasis on the racial and cultural differences between the North and the South is an exaggeration that has since become recognized and modified, but it still reflects the divergence of self-perceptions if not the objective realities in the identities of the two sets of people, thereby generating the crisis of national identity", F. M. Deng, 'Hidden Agendas in the Peace Process', in M. W. Daly, A. A. Sikainga (eds), *Civil War in the Sudan*, p. 187.

8   M. Wenger, 'Sudan: Politics and Society', *Middle East Report*, p. 3.

9   Human Rights Questions: Human Rights Situations and Reports of Special Rappoteurs and Representatives, *Situation of human rights in the Sudan*, Oct 1995. Online Available HTTP: http://www.un.org/documents/ga/docs/50/plenary/a50-569.htm, (accessed on 20 August 2007). M. Jok, *War and Slavery in Sudan* , p. 9 and p. 81; R. O. Collins, *Civil Wars and Revolution in the Sudan: Essays on the Sudan, Southern Sudan, and Darfur 1962-2004*, p. 341.

10 Human Rights Watch Africa, *The Lost Boys: Child Soldiers and Unaccompanied Boys in Southern Sudan* , p. 38; E. O'Ballance, *Sudan, Civil War and Terrorism, 1956-99* , p. 190.

NGOs in Southern Sudan

Within the thirty-three face-to-face interviews of NGO workers that this chapter explores, the following areas of analysis emerge: a critique of NGOs' approach, their understanding and interaction with child soldiers, and their conceptualisation of war.

NGOs' Approach

What is thought of as an 'international approach' or 'international policy', produces blanket policies which tend to overlook the case specific nuances and details that are vital to creating effective policies. Field knowledge is often highly regarded; however in transferring from one conflict to another, its value is limited as different groups of child soldiers present different demands and additional understanding. Such knowledge and experience in the field is not interchangeable between countries and conflicts. Resulting from this is a limitation in the value of DDR implementation.

Field Manager, Timothy Kilimo of Save the Children Sweden interprets NGOs' role in the community:

> The NGOs [are] pushing, of course, the standard, the international standards in child rights, and there is also a community that has beliefs, cultural beliefs and other things, and there is the political will of the people of each and every country. like now in Southern Sudan ... if all the players come to an understanding that children should not be involved and child soldiers who have been forcefully put into the army should be demobilised with an immediate urgency.[11]

How can one presume that because children can be found in the military, that this is accepted within the culture? A more successful solution might be found if those within the community who are against such practices are sought after for their participation in helping to eradicate children in the SPLA.

NGOs' Understanding of Child Soldiers

The interaction between NGOs and child soldiers is largely influenced by NGOs' epistemological perspective. For example, when NGOs are asking: what and how can we know about child soldiers? If asking child soldiers for

---

11 Ryan, *The Children of War*, p. 31. Interview with Timothy Kilimo, Save the Children Sweden – Field Manager of Lakes State, Rumbek.

their input is not one methodology employed in answering this question, then their understanding will be limited. Without understanding the child soldiers' experiences, an understanding of how best to care for child soldiers is strained. The danger of misrepresentation and lack of understanding is highlighted below by this DDR Officer at UNICEF:

Children went into slavery and the families kind of encouraged it because they would have one less mouth to feed, they would go into slavery for six months or one year, come back, instead of being fed, and then they can come back home. Everyone's a winner.[12]

This inaccurate understanding of the culture, history and how the conflict in Southern Sudan affected the people would thus influence how this DDR Officer approaches his work with child soldiers.

Although many NGO workers attributed children joining the armed forces to poverty, there was not demonstrated a further understanding as to how the conditions of poverty were created. Issues of poverty were simplified instead of linked to the conflict with the Northern government, thus removing a political context.

A lot of these children are coming from such impoverished backgrounds whereas the SPLA represented a higher economic standard than where they had actually come from before they had become child soldiers.[13]

The danger of an oversimplification of children's experience in Southern Sudan is that it removes their positioning, interaction and digestion of all that they are exposed to. When such opinions and experiences are simplified, there then becomes no need to ask further questions, or to delve into a more complex analysis. A stunted conceptualisation is formed by the NGO workers when they heavily rely on other country case studies for their interpretation of the Southern Sudan case study.[14] Similarly, looking at 'child soldiers' as one entity removes the uniqueness of each case study and time period.

These stunted conceptualisations by the NGO workers encompassed the ability for a child to have personal and political agency, rational thought, limited their ability to weigh advantages in the decision making process, and dismiss a reaction to emotion as immature. The nature of this stunted conceptualisation involves the NGO worker helping to remove the agency the child is capable of. This is demonstrated in the testimony by Bishop Mazzolari when he describes the children as 'followers'.[15] This further enacts their 'victim' status, disengages them from exercising their agency and interacting

12 Ryan, *The Children of War*, p. 32. Interview with Stuart Kefford, UNICEF – Child Protection/ DDR Officer Southern Sudan.
13 Ibid., Interview with Dean Piedmont. UNDP – DDR Reintegration Manager, DPT Regional Coordinator.
14 Ibid.
15 Ibid., p. 33. Interview with Caesar Mazzolari, Diocese of Rumbek – Bishop.

with their war environment.

As children they just get what the elders are telling them and they just follow their elders as such is what I would see is what their motives are.[16]

He looks at a father or a brother who is going to war and he's supposed to support that person you see in a way it becomes like an enforcement agent to that person or to the brother or other relative. These are the two differences here. But at the end of day he comes and does the same thing that that person who he has been following to the bush is doing.[17]

The level of participation the testimony above describes limits the children's capability and their value in contributing to child-based research. In other words, why ask for the children's interpretation if they were simply forced or were following their elders?

I think adults have the sense of reasoning and know the right from the wrong, they know why they are joining the military probably it's because they are going for personal wealth I think. Children, if they are not recruited and they just join the military voluntarily, it's because of maybe peer pressure or the way they see things going. Children get attracted to things, so maybe they see people in the cars, running up and down and they think it's something good they need to do.[18]

Dividing the child from the adult experience and how they would differ on thought process and decision making is speculative and tends to follow stereotypical roles rather than research. These stereotypical roles relate to adults conducting rational thinking, independent decision making and stress the ability to evaluate the any given situation critically.

As a child, a child needs somebody to make decisions for him/her because a child below the age of seventeen has not reached a certain standard of trying to decide for him/herself and this is why the SPLA Government decided to demobilise them from the military because they are not mature enough to decide for themselves, so they need people to decide for them.[19]

The NGO workers neglect to highlight that whatever a child's capacity is to have political or personal agency, they are still in a position to absorb their environment and have experiences to draw from in creating their own interpretations. The context of war the children find themselves in colours their understanding of the political world. They are often witnessing first hand human rights abuses or violations, and simply by being a child soldier

16 Ibid., p. 35. Interview with Ayalew Teshome, World Vision International – Operations Director, South Sudan Programme.

17 Ryan, *The Children of War*, p. 35. Interview with Colonel Manoah Alemi Peter, Southern Sudan War Veterans Association – Association Secretary.

18 Ibid., p. 33. Interview with Peter Wisseh, UNICEF – Consultant Child DDR.

19 Ibid., p. 34. Interview with Santo Domic Chol, Southern Sudan Disarmament Demobilisation Reintegration Commission – Child DDR Coordinator.

one could argue that they are an example of a human rights abuse themselves. So how could this experience not account for something valuable to the NGO's investigation into child soldiers?

NGOs' Interaction with Child Soldiers

I have very minimal contact directly. We have staff on the ground that are doing their project implementation who work directly with the child soldiers on a weekly basis.[20]

Despite being stationed in Juba, Southern Sudan for 6 months the testimony of the Peace Building and Protection Programme Manager above draws concern to the disconnection many NGO workers have with children their programmes aim to assist. The harm in having such minimal contact is that in order to judge effectiveness of DDR programmes, for example, one is left with statistics or second-hand information. Such disengagement encourages generalisations and impersonal policy making. What is the manager above equipped with in order to critique the staff she has 'on the ground' if she has never had contact with child soldiers herself? So the less a child has contact, the less they are able to influence policy that is created to help them.

A solution to creating more understanding could be to make the history, culture and conflict issues as part of the training of NGO workers in Southern Sudan. There also needs to be more direct contact for all levels of staff working on the topic of child soldiers to enable a point of reference that is their own experience. This would facilitate a greater understanding and serve as a starting point for getting familiar with the uniqueness of the Southern Sudan case study.

NGOs' Conceptualisation of War

Within policies to eradicate child soldiers in conflict there demands an investigation into what motivates children to join the armed forces to ensure effectiveness at preventing participation. In other words, removing their motivation is vital to long-lasting demobilisation. The environment of war needs to be understood in order to conceptualise the child soldiers' role in it. Many of the motivations for children to join the armed forces are elements of this war environment.

Q: What thought process do you think children go through in order to become a soldier? Whether forcibly recruited or they choose to do it.

---

20 Ryan, *The Children of War*, p. 36. Interview with Sarah Gerein, World Vision International –
   Peace Building and Protection Programme Manager. She had been in Sudan for 6 months and
   never had contact with child soldiers.

If you go back to the 90s I think it was very simple. They were roaming the bush and 'I want protection', 'I want to go the SPLA', 'I'll get fed, I'll get a roof over my head.' Simple thought process. 'I want to be safe.'[21]

The testimony above highlights issues of poverty and safety, however this is a simplified image of Southern Sudan and the motivations of children to join the SPLA. For much of Southern Sudan the reason that such conditions and insecurity existed was because the children were forced away from their homes by Northern forces, and in doing so these children witnessed human rights abuses against their community and themselves. This gave the children first-hand knowledge and political motivation for them to join in order to prevent further human rights violations.

Q: So what would you say, a former child soldier might say was their first motivation, their primary motivation (to join SPLA)?

Then again, I haven't talked to enough child soldiers to actually know, I would like to talk to a child soldier to know.[22]

To know the war environment that the children are living in is to have an insight into why they find motivation to join the armed forces. How for example, can the DDR Reintegration Manager above appropriately reintegrate the former child soldiers if he is not aware of their motivations?

Value of Researching Children in a War Context

Political alienation among war veterans has been researched within many returning troops.[23] Former child soldiers fall into two categories of possible alienation – children and soldiers. Child-focused research is concerned with the debate whether to involve children's participation or to what extent they act as a participant. The interview method of data gathering presumes there is a value to getting an opinion of those who are the focus of the research. Applied to children, this epistemological positioning is found within child-focused research and is concerned with involving children in participating in research. It is claimed that participatory research allows children to make a contribution to research affecting them.[24] My research supports the idea of

---

21 Ryan, *The Children of War*, p. 37. Interview with Stuart Kefford, UNICEF – Child Protection/ DDR Officer Southern Sudan.
22 Ibid., p. 38. Interview with Dean Piedmont, UNDP – DDR Reintegration Manager, DPT Regional Coordinator.
23 L. Johnson, 'Political Alienation among Vietnam Veterans', *The Western Political Quarterly*, pp. 398-409.
24 F. Thomson, 'Are Methodologies *for* Children keeping *them* in their Place?', *Children's*

involving children in research, and further expands on this idea to involve adult's reflections on their own childhood. When approaching the topic of conflict and war-torn areas, much can be learned about childhood experiences from adults who went through such experiences.

Simon Manoja, the Director of Centre for Peace and Development Studies at Juba University supports this:

> I'm glad you are raising very interesting questions because we need to explore more the area of the perception of the child soldiers themselves and I think that is very crucial if you really want to know more about the in-depth understanding of why children tend to go and get recruited as child soldiers; why they do that.[25]

The need for further research is paramount, and admitting there is a need for it is the first step. Without filling in the gaps in the research and literature on child soldiers the consequence is that it threatens how appropriate the policies pertaining to child soldiers are.

Simon Manoja, the Director of Centre for Peace and Development Studies at Juba University admits that:

> Very little I've heard being said about the child soldiers in the SPLA or SPLM and even child soldiers recruited by the government forces during the war in Southern Sudan and I think that's an area where I think a lot of people need to do a lot of research.[26]

In reflecting about how child soldiers are often presented in research and literature:

> Most of the young people go and join simply because that's the source of revenue for them, for earning their salary, for livelihood because many of the young people may not be able to get proper employment, so the military becomes a sort of recruitment agency so long as livelihoods are concerned, but on the other side those guerrillas side again that little monetary incentive because they are volunteers and probably they may be forced because of the circumstances during the guerrilla warfare.[27]

Geographies, pp. 207-218; S. Holland, E. Renold, N. Ross, A. Hillman, 'Power, agency and participatory agendas: A critical exploration of young people's engagement in participative qualitative research', *Childhood*, pp. 360-375; S. Punch, 'Research with Children: The same or different from research with adults?', *Childhood*, pp. 321-341.

25 Ryan, *The Children of War*, p. 38. Interview with Simon Manoja, Director of Centre for Peace and Development Studies at Juba University.

26 Ryan, *The Children of War*, p. 38. Interview with Simon Manoja, Director of Centre for Peace and Development Studies at Juba University.

27 Ibid., Interview with Simon Manoja, Director of Centre for Peace and Development Studies at

I don't think we have done enough research. Specialised groups have come to search here and there. I think you're making a much deeper study but some people have taken advantage of the situation maybe to write a nice book but to face the situation in many aspects of the life of Sudan is difficult.[28]

Not all those I interviewed shared the same opinion that more research was needed on the topic of child soldiers in Southern Sudan. One of those disagreeing was Stuart Kefford, a Child DDR Officer for UNICEF. As he explained to me before our interview, his opinion was that enough research had been conducted on child soldiers and he did not feel that his responsibilities allowed him enough time to read new studies. Among others who shared his view was Victoria Ngali a Child Protection Advisor at UNMIS:

I don't think so far there's been any study in regard to how the demobilised children actually got recruited in the first place.' However, when I asked what has been neglected to be researched she continues, 'No, no, no, there's so much written about child soldiers.[29]

The topic is actually neglected, that is why we fail to find more recommendation on how reintegration is to be handled even facing education. If many people had done research on it they should have actually informed various agencies and the government on the best practice that need to be done.[30]

The need for information to be Southern Sudan specific is evident from the testimony by Alpha Chabari below.

We are very interested in this and we get some information about child soldiers and demobilisation, disarmament and reintegration and rehabilitation and the pictures we tend to get are mostly from Western Africa, not from Southern Sudan, because very little has been documented about Southern Sudan and because of the nature of everything. Politics, infrastructure, all that and we need to develop very tailor-made, very locally decided programs and we need information for us to do that and sometimes we come in to implement and we don't have the system to be able to get all the information that is available, either in a more digestible manner and so this research if we could get feedback from you it would be perfect, it would be one of the things that we need to have

Juba University.

28 Ibid., pp. 38-39. Interview with Caesar Mazzolari, Diocese of Rumbek – Bishop.
29 Ryan, *The Children of War*, p. 39. Interview with Victoria Ngali, UNMIS – Child Protection Advisor.
30 Ibid., p. 39. Interview with Abraham Kur, UNICEF – Child protection officer. A former child soldier who joined the SPLA at 14 in 1998.

the information and make better use of it.[31]

How effective can a programme of DDR be if the information it is based on is not originating from local experiences and context?

Conclusion

Through testimonies from NGO workers in Southern Sudan this chapter brought to light a critique of NGOs' approach looking specifically at how the 'international' take on the issue of child soldiers can lead to oversimplification of the Southern Sudan case study. This chapter also investigated the degree of understanding and interaction NGO workers had with child soldiers, which could directly influence their point of reference for carrying out their role in the best interests of the child. Testimonies were also discussed in relation to NGO workers' conceptualisation of war and how the child was not considered to relate to the war context.

The value and extent of knowledge gained from involving children in researching their situation is interpreted by the NGO workers, and based on these judgements the appropriateness of their programmes are affected.

31 Ibid., pp. 39-40. Interview with Alpha Chabari, Save the Children Sweden.

Organisation	Priorities	Interviews
Save the Children (United Kingdom)	Child rights (based on CRC), child protection, education	2
Save the Children (Sweden)	Child rights (based on CRC), child protection, education	4[1]
World Vision International	Advocacy: child rights, peace and conflict, education, economic justice	2
Pact	Livelihood, natural resource management, and peace building	1
International Rescue Committee	Protecting human rights, post-conflict development, resettlement services, advocacy, rehabilitation	2
United Nations Children's Fund (UNICEF)	DDR, Child Protection	7[2]
United Nations Development Programme (UNDP)	Crisis prevention and recovery, DDR	1
United Nations Mission in the Sudan (UNMIS)	DDR, human rights, Gender Unit: DDR for female combatants	3
Centre for Peace and Development Studies, University of Juba	Programme headquarters in Khartoum	1
Southern Sudan Disarmament Demobilisation Reintegration Commission	Sudanese personnel working with DDR	6[3]
Southern Sudan War Veterans Association	Assists veterans over the age of 18	2
Diocese of Rumbek	Elevated in 1974	2
Total		33

Fig. 14.1: List of organisations interviewed[32]
(see Notes on page 268)

32 Ryan, *The Children of War*, p. 18.

NGO Interviews[33]

Name	Date	Organisation	Role	Time in Sudan	Other
Caesar Mazzolari	20/03/2008	Diocese of Rumbek	Bishop of Rumbek	He first arrived in 1981.	He has assisted, accompanied, and been responsible for the welfare of former child soldiers during his time in Sudan.
Mario Riva	20/03/2008	Diocese of Rumbek	Father	He first arrived in 1954.	Testimony not used. In 1964 he was sent away to where he stayed in Kakuma. He helped the refugees and travelled with them. From Kakuma he went to Koboko, Uganda with the Sudanese refugees.
Ali Aulia Ramly	28/02/2008	International Rescue Committee	Child Protection & Youth Livelihood Manager	One week.	He has been working on the child soldier issue since 1999. When starting his managing post, he had never been to Sudan or worked on the issue of child soldiers in Sudan. His references to Sudan were limited to literature.
Julius Tiboa	12/12/2007	International Rescue Committee	Child Protection & Youth Livelihood Coordinator	One year	
Simon Manoja	10/02/2008	Centre for Peace and Development Studies, University of Juba	Director of Centre for Peace and Development	Native	
Tim Hayden-Smith	03/11/2007	Pact	Project Manager: Community Security and Early Warning Posts.	Two years.	

33 Ryan, *The Children of War*, pp. 223–28.

Name	Date	Organisation	Role	Time in Sudan	Other
Alpha Chabari	29/10/2007	Save the Children Sweden	Programme Officer, Child Protection	Two years	He has been working on the topic of child soldiers for two years.
Timothy Kilimo	16/03/2008	Save the Children Sweden	Field Manager of Lakes State, Rumbek	10 months	He has worked for Save the Children Sweden for 10 months. Before that he was working with World Vision on child protection issues for 4.5 years.
Otto James Avelino	25/03/2008	Save the Children Sweden	Rumbek	Native – Former child soldier	He was a child soldier at the age of 14.
John Madol Puou	25/03/2008	Save the Children Sweden	Rumbek	Native – Former child soldier	He joined the SPLA at the age of 16 in 1996.
Emmanuel Zino Riko	05/11/2007	Save the Children UK	Care and Information Officer, Juba	Native	He has 4 years experience working on the topic of child soldiers.
Peter Dak Khan	10/11/2007	Save the Children UK	Child Protection Project Officer, Unity State, Juba	Native	Testimony not used. He has been working 2.5 years with Save the Children. He returned to Sudan in 1993.
Santo Domic Chol	05/12/2007	Southern Sudan DDR Commission	Child DDR Coordinator	Native	He has 6 years of experience working with DDR of child soldiers.
Oluku Holt	05/12/2007	Southern Sudan DDR Commission	Special needs group coordinator	Native	Testimony not used.
Stephen Dut Deng	05/12/2007	Southern Sudan DDR Commission	Assistant special needs group coordinator	Native – Former child soldier	Testimony not used.

Name	Date	Organisation	Role	Time in Sudan	Other
Diing Bul Arok	05/12/2007	Southern Sudan DDR Commission	Community Security Assistant coordinator	Native – Former child soldier	Testimony not used.
John Mayom Deng	01/12/2007	Southern Sudan DDR Commission	Information systems officer	Native – Former child soldier	Joined SPLA in 1991 and left in 1997.
Lt Col Dut Riak	19/03/2008	Southern Sudan DDR Commission	SSDDRC State Coordinator, Lakes State, Rumbek	Native – Former child soldier	Former child soldier, joined SPLA at the age of 17 in 1984. He started working for the SSDDRC in 2004. Currently stationed in Rumbek.
Colonel Manoah Alemi Peter	02/02/2008	Southern Sudan War Veterans Association	Secretary	Native	He started his position in November 2006. He joined the SPLA in 1987 and served for 30 years.
H.E. Kawac Makuei Mayar	02/02/2008	Southern Sudan War Veterans Association	Chairperson	Native	Testimony not used. He spent 10 years in an Ethiopian prison. He was elected Governor of Northern Bar El Ghazal. Then he was the minister of Labour. He was a member of one of the two first battalions and was a Major when he came from the bush. He was also Minister of Wildlife.
Dean Piedmont	03/11/2007	UNDP	DDR Reintegration Manager, DPT Regional Coordinator.	Two years	
Stuart Kefford	16/10/2007	UNICEF	Child Protection/DDR Officer Southern Sudan	Nine months	

Name	Date	Organisation	Role	Time in Sudan	Other
Jessica Alexander	28/11/2007	UNICEF	Child Protection office where she developed re-integration programs.	One year	
Frank Kashandof	19/10/2007	UNICEF	Consultant Child DDR.	6 months	He had been working for UNICEF for 3 years and has worked in both DDR and child protection.
Peter Wisseh	17/10/2007	UNICEF	Consultant Child DDR.	One year	
Abraham Kur	15/03/2008	UNICEF	Child Protection Officer	Native	Former child soldier, joined SPLA at 14 in 1998.
Dombek Deng Kuol	16/10/2007	UNICEF	Project Officer for Child DDR.	Native	
Garang Majak	03/10/2007	UNICEF		Native	Former child soldier, joined SPLA at 14 in 1987. He started working for UNICEF in 2002.
Victoria Ngali	25/11/2007	UNMIS	Child Protection Advisor	7 years	7 years of experience working with child soldiers in Southern Sudan.
Jean Lokenga	11/04/2008	UNMIS	Regional Child Protection Advisor in Southern Sudan	Two years	He has been working in Sudan for UNMIS since 2006. In 2002 he was working on the topic of human rights, which has encompassed the issue of child soldiers
Jacque Chiengnyang de Mabor		UNMIS	Rumbek	Native	Age 27, born 1980. At 15 started with SPLA. From Yirol county, Lake state. Marabol, Equatoria state he did 6 months of training.
Sarah Gerein	02/11/2007	World Vision International	Peace Building and Protection Programme Manager	7 months	She works with Southern Sudan military and UNICEF for the demobilisation of child soldiers. Her job is focused on the reintegration of the former child soldiers.
Ayalew Teshome	15/11/2007	World Vision International	Operations Director, South Sudan Programme	Two years	

Bibliography

Amnesty International, *Sudan: "The Tears of Orphans", No Future Without Human Rights*, London, Amnesty International, 1995.

H. Brocklehurst, *Who's Afraid of Children? Children, Conflict and International Relations*, Hampshire, Ashgate, 2006.

Coalition To Stop The Use Of Child Soldiers, *The Use of Children as Soldiers in Africa: A Country Analysis of Child Recruitment and Participation in Armed Conflict*, London, Coalition to Stop the Use of Child Soldiers, 1999.

Coalition To Stop The Use Of Child Soldiers, Child Soldiers Global Report, 2004. Online. Available site: www.child-soldiers.org/document_get. php?id=743, (accessed 2004).

R. O. Collins, *Civil Wars and Revolution in the Sudan. Essays on the Sudan, Southern Sudan, and Darfur 1962-2004*, Tsehai Publishers, Hollywood, Calif, 2005.

J. M. Davis, 'Understanding the meaning of children: A reflexive process', *Children and Society*, Vol. 12, 5, 1998, pp. 325-335.

F. M. Deng, 'Hidden Agendas in the Peace Process', in M. W. Daly, A. A. Sikainga (eds), *Civil War in the Sudan*, London, British Academic Press, 1993.

M. Fargas-Malet, D. McSherry, E. Larkin, C. Robinson, 'Research with children: methodological issues and innovative techniques.' *Journal of Early Childhood Research*, 2010, vol. 8, pp. 175-192.

F. Faulkner, 'Kindergarten killers: Morality, Murder and the Child Soldier Problem', *Third World Quarterly*, 2001, vol. 22, 4, pp. 491-504.

L. Gallacher, M. Gallagher, 'Methodological Immaturity in Childhood Research? Thinking through "Participatory Methods"', *Childhood*, vol. 15, 4, 2008, pp. 499-516.

I. Hakvoort, 'Children's Conceptions of Peace and War: A Longitudinal Study', *Peace and Conflict: Journal of Peace Psychology*, vol. 2, 1, 1996, pp. 1-15.

A. Høiskar, 'Underage and Under fire: An enquiry into the use of child soldiers 1994-8', *Childhood*, vol. 8, 3, 2001, pp. 340-360.

S. Holland, E. Renold, N. Ross, A. Hillman, 'Power, agency and participatory agendas: A critical exploration of young people's engagement in participative qualitative research', *Childhood*, vol. 17, 3, 2010, pp. 360-375.

A. Honwana, *Child Soldiers in Africa*, Philadelphia, University of Pennsylvania, 2006.

Human Rights Watch, *The Lost Boys: Child Soldiers and Unaccompanied Boys in Southern Sudan*, New York, Human Rights Watch, 1994.

Human Rights Watch/Africa, *Children of Sudan: Slaves, Street Children and*

Child Soldiers, New York, Human Rights Watch, 1995.

L. Johnson, 'Political Alienation among Vietnam Veterans', *The Western Political Quarterly*, vol. 29, 3, 1976, pp. 398-409.

M. Jok, *War and Slavery in Sudan*, Philadelphia, University of Pennsylvania Press, 2001.

A. M. Lesch, *The Sudan – Contested National Identities*, Oxford, James Currey, 1998.

E. O'balance, *Sudan, Civil War and Terrorism, 1956-99*, London, MacMillan Press Ltd., 2000.

S. Punch, 'Research with Children: The same or different from research with adults?', *Childhood*, vol. 9, 3, 2002, pp. 321-341.

D. M. Rosen, *Armies of the Young: Child Soldiers in War and Terrorism*, London, Rutgers University Press, 2005.

C. Ryan, *The Children of War: Child Soldiers as Victims and Participants in the Sudan Civil War*, London, I.B. Tauris, 2012.

F. Thomson, 'Are Methodologies *for* Children keeping *them* in their Place?', *Children's Geographies*, vol. 5, 3, 2007, pp. 207-218.

UNICEF, *The Decentralization of the National Programme of Action: A Case of Sudan*, Florence, UNICEF, 1994.

UNICEF, *Framework for Addressing the Problem of the Abduction of Children and Women in Sudan*, Khartoum, UNICEF Sudan Country Office, 1999.

United Nations, *Promotion and Protection of the Rights of Children: Impact of Armed Conflict on Children*, New York, United Nations, 1996.

United Nations Committee on the Rights of the Child, *Optional Protocol on the Involvement of Children in Armed Conflict*, Geneva, OHCHR, 2000.

United Nations General Assembly, *Report of the Special Representative of the Secretary-General for Children and Armed Conflict*, New York, UN, 2005.

United Nations Institute for Disarmament Research, *Disarmament Forum: Children and Security*, Geneva, UNIDIR, 2002.

United Nations Security Council, *Children and Armed Conflict: Report to the Secretary-General*, New York, UN, 2003.

E. N. Wakoson, 'The Politics of Southern Sudan 1972-83', in M. W. Daly, A. A. Sikainga (eds), *Civil War in the Sudan*, London, British Academic Press, 1993.

M. Wenger, 'Sudan: Politics and Society', *Middle East Report*, vol. 172, 1991, pp. 3-7.

W. Yule, 'Emanuel Miller Lecture, From Pogroms to "Ethnic Cleansing": Meeting the Needs of war affected Children', *Journal of Child Psychology and Psychiatry*, vol. 41, 6, 2000, pp. 695-702.

Notes to Fig. 14.1

1   Includes two former child soldier: John Madol Puou (Interviewed 17.3.08. From Rumbek. Joined the SPLA at the age of 16 in 1997) and Otto James Avelino (Interviewed 25.03.2008 From Rumbek. Joined SPLA at the age of 14 in 1994).
2   Includes two former child soldiers: Abraham Kur (Interviewed 15.3.08. Joined SPLA at 14 in 1998. Now works for UNICEF as a child protection officer) and Garang Majak (Interviewed 3.10.07. From Aweil. Joined SPLA at age 14 in 1987. He now works for UNICEF in Rumbek).
3   Includes four former child soldiers: Diing Bul Arok (Interviewed 20.1.08. From Bor. Joined SPLA at age 14 in 1995. SSDDRC Community Security Associate Coordinator), Lt Col Dut Riak (Interviewed 19.03.08. Joined SPLA at age 17 in 1984. Lakes State Coordinator) John Mayom Deng (Interviewed 01.12.07. Joined SPLA at age 12 in 1991. Information Systems Officer) and Stephen Deng (Interviewed 20.1.08. SSDDR Commission Assistant Special Needs Group Coordinator).

Stephen Deng's testimony was not used: He felt that journalism is just a profession where they simply reported visual observations rather than getting the opinion of children. They should have interviewed the head child. He thinks my questions are relevant because "it touches on political engagement of Sudan" from the perspective of child soldiers. It's not like there were several political parties to choose from. He thinks his former child soldier colleague will have very different opinions.

15   How to make international justice a reality for children affected by armed conflicts?

Laurene Graziani

A children's rights perspective

"What is the reason for armed conflicts? There is no reason.
They lead to nothing; they are a desperate race towards nothing.
All combatants become pathetic objects of the conflict.
They no longer think; they just kill, abduct children (ending their
innocence and identity), and become engines of destruction.
They are unable to think, because they have entered the vacuum
of nothingness. They have brutalized themselves, because killing
and destroying is their profession; for nothing. Absolutely nothing"
Antonio Augusto Cançado Trindade[1]

Protection of children in armed conflict situations is not a recent issue. In the early 20th century, the founder of *Save the Children*, Eglantyne Jebb, lobbied strongly in favor of children affected by the First World War and pressured the international community to adopt special measures to protect them.[2] As a result, the first Declaration of the Rights of the Child was adopted in 1924. It is a major step as it unambiguously states that "mankind owes to the Child the best that it has to give".[3] The international community has paid constant attention to this issue ever since. UNICEF was created after the Second World War in order to assist children in times of emergencies, especially to protect them against starvation and sickness brought about by the war.[4] The Geneva Conventions, first adopted in 1949 and further complemented by two protocols in 1977, also contain specific rules concerning the special protection

---

1 Dissenting Opinion, *Serrano Cruz Sisters Vs. El Salvador*, 2005, § 34.
2 C. Mulley, *The woman who saved the children: a bibliography of Eglantyne Jebb the founder of Save the Children*.
3 E.M. Belser, K. Hanson, A. Hirt, *Sourcebook on International Children's Rights*.
4 See: UNICEF, *À props de l'UNICEF: Qui sommes nous?* Online. Available HTTP: http://www.unicef.org/french/about/who/index_history.html.

of children. But it is the International Convention on the Rights of the Child (CRC) adopted in 1989, which constituted the landmark for the protection of children's rights, as it is the first binding instrument in this field. It critically reinforces the protection of children's rights both in times of peace and in times of war, as it contains specific rules on the treatment of children during armed conflicts, mainly contained in Article 38.[5] In addition, children affected by armed conflicts also benefit from the general legal protection under other Human Rights instruments. This legal framework was further complemented by the African Charter on the Rights and Welfare of the Child in 1990, the Rome Statute in 1998, the ILO Convention n°182 concerning the worst forms of child labor in 1999 and the Optional Protocol to the CRC on the involvement of children in armed conflicts in 2000.[6] Thus, by the end of the 20th century, the legal framework for the protection of children in armed conflicts was already substantially developed.

Despite all this progress, international justice remains very exceptional as showed by a very limited case law on this issue and violations are most of the time committed with total impunity (Siegrist, 2006).[7] The Special Representative for Children in armed conflicts (A/HCR/15/58, 2010) recently highlighted that the situation of children affected by armed conflicts remains particularly critical:

> Children affected by armed conflict is an issue which is of prime importance, both as a threat to international peace and security and also as a human rights concern, which never ceases to shock and horrify. Their suffering bears many faces in the midst of armed conflict and its aftermath. Appalling numbers of children are being killed and maimed, while many more are left orphans. Thousands are raped, sexually abused and left profoundly traumatized. Children are compelled to bear arms as child soldiers, act as spies, suicide

5   Belser, Hanson, Hirt, *Sourcebook.*
6   No Peace Without Justice (NPWJ) & UNICEF Innocenti Research Center, *International Criminal Justice*, pp. 36-46.
7   As of today, there are only some jurisdictions that examined children rights violations: mainly the International Court of Justice (ICJ), the European and Inter-American Courts of Human Rights (ECHR and IACHR), the International Criminal Court (ICC), the International Criminal Tribunals for the former Yugoslavia (ICTY) and Rwanda (ICTR), the Special Court for Sierra Leone (SCSL). For an overview of this case law, see M. Feria Tinta, *The landmark rulings of the Inter-American Court of Human Rights on the Rights of the Child*; Mole, 2006; I. Berro-Lefèvre, 'Improving children's access to the European Court of Human Rights', in *International Justice for Children*; F. Tulkens, 'The European Convention on Human Rights and children's rights', in *International Justice for Children*; D. Tolbert, 'Children and international criminal law', in K. Arts. V. Popovski, *International Criminal Accountability and the Rights of Children*; Kuper, 2006; M. A. Drumbl, 'Prosecutor v. Thomas Lubanga Dyilo', *AJIL*, vol. 101(4), pp. 841-848; V. Oosterveld, A. Marlowe, 'Special Court of Sierra Leone judgement on recruitment and use of child soldiers', *AJIL*, vol. 101(4), pp. 848-857.

bombers, human shields, or become sexual slaves by armed forces or groups. They are disproportionately affected by displacement and forced to flee their homes to ensure their survival. They are deprived of education, health care and access to justice mechanisms [...] The international community must be seen to be responding, as a matter of priority, to mitigate the impact of conflict on children, to ensure the enforcement of international norms and standards and to end the impunity of violating parties (§3-4).

Therefore, the main question that is addressed in this study is how to make international justice a reality for children affected by armed conflicts?

This question is, however, closely linked to the general discussion on the critical gap in accountability for violations of children's rights. As Isabelle Berro-Lefèvre recalled in 2008: "everyone is aware of the gulf that exists between the legal and political commitments and the fate of many children".[8] Several discussions on this issue took place at the international level: in 2005, the Hague Academic Coalition and the United Nations University organized a conference on the international criminal accountability and children rights;[9] in 2007, the Council of Europe organized a conference on the "International justice for children";[10] in 2009, the establishment of an Open-ended Working Group on an optional protocol to the CRC to provide a communication procedure was also the opportunity for many experts to discuss important challenges in the field.[11] For example, Santos Pais (2008) recognizes that human rights mechanisms and complaint procedures still need to be made genuinely accessible to children. Some authors also believe that the approach is still not appropriate, such as Cantwell (2004) who stressed that the "charity legacy" approach is an extremely powerful brake on efforts to realize the rights of the child.

---

8   Berro-Lefèvre, 'Improving children's access', p. 78.
9   K. Arts. V. Popovski, *International Criminal Accountability and the Rights of Children*.
10 *International Justice for Children,* The Council of Europe.
11 Human Rights Council, *Annual Report of the Special Representative of the Secretary-General for Children and Armed Conflict* (UN doc. A/HRC/11/L.3, 2009). If these are the main references for this article, NGOs reports and UN documents, referred to international law experts, international judges and others experts working in non-judicial bodies were also used. Legal instruments and case law, statutes and rules of procedure of the different international jurisdictions also constituted important support. The approach adopted in this study is foremost legal. However, it was also necessary to link it to other disciplines to better understand the complexity of this issue. More general discussions on children's rights were taken into account such as the debate on competence, the reconstruction of childhood, the balance between emancipation and protection, the status of the child, the universality of children's rights and the debated legal nature of the CRC. Indeed, our intention was to adopt a children's rights perspective which can be defined as an interdisciplinary, a comprehensive and a child centred approach towards children's rights. Although it reflects a personal understanding of children's rights, it was also appropriate to define the methodology, the reasoning and the overall structure of this study.

In 2002, the international community committed to creating a "World Fit for Children".[12] However, as underlined by David (2002), there are still major challenges ahead ensuring the protection of children. This article which is divided into two main parts aims at looking at the main challenges at the institutional level and the main challenges at the level of the child.

I. Challenges at the institutional level

Reinforcing the international justice system is fundamental. A better cooperation among the different mechanisms is necessary. The development of a new optional protocol to the CRC to provide a communications procedure could significantly reinforce the role of the Committee which could, therefore, act as a universal and central focal point. Finally, the role played by NGO will also be highlighted.

1. A better cooperation among the different mechanisms

A better cooperation between the different jurisdictions and between judicial and non-judicial mechanisms is a challenge: the universality and unity of the human rights system are still important issues at stake.[13] As stressed by Santos Pais "enhanced collaboration should be promoted amongst international bodies and mechanisms with a view to enhancing synergies between their mandates and enabling the regular exchange of information to advance the realization of children's rights."[14] For example, the Prosecutor of the ICC recognized that the cooperation between the ICC and other mechanisms was fundamental.[15] The importance of the cooperation between the regional Courts has also been emphasized by the President of the European Court. Due to the multiplicity of international mechanisms, organizing frequent meetings between the different bodies is an interesting solution to compare practices, approaches and case law.[16] In aid of this, an international conference entitled "International Courts and Tribunals –The challenges ahead" was organized in 2008 between the three regional courts. It was only the first time that these bodies met together, but it already showed very positive results. The European and the Inter-American Courts could share their experiences

---

12 UN General Assembly, *Resolution S-27/2: A World Fit for Children* (UN doc. A/RES/S-27/2, 2002).

13 Shelton, 2009

14 M. Santos Pais, 'International law and children's rights: a critical review and a wish list', in *International Justice for Children*, p. 65.

15 L. Moreno-Ocampo, 'The rights of children and the international criminal court', in K. Arts, V. Popovski, *International Criminal Accountability and the Rights of Children*, pp. 111-17.

16 J.P. Costa, *Discours d'ouverture du colloque « Les cours régionales des droits de l'homme » à l'occasion du 60ème anniversaire de la Déclaration universelle.*

with the African Court, which not only needs to develop its own case law more quickly and ensure increased efficiency, but also needs to be better prepared to respond to problems that other regional Courts already face, such as delay and overloading. For example, the European Court has been forced to deal with an increased number of applications but cannot examine them within a reasonable time.[17] This fundamental principle enshrined in the ECHR article 6 is particularly important when dealing with children not only because violations should cease as quickly as possible but also because they have a serious impact on the development of the child, which is one of the major principles contained in the CRC – Article 6. One can imagine that the African Court could face such a problem due to massive violations of children's rights in armed conflicts on this continent.

Furthermore, it is important to avoid contradictions in order to reinforce the quality and effectiveness of the international justice for children. For that reason, international jurisdictions need to be inspired by decisions of other courts. In this regard, the Inter-American Court often refer to the European Court cases, such as for example in its advisory opinion on *the Legal Status and Rights of the Child* (2002, §72-74). The expertise of the Inter-American Court on the issue of children in conflicts situation could also be useful in helping other jurisdictions develop their own case law, as the Inter-American case law is quite well developed. The European Court could therefore refer more frequently to the Inter-American Court's cases. This is also true for the ICJ which also had the opportunity to deal with the rights of the child in such situation. For example, the ICJ in the case of the *Armed Activities on the Territory of Congo* (2005) recognized that Uganda had incited ethnic conflict and concluded that this State failed to protect the civilian population. However, the Court did not take into consideration the specific case of children such as the Inter-American Court did in some cases, concerning where it paid sufficient attention to the specific situation of children and highlighted that States have specific obligations towards children in this context.[18] Therefore, it would be very interesting to develop such meetings specifically on children's rights, to establish best practices and to make case law widely accessible, as suggested by Santos Pais.[19] For example, "Theseus" which is the case law database of the Council of Europe on children's rights is a very interesting initiative that could be developed at the international level.[20]

Because these mechanisms are still limited and recent, the relation

---

17 J.P. Costa, *Discours d'ouverture à l'audience solennelle de la Cour européenne des droits de l'Homme à l'occasion de l'ouverture de l'année judiciaire.*
18 For example: *The Massacre of Maripirán vs. Colombia*, 2005 and *The Massacres of Ituango vs. Colombia*, 2006.
19 Santos Pais, 'International law and children's rights'
20 See http://www.coe.int/t/transversalprojects/children/caselaw/caselawchild_FR.asp.

between judicial and non-judicial mechanisms is also of extreme importance. As underlined by De Boer-Buquicchio "One way to improve the protection of children's rights is through a combined approach between mechanisms with specific, but complementary advantages and approaches".[21] The Monitoring and Reporting Mechanism on Children and Armed Conflicts illustrates well the complementary nature between judicial and non-judicial mechanisms.[22] Established by the Security Council in order to monitor the gravest violations suffered by children in armed conflicts, it reflects the possibility to develop an effective cooperation between actors on a vertical basis. The Special Representative for children and armed conflict establishes a yearly report which is based on information received from the field. This report, which is presented by the Secretary-General, includes an annex of named parties that recruit and use children as child soldiers. This procedure was further developed by the resolution 1882 and the report also includes crimes of sexual violence committed against children and killing and maiming.[23] The Special Representative stressed the importance of incident based reporting and perpetrators identification.[24] This mechanism is a useful means for gathering evidence and then for taking concrete action at the judicial level in order to ensure that children's rights violations are effectively redressed, and to prevent further violations. Indeed, the Security Council has the possibility to report a situation to the ICC, such as it did for the situation of Sudan (ICC 02-05). At the moment, the Security Council has not yet decided to refer any situation mentioned by the Special Representative to the ICC and has only reemphasized in 2009 that sanctions against perpetrators may be considered.[25] Could the procedure through the Committee on the Rights of the child be an alternative to address children's rights violations?

2. Reinforcing the role of the Committee on the Rights of the child

Since December 2009, an Open-ended Working Group is drafting a new optional protocol to the CRC to provide a communications procedure. The proposed draft will be discussed by the States in December 2010, and if consensus is reached, it will go to the Human Rights Council for adoption.[26]

---

21 M. De Boer-Buquicchio, 'Preface', in *International Justice for Children*, p. 12.
22 UN Security Council, *Resolution n° 1612* (UN doc. S/Res/1612(2005)).
23 UN Security Council, *Resolution n° 1882* (UN doc. S/RES/1882(2009)).
24 R. Coomaraswamy, *The Security Council and Children and Armed Conflicts. An Experiment in the Making.*
25 UN Security Council, *Resolution n° 1882* (UN doc. S/RES/1882(2009)).
26 Committee on the Rights of the Child, *General Comment No. 12 on the right of the child to be heard* (UN doc. CRC/C/GC/12). It is important to underline that this article was written in October 2010. Since then, the situation has changed. The Optional protocol has been adopted with important modifications. For example, NGOs do not have anymore the possibility to introduce a

This new protocol will critically increase the role of the Committee on the Rights for the promotion and protection of the rights of the child at the international level. Accountability mechanisms for children's rights will be further consolidated, as it will offer to all children a real chance to see the violations of their rights addressed by a universal organisation.[27] Indeed, the CRC has been ratified by all the UN Members, except USA and Somalia. In cases they do not have access to domestic remedies or that regional remedies do not exist,[28] children could access the Committee direct or indirectly via a representative. Beside the individual complaints, the draft of the Protocol also establishes a collective complaint procedure and an inter-state communications procedure.[29] Furthermore, the justiciability of children's rights will be reinforced. Any alleged violations will be addressed through the lens of the indivisibility and interrelationship of the CRC.[30] This mechanism will cover all civil, political, economic, social and cultural rights of the child and the Committee will have the possibility to look at new cases and develop an interesting jurisprudence. It will also be an opportunity for the Committee to further interpret and clarify the CRC provisions and the Protocol. Santos Pais adds that this mechanism will preserve the holistic perspective of this treaty and that the communications procedure will be pursued in conformity with the rights recognised by the Convention and guided by the general principles of the CRC, such as the best interests of the child.[31] Furthermore, this mechanism will complement the reporting process and provides another context for influence beyond the issuing of concluding observations.[32]

Concerning more specifically children in armed conflicts, this mechanism will also constitute an important avenue for violations redress as the Committee will apply the CRC and its optional Protocol on the involvement of children in armed conflicts. The Committee has been paying close attention to this issue since the beginning of the 1990s. In its general discussion on Children and armed conflicts in 1992, it emphasized the complexity of this issue that should not be reduced to the consideration of a single provision of the CRC, namely Article 38. It considered that it needs an urgent, specific and adequate response. Through the new communication procedure, the Committee will

complaint.

27 M. Santos Pais, *Human Rights Council Working Group and an optional protocol to the Convention on the Rights of the Child to provide a communications procedure* (UN doc. A/HRC/WG.7/1/CRP.7).

28 Such as in Asia for instance.

29 Committee on the Rights of the Child, *General Comment No. 12 on the right of the child to be heard* (UN doc. CRC/C/GC/12), Article 3 and Article 12.

30 Ibid.

31 Ibid.

32 P. Newell, *Submission to Open-ended Working Group of the possibility of elaborating an Option protocol to provide a communications procedure for the Convention on the rights of the child* (UN doc. A/HRC/WG.7/1/CRP.2).

also have the possibility to establish an inquiry procedure for grave and systematic children's rights violations.[33] Thus, the Committee has the sound expertise to give to the Convention the role it can play to strengthen the protection and promotion of children's rights affected by armed conflicts.

It is important to underline that the Committee is the only international body focusing on children's rights. The Committee is composed of independent children's rights experts that can understand the complexity of children's rights and the main challenges that are at stake. Most of them have been working for a long time in this field and can therefore adopt a children's rights based approach that reflects the multidisciplinary character of the CRC.[34] Moreover, they can guide other jurisdictions in the interpretation of children's rights. Indeed, even if the international jurisdictions paid an increase attention to children's rights violations since the adoption of the CRC, the aim of these jurisdictions is not to focus specifically on children's rights and apply the CRC. For example, Françoise Tulkens highlighted that children's rights are not the only priority for the European Court: it considers all different kinds of human rights violations but within the limits of the ECHR.[35] It is true that references to the CRC are actually not frequent in the jurisprudence of the European Court concerning children. As a result, the Committee could become a real international focal point on children's rights at the international level and could become the unique child-sensitive universal mechanism.[36]

3. Increasing the role of NGOs

NGOs working in the field of children's rights have an important role to play in the implementation of children's rights at the national level. They can pressure the government to enforce judicial decisions and improve legislation on children's rights by means of various actions: issuing report and public statement on individual cases or patterns of human rights violations; organising campaigns to mobilise the public opinion; attempting to affect the foreign policy of countries in their relationship with countries which violate human rights; undertaking diplomatic initiative; securing direct relief to victims; raising action through judicial actions in national courts.[37]

NGOs also have the possibility to introduce a complaint before some

---

33 Committee on the Rights of the Child, *General Comment No. 12*, Article 10 Draft Procedure.
34 P. David, 'Implementing the rights of the child: Six reasons why the human rights of children remain a constant challenge', *International Review of Education*, pp. 259-263.
35 C. Maisin, 'Françoise Tulkens, juge à la "Conscience de l'Europe"', *Journal Droit des Jeunes*, pp. 24-26.
36 Santos Pais, *Human Rights Council Working Group*.
37 S. Parmentier, 'The significance of mechanisms to monitor human rights at the international level', in E. Verhellen (ed.), *Understanding Children's Rights*, pp. 341-374.

international jurisdictions, and are particularly involved in this process at the Inter-American level. The ACHR, Article 44, and Inter-American Commission Rules of Procedure, Article 23, provide that NGOs which are legally recognized in the OAS State members can introduce petitions before the Commission on their own behalf or on behalf of third persons. Indeed, most of the cases concerning children and armed conflicts were introduced by NGOs. For example, in the case of the *Gomez Paquiyauri Brothers vs. Peru* (2004), the petition was introduced by the *Centro de Estudios y Acción para la Paz* and in the case of *Massacres de Ituango v. Colombia* (2006) it was introduced by the *Grupo Interdisciplinario por los Derechos Humanos* and the Colombian Commission of Jurists. Participation of NGOs at the European level is limited to the victim's support as they are not allowed to introduce a case before the European Court on behalf of the victim. However, such an initiative could be developed in the future. For example, Françoise Tulkens stated that the Court should accept actions by associations or groups even if not directly affected by violations to "speak on behalf of those who have no voice".[38] In this regard, the establishment of the European Committee of Social rights is already an important evolution as NGOs have the possibility to lodge complaints against States for alleged violations of the Social Charter. This procedure also has a lot of advantages: it is relatively speedy, accessible and simple. As there is no victim requirement it constitutes an important means for NGOs to oblige State parties to respect children's rights independently of the existence of individual rights violations.[39]

The development of such collective complaint procedure has been supported because of its efficiency. First, this procedure is of particular interest when the State's action has affected several people, such as for example in the cases concerning collective violations. A concrete example is the one of the cases concerning massacres in Colombia, mentioned before, or when a State is continuously violating the rights of children, such as the cases concerning violations of illegal migrant children's rights examined by the European Committee of Social Rights.[40] Even if justice is normally apprehended through an individual perspective and not a collective one, it is important to underline that individual petitions do not have such a large impact.[41] Furthermore, protection and redress for victims can be achieved more quickly as they are not obliged to pass through the lengthy process of individual petitions. Thus collective action appears to be an appropriate tool to develop quickly and effectively the judicial protection of children. It could also be linked with

---

38 F. Tulkens, 'The European Convention', p. 19.
39 M. De Boer-Buquicchio, 'Preface', pp. 9-13.
40 *International Federation of Human Rights Leagues (FIDH) vs. France*, 2003.
41 O. De Schutter, *Fonction de juger et droits fondamentaux. Transformation du contrôle juridictionnel dans les ordres juridiques américain et européens.*

strategic litigation: this technique aims to create broader changes in society by selecting a specific case and bringing it to the court. Strategic litigation is a creative and powerful means of advocacy which effects are enhanced if the action is part of an overall advocacy campaign designed to raise awareness on a particular issue or promote the rights of a disadvantaged population.[42] For example, the campaign launched by Amnesty International to support Omar Khadr, a former child soldier held in Guantanamo, is an interesting example of an action taken by an NGO to address the issue of children and armed conflicts with a combination of political and judicial strategy. Amnesty International has been actively supporting his repatriation to Canada using traditional activist tools such as public marches, urgent actions and petitions in order to pressure the government.[43] Furthermore, with other NGOs such as Human Rights Watch or the Canadian Coalition for the Rights of Children and Justice for Children and Youth, they introduced a case before the Supreme Court of Canada claiming that the government of Canada was not protecting one of its citizens. Although the Supreme Court of Canada unanimously declared that Omar Khadr's ongoing detention constitutes a human rights violation, he has still not been repatriated to Canada.[44] He is currently judged by a US military commission, and Amnesty International created a specific blog in order to keep public informed about this trial.[45] In Belgium, NGOs played an active role in the *Mubilanzila Mayeka and Kaniki Mitunga vs Belgium* case before the European Court in 2006 concerning a five year old girl from the war-torn Congo. The decision was followed by the establishment of a Court of Opinion organized in Brussels in January 2008 by Defence for Children International and UNICEF. Chaired by Jaap Doek, the objective was to denounce the detention of minors in illegal situations or asylum seekers.[46] This is an example of a broad and concrete action initiated by NGOs to oblige a State to comply with its obligations towards children, not only when they are citizens but also when they are migrating or fleeing from their countries because of armed conflicts.

Beside these challenges at the institutional level, there are also important issues concerning the role and the treatment of the child in this process. A child centred approach. Children should be participating and justice should be adapted to their specific needs. Furthermore, children's rights should also

---

42 CRIN, *Children's Rights: A guide to Strategic Litigation.*
43 See: http://www.amnesty.ca/take_action/actions/canada_bring_khadr_justice.php.
44 *Canada (Prime Minister) v. Khadr*, 2010.
45 Online. Available HTTP: http://livewire.amnesty.org/2010/08/12/omar-khadr-trial-%E2%80%93-%E2%80%98jury%E2%80%99-selected-for-omar-khadr%E2%80%99s-military-commission-trial/ (October 15, 2010).
46 UNICEF Belgique & Défense des Enfants International Belgique, La détention des enfants en centres fermés.

be translated in a way that children are taken more seriously. The international law on the rights of the child (and international justice for children) could not become a reality if the rights for the child and the rights by the child are not incorporated into this framework.

II. Challenges at the child level

In its general comment n°12, the Committee on the Rights of the child stressed that "proceedings must be both accessible and child-appropriate".[47] Therefore, we will mainly focus on the development of an appropriate access to international justice for children and a child-friendly justice. The optional protocol to the CRC to provide a communications procedure highlighted that the special status and rights of the child are taken into account in the development of an international child-friendly justice.[48] Thus, we will also pay attention to these two aspects.

1. Encouraging appropriate access to international justice for children

How to translate the maxim "*ubi ius ibi remedium*" in a children's rights language? Access to justice is a fundamental right: individuals whose fundamental rights have been violated should have access to effective remedies to oblige States to comply with their obligation, to redress violations and to obtain compensation. Even if international justice is still subsidiary, it is essential when national remedies are inexistent or inappropriate. However, it is still an important challenge for children to access international justice. The legal capacity of the child is one of the major obstacles.[49] The European Court on Human Rights is actually the first mechanism that examined petitions lodged by victims under 18 years old. The ECHR states that "any person" claiming to be a victim can introduce a complaint in Article 34. Thus, children – even though they are not entitled to access justice at the national level because of the lack of legal capacity – can introduce a petition if they suffered human rights violations.[50] Some of the applications lodged by children concern armed conflict situations. For example, three cases concerning the conflict between Turkey and the PKK: two petitions were lodged by minors unlawfully detained,[51] and one was introduced by a girl raped and ill-treated while in detention.[52] Some children were also co-petitioners such as in the *Muskhadzhiyeva v. Belgium* case, 2010,

---

47 Committee on the Rights of the Child, *General Comment No. 12*, § 34.
48 Human Rights Council, A/HCR/WG. 7/2/2.
49 Tulkens, 'The European Convention'.
50 Berro-Lefèvre, 'Improving children's access', pp. 69-78.
51 Güveç v. Turkey, 2009 and Salduz v. Turkey, 2008.
52 Aydin v. Turkey, 1997.

and the *Mubilanzila Mayeka and Kaniki Mitunga vs. Belgium* case, 2006. Both cases are also interesting to underline that the Court is also opened to non-citizens regardless of their age.

Such an approach is still exceptional, but this possibility is also foreseen in the Protocol to the African Charter on Human and Peoples' Rights on the establishment of an African Court on Human and Peoples' Rights in 1998, and the proposal for a draft optional protocol to the CRC to provide a communications procedure in 2010. The Inter-American Commission might also receive petitions lodged by children.[53] However, the Inter-American Court adopted a broader approach regarding the role of the family in the procedure.[54] In fact, the Court has a large interpretation of the notion of victim and admitted that the closed members of the family might also be considered as victims when children suffered cruel, inhuman and degrading treatment, such as in the cases of conflicts.[55] The interpretation of the bounds between the child and his family is very interesting and is particularly well reflected in one dissident opinion of judge Cançado Trindade: "The intense suffering caused by the violent death of a beloved person discloses one of the great truths of the human condition: that the fate of one is ineluctably linked to the fate of others. One cannot live in peace in face of the disgrace of a beloved person."[56] Thus, victim's relatives are generally involved and children can also be considered as indirect victims.

As of today, only a few children lodge applications on their own.[57] Indeed, because children lack legal capacity, the exhaustion of all available domestic remedies can be an important barrier.[58] Berro-Lefèvre stressed that "consideration should be given to the admissibility problem posed by failure to exhaust domestic remedies, where a minor has been unable to assert his or her rights in the national courts."[59] An interesting approach was adopted in the draft for the optional protocol to the CRC to provide a communications procedure: Article 4. It provides that all available domestic remedies should have been exhausted, but "This shall not be the rule where the application of the remedies is unreasonably prolonged or unlikely to bring effective relief." Moreover, "The Committee shall interpret the application of the remedies in a manner sensitive to the impact that delays may cause to a child's well-

---

53 P. S. Pinheiro, *Reasons and timing to elaborate a communications procedure under the Convention on the Rights of the Child* (UN doc. A/HRC/WG.7/1/CRP.4).

54 Feria Tinta, *The landmark rulings*.

55 Gomez Paquiyauri Brothers v. Peru, 2004, Serrano Cruz Sisters v. El Salvador, 2004 and Molina Theissen v. Guatemala, 2004.

56 Feria Tinta, *The landmark rulings*, p. 20.

57 Berro-Lefèvre, 'Improving children's access', pp. 69-78.

58 The exhaustion of national remedies is one of the major conditions to introduce a petition, see for example ECHR Article 35 and ACHR Article 46.

59 Berro-Lefèvre, 'Improving children's access', p. 76.

being and development".[60] This approach could also be adopted by other jurisdictions.

It is also fundamental to ensure the right to information. In this regard, Cançado Trindade considered that "*le droit au droit*" should be considered as a rule of jus cogens.[61] This right is entitled in the CRC in Article 17. Berro-Lefèvre considered that "the right to appropriate information is a prerequisite for children to be able to assert other rights" and emphasized that "Each country should set public or private information agencies for young people, aimed firstly at promoting the exercise of children's rights and secondly at providing information and advice on how to lodge an application."[62] On that specific point, Santos Pais adds that providing children with relevant information on existing complaint mechanisms and procedures is not sufficient, it is also necessary to raise awareness of what these instruments mean and how they can be used and to employ child sensitive language, materials and tools in the performance of these tasks.[63] Thus, education to children's rights should be systematised in and outside schools.[64] Children's rights should be included in curriculum and children should have the possibility to ask information not only at home or at school but also have access to children's rights offices, judicial services and online forums on that question.

Finally it is also important to emphasize that the recognition of children as autonomous actors does not exclude protection. For example, it can be difficult for them to endure the whole judicial procedure alone. They need to be represented and supported by responsible adults. Parents are supposed to be the first child carer, in application of parental authority. Actually, most of the cases concerning children's rights violations in Europe have been introduced by parents.[65] Children can also be represented by professionals such as a social worker, an NGO or a children's ombudsman.[66] It is necessary when parents do not want or are not able to do so, or when there are conflicts of interest between the child and its parents. Thus, it is important to define broad criteria to allow all the different actors to act such as in the draft for the optional protocol to the CRC to provide a communications procedure which establishes that "communications may be submitted by or on behalf of an individual or group of individuals [...] claiming to be victims of a violation

---

60 Human Rights Council, A/HCR/WG.7/2/2.
61 A. A. Cançado Trindade, *Evolution du droit international au droit des gens. L'accès des individus à la justice internationale, le regard d'un juge*, p. 119.
62 Berro-Lefèvre, 'Improving children's access', p. 74. In her opinion, these agencies should cooperate with local bars associations, child welfare services and NGOs.
63 Santos Pais, *Human Rights Council Working Group*.
64 David, 'Implementing the rights of the child', pp. 259-263.
65 Berro-Lefèvre, 'Improving children's access'.
66 Newell, *Submission to Open-ended Working Group*.

by that State party of any of the rights."[67] We will now look more deeply at the adoption of specific measures to ensure that justice is adapted to children.

2. Adapting international justice to children

Adopting measures to establish an appropriate justice for children are necessary whether children are directly involved or not in the procedure. This is an issue of foremost importance in cases concerning children affected by armed conflicts, as it has been reflected in the Lubanga case before the ICC. If we take the previous example of the right to trial within a reasonable time, this right must be adapted to the needs of children and be respected anytime children are concerned. The experience shows that justice can take time.[68] The temporal dimension is an important factor to be taken into account in cases related to children. It is true that, in general, human rights violations have to stop as soon as possible, but children have nether the time nor means to wait. As underlined by Berro-Lefèvre cases involving children should be treated as a matter of priority. For instance, in the European context, the European Court Rules establish that some cases must be given priority, especially those raising serious and urgent issues in Article 41, and Berro-Lefèvre underlines that this rule should be systematically applied when the case concerns children.[69] It was recently highlighted by the Council of Europe: "in all proceedings involving children, the principle of immediacy should be applied to provide a speedy response and protect the best interests of the child, while respecting the rule of law."[70] Furthermore, some courts decided to adopt provisional or interim measures in order to prevent further violations and ensure protection while awaiting the final decision. For example, the Inter-American Court Rules of Procedure (Article 26) and the ACHR (Article 63.2) establish that at any stage of the proceedings involving cases of extreme gravity and urgency, and when necessary to avoid irreparable damage to persons, the Court may order provisional measures as it deems pertinent. The Inter-American Court underlined that adoption of provisional measures is of utmost importance in cases where vulnerable children are concerned (*Case of the Children and Adolescents Deprived of Liberty in the "Complexo do Tatuapé" of FEBEM*, 2008). This possibility has also been foreseen in the draft of the new optional protocol to the CRC (Article 5).

Santos Pais (2009) also stressed the importance to establish specific legal

---

67 Committee on the Rights of the Child, *General Comment No. 12*, Article 2.1.
68 N. Vuckovic Sahovic, *Feasibility of a communication procedure under the Convention on the Rights of the Child* (UN doc. A/HCR/WG.7/1/CRP.1).
69 Berro-Lefèvre, 'Improving children's access'.
70 Council of Europe, *Final draft Guidelines of the Committee of Ministers of the Council of Europe on child-friendly Justice* (CJ-S-CH (2010) 12).

safeguards for children. Guidelines on Justice in Matters involving Child Victims and Witnesses of Crime (2005) provide that children need protection, assistance and support appropriate to their age and maturity but also to their individual needs. The Inter-American Court also establishes important measures in its advisory opinion on the *Juridicial status and human rights of the child* (2002). This is consistent with the CRC's Preamble: "the child [...] needs special safeguards and care, including appropriate legal protection" (Belser, Hanson and Hirt, 2009). The Council of Europe is currently developing guidelines on child friendly justice (CJ-S-CH (2010) 12, 2010). Those guidelines are going further than the ones of the ECOSOC as they include all the steps of the procedure, and as they concern not only children as victim or witness but also children in conflicts with the law. For example, it is established that children should receive appropriate assistance in an effective manner throughout the process, they should receive legal counsel and legal aid, and their anonymity should be guaranteed.

International criminal tribunals are particularly ahead on this subject as they had to implement special measures to protect child witnesses. The experience of the SCSL is significant. Michels (2006) explained that in this context of systematic violence and massive violations of human rights, children have suffered important emotional and psychological traumas. For instance, it can be extremely painful for child witnesses to narrate their experiences. As a result, child witnesses have been recognized as a particularly vulnerable group. For example, the SCSL Rule 34 of Procedure and Evidence states that children should receive adequate support, including medical and psychological assistance. Furthermore, children tend to be daunted by the whole judicial procedure. Protection Units for Children and Witnesses were established to guarantee the protection of children (Tolbert, 2006). During the whole judicial procedure, the members of the protection unit have to assist child witnesses and have to explain to them exactly what is happening as well as the meaning of the terms being used. It is also important to ensure the physical security of these children. Their anonymity should therefore be protected as they can be easily threatened or stigmatized (Michels, 2006, p. 138-139). As a result, the Court decided that children will be testifying via closed circuit television (*Prosecutor v. Sam Hinga, Moinana Fofana, Allieu Kondewa*, 2004) and that a voice distortion system could also be used (*Prosecutor v. Issa Hassan Sesay, Augustine Gbao and Morris Kallon*, 2004).

Thus, international jurisdictions took into account the fact that children are human beings entitled to a full array of rights: they do not only need protection but they also have the right to participate. For instance, they can bring a case before the European Court of Human Rights or they can testify before the ICC. In this regard, the CRC initiated an important evolution with an emancipatory approach reflected mainly in article 12 on the right to participation. As mentioned by De Boer-Buquicchio (2008), children's rights need to be incorporated in the functioning and decisions of the monitoring mechanisms. However, international jurisdictions paid more attention to the protection of children and less to their participation. A comprehensive approach seems to be missing. Furthermore, many experts think that the gap between theory and practice cannot be addressed because the approach to children's rights is still not appropriate. Hanson (2008) explains that "a consensus on the extent, priorities or even precise content of children's rights is not readily available." In his opinion, the phrase "children's rights is a slogan in search of definition" launched by Hillary Rodham in 1973 has lost nothing of its relevance. Thus, how could the rights of the child can become a reality if there is still not a homogenous understanding and common approach? If we follow the reasoning of Tomaševski (2007), children's rights are even in danger of becoming "a weasel word". Finding an appropriate approach to children's rights is another challenge, if not the most important one.

3. Developing an appropriate approach to children's rights

Since the World Conference on Human Rights in 1993, the "First Call for Children" established that the rights of the child should be a priority in the United Nations system-wide action on human rights (Newell, 2009). However, in December 2009, the Chairperson of the Committee on the Rights of the child stressed that nearly a century of work has been dedicated to children and their rights but still children's rights are not realized (Lee, 2009). Thus, she comes to the following conclusion:

> Are children really recognized as true holders of rights? Are the States doing everything possible for children to exercise their rights? Is the international community doing everything possible to monitor this? What are the fundamental reasons why children continue to live in a world that is not 'fit for children'?

The welfare approach, i.e. the dominant ideology in the field during the twentieth century which is merely based on the children's needs is no longer valid. However, it is still dominant (Hanson, 2008). For example, Verhellen (2008) explained that adult centrism, paternalism, manipulation and tokenism are prevalent and Pupavac (2006) stressed that children are considered as rights-holders but are still not treated as moral agents who determine those rights. Indeed, the emancipation of children met with widely varying degrees of enthusiasm from different degrees of society, as many groups still feel that recognising rights of children will infringe their own rights (David, 2002). Furthermore, the reality of childhood is often under estimated. It is fundamental to recognize that children are actually taking an active role in their own community. Indeed, children can play a fundamental role and assume important responsibilities, such as taking care of relatives or working (Verhellen, 2000).

This is particularly true in armed conflicts situation where children play a critical role. Often this reality is also oversimplified with sharp distinctions such as adulthood/childhood or innocence/guiltiness. Honwana (2000) explains that most of the time children in armed conflicts are considered either as victims or as perpetrators. But the situation is more complex as they can play several roles at the same time. When we look at how international law and justice dealt with this issue, it is interesting to see that the debate was mainly focused on the recruitment of child soldiers for the last years and international criminal courts did not pay enough attention to other crimes, such as sexual crimes committed against girls. For example, in the AFCR case, although thousands of girls had been victims of sexual violence, sexual slavery and forced marriage, the judges concluded that it was a war crime of outrage upon personal dignity but did not develop further the case law on sexual violence against women and girls (Oosterveld and Marlowe, 2007). The Special Representative for Children and Armed Conflict encouraged some improvements on this issue. As a result the Security Council in its latest resolution on children in armed conflicts (S/RES/1882, 2009) designated rape and other sexual violence as critical priorities.

The actual conceptualization of children affected by armed conflicts reflects very deep problems in the way the international community responds to children's rights violations. For children's rights norms to be effectively put into practice and children's rights violations effectively redressed, it is necessary to take into account the reality in the lives of these children. The international system is still based on the idea that children should be protected from the adult world and does not actually take into account the fact that children are also important actors. As Pupavac (2006) stressed it is necessary to reconstruct the image of the child. The child agency theory can help to overcome this deadlock. The recognition of children as actors offers another image of childhood: these children are not "empty" innocent victims as Honwana (2000) stressed about children in armed conflicts but agents able to take decisions and to have real life knowledge. Nieuwenhuys (2005) explains that:

> Recognizing child agency means understanding that get what they need children must be cunning and be able to manipulate even a highly oppressive situation to their own advantage and that this may involve trying to improve their situation by looking for opportunities outside the family and neighbourhood. Of course the latter children are particularly vulnerable to abuse and exploitation, but at

the same time they are also strong, for they often show remarkable resilience and resourcefulness in facing unknown situations (p. 12).

An appropriate children's rights approach also requires a fair balance to be struck between emancipation and protection. This challenge could be addressed through the concept of evolving capacities. Lansdown (2009) explains that this concept is the basis for an appropriate respect for children's agency without exposing them prematurely to the full responsibilities normally associated with adults: children must be recognized as active agents in their own lives, while also being entitled to protection in accordance with their relative immaturity and youth.

Finally, we conclude by underlining that the evolution towards a children's rights based approach requires, as David (2002) said, "a fundamental change of legislation, policies, programmes and institutions, but even more importantly, of mentalities and beliefs" (p. 2).

Bibliography

E.M. Belser, K. Hanson, A. Hirt, *Sourcebook on International Children's Rights*, Bern, Staempfli, 2009.

I. Berro-Lefèvre, 'Improving children's access to the European Court of Human Rights', in *International Justice for Children*, Strasbourg, The Council of Europe, 2008, pp. 69-78.

A.A. Cançado Trindade, *Evolution du droit international au droit des gens. L'accès des individus à la justice internationale, le regard d'un juge*, Paris, Pedone, 2008.

N. Cantwell, 'The Convention on the Rights of the Child, Vini, vici ... et vinci?', in E. Verhellen (ed.), *Understanding children's rights*, Ghent, Ghent University – Children's Rights Centre, 2004, pp. 395-407.

Committee on the Rights of the Child (2009) *General Comment No. 12 on the right of the child to be heard* (UN doc. CRC/C/GC/12). Online. Available HTTP: http://www2.ohchr.org/english/bodies/crc/comments. htm, (accessed 6 October 2010).

R. Coomaraswamy (2010) *The Security Council and Children and Armed Conflicts. An Experiment in the Making.* London, Online. Available HTTP: http://www.un.org/children/conflict/english/12-apr-2010-the-security-council-and-caac.html, (accessed 6 October 2010).

J.P. Costa (2008) *Discours d'ouverture du colloque « Les cours régionales des droits de l'homme » à l'occasion du 60ème anniversaire de la Déclaration universelle.* Strasbourg. Online. Available HTTP: http://www.echr.coe. int/NR/rdonlyres/8C470BE2-687E-4D5C-9546- 0EBD3421CB1E/0/ DiscoursdouvertureduColloquecoursregionalesDHStrasbourg08122008.

pdf, (accessed 30 September 2010).

Idem. (2009). *Discours d'ouverture à l'audience solennelle de la Cour européenne des droits de l'Homme à l'occasion de l'ouverture de l'année judiciaire.* Strasbourg. Online. Available HTTP: http://www.echr.coe.int/NR/rdonlyres/4945592B-0229-4F71-ACC9-02B54A842250/0/30012009PresidentCostaAudience_fr_.pdf, (accessed 8 October 2010).

Council of Europe (2010*) Final draft Guidelines of the Committee of Ministers of the Council of Europe on child-friendly Justice* (CJ-S-CH (2010) 12). Online. Available HTTP: http://www.coe.int/t/dghl/standardsetting/childjustice/CJ-S-CH _2010_ 12 E - Final draft _rec containing_ guidelines of the CM of the CoE on Child-friendly justice.pdf, (accessed 6 October 2010).

CRIN (2009) *Children's Rights: A guide to Strategic Litigation*, Online. Available HTTP: http://www.crin.org/docs/Childrens_Rights_Guide_to_Strategic_Litigation.pdf, (accessed 8 October 2010).

P. David, 'Implementing the rights of the child: Six reasons why the human rights of children remain a constant challenge', *International Review of Education*, 2002, vol. 48, pp. 259-263.

M. De Boer-Buquicchio, 'Preface', in *International Justice for Children*, Strasbourg, The Council of Europe, 2008, pp. 9-13.

O. De Schutter, *Fonction de juger et droits fondamentaux. Transformation du contrôle juridictionnel dans les ordres juridiques américain et européens*, Bruxelles, Bruylant, 1999.

M. A. Drumbl, 'Prosecutor v. Thomas Lubanga Dyilo', *American Journal of Internationa Law*, 2007, vol. 101(4), pp. 841-848.

ECOSOC (2005) *Resolution 2005/20: Guidelines on Justice in Matters involving Child Victims and Witnesses of Crime*. Online. Available HTTP: http://www.apav.pt/portal/pdf/ECOSOC_RESOLUTION_2005-20.pdf, (accessed 6 October 2010).

M. Feria Tinta, *The landmark rulings of the Inter-American Court of Human Rights on the Rights of the Child*, Boston and Leiden, Martinus Nijhoff, 2008.

K. Hanson, *Schools of thought in children's rights*, Unpublished manuscript, IUKB, Switzerland, 2008.

A. Honwana, 'Innocents et coupables. Les enfants-soldats comme acteurs tactiques', *Politique africaine*, 2000, vol. 80, pp. 58-78.

Human Rights Council (2010) *Annual Report of the Special Representative of the Secreatry-General for Children and Armed Conflict* (UN doc. A/HCR/15/58). Online. Available HTTP: http://www2.ohchr.org/english/bodies/hrcouncil/docs/15session/A.HRC.15.58_en.pdf, (accessed 9 October 2010).

Human Rights Council, *Annual Report of the Special Representative of the Secreatry-General for Children and Armed Conflict* (UN doc. A/HRC/11/L.3, 2009).

G. Lansdown, *The evolving capacities of the child.* Florence, Italy, UNICEF Innocenti Research Centre, 2009.

Y. Lee (2009) *Reasons and timing for a communications procedure under the Convention on the Rights of the Child* (UN doc. A/HRC/WG.7/1/CRP.6). Online. Available HTTP: http://www2.ohchr.org/english/bodies/hrcouncil/OEWG/1stsession.htm, (accessed 9 October 2010).

C. Maisin, 'Françoise Tulkens, juge à la "Conscience de l'Europe"', *Journal Droit des Jeunes*, 2010, vol. 296, pp. 24-6.

A. Michels, 'As if it was happening again: supporting especially vulnerable witnesses, in particular women and children, at the Special Court for Sierra Leone', in K. Arts, V. Popovski, *International Criminal Accountability and the Rights of Children*, The Hague, Hague Academic Press, 2006, pp. 133-145.

L. Moreno-Ocampo, 'The rights of children and the international criminal court', in K. Arts, V. Popovski, *International Criminal Accountability and the Rights of Children*, The Hague, Hague Academic Press, 2006, pp. 111-17.

C. Mulley, *The woman who saved the children: a bibliography of Eglantyne Jebb the founder of Save the Children*, Oxford, Oneworld Publications, 2009.

P. Newell (2009) *Submission to Open-ended Working Group of the possibility of elaborating an Option protocol to provide a communications procedure for the Convention on the rights of the child* (UN doc. A/HRC/WG.7/1/CRP.2). Online. Available HTTP: http://www2.ohchr.org/english/bodies/hrcouncil/OEWG/1stsession.htm, (accessed 9 October 2010).

O. Nieuwenhuys, 'The wealth of children: Reconsidering the child labour debate', in J. Qvortrup (ed.), *Studies in modern childhood, society, agency, culture*, Basingstoke, England, Palgrave MacMillan, 2005, pp. 167-183.

No Peace Without Justice (NPWJ) & UNICEF Innocenti Research Center (2002) *International Criminal Justice.* Online. Available HTTP: http://www.juvenilejusticepanel.org/resource/items/N/P/NPWJInnocentiIntCrimJusticeAndChildren02.pdf, (accessed 7 October 2010).

V. Oosterveld, A. Marlowe, 'Special Court of Sierra Leone judgement on recruitment and use of child soldiers', *American Journal of International Law*, 2007, vol. 101(4), pp. 848-857.

S. Parmentier, 'The significance of mechanisms to monitor human rights at the international level', in E. Verhellen (ed.), *Understanding Children's Rights*, Ghent, Children's Rights Centre, Ghent University, 2004, pp. 341-374.

P. S. Pinheiro (2009). *Reasons and timing to elaborate a communications procedure under the Convention on the Rights of the Child* (UN doc. A/ HRC/WG.7/1/CRP.4). Online. Available HTTP: http://www2.ohchr. org/english/bodies/hrcouncil/OEWG/1stsession.htm, (accessed 9 October 2010).

V. Pupavac, 'Misanthropy without borders. The international children's rights regime', *Disasters*, 2001, vol. 25(2), pp. 95-112.

M. Santos Pais, 'International law and children's rights: a critical review and a wish list', in *International Justice for Children*, Strasbourg, The Council of Europe, 2008, pp. 49-65.

Idem. (2009) *Human Rights Council Working Group and an optional protocol to the Convention on the Rights of the Child to provide a communications procedure* (UN doc. A/HRC/WG.7/1/CRP.7). Online. Available HTTP: http://www2.ohchr.org/english/bodies/hrcouncil/OEWG/1stsession. htm, (accessed 9 October 2010).

B. Santoscoy, 'La protection des droits de l'Homme dans le continent américain : référence spéciale au cas d'Haïti et Cuba', *Revue québécoise du droit international*, 2000, vol. 13.2, pp. 1-44.

S. Siegrist, 'Child participation in international accountability mechanisms', in K. Arts, V. Popovski, *International Criminal Accountability and the Rights of Children*, The Hague, Hague Academic Press, 2006, pp. 53-65.

K. Tomaševski, 'Are we educating children as people with rights or just talking about it?', in A. Alen et al. (eds), *The UN Children's Rights Convention: Theory meets practice*, Antwerp, Intersentia, 2007, pp.165-179.

D. Tolbert, 'Children and international criminal law', in K. Arts. V. Popovski, *International Criminal Accountability and the Rights of Children*, The Hague, Hague Academic Press, 2006, pp. 147-154.

F. Tulkens, 'The European Convention on Human Rights and children's rights', in *International Justice for Children*, Strasbourg, The Council of Europe, 2008, pp. 17-33.

UN General Assembly (2002) *Resolution S-27/2: A World Fit for Children* (UN doc. A/RES/S-27/2, 2002). Online. Available HTTP: http://www. unicef.org/specialsession/docs_new/documents/A-RES-S27-2E.pdf, (accessed 6 October 2010).

UN Security Council (2005) *Resolution n° 1612* (UN doc. S/ Res/1612(2005)). Online. Available HTTP: http://daccess-dds-ny.un.org/ doc/UNDOC/GEN/N05/439/59/PDF/N0543959.pdf?OpenElement, (accessed 6 October 2010).

UN Security Council (2009) *Resolution n° 1882* (UN doc. S/ RES/1882(2009)). Online. Available HTTP: http://www.un.org/ children/conflict/_documents/SC-RESOLUTION1882-2009.pdf, (accessed 6 October 2010).

UNICEF Belgique & Défense des Enfants International Belgique (2008)

La détention des enfants en centres fermés. Online. Available HTTP: http://www.dei-belgique.be/docs_outils/Trib Opinion Dossier Final FR OCT 2008.pdf, (accessed 7 October 2010).

E. Verhellen, 'Citizenship and participation of children – In search of a framework and some thoughts.', in D. Ferring et al., *Les droits de l'enfant: citoyenneté et participation*, Luxembourg, Université du Luxembourg, 2008, pp. 14-32.

Idem., *Convention on the Rights of the Child. Background, motivation, strategies, main themes*, Leuven, Garant, 2000.

N. Vuckovic Sahovic (2009) *Feasibility of a communication procedure under the Convention on the Rights of the Child* (UN doc. A/HCR/WG.7/1/CRP.1). Online. Available HTTP: http://www2.ohchr.org/english/bodies/ hrcouncil/OEWG/1stsession.htm, (accessed 9 October 2010).

Index

CPSIA information can be obtained at www.ICGtesting.com
Printed in the USA
BVOW06s2049131016

R7525500001B/R75255PG464499BVX18B/1/P

9 781911 096719